Books by Dan Kurzman

Kishi and Japan
Subversion of the Innocents
Santo Domingo: Revolt of the Damned
Genesis 1948: The First Arab-Israeli War
The Race for Rome
The Bravest Battle
Miracle of November

MIRACLE
OF
NOVEMBER

Madrid's Epic Stand
1936

Dan Kurzman

G. P. PUTNAM'S SONS
NEW YORK

ST. PHILIPS COLLEGE LIBRARY

946.081
K96

Copyright © 1980 by Dan Kurzman

All rights reserved. This book, or parts thereof, must not be reproduced in any form without permission. Published simultaneously in Canada by Longman Canada Limited, Toronto.

Library of Congress Cataloging in Publication Data
Kurzman, Dan.
  Miracle of November.
  Bibliography: p.
  1. Madrid—Siege, 1936-1939. 2.   Spain—History—
Civil War, 1936-1939—Campaigns and battles.
I. Title.
DP269.27.M3K87 1980   946.081   79-12555
ISBN 0-399-12271-0

Printed in the United States of America

For my dear wife, Florence,
*whose faith, devotion, and patience eased
the agony of putting it all together*

60360

Madrid; Florentino González—Biblioteca Central Militar; Edward M. Harper—press attaché, U.S. embassy, Madrid; Gervasio Huertas—Spanish Communist party official; Colonel Earl L. Keesling—military attaché, U.S. embassy, Madrid; Armando López Salinas—Spanish Communist party official; Colonel Luis López Anglada—Ministry of the Army official; José Martínez—editor, *Rueda Iberico*, Paris; José Manuel Martínez Bande—Spanish military historian; Angel Mullor—Spanish Communist party official; Dory Otero—secretary, Lawyers' Bureau, Madrid; Jesús Pardo de Santayana—director, *Historia 16*; Celestino Plaza Rivera—Servicio Histórico Militar; Ramón Salas Larrazábal—Spanish civil war historian.

Characters in this drama who kindly permitted me to interview them include the following: Rafael Alberti—Communist poet; Rufina Alonso—Madrid citizen; Mariano Alvarez Galindez—Falangist inmate in Model Prison; Aldea Amancio—Fifth Regiment militiaman; Luisa María de Aramburu—founder of Falangist Women's Association and sister of murdered Josefina Aramburu; María Luisa Asensio Torrado—sister of General Asensio; Mario Asensio—son of General Asensio; Pedro Barrios—anarchist militiaman; Fernand Belino—French officer in International Brigades; Antonio Beltrán Marin—son of Loyalist Colonel Antonio Beltrán; David Ben Dayan—Jewish rebel soldier; Antonio Bernal Gutierrez—son of General Carlos Bernal García; Father José Caballero—rebel priest; Cristobal Caliz Almiron—UGT official; José Calvo Sotelo—son of rightist leader; Sifre Carbonel—rebel captain; José Carratelá García—son of murdered Colonel Carratelá; Santiago Carrillo—head of Socialist Youth, later chief of Spanish Communist party; Rafael Casas de la Vega—son of murdered suspected rebel; Paco Castillo—brother of Lieutenant Castillo; Mirko Deucht (Ben-Yehuda)—Yugoslav soldier in International Brigades; Fernando Escribano—militiaman in United Socialist Youth; Irene Falcón—secretary of Dolores Ibarruri; Juan Manuel Fanjul Cedeno—son of General Fanjul; Enrique Fernández Heredia Castanaga—Loyalist officer; Manuel Fontengla—Loyalist officer; Gregorio Gallego—anarchist leader; Juan José Gallego Pérez—Loyalist officer; Paulino García Puente—Loyalist officer; Rafael García Serrano—Falangist soldier; José María Gil de Santibanez—Falangist soldier; Antonio Gómez—Communist worker-militiaman; Felipe Gómez Acebo—Falangist soldier; Carmen González de Lain—Madrid citizen; M. González Frias—member of Calvo Sotelo's party; Miguel González Inestal—anarchist leader; Yitzhak Gruber—Palestinian Jewish soldier in International Brigades; Boris Guimpel—French officer in International Brigades; Eduardo de Guzmán—anarchist newsman and author; Manuel Hernández Roldan—republican government official; Carlos Iniesta Cano—rebel captain, later commander of Civil Guard; Lorenzo Inigo—anarchist leader; David Jato—Falangist refugee in Finnish embassy; Carmen Kindélan—Ultano Kindélan's wife; Ultano Kindélan—prisoner in Madrid; Enrique Lister—commander of Fifth Regiment; Carmen Machado—Communist militiawoman; Hernando Martín Calvarro—Falangist soldier; Regulo Martínez Sánchez—a leader of Azaña's Left Republican party; Roger Mechaut—French soldier in International Brigades; Elena Medina—General Mola's secretary; Emilio Mola—son of General Mola; Consuelo Morales Castillo—wife of murdered Lieutenant Castillo; Colonel Félix Muedra—Loyalist commander; Eusebio Muñoz—anarchist militiaman; Nicolas Muñoz Pando—student in Madrid; Urbano Orad de la Torre—socialist army captain; Luciano Otero—Socialist Youth militiaman; Miguel Palacios—officer commanding anarchists; Vicente Peragón Herranx—Communist militiaman; Michel Perlman—Russian-French officer in International Brigades; Sacramento Piedrabuena—Loyalist policeman; Yehezkel Piekar—Palestinian Jewish flyer in André Malraux's air force; Eduardo Prada Manso—militiaman son of Colonel Adolfo Prada Vaquero; Juan Pradillo de Osna—chief of Madrid's industrial services; Eduardo Rodrigo—anarchist militiaman; Antonio Rodríguez Sastre—Loyalist official who helped rebels escape from Madrid; Mariano Román—anarchist commander; Antonio Remis—Left Republican party official; Colonel Luis de Ribera Zapata—rebel officer; Ricardo Rionda—anarchist commander under Durruti; Angel Rojo—son of Major (later General) Rojo; Vicente Rojo—son of Major Rojo; José Luis Sáenz Heredia—film director and cousin of José Antonio; Gabriel Salinas Rodríguez—militiaman in United Socialist Youth; José Antonio Sánchez—fourteen-year-old fifth columnist; Modesto Sánchez de las Casas—Loyalist newsman; Simon Sánchez Montero—Communist militiaman; Teodoro Sánchez—rebel soldier; José Sandoval—Communist militiaman; Fugencio Sanudo Palazuelos—food administrator in Madrid; Enrique Segura—son of suspected rebel colonel who was captured by García Atadell; Mercedez de Semprun—Madrid aristocrat; Shalom Shiloni—Palestinian Jewish soldier in International Brigades; María Teresa de Solas Rafecas—Madrid citizen; Vicente Solis—Madrid student; Ramón Serrano Suñer—Franco's brother-in-law and later foreign minister; Alexander Szerek—Polish soldier in International Brigades; Carlos Torres—son of Loyalist officer who turned rebel; Segunda Ugarte Mendia—maid of María Luisa Asensio Torrado; Fernando Valera—deputy minister of communications, later president of republican government in exile; Luis Valero Bermejo—rebel soldier; Salvador Vallina—Falangist soldier; Justo Villanueva—anarchist militiaman.

Contents

PREFACE

The story of Madrid in the first months of the Spanish civil war must rank as one of the most inspirational, terrifying, and historically important epics of our time. It opens in July 1936 when General Francisco Franco's rightist army revolts against the left-leaning republican government, weaves through the tensions and euphoric delusions of a nightmare anarchy, and climaxes with a miracle in November when the professional rebel forces assault a desperate but suddenly aroused populace that holds out even after its leaders flee in panic.

None of the hundreds of nonfictional works about the civil war have told this story in the comprehensive human detail it deserves. And except for some vivid personal diaries and memoirs that contribute fragments, mostly in Spanish, even books that concentrate on Madrid are largely technical, academic accounts of battle tactics and strategy.

This book, however, is neither technical nor academic and is not simply about battle. It is about the trial of a beleaguered city as seen through the eyes of the people who were there. The emerging portrait of Madrid at war almost allegorically reflects the Spanish character, with all its subtle complexities and sharp conflicts. It also reflects the resilience of the human spirit—and the wretchedness of Soviet dictator Josef Stalin and some of his henchmen who would use and then betray this spirit for their own purposes.

This small but vital segment of history has been explored in little depth up to now because in the end, three years later, Madrid fell to Franco as did all Spain. He simply marched in after the last shots of the war had been fired, and by then

13

ST. PHILIPS COLLEGE LIBRARY

the early days had faded into a vague memory of hope and horror, exultation and despair.

Yet, as this book points out, the final Loyalist defeat could not diminish the luster of Madrid's heroic stand in November 1936, which even government leaders had thought impossible. History will not forget the suicidal efforts to stop tanks at Carabanchel with little more than bare hands; the fighting for every room and floor in every building in University City; the brutal, if vain, attempt to bomb Madrid into surrender in the first mass aerial bombardment of a metropolis ever launched—a Hitler-inspired model for the total-war tactics of World War II.

Nor will history ignore the savagely eloquent attack on Montaña Barracks in central Madrid when the army rebellion broke out, an assault by the people comparable in scope and spirit to the storming of the Bastille in the French Revolution; or the lurid crimes committed by some *Madrileños* against suspected fifth columnists, and simply personal enemies, in the frenzy of a civil war that spurred both sides to unimaginable atrocities; or the murder and treachery that ironically splintered the Loyalist forces after they had, during one glorious, spontaneously improvised moment in time, merged their conflicting ideals into a spirit of resistance that the enemy could not shatter.

The story is described in this book through democrats, Communists, anarchists, Fascists, monarchists, Russians, Germans, Italians, Americans, Britons, Frenchmen, Poles; through young men and women fighting to create a new world or to return to an old; through brothers and sisters, fathers and mothers who suddenly found themselves mortal foes; through prime ministers and generals, mercenaries and militiamen, spies and traitors, opportunists and adventurers, priests and priest-killers; through simple *Madrileños* who felt they must save Madrid in order to save themselves—not only from the enemy but from the damnation of history and their own conscience.

While Madrid was the hub of a civil war, it was also the symbol of a worldwide ideological struggle, and a turning point in history. Until the battle of November, Franco's victory seemed assured, and if he had captured Madrid then, the war might have ended soon afterward. But when the *Madrileños* stopped him at the gates of the city, the military situation was suddenly reversed and the Loyalists began taking the offensive.

Realizing now that he could not win the war with the men and equipment he had, Franco put the problem squarely to Hitler and Mussolini: Either they supplied him with all he needed for final victory or he would lose, and this would mean a disastrous setback for fascism in Europe. The two dictators, who had already been giving him limited aid, agreed, despite the danger that Stalin might react by sending comparable help to the Loyalists and thereby escalate the chances of a general European war.

But Stalin was more devious than daring. He decided to give the Loyalists only enough aid to keep the war going in Spain and Hitler tied up there until

Russia grew sufficiently powerful to meet a possible Nazi attack, or to bargain with the Führer for an alliance. Thus, in a strange and momentous twist of history, the Loyalist stand in the November battle doomed the Loyalist cause—and helped to determine the path that would lead to World War II.

In preparing this book, I interviewed more than five hundred people, read about four hundred books and innumerable articles in several languages, and studied thousands of original documents. With the liberalization of Spain after the death of Franco in 1975, many of his enemies who had previously been afraid related their experiences for the first time to me, while countless documents in the Spanish archives that had been withheld from researchers were made available. This book, therefore, contains a large amount of material never published before.

None of the details presented here are fictionalized; all are the fruit of more than two years of intensive research in Spain, Britain, France, Italy, Israel, West Germany, and the United States. The dialogue and other quotations, as well as thoughts attributed to characters in the book, come directly from diaries, memoirs, or verbal reconstructions by the characters themselves, and so have the authenticity of autobiography. The sources of all quotations are indicated in the Notes. I have exhaustively checked all statements and claims, taking into account possible self-serving distortions, and have omitted any material that appeared to be doubtful or inconsistent with known facts.

The drama of Madrid in 1936 is closely linked to the drama of Madrid today as Spain returns to democracy, with even some of the main characters unchanged. It is as if life is resuming for the Spanish after a time freeze of forty-one years. Most, it is true, have considerably matured politically and emotionally, but few have changed their basic ideas. Therefore, to understand the forces that are rekindling democracy in Spain today, one must understand those that snuffed it out yesterday. This story of a brave, besieged city caught in the tempest of the times will, it is hoped, foster that understanding.

—Dan Kurzman
Madrid, Spain

PROLOGUE

The first shells whistled through the cold murky sky just before dawn and crashed into buildings on the Gran Vía, the Broadway of Madrid, illuminating the whole center of the city. Like a black parable by Goya, Madrid lay naked in the dazzling glare, its wounds open and ugly from weeks of air bombardment and now from artillery fire.

Some buildings had their fronts completely ripped away, and stood with rooms exposed like model toy houses. Pieces of furniture, twisted steel girders, shredded clothing, kitchen utensils, and other mementos of a bygone life littered the streets in the modern downtown area and the ramshackle workers' quarters at the edge of town, the prime targets of the enemy.

In an alley near the Gran Vía, a woman, silhouetted like a Madonna against the flickering glow of some wreckage, sat on a curb stroking the head of a charred corpse. In a pile of debris nearby lay the fragment of a child's body with a hand still clutching a doll. The smell of death was everywhere, carried by the wind from the northern Guadarrama Mountains, a bitter wind that, it was said, "does not blow out a candle but kills a man." Leaves from the trees lining the boulevards danced amid the carnage—tiny tokens of life that perhaps might augur another day of survival.

Today, November 7, 1936, Madrid faced the supreme challenge. It was a day that would test its resolve, its fortitude, its soul. The right-wing Nationalist rebel forces, which had revolted against the left-leaning republican government on July 17, 1936, were at the gates of this "very noble, very loyal, very heroic and

17

most excellent city," as it is described in the formal royal coat of arms. Generalissimo Francisco Franco's professional army of Moors and foreign legionnaires,
after being airlifted from Spanish Morocco to Seville in southern Spain, had driv-
en northward all the way to Carabanchel, two miles from the center of the capital. And some troops had even entered the wooded Casa de Campo on the western fringe of the city, where kings once went for morning gallops along the curl-
ing Manzanares River.

Franco had only about twenty-five thousand men, including reserves, to capture a metropolis of more than a million people. But the fifty thousand or more
Loyalist defenders, among them young women, hardly formed a real army. Most
were civilians, with little or no military training, who wore tattered working
clothes and carried ancient rifles. Others bore no arms at all, hoping to seize
those dropped by fallen comrades.

The night before, on November 6, American journalist John T. Whitaker had
cabled a dispatch to the New York *Herald-Tribune* echoing the sentiments of almost everyone, even those who were determined to die fighting: "Madrid
is . . . a doomed city . . . which will haul down its republican flag whenever . . . Franco so decides. Today's barbs have lowered her proud head, as
surely as the *picador's* lance and the *banderilleros* drive darts into the lowered
head of the bull so that the [*torero*] can lean over the horns with his sword and
kill it. Franco is now ready for the kill . . . Madrid's hour is near."

The *Madrileños* had little reason to disagree. After all, even the republican
government—they would learn later in the morning—had quietly packed its bags
and slipped out of town during the night to seek safety in Valencia on Spain's
eastern coast, expecting the capital to fall at any moment. It had been afraid to
tell its own people, as the reporters told the outside world, that "Madrid's hour is
near," and that Madrid's fall would probably mean Spain's as well, since Madrid was Spain's heart. It had feared that the population would panic and prevent
it from leaving. Only the government, apparently, had a right to panic.

Almost all Madrid had remained sleepless that night awaiting the thrust of the
sword. For rebel sympathizers, as they listened excitedly in back rooms and foreign embassies to the boom of Franco's guns, the sword would kill a horde of
barbarians who had slain their sons in nightly orgies of murder. But for Loyalist
sympathizers, the majority of *Madrileños,* it would kill the defenders of freedom
and justice—*their* sons. And while Loyalist leaders deplored the murder of rebel
civilians, though helpless to halt the savagery, rebel leaders would certainly *order* the murder of loyalist civilians, to judge by their past behavior. Most *Madrileños* knew what had happened during Franco's drive from Seville to Madrid:
the slaughter in every village of people even suspected of leftist sympathies, the
machine-gunning of hundreds in the bullring of Badajoz, the massacre of all
wounded Loyalists in their hospital beds in Toledo.

The previous day, Franco had instructed the *Madrileños* to stay indoors for forty-eight hours, until the city was safely in his hands. Then he would deal with them. A few days earlier, his planes had dropped leaflets telling them how:

"For every murder committed against our followers in Madrid, ten of your men will be shot. In the capital the twenty-five thousand wounded will be held responsible for your excesses."

Another Badajoz! Another Toledo!

Soon after dawn, panic spread among many civilians as they learned of the government's flight, just as the ministers had feared. They streamed out into the streets to join a chaotic procession of cars, trucks, and wagons piled high with household goods and store merchandise, all heading toward Valencia on the heels of their leaders. Their prayers, their laments, their cries of anguish melded with the honking of horns, the clanging of streetcar bells, the braying of donkeys belonging to peasant refugees from nearby villages, and the shouts of street-hawkers trying to unload their stock of trinkets, republican flags, and toy militia-men at rock-bottom prices before Franco arrived and put them out of business altogether. In the seething tumult, even a hearse with a corpse inside was left abandoned on a street corner. Just one more dead man.

And helping to fuel the panic were thousands of beaten demoralized militia-men who had scrambled into the city in the past few days. With their lack of training and discipline, they had fallen back from the southern approaches to Madrid while Franco's German and Italian planes and tanks spurted withering fire. This ragtag army, suffering enormous casualties, had fled northward from village to village, town to town, before the relentless rebel advance. Finally, they had crowded into Madrid to join other *Madrileños* suicidally resigned to their fate.

The night before, some of the more desperate ones had reacted to their humili-ation with bestial fury, especially after a fifth column of rebel conspirators hurled bombs from balconies and rooftops and raked the streets with gunfire to help pave the way for Franco. These militiamen herded hundreds of rebel suspects from Madrid's packed jails into trucks and drove them to nearby villages, where they mowed them down en masse. Caught in the middle of the turmoil, some for-eign embassies, jammed with terrified Francoist refugees, set up machine guns in their gardens—just in case.

But while many Loyalists panicked, most were now steeled for battle, harbor-ing a dim hope that the sword would somehow miss its mark. There was hope in the appearance at sunrise of the street cleaners, who began sweeping up the rub-ble as if unaware that today these streets might run with blood. There was hope in the optimism of the bootblacks, kneeling by their stands at the corners to await customers who would need a shine, battle or no battle.

There was hope in the courage of housewives and children who formed long queues in front of the food shops to buy their meager rations—and were deter-mined not to move and lose their place even during an air raid—though many of their friends and relatives had been killed in recent days by bombs dropped in their midst. There was hope in the boldness of old men who sat in their favorite cafés as they did every morning and analyzed the latest war news with diagrams sketched on the tablecloth. There was hope in a cold cup of coffee that stood untouched on a table in Café Molinero reserved for rebel General Emilio Mola, who had boasted weeks earlier that he would be having coffee there within days.

There was hope in the zeal of citizens who were building barricades across the roads with logs, stones, and furniture from their own homes. Most important of all, there was hope in the massive march to the front that morning of tens of thousands of militiamen—the same ones who had fled from their positions south of Madrid. Even many of the *Madrileños* who were now stumbling down the Valencia road would soon halt, sit beside the road, and ask themselves why and where they were going. They would come back as the sword was being thrust, returning to destroyed homes, to burning barricades. If they were too old or too weak to fight, they would feed those who could or build new barricades or make bombs.

The Spaniard who panicked and ran was the same Spaniard who would stand and fight. He was the product of generations that had known many lost wars and aborted revolutions, economic and social upheavals, bitter, hapless struggles to entice life from stubborn land. He was a man with a zigzag fever chart reflecting the deep inner conflict born of these inherited pressures.

His clashing visions of how to manage his life and his nation drove him to alternate between submission and rebellion. When he submitted, he collapsed completely. But when he rebelled, he showed extraordinary courage. For ingrained in him was the cult of virility, or *machismo,* which pushed him to defend his beliefs regardless of cost. Was it not such bloated bravery that had permitted him to survive centuries of crushing adversity? Thus, the greater the challenge, the greater his tenacity. He was Cortés against the savage hordes, Columbus against the raging ocean.

And so the *Madrileños* decided to stay in Madrid and die.

In fact, the prospect of death in battle seemed almost appealing to the Spaniard, feeding his fantasies of heroism and tragedy bred by the turbulent past, and helping to explain why he killed with almost innocent pleasure and died with a philosophical shrug. And death had its pragmatic side, too. It was a clever way to cheat the exploiter, a means of solving the conflicts within one's self, a method of achieving a degree of martyrdom.

Death had always been an intimate companion of the Spaniard's. Since childhood, he had thrilled to the sight of brave bulls, symbols of brute strength and the macabre majesty of doom, falling bloodily, thrusting their horns to the last throb of life, while bugles blared and crowds cheered. And sometimes he saw the *torero* die as well, to be honored eternally for his courage and daring. Death could even be elegant. The undertaking parlors were always furnished in exquisite taste, and funerals were elaborate, often grandiose—though, of course, processions had to be dispensed with during the war.

Madrid had always valued *machismo* and scorned danger more than most other Spanish cities because it was traditionally a jealous, arrogant capital. Threatened for centuries by foreign invasion, civil war, and regional pressures for independence, it had tried to rule the nation with a cunning mixture of military muscle and political paternalism.

But despite resentment of Madrid's swagger, in moments of national crisis the provinces had usually rallied round it, for it was not only a political capital but a cultural melting pot in which each region could find something of itself. Madrid was a mirror of the national character.

It had not always been. Only about four-hundred years earlier Madrid was a minor provincial town itself, a mere clump of houses perched on the high, bleak plains of Castile in the shadow of the towering Guadarramas to the north. Aware of its apparently small potential for growth and grandeur, Emperor Charles V, in 1561, gave some advice to his heir, future King Philip II: "My son, if you want to extend your domains, set up your courts in Lisbon, facing the Atlantic. If you simply want to keep what I bequeath to you, stay here in Toledo. But if you want to lose territory and power, choose Madrid as your capital."

Intrigued by the challenge, Philip II moved his court to Madrid. When forty years later his son, Philip III, switched it north to Valladolid, the landowning *Madrileños* were horrified as their land values suddenly plummeted. They sent an emissary to the king with an irresistible offer—a huge sum of money plus one-sixth of the city's revenue from rent. Philip III thus returned in 1606 amid great pomp and joy, this time to stay.

Madrid's reputation for valor soared to a peak in 1808 when the *Madrileños* revolted against Napoleon, who had placed his brother, Joseph, on the Spanish throne. Napoleon attacked Madrid in a spectacular cavalry charge, but the men and women of the city swarmed into their crooked streets, frenziedly threw up barricades, and greeted the invader with the few guns they had, as well as with knives, sticks, stones, and spears.

After a sanguinary battle in which hundreds of captured defenders were lined up and shot, the city finally surrendered. But it had roused the whole nation to arms. Five years later, after changing hands several times, Madrid was finally free of the invader.

But not of its chronic internal torment. In the next decades, coup followed coup, and three civil wars raged over which royal line should reign, while each new government floundered in the muck of intrigue and corruption. Then, in 1898, the United States seized Cuba, Puerto Rico, and the Philippines, and Spain lost its last scraps of empire as well as its national self-esteem.

During World War I, the Spain of King Alfonso XIII polarized into two hostile blocs—a leftist group of cruelly exploited workers and peasants and a rightist one of privilege-loving clerics, military men, and big landowners.

Workers and peasants, awakening to their latent power, flocked into anarchist and socialist trade unions. The anarchists, who viewed all governments as rotten, corrupt, and contemptuous of society, were disciples of Mikhail Bakunin, a contemporary of Karl Marx's. Though both men favored the collective ownership of property, Bakunin, unlike Marx, wanted a confederation of communes rather than the government to be the owner. He and his followers would perfect man, purge him of greed, selfishness, and vanity, teach him to live and work in harmony with his neighbors under a system of complete freedom. There would be no police, no jails. If anyone committed a crime or acted against the collective interest, he would simply be ostracized, isolated from his fellows, until he saw his error and repented.

The socialists, by contrast, were disciplined Marxists, though they were divided on how to achieve a Marxist state; some wanted revolution, others, evolution.

The growing leftist threat alarmed the rightists, who saw their power shrinking daily. For the clergy, it was no longer the golden sixteenth century when the Church held Spain in an iron grip, presiding over an Inquisition that condemned thousands of "heretics" to exile and death. The leftists now "robbed" the Church of believers, land, and influence over the government.

Yet, though only about a third of the people went to church regularly, most were by no means atheists. On the contrary, they hated the average priest so fiercely because they saw him as a false servant of God who betrayed His wish to help and comfort the people. They were anti-Church, not anti-God. But the religious leaders would not dare let themselves make this distinction.

The big landlords were also frightened. Those owning more than two hundred and fifty acres held over half of the cultivated land in Spain, and in their huge olive groves and vineyards peasants slaved for a few pesetas a day. After all, how much bread and olive oil did a peasant need to stay alive?

The army, too, had a stake in keeping things as they were. Since the Middle Ages it had steered the nation's political life, usually from behind the scenes. It considered itself the guardian of the *Patria,* the Fatherland, and since the *Patria* was sacred, so was its keeper. Neither the people nor the king or president could claim to be sovereign. But the army could. And anybody who even criticized it publicly was committing a punishable crime. Some officers, no doubt, were true believers in the army's "sacredness," but many others simply used their exalted status as a front to cover their lust for power, privilege, and wealth. This lust led to an incurable addiction to conspiracy. And whenever the government neglected its "obligations" to the army, the ambitious, dissatisfied officer who earned a meager salary saw in the coup, or *pronunciamiento,* the best way to get what he "rightfully" deserved.

Feeding the lust was pride. For the military found itself bogged down in a Moroccan campaign that had been plaguing it since Spain and France divided Morocco between them in 1904. Year after year, the cream of Spanish youth died trying to snuff out native revolts, and there was nothing but humiliation—even though Morocco did give the oversized Spanish army something to do after it no longer had a great empire to defend.

The army launched one of its most successful *pronunciamientos* in 1923 when General Miguel Primo de Rivera seized power with the approval of Alfonso XIII, who remained a figurehead king, and ended the chaos. But Primo soon found himself the newest public target, with even his fellow officers determined to oust him. The army had finally managed to crush the Moroccans in 1927, but grew more restless than ever, especially since it no longer had an outlet for the *machismo* drive. There were no more medals to be won "proving" one's courage. Besides, Primo dared change the traditional promotion system to favor his friends.

Thus, under the mounting pressure, Primo finally stepped down in 1930, and in the following year the unpopular king ran out of the palace through the back door—"never to return . . . until my people call me."

A republic was proclaimed in 1931 and, though the army had expected the new government to slant right as usual, the hysterical masses overflowing the squares hoisted to power a social democratic regime under the leadership of an intellectual reformer, Manuel Azaña. Now, thought many people, medieval Spain would be modernized overnight. However, the new government's program for pruning the Church's might and reapportioning the landlords' vast estates dissatisfied the Left, which wanted swifter reform, and outraged the Right, which wanted none at all.

And adding to the discontent was dissension within both camps. On the left, socialists and anarchists engaged in an often bloody feud, while the Communists opportunistically sought to profit from it. And on the right, monarchists and reactionary republicans bitterly vied for influence—with the modern Fascists in the opportunist's role.

General Primo de Rivera had faded away, but his name had not. For his son, José Antonio, soon became an even more impressive figure. Unlike the father, who was strictly a military dictator, the son preached a virulent ideology, founding, in 1933, the Falange, a fascistic movement that vowed to halt the march of Marxism with a fiery blend of nationalism, socialism, and terrorism.

In some respects, ironically, José Antonio's announced program did not sound much different from that of the Stalinists he deplored. To the fury of the conventional rightists, it ambiguously called for an end to capitalism and a division of large landholdings—though it would preserve the traditional social structure. But more important than the program was the man. Brilliant, handsome, urbane, personally liked even by many of his enemies, José Antonio became, at thirty-three, one of the most charismatic personalities in Spain. Middle-class youth, especially, flocked to him, and even some Communists and anarchists did, turning into fine Fascist gunmen.

Despite their differences, however, the rightist groups joined together to fight the new moderate government and, with the help of equally hotheaded leftists, brought it down in 1933. In the confusion, the rightists won a new election the following year, but in February 1936 lost again to the leftists, who had banded in a Popular Front under Azaña. The rightists were now convinced that Azaña, who became president, would lead Spain to revolution. Was he not switching top officers to relatively minor posts or trying to induce them to resign, even offering to pension them off with full pay for life? Had he not refused to modernize Spain's archaic military equipment? Azaña, most officers believed, clearly wanted to destroy their army and replace it with a "red army." Many thus joined the Spanish Military Union (UME), a thinly disguised organ for conspiracy led by General Mola. (General Franco at this time was still wary of revolt, preferring to let others take the risks.)

Meanwhile, José Antonio, who was arrested on trumped-up charges in spring 1936, ordered Falangist colleagues visiting him in jail to fan the flames of revolt. And his followers, many of them more violent-minded than he, went wild, assassinating leading leftists and provoking gunfights in the streets.

The leftists gladly accepted the challenge and struck back, not only to avenge but to generate an atmosphere favorable to their own varying brands of revolution. They even agreed finally to unite in the face of the common danger, as the rightists had. And with no significant middle class to mediate between the two extremist-led groups, the stage was set for civil war. . . .

So now, on November 7, 1936, as on that day in 1808 when Napoleon attacked, the people of Madrid would fight for every street, every house, every room with only their few guns and even boiling water if necessary. The paralyzing sense of impotence and fatalism that had psychologically disarmed many of them until this morning vanished like ice in fire. What had sparked this miraculous transformation between midnight and dawn? In large measure, the sudden emergence of a typical, if most unlikely, Spaniard as their leader.

General José Miaja, fifty-eight, bald, puffy-cheeked, bespectacled, looked like an owl, seemed as gentle and inoffensive as a lamb, and sometimes acted like a chimpanzee, pounding his chest when he was angry and slapping his ample belly when he laughed. No one, including his fellow officers on either side, had ever taken him seriously, and people even joked about his name, since a similarly pronounced word, *miga,* means "crumb" in Spanish. He was a bastion of military mediocrity, amiably indecisive, utterly dispensable. He was the perfect sacrifice, the ideal man to surrender Madrid to the enemy. And so the government appointed him commander of the city before retreating to safety.

But Miaja was a vain, sensitive man. Whatever animal he resembled, he would not be the goat. He rushed to the War Ministry at 2:00 A.M., gathered together all the officers he could find, formed a governing *junta*, made dramatic radio appeals, and sent messengers to knock on every door in search of fighters. With daybreak, newspaper vendors were shouting the headline, *NO PASARAN!* (''THEY SHALL NOT PASS!''), and posters and slogans on every wall were crying, TO THE FRONT!

The response was volcanic as thousands of people marched to the trenches and the barricades. Just behind the lines were their homes, their wives, children, parents. They would run no farther. There seemed to be something more important at stake than political or ideological victory, or even their lives and the lives of their families. They were *Madrileños*. They were Spaniards. They were men. Men driven by all the bitter passions accumulated for centuries.

Madrid had become not just a city but a reflection of each man's judgment of himself, a mirror of the human spirit. To die in this martyred capital would be to live forever.

PART I

The Rising

CHAPTER I

Conspiracy

1

July 9, 1936, was a joyous day in Pamplona. Tens of thousands of people had come from all over Spain to celebrate the week-long festival of San Fermín in this northern Navarran town, releasing their multiple tensions in an explosion of unrestrained merriment. The previous night dozens of bars had overflowed with raucous, rollicking celebrants who wore the traditional red beret and scarf of San Fermín and lifted to their lips a *bota* of wine while brass bands blared the music of Navarre.

Outside, in the warm evening air, little groups of musicians marched through the brightly lit streets from one sidewalk café to another, beating on drums and puffing on oboes that wailed haunting tunes. In the distance a familiar rumble aroused heady expectations of tomorrow as a herd of bulls galloped through the darkness to a corral where they would await the battle they were doomed to lose.

All night long Pamplona echoed with the festive sounds of carnival, though finally, in the wee hours, some people staggered out of the bars, singing less coherently now, and helped one another through the streets to their homes, their hotels, or to the park or any patch of grass they could find. Soon, under every tree, on every stretch of green, an ecstatically exhausted body smelling of beer or wine sprawled as if in eternal sleep.

But eternity lasted only two or three hours, because by 6:00 A.M. the merrymakers had to be up and ready to take part in, or at least watch, the highlight of the festival—the running of the bulls. At exactly 7:00 A.M., a rocket zoomed into the sky and exploded, and the corral housing the bulls swung open. The animals charged out and galloped down a narrow street chasing hundreds of daring youth toward the bullring about nine hundred yards away. While excited spectators jamming the balconies along the streets cheered them on, the amateur *toreros* raced for their lives, and for the thrill of it.

They reached the arena shortly before the bulls, and as they entered, thousands of people in the grandstands rose with a mighty roar to greet them. When the bulls had been enticed into another corral where they would remain until their afternoon battle debut—and finale—the crowd gleefully watched the hysterical antics of the young men in the ring as they teased the leaping baby bulls, pulling their tails and harassing them from all sides in a splendid display of mass *machismo*.

Late in the afternoon, another capacity crowd turned out to see the real *toreros* exhibit their skills. And among the spectators were the occupants of a special box for important persons. One of the men in the box was tall and slightly stooped, with an olive complexion and hard piercing eyes that peered through round glasses. He was General Mola, the forty-nine-year-old commander of the Northern Military Region, based in Pamplona. Beside him was an officer whose sensitive white-bearded face reflected a tension in strange disharmony with the exhilaration of the crowd. General Joaquin Fanjul was not in the mood for fun, even the fun of San Fermín, which he knew so well from his early years, since he was a Navarran.

Fanjul had arrived in Pamplona the day before from Madrid after being invited by Mola to attend the festival with him. Mola was the leader of an army plot to overthrow the republican government and set up a military dictatorship, and the key to a quick coup was Madrid. It was not only the capital of Spain, but the hub of its communications system and an enormous reservoir of manpower and economic resources. Besides, the fall of Madrid would convince the nation, and the world, that the rebels controlled Spain. Even more important, if the insurgents could seize the capital before the government had time to react effectively, the rest of Spain would probably be shocked into surrender within days. But if the government could hold out in Madrid, civil war seemed inevitable, and no one could predict its outcome.

Mola had picked Fanjul as one of the two generals who would lead the uprising in Madrid and had asked him to come to Pamplona with a report on preparations there. He had invited other leading plotters as well, for San Fermín offered an ideal cover for conspiracy. People flocked to the festival from all over Spain, and it was perfectly natural for generals to be among them, especially a native like Fanjul. Government spies would not be likely to draw dangerous conclusions from the congregation of high-ranking military men at San Fermín. And to mask his intentions, Mola had conspired with his colleagues in the past few days

not only in his headquarters, but in the barracks, in the street, in the cafés and
bars, at Mass, and at the bullfights.

But not at this bullfight for, to Mola's discomfort, sitting on the other side of
him was the civil governor of Pamplona, who firmly supported the republic that
the general was plotting to destroy. With a thin smile, Mola introduced Fanjul to
the governor.

"Mr. Governor, here is a good Navarran who has not forgotten San Fermín."

Fanjul and the governor exchanged greetings.

"How long are you staying?" the governor asked.

"I'm returning to Madrid this evening," Fanjul replied. "The summer vacation is almost here and I must get ready for it. A supper with friends, a bull run, a
corrida—what else could I ask for? It's been an enjoyable two days."

The governor smiled, apparently unable to detect the contradiction in Fanjul's
eyes. Fanjul was, in fact, returning to Madrid a dejected, even despairing, man.
Upon arriving in Pamplona the day before, he had discussed Madrid with Mola at
Mola's headquarters while the rhythms of San Fermín wafted through the windows as if to mock his agony.

How were things going in Madrid? Mola wanted to know.

There seemed little chance of success, Fanjul replied. The government had the
forces to crush an uprising in the city. True, there was a core of army officers and
civilians ready to join the revolt, but it was practically impossible to coordinate
their efforts because key officers in most units could not be trusted.

"So we are exactly where we were before," Mola responded with disappoint-
ment. "Heading straight for failure."

But unlike Fanjul, who considered his role suicidal and understandably viewed
the plot through the prism of Madrid, Mola refused to be pessimistic. No plot
could be perfect. And even if the revolt in Madrid failed, it would succeed elsewhere, and Madrid, isolated, would fall in the end anyway. Besides, it could be
fatal to delay the insurrection any longer, especially with rumors spreading that
one was imminent. Little wonder that the government was sending spies to check
on his activities—information he had learned from his own intelligence agents.

Furthermore, Mola had heard that the Communists were planning to rebel in
late July, with the left-wing socialist leader Francisco Largo Caballero, known as
the Spanish Lenin, playing the role of Stalin's chief puppet. And the anarchists
were plotting their own revolution, which would wipe out government altogether. Though there was no evidence to support either report, Mola apparently
believed them because they helped to justify his own conspiracy. The "reds"—a
word referring to all supporters of the government—had to be headed off
quickly.

Mola's optimism, his Prussianlike methodical mind, his rigid mores leavened
with intellectualism, were traits that had led to his swift rise in an army overload-
ed with officers—one out of every ten men. He was wounded in Morocco while

hardening himself for seventeen years in the bloody campaign to subdue the Moors. In 1928, shortly after the Spanish had finally conquered Morocco, he was appointed its military governor, and in 1930 became Spain's chief security officer.

When the republic swept into power in 1931, Mola was jailed for his persecution of republicans though he had also criticized the monarchy. Not long after he was released, he went to work for Franco, who had risen to chief of staff. Later he was sent back to Morocco to command the forces there and took over Franco's task of conciliating the Moors, who even agreed to join the Spanish army as mercenaries. But President Azaña decided to move Mola and other distrusted officers to new, more obscure, posts where presumably they would be less able to make trouble. Franco was sent to the Canary Islands, Mola to Pamplona.

Now all officers favoring a revolt looked to Mola for leadership, calling him *El Director.* They considered him not only the brightest of them but in the best position to direct a *pronunciamiento.* For though the government had given him a rather unimportant post, it had ironically facilitated a conspiracy, since Pamplona was right in the heart of the most reactionary, antirepublican region in Spain—Navarre. The general could therefore count on the people of that region to support him and supply many of the men he would need.

Convinced that Madrid could not be captured from within, Mola called for an initial rising in the northern cities. From these towns, including Pamplona, rebel troops would swiftly converge on Madrid, storming the Guadarrama passes as Napoleon had done 128 years earlier. At the same time, Franco would fly from the Canary Islands to Morocco and with his army there cross over to Spain in naval vessels and attack from the south.

Meanwhile, shortly after the revolt broke out, General José Sanjurjo, Spain's most senior and respected officer, who led an abortive coup in 1932 and was now living in Portugal, would fly to Burgos to be proclaimed chief of a new governing *junta,* which would include Mola and Franco.

If the rebels in Madrid found they could not capture the city, they should try to flee northward to join Mola's troops in storming the capital. By no means should they let themselves be surrounded in their barracks.

Since Spanish noncommissioned officers and soldiers generally came from the lower classes, which backed the republic, they could not be trusted. Therefore, few would be used in this complex operation. Franco would rely mainly on the Moors and foreign legionnaires, a volunteer group of adventurers and social misfits, 90 percent Spanish despite their name. The legionnaires, like the Moors, were reputed for their ruthlessness and their utter scorn of danger, as reflected in their motto: Long Live Death!

Mola had a more difficult problem. He had to depend mainly on two amateur forces: the Falangists, young followers of José Antonio Primo de Rivera, with little or no military training; and the *Requetés,* the self-trained paramilitary organization of the Carlists, mostly Navarrans, who wanted to set up a medieval-type monarchy.

While there were many question marks, the biggest remained Madrid itself. As Fanjul told Mola, most officers did not seem cooperative, though at H-hour, Mola assured his visitor, the situation in Madrid would be resolved. He promised to send last-minute orders when the final date for the rising was set. There were still a few hurdles to clear. For one thing, Mola was waiting for word from Franco that he was ready to leave for Morocco.

Despite his pessimism, Fanjul showed a courageous spirit and even refused the opportunity to take another command. The son of a professional soldier who had worked his way up through the ranks, he was a simple, unimposing though intelligent man, a lawyer and former parliamentary deputy thoroughly imbued with Navarran conservatism. He had been vice-minister of war until the February election won by the Popular Front, a man who had gone far through dedication to duty and hard work.

Now, at fifty-six, it appeared he would die—probably before he could enjoy the sight of his beloved army marching triumphantly through Madrid. But what concerned him more was the fate of his two sons, both of them officers in Madrid. One, Juan Manuel, a Falangist, had accompanied him to Pamplona. His sons, like himself, might be trapped in a hostile, murderous city. His family might be wiped out.

On the evening of his arrival in Pamplona, Fanjul and his son had joined some old friends for supper at a farm outside the town. It was a happy occasion, as Fanjul would remark to the civil governor at the bullfight on the following day, and one of his hosts invited him to celebrate San Fermín next year at the same place.

"I promise you I'll be here," Fanjul replied doubtfully. "If my head is still on my shoulders."

2

Sunday, July 12, was a steaming summer day in Madrid. The sun beamed down from a luminous Velázquez sky upon a city in lazy repose, a half-deserted city, for many people had gone on vacation or to the country for the weekend, a city that echoed with the cheerful sounds of leisure. Children played in the West Park under shady trees or along the sandy pathways that led to a huge rose garden near the bank of the Manzanares River. Lovers went rowing in Retiro Park under the gaze of white stone lions, while statues of kings and queens peered out from the surrounding shrubbery.

Thousands of bargain hunters swarmed through the Rastro, the Madrid flea market, and thrilled to the discovery of a candlestick from ancient times or an out-of-print edition of Shakespeare. Passengers streamed endlessly from yellow Toonerville trolleys gathered in gayly clanging pandemonium at the Puerta del Sol in the heart of the city, and strolled unhurriedly past the fine shops and restaurants lining the winding alleys that extended from the plaza like the crooked legs of a giant spider. People who strolled to Plaza Mayor entered a huge enclosed square bordered by seventeenth-century buildings and stone arcades where they sipped coffee or wine at outdoor cafés under balconies from which ancient kings once watched bullfights, tournaments, pageants, and the burning of heretics.

Other *Madrileños* crowded into Madrid's more modern bullring to see blood under the sun, attended a morning concert, went to an exhibition of "catch-as-catch-can" wrestling, or stood in the long queues in front of a theater showing *The Gay Divorcee* with Fred Astaire and Ginger Rogers. And many went with their family or friends for lunch at a favorite restaurant.

Lieutenant José Castillo and his bride, Consuelo, however, lunched at home. They were celebrating her father's birthday with her parents, and they joked and laughed and enjoyed the afternoon immensely. And yet, an almost morbid melancholy showed through their good humor. The young couple, who had been married just fifty-two days, were to be parents themselves, and their baby would be born at an uncertain time, when no one could foresee Spain's fate—or his own.

They were not alone in their inner gloom. Tension also gripped many other *Madrileños* who were making the most of this fine day, even as they hummed the latest hit tune, "The Music Goes Round and Round," and talked excitedly about the Verbena de San Juan, the annual summer festival that would open the following day and turn Madrid into a mecca of music and amusement. Contrary to the ostrich-like attitude of some government figures, most people had little doubt that an explosion was at hand that could radically change their lives and futures.

But the Castillos had more reason for concern than most, for the lieutenant, a member of the progovernment Assault Guards, was a marked man. He had been one since April 17. On that day took place the funeral of a leading Falangist, Lieutenant Anastasio de los Reyes, who had been killed two days before during a parade celebrating the fifth anniversary of the republic. A bomb had exploded near the tribune where President Azaña was seated, setting off a shooting match between republican guards and Falangist gunmen that resulted in Reyes's death.

About four hundred Falangists and other rightists further inflamed the atmosphere during the funeral when they carried the body to the cemetery in a procession through the main streets of Madrid. The marchers gave the Fascist salute, and the leftists fired at them from buildings along the way, provoking another gun battle. Lieutenant Castillo rushed to the scene with a group of Assault Guards to restore order, and a rumor spread like dust in a storm that he had killed a cousin of José Antonio Primo de Rivera's. But the truth was—as told to the author by another cousin of José Antonio's, José Luis Sáenz Heredia, who was there—that the victim had been shot before Castillo had even arrived on the scene. The Falangists vowed revenge whether or not they believed the rumor, for Castillo had become a symbol of government authority.

The lieutenant moved in with his future in-laws but he would not flee Madrid, feeling it his duty to remain with his colleagues, who loved him, the young socialists he was training to fight, and the workers he protected. He did not look like a man of great physical strength, with his tall slim build and small face decorated with a thin mustache and dominated by round black-rimmed spectacles. But he had a powerful hold over all who knew him, and he now reciprocated their faith by refusing to abandon them even at this moment of great personal danger.

Still, as a marked man Castillo wondered how effective he could now be, and his bride lived in constant fear for her husband's life. In May, a colleague, Captain Carlos Faraudo, had been shot dead by Falangists while walking down the street with his wife. And Castillo himself received threatening notes almost daily. On one visit to a neighborhood bar he barely escaped assassination when the would-be killer suddenly dashed out shouting, "I can't do it!" Castillo's tormentors would not even let Consuelo alone. Just before their wedding, an anonymous message arrived for her, saying: "Do not marry Castillo. He is on our list. You will be a widow within a month. You have been warned."

While Lieutenant José Castillo lunched with his wife and in-laws, another prize target, who had the same first name but held diametrically opposed political views, was also dining with his family at home. José Calvo Sotelo, the chief spokesman for the Right in the Cortes, normally went with his wife and children to the country on weekends. But this weekend, the family remained in Madrid.

Calvo Sotelo was close to the army leaders, and he knew that General Mola would probably launch a coup in the coming week. As soon as he got the signal, he would have to flee the country immediately with his family, for the "reds" would surely come for him before anyone else. Indeed, he had heard that they might come for him even before then. That was why he had stayed home this weekend.

"If we left the house, it would be easier for them to get me," he told his wife, according to his son, José junior. "But they wouldn't dare come to my home."

And besides, two soldiers were standing watch outside. But could he trust these new guards? He wasn't sure. The last two were suspect and had to be removed. Calvo Sotelo heard rumors that the chief of police had ordered them not to disturb any attempts to kill him in the city, and to actually assist in murdering him in the country.

Friends had pleaded with him for weeks to leave Madrid but, like Lieutenant

Castillo, he refused. The "reds" could not drive him out. He would go only at the last moment. And when Madrid fell to the army, he would return and help to set up the kind of government he felt Spain needed. He had explained to a journalist what that was: a blend of Portuguese military dictatorship and Italian fascism within a monarchy.

Calvo Sotelo came from a distinguished Galician family and was a man of grace and good manners. His world was the world of old Spain in which men like himself ruled benevolently over a people blessed with the peace and order imposed by social hierarchy. Spaniards had to know their place. He knew his, and the masses being excited to violence by crude, power-hungry leaders would have to learn theirs. No peasant or worker should starve, but neither should he expect to live so well that he would forget his place. Calvo Sotelo was thus impatient with social reforms. After all, where did reform end and revolution begin?

Calvo Sotelo had skyrocketed to prominence at a remarkably early age. At twenty, only fresh out of university, he was already serving as secretary to Antonio Maura, the prime minister under King Alfonso XIII. Five years later he was sitting in the civil governor's chair in Valencia, and when General Primo de Rivera took over as dictator in 1923, he emerged as minister of finance. After the dictator fell in 1930, followed by the king the next year, Calvo Sotelo fled to Paris. But a few years later, he was back and in the limelight again—as a deputy in the Cortes, representing the monarchist Spanish Renovation party he led.

Calvo Sotelo proved to be a cool, eloquent debater and seized the reins of rightist leadership from Gil Robles, the head of the Spanish Confederation of Autonomous Movements of the Right, a Catholic party known as CEDA. Robles did not want a Fascist-type dictatorship as did Calvo Sotelo, but simply a conservative republic that would keep the class structure intact and the Church powerful. He thus crushed a leftist rebellion in the Asturias region with great brutality when he became war minister in 1933, a post he held until the Popular Front surged to power in February 1936.

With Robles's influence flagging, only Falangist leader José Antonio Primo de Rivera stood out as a strong rival to Calvo Sotelo, and the government had jailed him. Thus, Calvo Sotelo was clearly the star of the Right in the summer of 1936. And on June 16, in the midst of murderous street fighting, he sardonically warned the Cortes what might happen:

"When I hear talk of the danger from monarchist generals, I smile a little, for I do not believe . . . that there is, in the Spanish army, a single soldier disposed to rise on behalf of a monarchy and against the republic. If there were such a person he would be mad—I speak with all sincerity, mad indeed—as would be any soldier who, before eternity, would not be ready to rise on behalf of Spain, and against anarchy—if *that* should be necessary."

Azaña's prime minister, Santiago Casares Quiroga, stood up and replied with choked fury at this hint of a possible coup: "After Your Excellency's words, the responsibility for whatever happens will be yours. You come here today with two aims only: to condemn the Cortes as impotent, and to inflame the army, trying to detach units from their loyalty to the republic. But I give my assurance. The Cortes *will* work. The army *will* do its duty."

Choosing to interpret this statement as a personal threat, Calvo Sotelo rose again, poised, arrogant, and proclaimed: "My shoulders are broad. I do not shun, indeed I accept with pleasure, the responsibility for what I do . . . I recall the answer given by St. Dominic of Silos to a Spanish king: 'Sire, my life you may take from me, but more you cannot take!' Is it not, indeed, better to perish gloriously, than to live in contempt?"

Now, almost a month later, Calvo Sotelo felt that these words might have been prophetic. Certainly there were those who would like to see him perish . . . But what nonsense to meditate on such things on this bright, beautiful day.

After lunch, while his two young sons went outside for a soccer game with the neighborhood children, he sat down in his study and played classical gramophone records, listening raptly to the music of his favorite composers, Wagner and Albéniz. He had once been a music critic for a leading Madrid newspaper, and often regretted that he had not become an orchestra conductor.

Life would have been happier—and perhaps longer.

About 9:45 P.M., Lieutenant Castillo and his wife walked slowly along Calle Augusto Figueroa toward their home after going for a stroll with Consuelo's parents. It was still warm, and the couple had wanted to continue their promenade, but Castillo was scheduled for duty that night at nearby Pontejos Barracks in the Puerta del Sol.

"Please let me walk with you to the barracks," Consuelo urged.

She not only would enjoy the walk but she didn't want him to be on the streets alone. She imagined that somehow her presence might protect him.

But her husband refused, insisting that she stay home. Consuelo felt that he was jealous and simply didn't want her to meet his colleagues. A typical Andalusian! When they reached the corner of Calle Hortaleza near their house, they stopped and embraced, and he promised to return in a few hours. After a final kiss, he turned and walked on toward Calle Fuencarral, while she started toward the house.

In the soft shadows of evening, three men loitered on the opposite side of Calle Augusto Figueroa near the corner of Calle Fuencarral while a fourth walked directly toward Castillo, according to Castillo's brother, Paco. Suddenly the man approaching the lieutenant shouted, "That's him!" And those across the street fired several pistol shots. When the bullets whizzed over Castillo's head, the man who had pointed him out ran toward him firing his own pistol. He collided with his victim, and the two men fell together on the sidewalk. The killer immediately got to his feet, picked up Castillo's glasses by mistake, and joined his accomplices in flight.

A short time later, Paco told the author, the man audaciously went to the clinic where Castillo's body had been taken and asked for his own spectacles, apparently to avoid identification, and bluffed a clerk into giving them to him!

Consuelo was about to enter her house when she heard the cry and the shots, and in panic rushed to her husband's side. He was already dead.

News of Lieutenant Castillo's assassination spread rapidly and stunned government supporters. "Vengeance! Vengeance!" the cry went up. And nowhere more vehemently than in Pontejos Barracks, where Castillo had been heading when he was killed. Within two hours, not only dozens of Assault Guards but also friends from the army and the Civil Guard and some civilians came streaming in. Most were members of the Anti-Fascist Republican Military Union (UMRA), which had been formed in 1935 to counter the activities of the rightist military organization, UME.

It seemed clear to them that the assassins were Falangists working together with the UME—though the identity of the killers is unknown to this day. UMRA had vowed after Lieutenant Faraudo was assassinated in May that if the rightist murders continued, its members would strike back with a sensational retaliatory act. They would not stand by and be eliminated one by one. And now the time had come.

The chief of police learned of the meeting at Pontejos. Remain calm, he advised, and don't take any action that would perpetuate the chain of killings. The government would find the murderers of Castillo and bring them to justice. But as moderate socialist leader Indalecio Prieto would write later, the chief of police "did not know how to impose his authority and energetically call on them [the leftist plotters] to obey him."

At about midnight, one of Castillo's closest friends, Assault Guard Lieutenant Alfonso Barbeta, shouted above the tumult the sentiment of all: "We must avenge our comrade's death. I, for one, will do so regardless of the consequences." Everybody agreed, and now the only question was: Who was to be the victim?

The guards chose Antonio Goicoechea, Calvo Sotelo's deputy in the Spanish Renovation party, according to Urbano Orad de la Torre, a socialist artillery officer who was a comrade of the plotters. Who would head the grisly mission? They drew lots, and Captain Fernando Condés of the Civil Guard "won." A sensitive young officer, Condés was, ironically, one of those least enamored with the idea of assassination. But no one could have resisted the pressures that had been generated for vengeance. And even Condés felt that there was no longer an alternative to murder, though he later claimed he had intended merely to take a hostage and not to kill anyone.

At about 2:00 A.M., July 13, only five hours after Castillo's death, police wagon 17 raced out of Pontejos Barracks carrying sixteen men dressed in civilian clothes. Within minutes, the vehicle ground to a halt in front of Goicoechea's house—but no one was home. Who was next on the list? Someone suggested Gil Robles. The car sped to *his* house, but *he* was in Biarritz. The men were despondent. They had to kill somebody.

"What about Calvo Sotelo?" one of them exclaimed.

There was a moment of silence. The idea of killing the chief, the top man, was somehow frightening, though some of the plotters had thought about this for weeks. The repercussions could be staggering. His murder might easily trigger the *pronunciamiento* they were sure was being planned, perhaps even a civil war. But in this moment of unreasoned fury the assassination of Calvo Sotelo seemed utterly logical.

Calvo Sotelo had spent the evening in his study catching up on his correspondence, typing rapidly with two fingers. There was a lot to do before he left Madrid, and he had to make sure that everything was done by the time he received word that the revolt was starting. At about 10:00 P.M. he sat down to dinner. Normally when he was finished, he would call up the monarchist newspaper, *ABC,* and ask for the latest news. But this was Sunday, and there was no Monday paper. Probably nothing important had happened that day anyway, or someone would have called him. He didn't even bother to turn on the radio.

At about midnight, Calvo Sotelo went to bed, no doubt wondering when he would spend another peaceful day at home listening to his records and working quietly in his study.

Police wagon 17 sped down Calle Diego de León and turned into fashionable Calle Velázquez, pulling up at apartment building number 89. Captain Condés jumped out, gave orders to three men to stop and question all drivers passing the house, and posted two, armed with submachine guns, on adjacent corners. He then approached two security guards who were standing by the gate of the house and flashed his identity card, showing him to be a captain in the Civil Guard. Before they could respond, he announced with grim authority:

"We're going up to Calvo Sotelo's flat to do our duty."

The two guards, intimidated and apparently unaware of the mission of this carload of armed men, did not object. A night watchman appeared and Condés ordered him to unlock the front gate. Condés then led a group of his men up to the third floor, and rang the doorbell.

"Who is it? What do you want?" asked the maid.

"Open up. It's the police," Condés replied.

The maid knocked on Calvo Sotelo's door and awakened him. He rushed to the balcony and called down to his guards: Had they checked the policemen's identity? Yes, one of them shouted back. As soon as Condés and his men were let in they immediately went into the study and cut the telephone cord. Condés then ordered Calvo Sotelo to come with them to police headquarters for questioning.

"There must be some mistake," Calvo Sotelo replied, apparently with growing suspicion. "As a deputy I enjoy parliamentary immunity and cannot be detained unless caught in a criminal act, and this is not the case. I'll call police headquarters and straighten this out."

When he found that his telephone had been cut, his children's governess tried to go out to use a neighbor's phone, but she wasn't allowed to leave. He had orders, said Condés, not to let Calvo Sotelo communicate with anyone. However, he needn't worry. In five minutes he would be at police headquarters where he could make any statement he wished.

Calvo Sotelo clearly felt he had no choice. They might kill him right there in front of his family if he refused to leave. So he agreed. He and his wife then went to their bedroom where he dressed while she packed a small valise with toilet articles, writing paper, and a pen. Suddenly she looked at him with a sense of dread and pleaded:

"Don't go, don't go."

"Be quiet," Calvo Sotelo replied gently, "or they'll laugh at you, and then I won't be responsible for what I might do."

When his wife had escorted him to the door, he turned to her and said: "I'm sorry for you because of all this. You're always the victim."

"When will I hear from you?" she asked.

"When I get to police headquarters I'll try to get in touch with you . . . if these gentlemen don't blow my brains out."

Calvo Sotelo then walked downstairs and entered the wagon, with the others following him, and the vehicle raced down Calle Velázquez. When it turned into Calle Ayala, he exclaimed:

"Where are we going? This is not the way to police headquarters!"

At that moment, the man sitting directly behind Calvo Sotelo, Victoriano Cuenca, pulled a pistol from his pocket and fired two shots into the back of the prisoner's head. The victim slumped forward.

Speeding up, the wagon raced on to the East Cemetery, where the killers left the body, explaining to the caretaker that they had found it abandoned on the street. As the vehicle roared away, one of the men warned: "Whoever breathes a word of this will be committing suicide. We'll kill him just like we killed that swine."

3

On the afternoon of July 13, a tall thin man with a sallow complexion stepped into an elevator that soared to the top of one of the highest business buildings in Madrid, overlooking Calle de Alcalá. He entered a suite of offices and morosely contemplated sitting in his "cage of glass and iron" and listening to more inventors explain how their new gadgets could revolutionize a whole industry, perhaps the whole economy.

Arturo Barea was a hardworking disgruntled bureaucrat who was bored with both his wife and his mistress and dreamed of a new Spain and a new life. He worked in the government patent office, a job, he felt, that was growing less vital each day. This was a time not of constructive but of destructive change. One needed no patent for that kind of change, only bombs, bullets, and blood. Barea was a socialist, a true believer in the betterment of mankind, yet a tormented cynic. He envisioned the world being destroyed in the name of human justice.

Barea was startled to see only unoccupied desks as he walked toward his own office. Everyone had gathered around the desk of the chief administrator, who was speaking with a broken voice and defiant gestures.

"What the devil is going on here?" Barea asked an employee.

"Good Lord, don't you know? They've killed Calvo Sotelo!"

Only a few hours earlier, the body at the cemetery had been identified and the volcano had erupted. Most of the employees, from "good families," were aghast.

"It's a crime against God!" the chief administrator shouted. "Such a man, so clever, so good, such a Christian, such a gentleman, killed like a dog."

"We'll settle the account," someone promised. "They'll have little time to rejoice. Now the only thing we can do is to go out into the street."

Barea, stunned by the news, turned and left. Who would be registering patents today?! He walked past the fairgrounds of the Verbena de San Juan, at the Glorieta de Atocha, where workmen were feverishly setting up a merry-go-round, building wood-and-canvas stalls, unloading packing cases. Tonight the fair would start and everything had to be ready. Madrid would amuse itself even as it prepared for catastrophe. And Calvo Sotelo's murder, Barea was sure, would lead to just that.

His dilemma was painful. Unlike many Spaniards, he abhorred violence, and vomited at the very sight of blood. But like many, he was prepared to see Spain destroy itself in fratricidal battle to clear the way for the building of a new and more just society. He had been brutalized by the Spanish lawyer of the German embassy, a business contact, who had become an honorary member of the SS and suggested to him that what Spain needed was "a whiff of German civilization." And by the village priest, who had told him with a pleasant smile shortly after he had bought a country house in the Guadarramas:

"I've noticed, of course, that you don't go to church on Sundays. I know you are one of those socialists and have dealings with the lower-class people of our village. I must tell you, when you set up house here and I saw your wife and children, I thought: *They seem the right kind of people. Pray God it be so.* But—it seems I was mistaken."

Yes, mistaken. He was not, Barea agreed, one of the "right kind of people," the kind who would preach love to the "lower-class people" without giving them love, who would preach justice to them without giving justice.

And so, as the employee in his office had said on hearing of Calvo Sotelo's murder: "Now the only thing we can do is to go out into the street."

Arturo Barea's pessimism was shared by other Spaniards after the two ruthless murders. Captain Condés visited Indalecio Prieto, the moderate socialist leader, and told him of the slaying. Despondently, he said that he contemplated suicide. His mission, he insisted, had been one of honor, but he nevertheless could not live with the thought that he had helped to murder someone in cold blood. Prieto was shocked and replied that the crime was inexcusable. But, being a practical man, he added:

"Don't worry. It won't be long before you'll have to risk your life defending your ideals, and you'll then have an important mission to accomplish."

If one was going to die at this point, why not die usefully?

And while Prieto deplored the thought of civil war, he went to Prime Minister Casares Quiroga and urged him to let the people have arms before it was too late.

The answer was no.

"If I do what you want Señor Prieto," responded Casares, "you, not I, will be running the country. It happens that I am prime minister. I shall guide the nation through the storm."

Casares—and his overseer, President Azaña—feared a rightist revolt, but they also feared a leftist revolution. And while Casares arrested some suspected army officers, broke up rightist parades, and ordered several ships to anchor in Moroccan waters to block troops from sailing to Spain, he and Azaña still felt the storm would blow over. Even the thunderous oratory in the Cortes seemed to them like empty bombast. True, the monarchists walked out and promised never to come back. And Gil Robles told Popular Front deputies that the "blood of Calvo Sotelo . . . falls on your head! . . . The day is not far off when the violence you have unleashed will turn back on you." But while this sounded like a declaration of war, so had dozens of other political statements in recent months.

In fact, Cortes leaders optimistically scheduled a session of parliament for July 21—though with the discreet request that all members kindly check their weapons at the cloakroom.

* * *

The two Spains that had crystallized, each incapable of understanding the other, were tragically symbolized on July 14 by two emotion-charged funerals in Madrid's East Cemetery. In one part of the cemetery, thousands of people lifted their arms in the Fascist salute as the body of Calvo Sotelo, wrapped in a monk's hood and gown, was laid to rest.

Antonio Goicoechea, Calvo Sotelo's deputy in the Spanish Renovation party, who might have been lying in the coffin himself if he had been home on the night of Lieutenant Castillo's murder, called upon the mourners to take an oath of vengeance. Fervently they replied, "We swear, before God and before Spain!"—as bullets whizzed by in another riot between rightists and leftists that cost several more lives.

A little earlier in a different part of the cemetery, thousands of others had raised the clenched fist, the Popular Front salute, as Castillo's coffin, draped in a red flag, was lowered into his grave.

One of the mourners at this funeral was a tall, middle-aged, black-garbed woman with ascetic features and eyes that radiated burning intensity under heavy lids. She had a wide sloping forehead and long black hair that was wound into a bun at the nape of her neck. Dolores Ibarruri, known as *La Pasionaria*. "The Passion Flower" was a Communist deputy whose dramatic, accusing voice sent tremors of emotion through people sitting in the Cortes, at meetings, or by the radio. While her hands danced before her as if she were directing an orchestra, words gushed from her throat in raging torrents that overwhelmed the listener, impelling him to love or hate her, worship or fear her.

Dolores was the purest kind of Communist, utterly uncorrupted by opportunism. Needing a god to replace the one she had long since abandoned, she found Stalin the perfect substitute. For whatever his faults, and at whatever price, she felt, he was creating an egalitarian society in which simple people could occupy a dignified place. But if she had a Stalinist mind, she did not have a Stalinist heart. Indeed, it was the warmth and basic humanity showing through the imperial arrogance of her voice that won over thousands of sympathizers who otherwise deplored communism. To synchronize the dictates of mind and heart, Dolores carried rationalization to the ultimate, and she could do this because she had experienced the ultimate in human misery and degradation.

Born into a Basque miner's family in 1895, she would always remember her first home, a bunkhouse that seemed out of a "scene from Dante": the smell of sweat, urine, harsh tobacco, and fermented food; the blurred lamplit vision of half-naked exhausted miners sleeping on sacks stuffed with cornshucks; the cries of men with smallpox or typhus as they were removed from their cots to a hut of death while others replaced them as soon as lime water could be sprinkled on the infected bunk.

And she remembered also her father, an old man, standing knee-deep in mud and shivering in the icy cold as he shoveled ore wastes; the nuns dressing a scarecrow in purple velvet to look like the Virgin so they could use it to frighten people into obeying the "authorities"; the rebellious miners who had been arrested and thrown into the "kennel," the jail right under her school where children, taught that anyone who acted against the established order was a criminal, cruelly urinated upon them through cracks in the floor.

And then her marriage to a miner, who was soon jailed for striking; the birth of six children, including triplets, fed with food and diapered with rags provided by a compassionate beggar; the four little graves side by side, as all but two children succumbed to hunger and disease.

Life, Dolores later wrote, was "like a deep pit without horizons, where the light of the sun never reached, illuminated at times only by the bloody glare of the struggles that burst out in flames of violence when the capacity to bear brutal treatment had reached the limits of human endurance." She was filled with a "bitter, instinctive resentment which made me lash out against everything and everybody."

Communism seemed the most natural outlet for her resentment, the most suitable instrument for lashing out. She went to jail several times, but the jailers were glad to be rid of her since she was always haranguing the prostitutes and other women prisoners about their rights and demanding better prison conditions. When she was elected to the Cortes, the rightists would also have liked to be rid of her, for she was the Left's most eloquent speaker, what Calvo Sotelo was to the Right.

Though the Communist party was small, Dolores, who now headed its Political Bureau, was giving it a voice far out of proportion to its size. For one didn't have to be a Communist to be dazzled—and disturbed—by this woman, whose own festering wounds somehow lent credence to her promises to pull the people out of the deep pit into the sunlight.

As she stood with clenched fist saluting the body of Lieutenant Castillo, Dolores was sure the moment was near for the final showdown with the mine owners, the police, the soldiers, and the Church that had backed them, with all those who reminded her of the foul odors and desperate cries in the bunkhouse of her childhood. The Communist party would burgeon as a result, for it was the most militant and determined group in the Popular Front. And it had Stalin.

Late that afternoon of July 14, two other Communists left the office of the Communist newspaper *Mundo Obrero* and cautiously walked down the street, glancing behind them every few moments to see if they were being followed. The Falangists were looking for people who worked for that paper, especially on this day of Calvo Sotelo's funeral.

The two men entered the nearby Arquelles Bar and ordered coffee. Enrique

Castro Delgado, short, stocky, cold-eyed, often relaxed over coffee with his comrade, Luis Sendín, after work, and this was a grueling day, with two funerals to report on and a *pronunciamiento* likely to explode soon. Castro was a kind of handyman for the party. He agitated in the trade unions in Madrid and wandered all over Spain clandestinely seeking new party members. Now he was writing inflammatory articles for *Mundo Obrero*. And he hoped soon to command a new Popular Front militia—if fighting broke out—though he had had only about two years of army training.

It was his experience in the army that had triggered his decision to join the party. He came from a poor Madrid family; his father couldn't find work, his mother scrubbed floors, and the numerous children had little to eat. Castro had quit school at an early age when his teacher, a priest, struck him for some minor offense, and he went to work for a tailor, then an electrician. The proud officers in the army had little patience with soldiers of such lowly station, and treated him brutally.

Castro decided to fight back. He joined the Communist party. And now, at twenty-eight, he was a man of considerable stature. He was finally respected for his toughness, his tenacity, his ability to be as brutal as those who had made him so. These were the qualities that the party needed at this time of crisis—and opportunity.

"Will they rise?" Sendín asked Castro, referring to the army.

"What else can they do?" Castro replied. "They either accept final defeat or make one more attempt to save themselves. . . . For years we have been working for the sake of the revolution. Let it come . . . as soon as possible."

"To kill . . ."

"Yes, Sendin, to kill. The old has to be killed, broken into pieces. Into dust. Close your eyes and dream of tomorrow. When I do, I think of the Russian revolution, of the red battalions of workers and peasants. It seems to me I see one world dying and another being born."

"To kill . . ."

"There's no revolution without blood. For a long time we've been talking to workers about salary increases, shorter working hours, more freedom. But those were all intermediate stages. It was a gradual approach. Now it's a question of the fundamental thing, of the last great battle."

"To kill . . ."

"Is there another way?"

The undersized Communist party would probably have no influence at all if it were not for *La Pasionaria*'s personal magnetism. But if the Right attempted a coup, Castro's militia would lead the way in crushing the rebels. The party would then suddenly be at the top of the political heap—and Castro would have his revenge on the pompous officers who had humiliated him.

Everything now depended on the cooperation of Mola and Franco—on whether the Right would try to "save itself."

Elena Medina looked pale as she stepped into General Mola's apartment in Saragossa, one of his command posts. It was about 10:00 A.M., July 14, a few hours before Calvo Sotelo was to be buried, and rightists all over Spain were in an uproar over his murder, demanding swift revenge. And she was coming with news that could determine whether their hopes would crystallize.

Elena was Mola's private secretary, an aristocratic woman whom the general entrusted with his most delicate missions. She had just returned from Madrid with a coded message from two generals who served as Franco's contacts. Earlier, Mola had sent a message to Franco in the Canary Islands. A private plane would pick him up at a still undetermined time and fly him to Morocco. There he would take over command of the Moors and foreign legionnaires from Colonel Yagüe and pack them into naval vessels that would sail to Spain for the attack on Madrid. Now Elena stood waiting for Mola with Franco's reply, impatiently tapping her heels on the floor.

According to Elena, Mola finally entered and said, noting her unhappy expression: "Good morning, señorita. Please sit down and don't look so glum. Is anything wrong? What's going on in Madrid?"

"It's not in Madrid, señor. It's in the Canaries. I've got a message in my belt. Have you a scissors?"

Elena removed her cloth belt, cut some stitching in it, and took out a neatly folded piece of paper. The message had been invisibly written in chlorine and would only emerge when a hot iron was applied.

The general and his secretary went into a small laundry room and he heated the paper with an iron. As he saw the emerging words, his face grew red. The message said: *Geografía Poco Extensa* ("Geography too small").

In a fit of rage, Mola crumpled the paper in his hand and threw it to the floor, together with the belt. But he quickly picked them up, handing the belt back to Elena with apologies.

Then he said, trying to control himself: "I suspected this. I'm not really surprised. Those three words mean three others: 'Franco won't come.'"

The revolt would go on without Franco, Mola added coldly. There was little choice. Some army forces were so stirred up by Calvo Sotelo's death that they were ready to rebel on their own. The general left for several minutes, then returned with another folded piece of paper.

"Put this in your belt," he said, "and go to Morocco without telling anybody. Give this to Colonel Yagüe personally and explain our situation to him. If he thinks he can bring the troops from Morocco to Spain without help, don't send me a cable. If he needs help, I'll send General Sanjurjo to Morocco. In that case, send me a cable saying, 'The feasts are incredible in Pamplona. Please tell me if there is an extra place.' And sign it 'Consuelo.' ''

And he added: ''If Yagüe needs Sanjurjo, don't forget to tell him to paint a white line on the runway ten meters long and one and a half meters wide, which will mean the airport belongs to the movement. I don't want them to take Sanjurjo prisoner.''

Under Mola's original plan, Sanjurjo was to fly from Lisbon to Burgos shortly after the revolt in Morocco started, and there take command of the rebel movement. But now plans would have to be changed—if Yagüe felt he could not handle the situation alone. One of Mola's aides suddenly grew fearful. Without Franco the revolt might fail.

''General,'' he said, ''if things go wrong they'll kill you.''

''Don't worry about me,'' Mola replied brusquely. ''Nothing can stop the revolt.''

And he ordered his aide from the room.

Elena departed with her urgent message but the next day, before she could reach Morocco, another message arrived from Madrid. Franco had changed his mind. With Calvo Sotelo's killing, the revolt could not be canceled or even postponed. The pressures were too great. And if the rebellion started without him, Franco would be frozen out of its leadership. He wasn't one to take unnecessary risks, but he would have to take the risk now—if he were not to abandon his dream of becoming the caudillo of Spain.

Mola was greatly relieved; with Franco taking part, the machinery was finally in high gear. Madrid, of course, was still a grave problem. The rebels there were in greater disarray than ever since the killing of Lieutenant Castillo, and some officers were fleeing the city or going into hiding, for the masses were starting to demand arms and preparing to crush an expected rebellion. However, it was foolish to worry about the inevitable snags at this stage.

In midmorning, July 17, Colonel Yagüe, who was awaiting the arrival of Franco in Morocco, transmitted a coded message to his fellow conspirators in Madrid: JACINTO LEAL ASKS ME TO CONGRATULATE YOU ON YOUR NAME DAY. Signed FERNANDO GUTIERREZ.

The recipients counted seventeen letters in the signature. This meant the revolt in Morocco would begin that day at 5:00 P.M.

CHAPTER 2

Retribution

1

Probably the most famous bull in Spain at this time was a huge ferocious-looking animal called Civilón. For despite his presumed fierceness, Civilón seemed to like children, and hundreds of photographs appeared in the press showing tots stroking him while he stood patiently, not even bothering to snort. The day came when Civilón was let loose in the bullring in Barcelona and the crowd wondered whether any *torero* could survive a bout with this savage beast. It soon found out. Civilón fled at the sight of the *torero* and finally had to be driven out of the ring.

Civilón was turned into supper beef, but his name lived on—in the person of Prime Minister Casares Quiroga. Many of his officers quietly referred to him by this name because he spoke with a ferocious voice against the rightists but did little to prevent them from plotting or to prepare for a showdown with them.

"If they throw a chair at me," he would simply say, "I shall throw a table at them."

Casares was a slender, sickly man with sunken cheeks and cynical eyes that mocked anyone who differed with him, and this meant almost everybody. Sensitive to charges that he was little more than a tool of President Azaña, Casares tried to give an impression of authority by ridiculing anyone who offered him unsolicited advice.

Shortly after noon, July 17, Casares was presiding at a cabinet meeting when a messenger brought him a note. He casually read it, put it in his pocket, and went on discussing with the other government members the usual daily business. He even told a joke. When the meeting was about to end, Casares suddenly remembered the note in his pocket. He drew it out and said:

"Oh, by the way, gentlemen, there's one other thing."

He read the note aloud, and his listeners gasped. The "other thing" was that an uprising had started in Morocco!

At about this time, General Franco was attending a funeral in Las Palmas, capital of the Canary Islands. General Amadeo Balmes, military governor of Las Palmas, had been killed at target practice the preceding day, July 16, and his funeral gave Franco an ideal excuse to leave his headquarters in Tenerife for that city, where a private plane was waiting to take him to Morocco. The War Ministry had approved the trip, so shortly after midnight Franco, his wife, daughter, and cousin boarded a boat sailing there.

Franco was officially supposed to return to Tenerife the day after the funeral, but his plans were a bit hazy. He had heard that the revolt had already broken out in Morocco. Something had gone wrong, he realized. It shouldn't have started until 5:00 A.M. the next morning, July 18. He would learn later that a rebel "traitor" in the Moroccan town of Melilla had tipped off the government about the planned rising early in the afternoon, forcing the rebels to act immediately before they were arrested. At pistol point, the conspirators took over the military government in Melilla and a fierce battle with socialist militia was now raging in the city.

With the funeral over, Franco could have left for Morocco immediately to lead the revolt, but he decided to wait until morning. Perhaps the haze would clear by then. After all, why rush into a possibly hopeless cause—and perhaps lose his head? Better to be cautious. If things went wrong, he could fly to Madrid and claim that he wanted to help the Loyalists crush the revolt. Just in case, he had in his pocket a letter addressed to the government saying that he wished to go to Madrid for this purpose.

Franco was a paradox. He was a small shy man with an effeminate air, the soft damp hands of a woman, and a shrill high-pitched voice—not at all the physical embodiment of *machismo*. Yet, he was a legend among both Spanish and Moorish fighting men for the bravery, ruthlessness, and iron determination he had displayed in the Moroccan war, qualities which, combined with his Galician slyness, sent him soaring to the top. At forty-four, he was the youngest general in the Spanish army.

Caution was the key to his remarkable rise. He was always on the side that was in power or seemed likely to be. King Alfonso XIII had been convinced that he was the most monarchist of all Spanish generals and had even appointed him his gentleman of the bedchamber, a job that only the most loyal supporter would get. Yet Franco refused to join a revolt planned by General Sanjurjo in 1932 that was to bring the king back. The plot, he felt, would fail—as it did.

Again, in 1934, when leftist miners in Asturias tried to set up an independent state, the monarchists approached Franco about another coup, and he refused, forcing the plotters to back off. He could better serve his own career by supporting the conservative but antimonarchist government then in power and crushing the miners' revolt. He did this as War Minister Gil Robles's chief of staff, using the Moors and foreign legionnaires, who not only ended the rebellion but murdered thousands in the bloody aftermath.

Since Franco earned the bitter enmity of the Popular Front for this barbarism, he saw his career tottering when it came to power in February 1936. Even before all the votes were counted, he tried to get the conservative prime minister still in office to declare a state of siege, which would permit the army to rule the country. But the prime minister refused, and the Popular Front took over the reins.

So once again, Franco waited patiently, this time in "exile." Too much was at stake to gamble recklessly. Let the others take the risk—until he was certain he would not lose. Then he would step in and take over. Of course, he would support the monarchy, but not as gentleman of the bedchamber; he would be the *occupant* of the king's bedchamber.

Yet, so skillfully did Franco hide his ambitions that American ambassador to Spain Claude G. Bowers, who was out of Madrid on vacation at this time, cabled the State Department: "Franco undoubtedly has the most brilliant mentality of any of the officers . . . everyone has agreed that he is not of the dictator type . . . he is generally thought a bit academic. He is reputed to be a great strategist. But many think that he would be best employed as a teacher of military tactics than as a practitioner."

Meanwhile, Franco the practitioner waited to see if the time was ripe to step in.

The National Palace stood with colossal dignity upon a bluff overlooking the trickle called the Manzanares River. Napoleon was so impressed with the building that when he blasted his way into Madrid in 1808, he told his brother, whom he was trying to keep on the Spanish throne: "You're better lodged here than I am in the Tuileries."

The newest lodger was a pudgy, balding intellectual with a large head, a pallid complexion, and sensuous lips. His greenish eyes behind small round glasses blinked sleepily, but always lit up when he was speaking. And the eyes of most people who listened to him did, too, with either deep admiration or unbounded hatred.

To his supporters, President Azaña, though cold and aloof, was the father of Spanish democracy, a political messiah who had delivered them from a corrupt, dictatorial monarchy and promised to turn medieval Spain into a modern, socially just nation. To his enemies, Azaña was, as General Mola characterized him, "a monster who seems more the absurd invention of a doubly insane Frankenstein than the fruit of the love of a woman."

Despite this great disparity of view, many of Azaña's supporters agreed that he was the wrong man to run the country at this time of national ferment. Not because he was a monster, as his foes thought, but because he was a messiah. With the nation's deliverance, his mission should have ended. He was too moralistic, too idealistic to lead an unmanageable people suddenly unleashed, after hundreds of years of political bondage, in a world convulsed by extremism. Though warned numerous times that a revolt was imminent, he would simply reply that he had faith in the army—in the men who furtively called him a monster.

But if Azaña felt that common sense would ultimately win out even in the enemy camp, he clearly saw, as Prime Minister Casares Quiroga did not, what the rising in Morocco implied. As soon as the news reached him on the afternoon of July 17, he called in several trusted political colleagues. One of them was Mariano Anso, a Cortes deputy.

Anso rushed to the palace, passed through several huge antichambers draped with priceless tapestries, and entered the president's throne room. Azaña was alone, intensely pale but calm as his bulbous figure slouched in an enormous armchair behind a desk piled high with books and papers. He informed his visitor at once about the revolt in Melilla.

"And this very night or tomorrow," he added, "it will spread to other parts of Morocco. Afterward, to the mainland."

There followed a long silence, which the shocked deputy did not dare interrupt. Then Azaña continued:

"This test of presiding over a civil war is the most terrible test that destiny could hold for me. I am fully aware that I don't deserve it. I have always tried to create a tranquil national climate without being a traitor to the objectives of the republic. Many blind, passionate Spaniards have refused to see it this way. Violence can only yield violence; we're already in the midst of it."

Another silence. Azaña was a broken man, when he had once been vain, arrogant, utterly self-confident. He alone could lead Spain through the agony of transformation. He alone could control the centrifugal forces that had always threatened to tear the nation apart. He alone could produce progress without the bloodshed of revolution. But now he alone might have to preside over a civil war that could only bring disaster to Spain, whoever won. For his tiny moderate constituency would be blown aside by the cyclone of extremism—in both camps—that would ravage the country.

Azaña, it seemed, would end his career in the same bitter gloom that had engulfed him since his earliest days. Born in 1880 in Cervantes's native town of Alcalá de Henares near Madrid, Azaña was brought up as an unloved orphan by his patrician grandmother in a great dark forbidding house. He attended a Jesuit college where he studied under stern Augustinian friars, then earned a law degree in Paris while writing political articles for French and Spanish intellectual publications. In Madrid, he founded a literary review, edited a liberal political magazine, and wrote numerous novels.

His writings sounded revolutionary, for they called for political and social reforms when such ideas were little short of heresy. With the monarchy's fall he emerged as war minister and began to pare the army. Soon he was prime minister, and though voted out of power in 1933, bounced back three years later as president.

He became both the symbol of the republic and its driving force. He was sure he could reason with his enemies, as the French logicians had taught him. Logic could tear through the emotional fabric of the Spanish character. If it could not, were his enemies not right? Was democracy not doomed?

Now Azaña asked Anso about the atmosphere on the street, in the Cortes. There was no reaction yet. Few people knew about the revolt. Anso departed and Azaña was alone again in the great dark forbidding house he had never left.

Constancia de la Mora could hardly wait to leave Madrid and get away to the island of Ibiza on a long-planned vacation. But her husband, Air Force Major Ignacio Hidalgo de Cisneros, was aide to the war minister, the second job of Prime Minister Casares Quiroga, and couldn't leave immediately because of the crisis sparked by Calvo Sotelo's murder. Constancia worried about her husband. He was, she knew, the next Fascist target since police had found a death list of twenty "sentenced" officers on a captured Falangist, and Cisneros was named after the assassinated Captain Faraudo and Lieutenant Castillo. Anyway, her husband was at the War Ministry day and night and was utterly drained. She desperately hoped that the crisis would pass soon so that he could get some rest.

On this morning of July 17, Cisneros left early for the ministry, but he was so exhausted that Casares sent him home for a nap. While he and his wife were having coffee that afternoon, the telephone rang.

"Yes," Cisneros said after a moment, "I'll come over if you want me, but I'm very tired and need sleep. Can't you manage without me?"

Another pause.

"Very well," he said in a tense voice, "I'll be there at once."

Cisneros returned to his wife.

"An army uprising," he said excitedly, "has taken place in Morocco. All communications are cut with the African side. Some posts in Spain seem to be revolting."

Constancia rose, her throat tightening.

"When?"

"Early this morning. Casares knew but he went to a cabinet meeting and only told the other ministers casually at the end of the meeting. Now he thinks it might be of some importance. And the man sent me home to take a nap!" He added: "We shall see whether Spain will be Fascist."

Constancia had never seen her husband speak with such bitterness. But she understood. How many times in the last several weeks he had pleaded with the prime minister to crack down on the plotters. Everyone in Madrid, it seemed, knew about the plot, but nothing could make Casares act.

Once, when Cisneros revealed a conspiracy by officers at the flying school in Alcalá, the prime minister agreed to take him to see Azaña. The president addressed him imperiously:

"According to Casares, you have something important to tell me."

Yes, explained the major, he had proof that a *pronunciamiento* was being prepared.

Azaña interrupted: Cisneros was "very excited." Didn't he realize that it was dangerous to make such charges? Above all, he should not forget that he was speaking to the president of the republic!

Azaña then rose and walked out of the room.

Later, Casares assured his aide that Azaña was basically a good man.

"After what you have witnessed," he said, "you'll realize how difficult it is for me to take steps against the suspects."

The prime minister spoke, it seemed to Cisneros, as if he would take such steps if it weren't for the president. However, only a few days before Colonel Yagüe would lead the uprising in Morocco he had visited Casares, and the prime minister commented after the meeting: "Yagüe is a gentleman, a perfect soldier. I am sure he will never betray the republic. He gave me his word of honor and his soldier's promise that he would always serve it with loyalty, and men like Yagüe keep their promises." . . .

Yet, Constancia perhaps realized, Casares—and most other government leaders and supporters as well—could hardly have comprehended the rebel mentality as clearly as she and her husband did. For both came from the aristocracy that was vigorously supporting a revolt. The two had been virtually disowned by their families for backing a regime of "radicals," men of inferior breeding who wanted to take their property and wealth and distribute it to the "rabble." Constancia had a sister who was a Falangist, and Cisneros, a brother who was among the army plotters.

Constancia was born in 1906 in the warmth of a large luxurious Madrid home while the cruel wind from the Guadarramas sent chills through the beggars squatting on the steps of the Church of Las Salesas nearby. Her family was of noble blood and one of her most vivid memories was of a crowd milling outside her house shouting: "Maura *sí*! Maura *sí*!" Prime Minister Antonio Maura, her grandfather, had just made the greatest speech of his career—though at eleven Constancia was too young to understand what he had said. It was her grandfather who had launched José Calvo Sotelo's career by appointing him his private secretary.

Constancia's Irish governess would take her for walks almost every day along the Paseo de la Castellana, a wide tree-shaded avenue reserved for only the richest strollers, who would show off the latest fashions and exchange the choicest bits of gossip. She hardly knew that people lived on the run-down side streets until a scrawny, raggedly dressed little boy with contempt in his eyes suddenly emerged from one and splattered her beautiful Scotch plaid frock with mud. For the first time, she experienced fear—and glimpsed the other Spain.

Shortly afterward, Constancia learned what often happened to children with tattered clothes, even if they didn't throw mud. Someone had stolen a tire from a car on her father's vast country estate, and he called the Civil Guard, whose job was mainly to keep peace in the rural areas. The guards, unable to find the guilty party, arbitrarily picked up a young shepherd boy and beat him mercilessly.

"Who did it?"

"I don't know; nobody told me; I never heard."

"You know, you little rat."

More blows and screams.

"They're killing him," Constancia sobbed to her father's steward, and she begged him to stop the beating.

"You must learn, little Constancia," the steward said gently, "that the authority of the Civil Guard is the authority of your father. One cannot interfere with it."

The screams went on and on, burning into her heart.

But there was charity, too—the humiliating annual ritual of black-uniformed children from her exclusive convent school parading to a school for poor children with orders to give them chocolate bars and buns, but not to play with them.

Constancia learned what freedom was for the first time when, as a beautiful young woman, tall, black-haired, and olive-skinned, she was sent to school in England. But her parents soon snatched her back for her debut in the marriage market. Back to the silk-lined cell to which she was condemned—the maids who knelt to dress her, the dull, polo-playing young men at the balls, the ugly old society matrons who wore tight corsets to confine flesh grown flabby from excessive leisure.

Then, finally, the last ball of the season, and a chance to romp in the country with a visiting schoolmate from England. As the two girls strolled through her father's estate, Constancia saw the shock in her friend's eyes as they passed the mud-and-stone huts that the nearly starving peasants inhabited. Suddenly a sight that had been commonplace since childhood struck her like a mystical revelation.

For the first time she entered a hut, where a peasant family and its animals lived together in fetid darkness. A lady from England? But there was no world outside of Spain. There was no language other than Spanish. If the "English" girl didn't know Spanish she could only be deaf. A lunch of sausages from last year's pig, a piece of hard cod that had been put aside for the winter. Constancia's uncle used to make fun of the peasants and laugh at them. And she had considered such ridicule perfectly natural, as if he had been commenting on farm animals. But now they were people, human beings with feelings, with sadness in their eyes. Could they see the shame in hers?

And then the visit with her mother to a village priest who was thought to have voted against the landlords' party. The church was dirty and decrepit, and her mother promised the priest that soon he would have a new carpet, new images, new cloth for the altar. Then the two women sped in their chauffeured limousine past villagers who had no school or doctor, nor children under three, since all had perished in an epidemic. Constancia's mother said with satisfaction: "He will never vote again against the conservatives."

There followed work in charity institutions, a disastrous marriage to a fortune hunter, a separation that scandalized her family, a job as salesgirl—and a chance meeting with dashing, handsome Major Hildago de Cisneros when she chaperoned her sister to a rendezvous with his pilot friend.

"You are married?"

"I am separated from my husband."

"You live with your parents, I presume?"

"No, I am working. I live alone with my little girl and my maid and nurse."

"Is it difficult?"

"I would rather be independent than live in security."

She waited. This was a daring thing to say.

"Good for you! I admire you!"

Constancia was the first woman to divorce under the government's new divorce law, and she and Ignacio were the first couple to wed under the new marriage law permitting a divorced person to remarry. But the civil ceremony couldn't take place until a republican town clerk replaced a monarchist who had refused to marry the couple. Constancia and her new husband had broken with their families, with their pasts, with their traditions.

And now that the revolt had started, they would fight their fathers and brothers and sisters to the death with the terrible rage of the little raggedy boy who had muddied Constancia's plaid dress, with the screams of innocent children ringing in their ears, with the vision of peasants unaware of a world beyond Spain searing their consciences.

Cisneros left for the War Ministry to help lead the fight.

At 2:15 A.M., July 18, Franco's cousin burst into the general's hotel room in Las Palmas and awakened him. The rebels had captured Melilla and were doing well throughout Morocco! Franco could now take the risk. He jumped out of bed, rushed to local military headquarters, and telegraphed Morocco: "All glory to the heroic African army. *Arriba, España!* (Rise up, Spain!) Long live Spain with honor."

He then scribbled out a statement that Radio Tenerife would broadcast at 7:00 A.M., condemning the anarchy in Spain and calling upon all Spaniards to join the revolt. Their loyalty was to the *patria,* and not to the government.

"Can we tolerate one day longer the shameful example we are giving the world?" he asked.

Then he rushed to the airport where Captain Bebb, a British pilot, was waiting to fly him to Morocco.

Captain Bebb had no idea who his passenger would be. His role in the plot had started one day in early July when two rebel agents in London invited an English friend named Douglas Jerrold to lunch. During the meal, one of the Spaniards asked Jerrold a favor.

"I want a man and three platinum blondes to fly to Africa tomorrow."

The puzzled Englishman replied: "Must there really be three?"

Well, two would do. But please, no questions.

After lunch, Jerrold called Major Hugh Pollard, an adventurer and journalist he knew, and Pollard agreed to help. He supplied the girls—his daughter and her friend—and the pilot, Captain Bebb of Olley Airways, Ltd.

On July 11, Bebb's *Dragon Rapide* took off from Croydon Airport with Pollard and the two girls, who were to act as typical British tourists out for a roaring time. After two stopovers, the plane arrived in Las Palmas three days later without official permission, to the great annoyance of airport authorities.

"It's just like the English to land here without papers," one of them scowled. "They think they own the earth; I shall remove the propeller after dark."

But the official backed down, and Bebb waited for the man he was supposed to pick up, while his three passengers sailed back to England. At dawn, July 18, the mysterious man arrived, together with his party. He was carrying a brown paper package, which he placed on his knees when he had taken his seat.

Twenty-four hours later, on July 19, as the plane approached rebel-controlled Tetuan, the capital of Spanish Morocco, the passenger opened the package, and when the aircraft taxied to a stop he was resplendent in the uniform of a general.

Franco was ready for the attack on Madrid.

2

Madrid awakened on the morning of July 18, still unaware of the revolt that had shaken Morocco. But in the Naval Ministry station at Ciudad Lineal on the outskirts of the city, Benjamín Balboa was only too aware of it. He struggled to keep his eyes open as he had been up all night furiously tapping away messages to ships at sea. Yet, for all his fatigue, he was excited by the small but vital role he was playing in Spanish history.

El Ferrol and Cartagena . . . Balboa radioed . . . all ships must urgently sail to Moroccan waters and sink any rebel troop ships headed for Spain. But would their commanders obey? Balboa was not at all sure. He was, however, comforted by the knowledge that most junior officers and sailors were loyal republicans like himself and were probably watching their leaders closely.

At about 7:00 A.M., as Balboa lit a cigarette and relaxed for a moment, a signal began stuttering through again—from Cartagena. He read the message and turned pale. General Franco was asking the armed forces to rise up throughout Spain! The message was to be sent to all ships and garrisons.

Balboa immediately signaled back: "Cartagena! Cartagena! What's this all about? How can you ask me to transmit it? Don't you understand?"

"I limit myself," came the reply, "to obeying orders from my superiors."

"Cartagena, what is going on? Is there an uprising in the naval base there?"

No reply. Balboa picked up the telephone and frantically called the War Ministry.

"Señor Minister, a radiotelegram from Tenerife, signed by General Franco, has just been received here. I'm reporting it to you before passing it to the station commander."

A shocked silence followed the reading of Franco's statement. The message must be delivered to him immediately, Casares Quiroga ordered. Balboa put down the phone and told an orderly to find a car. Meanwhile, he started to retype the message.

A few minutes later, the orderly returned with Lieutenant Commander Castor Ibañez, the station chief, at his side.

"Just a moment, Balboa," Castor shouted. "Who said you could give orders?"

The commander then dismissed the orderly and cried: "I'm the only one who gives orders here!"

He extended his hand and said: "Let's see that message. We are subordinate to the Naval Ministry and it is our duty to convey messages to the naval chief of staff and to no one else. He will decide what should be done. You have disobeyed orders."

Castor then hurried to a telephone, and Balboa ran to the switchboard to eavesdrop. He heard the naval chief of staff tell Castor to relay the message as ordered by Cartagena. Balboa confronted Castor:

"Sir, you shall not carry out the admiral's order."

"What's that you said, Balboa?" his superior gasped.

"In the name of the government you are under arrest!" exclaimed Balboa, and he drew a pistol.

He then locked the station commander in a room and sent a message of his own to all ships: Crews must keep an even closer watch over their commanders—and kill them if necessary.

A little later, Captain Urbano Orad de la Torre, the artillery officer and militant socialist, awoke and turned on the radio to listen to the morning news. The announcer calmly reported that there had been an uprising in Morocco. But "no one, absolutely no one, on the Spanish mainland," he said, "has taken part in this absurd plot,'' which, he promised, would be crushed soon. Orad de la Torre scoffed. Morocco was indeed the signal for a mainland revolt—just as he and other socialists had been warning Casares Quiroga for months.

Casares could not hold out any longer. He had to arm the people while there was still time. And Orad de la Torre would try personally to persuade him. He quickly dressed and drove to the War Ministry in the Palace of Buenavista, an imposing gray building set inside a large tree-studded garden on Calle Alcalá. As he entered the anteroom outside the minister's office, he found chaos reigning, with orderlies rushing in and out carrying papers. Low-ranking officers like himself were already waiting to see Casares. The generals and colonels, it seemed, were not yet committing themselves to the government.

When Casares finally received the officers, he looked nervous and pale, visibly shaken by Franco's message, as well as by reports that various garrisons were already rising or were on the brink. No, he at last realized, his government would not have an easy time smashing the insurrection. And his fear, it appeared, was mixed with guilt. For his agents had given him all the details of the planned revolt in advance—except for the identity of *El Director*, the signature on intercepted rebel messages. But was this information valid? Casares had doubted it until the last minute.

Even now, he hoped, he could somehow contain the rebellion without giving the people arms and almost inevitably sparking a leftist revolution. He had only just cautioned his civil governors: Anyone who distributed arms to the people would be shot! And now he repeated to Orad de la Torre and the other officers that there was no need to do so. The revolt would fail, as he had predicted all along.

The visotors left in disgust. But Orad de la Torre would not give up. He would go to Artillery Park, where he had once been based. There were certainly arms stored there. And the commander, Lieutenant Colonel Rodrigo Gil, was a good friend and a good socialist. But would he flatly disobey the orders of the government and risk being shot?

In the heat of midday, every window in Madrid was open, and the streets resounded with the blurred echoes of thousands of radios: ''People of Spain! Keep tuned in! Keep tuned in! Do not turn off your radios! Rumors are being circulated by traitors. Wild stories are causing panic and fear. The government will broadcast day and night—learn the truth from this station. Keep tuned in! Keep tuned in!''

But few *Madrileños* expected to learn the truth from the radio, which repeated almost every ten minutes that the government had ''the situation well in hand.'' And so rumors continued to spread. Franco had landed with troops in the south. This city or that town had fallen. The garrison in Madrid was about to revolt.

Arturo Barea, the bureaucrat in the patent office, was sitting in a neighborhood bar having coffee and exchanging the latest rumors with friends when the radio once more interrupted its music and the same familiar voice announced: ''An urgent order has been issued to the members of the following trade unions and political organizations to report immediately to the center of their respective groups.'' As the announcer listed the various groups, frenzy seized the men in the bar. The time had come to fight. At last they would get arms.

The bar immediately emptied, and Barea glimpsed Armageddon. But like the others, he registered at his trade union office, then headed for the Casa del Pueblo (People's House), the seat of several socialist organizations. He was caught up in a huge crowd of overalled workers, tieless clerks, bespectacled students, unshaven ruffians, rumpled idealists, all converging from a dozen directions on the house, which stood on a narrow short street and could be pinpointed from almost any attic in Madrid because of the huge red lamp that burned on its roof. The street became so choked with people that sentries started checking union cards two-hundred yards away on the blocked-off alleys.

Amid the bedlam, Barea wriggled toward the door as tens of thousands thundered in clipped rhythm: ''Arms! Arms! Arms!'' Barea had been an army sergeant in Morocco for four years, and though he was physically unfit to fight now, he could at least train youngsters how to fire a rifle and kill other Spaniards.

The problem was to get the rifles.

That afternoon, the Puerta del Sol was also packed with *Madrileños* standing outside the Ministry of Interior shouting the same battle cry: ''Arms! Arms!'' The Assault Guards in Pontejos Barracks nearby peered through the windows with impatience. Most were dressed in blue boiler suits, called *monos*, which would become the temporary uniform of the Loyalist militia.

''How could the government be so foolish?'' asked one guard. ''If the Fascists tried to take over Madrid now there would be no way to stop them.''

The government was not the only problem, commented Lieutenant Maximino Moreno. Hardly any of the fifty thousand rifles stacked in the armories of Madrid, he said, were equipped with bolts, almost all of which were stored in Montaña Barracks near the Plaza de España. And the officers quartered there were ''Fascists.'' They would never give up the bolts without a fight and there was no way to fight without the bolts.

Army Lieutenant Paulino García Puente (who later became a top Loyalist commander) told the author that he replied: ''Not all of the bolts are in Montaña. About five thousand are in Artillery Park.''

How did he know that? Moreno asked.

''A friend of mine, Virgo, who is based there, told me. Let's go to Artillery Park and see.''

''All right,'' said Moreno skeptically, ''but if you're wrong I'll kill you.''

The two men drove to Artillery Park and when a guard questioned them, Moreno drew his pistol.

"Take us to the commander's office!" he demanded.

Soon the visitors were confronting Lieutenant Colonel Gil, who was sitting at his desk.

"Colonel," ordered Moreno, "don't move or touch anything and give us the bolts."

Gil, according to García Puente, looked stunned. Here was a fellow socialist pointing a gun at him. How could they expect him to ignore government orders? Especially when the prime minister had warned that anyone who turned over arms to civilians would be shot! The bolts would be used, all right, but only when the government gave the word. If it hadn't been for him there would be none to distribute.

In 1934, a rightist war minister had stored the bolts in Montaña Barracks to prevent the people from seizing them in case of civil war or revolution. And the officers in Montaña were the caretakers. Gil had recently managed to obtain five thousand with the help of General Miaja, commander of the First Division, which included all the troops based in Madrid. Miaja, who sympathized with the republicans, ordered the Montaña commander to send the bolts to Artillery Park. They must be cleaned and checked there, he bluffed. But when an officer went to pick them up, he was arrested. Miaja phoned Colonel Moises Serra, the Montaña commander, and rasped: "Unless you hand over the bolts immediately, I'll come personally to get them."

An hour later, the bolts were in Artillery Park.

The trick, however, did not work a second time. Only about an hour earlier on this afternoon, Miaja, with Casares's approval, had sent some trucks to fetch the forty-five thousand remaining bolts, just in case it became necessary to arm the people after all. Many Montaña officers distrusted Serra because of his moderate and apolitical views, and one told him: "Colonel, do you know what the Marxist government wants them for? They're going to turn the rabble on us."

Serra replied: "Don't worry, gentlemen. I'm fifty-seven years old and I have no intention of dying a traitor."

And this time, Miaja couldn't get him to change his mind. But the Montaña officers had been forced to reveal themselves as rebels.

Gil now told Moreno and García Puente that "all the bolts are in Montaña."

"We know you have some here," Moreno said. "Come with us. Maybe you'll remember where they are."

As they walked through the corridor, García Puente suddenly recognized his friend, Virgo, and asked him about the bolts.

"They're in that room," Virgo said, pointing to a door off the corridor.

The group entered the room and saw piles of rifles on the floor, but none had bolts. García Puente then eyed stacks of ammunition boxes and looked inside. Bolts! Soon, soldiers were busy fitting them into the rifles.

Major Luis Barceló, an aide to Casares, entered and saw what was happening.

"No guns are to be distributed," he said, "unless the minister says so."

Morena hotly replied, waving his pistol: "Don't be an idiot! We're taking these guns right now and don't interfere or I'll blow your brains out!"

The men began loading about four thousand bolt-equipped rifles onto trucks—while Gil and Barceló looked on silently with no apparent displeasure. Who could blame *them* for disobeying orders?

When the trucks had left, Captain Orad de la Torre arrived, also seeking arms. Gil gave him five hundred of the thousand that remained. The time was past for worrying about stupid government orders. And besides, thousands of people were at the gates screaming for arms and were threatening to break in.

The massive arming of the militia had begun. Just in time, thought many, to face the revolt that would certainly start in Madrid within hours.

The revolt in Madrid would *not* start within hours because the rebel plotters were in a state of utter confusion. General Fanjul had been in a quandary ever since returning from Pamplona, where he had celebrated San Fermín with General Mola. His understanding was that old, indecisive General Montesinos Villegas was the leader of the Madrid rising because of his senior status, but in little more than name only; that he himself was the real chief. Mola, however, had not sent word to either of them, though the Moroccan garrisons were already rising.

Frustrated and alarmed, Fanjul had sent a messenger to Pamplona two days earlier, July 16, with a note for *El Director:* "It is impossible to wait any longer."

The following day, Mola simply sent back the reply: "The orders are already in Madrid."

But where were they? Fanjul checked with Villegas and several other top officers; no one seemed to know. Perhaps Mola's liaison, who had just been arrested, had them. Had Mola appointed someone else Madrid commander without informing either Villegas or himself?

One reason for the confusion was that the generals had to remain in hiding until the last minute; their political views were too well known, and so they were forced to depend on a few younger officers, who had formed a *junta,* to coordinate the plans of the various rebel forces. Why, at this critical time, didn't these officers tell their leaders what was happening?

Fanjul grew more restless, more pessimistic, more lonely by the hour as he listened to radio reports, which made no mention of any rebel advance from the north. Perhaps most frightening of all was the fervid call to arms by Dolores Ibarruri, *La Pasionaria:*

"Workers, anti-Fascists . . . rise up and defend the republic, the popular freedoms, and the democratic conquests of the people. . . . Communists, anarchists, and republicans, soldiers and all the forces faithful to the people's will are destroying the rebel traitors who have dragged into the mud the military honor they so often boasted about. The whole country throbs with rage in defiance of those inhuman individuals who want, with fire and destruction, to plunge democratic Spain into a hell of terror. *No pasarán!* They shall not pass!''

Pass? He could not even move!

Sharing Fanjul's agony, his sister-in-law suggested that he make some decision on his own and carry it out, but the general replied firmly, almost angrily: ''I cannot do anything. I have to wait. I received categorical orders not to act until ordered to. I have no choice. I am a soldier and must respect discipline.''

From his window, Fanjul glimpsed the growing crowds marching down the street shouting: ''Arms! Arms!'' Once they had them, it would probably be too late. And here he was just across the street from First Division Headquarters!

While General Fanjul awaited word on when to walk ''across the street'' and take over First Division Headquarters, another general was planning to capture it. Unknown to Fanjul, the young officers' *junta* now recognized General Miguel García de la Herrán, a retired engineering officer, as the ''real'' chief of the rising in Madrid. And General Mola apparently approved the switch, being concerned about Fanjul's pessimism.

Originally, García was to lead the revolt in the communities outside Madrid, but now he would march into General Miaja's office and demand that Miaja turn over his command to him so that he could order the whole Madrid garrison to rebel. If he refused, García's escort troops would seize the headquarters by force. The trouble was, these troops were to be Civil Guards, and the Civil Guards, though sympathetic to the revolt, voted not to support the rebels until it seemed that Madrid was about to fall. Thus, the plan fell through.

But the leader of the *junta*, Lieutenant Colonel Alberto Alvarez Rementería, decided to act without a general. Early that evening of July 18, he went to First Division Headquarters with another officer and burst into Miaja's office. The time was past for subtleties. Would Miaja join the rebels? Alvarez demanded to know. Miaja was just as blunt: No! Alvarez's companion, who was standing behind Miaja, suddenly aimed a pistol at the general's neck. But Alvarez glared at his comrade and the pistol was withdrawn. The two officers then angrily stalked out of the office, slamming the door behind them.

''This Miaja is a scoundrel!'' Alvarez exclaimed bitterly. ''But we can't start an uprising like ours by doing what you were going to do.''

Perhaps they would have better luck by going directly to Montaña Barracks—a wishful thought since they were to find the rebel commanders there unwilling to ''commit suicide'' by taking their troops into the streets without the support of other barracks.

On leaving First Division Headquarters, the *junta* officers walked past General

Fanjul's apartment building but didn't bother to stop by and let him know what was happening. Or even to tell him that he was no longer leading the revolt.

Late that night General Miaja was called to the prime minister's office and offered the job of war minister once more. He had served briefly in this post when the Popular Front had first come to power early in the year. The man who asked him was Cortes Chairman Diego Martínez Barrio, who had replaced Casares as prime minister.

After a day of shock and disillusionment, Casares had simply collapsed. His eyes were sunken and his skin scaly as he sat behind a cluttered desk with telephone receivers left unhooked. Announcing his resignation, he muttered pathetically to visitors:

"I've been calling the barracks and no one answers. There's nothing left to do but die, each one at his post."

Now Miaja would be a member of a "capitulation" government. President Azaña had made that clear at a series of conferences he held with Popular Front leaders. During one meeting, the socialist chiefs, Largo Caballero and Prieto, walked out in fury when Azaña and Casares still refused to arm the people, even though the dam had already started to crack.

The government, Azaña and Casares felt, had done everything it could to keep the rebellion from flaring into a civil war. The prime minister had discharged all members of the armed forces so that they would not feel bound to follow the orders of their superiors. And many garrisons were still loyal—in Barcelona, Valencia, Málaga, Granada, Huelva, Jaén, Almería. Perhaps the best news was that the navy remained in government hands; the noncommissioned officers and sailors had shot and thrown most rebel officers overboard, and the fleet was now blockading Morocco so that insurgent forces there could not cross over to Spain. The air force was also solidly in the republican camp, largely because Major Ignacio Hidalgo de Cisneros, Casares's aide, had made sure that almost all air bases were under the command of loyal officers.

Nevertheless, the bad news that day, in the eyes of the president and prime minister, seemed to eclipse the good. All Spanish Morocco had fallen, and Seville, Córdoba, Cádiz, Algeciras, and Jerez had either been captured or were about to be, while few officers anywhere could be trusted. Just about every time Casares had picked up the telephone to call a garrison, he would be greeted with the rebel battle cry, "*Arriba, España!*"

The situation looked hopeless. The revolt could not be quelled without a catastrophic civil war, and even then armed street mobs would hardly be a match for the professional rebel army. Nor was a revolution by the leftists better than compromise with the rightists. The government had to make a deal with the rebels at almost any cost.

Azaña's puffy, tormented face was gray with fatigue as he listened restlessly to his callers' suggestions. The one he liked best came from Felipe Sánchez Román, a centrist politician who had refused to join the Popular Front because of its leftist coloring. A general should go to rebel headquarters, he said, and propose forming a national government representing the entire political spectrum except for the Communists. The Cortes would be dissolved and a national advisory council would decide when to have new elections.

This was treason, shouted the proletarian leaders, but the idea made sense to Azaña. And so he selected Martínez Barrio, a moderate leftist like himself, to lead the capitulation government.

General Miaja seemed the obvious choice for war minister. He was a senior officer and a friend of the top rightist plotters, particularly Mola, who had served under him in Morocco. And he was loyal to the government, yet agreed that the people should not be armed. Miaja, thought Azaña and Martínez, would be the perfect go-between.

The general himself also thought so, for he was a man in the middle, a man of both Spains. Still, he favored the government, not only out of a sense of loyalty but because of his proletarian roots. His father had worked in an arms factory in Oviedo and had been barely able to support his family. It was only because he had made great sacrifices that young Miaja could finish secondary school and enroll in the Toledo Military Academy. There he felt the sting of discrimination as cadets from rich and aristocratic families enjoyed exclusive privileges withheld from those of humble background.

But the challenge of making good in a world that rejected him overcame the pain of his bruised sensitivities, as well as the limitations of his military competence. To meet the challenge, he suppressed his liberal instincts and cultivated the conservative, disciplined mentality of his military peers. Soon he was fighting in Morocco and being steadily promoted as the mounting casualties there drained Spain of its best officers.

He joined the rightist UME out of a feeling of camaraderie for Mola and other officers, but refused to be part of any conspiracy against the republic. Though he was a general, he was still a worker's son. He had tasted the poverty of those people the government was trying to help, and would not turn against them.

At the same time, he would not arm these people. He would not help them to kill his close comrades in the army, men with whom he had shared the horrors and heroism of the Moroccan war. Certainly they were vain, ambitious men, the kind his father would not have liked. But they were also warm and good and they laughed at his jokes.

And although Miaja would not admit it, he perhaps saw something of himself in them. He, too, was vain and ambitious; but he would never advance much further if he joined the rebels—not with his lower-class background, his less than brilliant military mind, and his folksy ways, which suggested that he lacked the hardness and ruthlessness required of a top military leader. However, with most of the hard, ruthless officers on the rebel side, a general who remained with the government could go far.

Indeed, he had become war minister!

And now Miaja felt his sacred duty was to prevent a bloody collision between the two worlds that he so agonizingly straddled. Hardly had he settled grandiosely in the war minister's chair at about 2:00 A.M., July 19, when he telephoned his old friend General Mola in Pamplona. Mola had not revealed his position yet, though he had proclaimed a state of siege in his region. But Miaja knew only too well that he was *El Director*. After all, Mola had tried, if subtly, to recruit him. Now, on the phone, he told Mola that he, Miaja, had been appointed war minister.

"Do you intend to shoot me?" Mola mocked.

"I?" exclaimed Miaja. "You know I've always considered you a friend. But why have you proclaimed a state of siege without orders from this ministry?"

"The very special circumstances here have made it advisable, Señor Minister," Mola replied vaguely.

"What circumstances?"

Mola hestitated and when he spoke his voice was barely audible. Miaja impatiently interrupted: "Let's finish this quickly. In one word: Have you rebelled?"

"Yes, señor."

"You could have told me."

"You could have figured it out."

"Then you must take the consequences," Miaja said abruptly, and he hung up the receiver.

"Yes, señor. . . ." Words stated with an unshakable firmness that Miaja understood from years of working and fighting beside Mola. Words, he knew, that doomed the new government at birth. Through the window he could hear the cries of the people, *his* people. They had just learned of the change in government and that capitulation was in the air and were besieging the War Ministry in clamorous protest.

"Attention! Attention! . . . . A new government has been formed!" Arturo Barea listened anxiously to the radio reverberating through the streets as he stood on the terrace of the Casa del Pueblo waiting for the dawn. He had been training people how to use a rifle until late into the night, and thousands were still jamming the street below and the adjacent alleys shouting for arms. The radio announcer began listing the names of the new ministers, but when he came to Sánchez Román nobody bothered to listen anymore. For Sánchez Román was the "traitor" who had refused to join the Popular Front. There was a great, furious roar. This was obviously a capitulation government.

The crowd on the street charged into the building as if somehow their very presence would produce arms. Then someone shouted, "To the Puerta del Sol!" Within seconds the word "Sol!" burst from thousands of throats, and the crowd

wildly stampeded toward that huge plaza to protest before the Ministry of Interi-
or, as others were doing in front of Miaja's War Ministry. Barea, as angry as his
comrades, found the socialist militia chief and said:

"I came here last night of my own will to help in any way I could . . . but
I'm not willing to serve under a Sánchez Román. You know as well as I do
. . . that this government will try to make a deal with the generals. I'm sorry."

Barea then marched out of the Casa del Pueblo and stopped for coffee in a bar
while the great sea of humanity flooding the Puerta del Sol rumbled in the distance like an angry tide.

"Attention! Attention!" blasted the radio again. "A new government has
been formed. The new government has accepted fascism's declaration of war on
the Spanish people!"

Barea knew it wasn't true. But he also knew that no government could calm
the tide, the overwhelming tide that would drown them all.

He was so weary. He longed for a few hours of peace, away from the world he
would hopelessly defend. Yet, he could not bring himself to go home to his wife.
Shortly after dawn, he went by train with his mistress, Maria, to his country
house in the Guadarramas, where they could lie under the pine trees a million
miles from Madrid.

Diego Martínez Barrio, the new prime minister, looked distressed as he sat at his
desk and phoned up commanders, governors, mayors, dispensing orders to
some, trying to reason with others. Even his closest aides couldn't be sure whether he was really as worried as he appeared since his eyebrows were perpetually
arched, giving his swarthy face an expression of dismay even when he was most
at ease. He was, however, clearly not at ease in the hours after midnight as he
desperately tried to end the rebellion.

His forte, as speaker of the Cortes, had been the art of compromise, a rare
quality indeed in a nation that viewed compromise as little short of treason.
Martínez Barrio, a Freemason, was strongly anticlerical and was therefore considered an implacable enemy by the Church-dominated Right; but as a moderate
republican he was seen as less dangerous than most Popular Front leaders. He
was President Azaña's last chance of staving off civil war and social revolution.

Martínez Barrio was having little luck so far. The situation was deteriorating
rapidly and no one would give in. The military was determined to grab all of
Spain, and the crowds surging through the streets were just as determined not to
yield a single pebble. Miaja had informed him of his futile talk with Mola, and
without Mola there could be no compromise. Martínez Barrio, however, was a
stubborn man. Now, at about 3:00 A.M., he would make one last effort to persuade Mola.

"This is General Mola. . . . Who? Señor Martínez Barrio? I'm listening
with all due respect."

"General, Señor President of the republic has conferred upon me the high

honor of . . . forming a government to satisfy the aspirations of the army. I
have reserved for you a portfolio that I hope you will accept after changing your
stand.''

''I thank you very much for your kindness, Señor Martínez Barrio, but with all
due respect I must state my opinion. Rather than remedying the situation, this
would only worsen it. No, it is impossible to reach a settlement. You have your
followers and I have mine. If we were to make a deal, we would be betraying our
ideals and our men. We would both deserve to be lynched. Of course, I understand what this means. The battle will be hard, painful, and long. But it is a
duty.''

''And that is your last word?''

''Yes, señor. It is my last word. . . . I say good-bye to you, Señor Martínez
Barrio.''

''But that means war!''

''War? But isn't that what they wanted?''

Martínez Barrio put down the phone. Then he went home to sleep for a few
hours. He had to stop the revolt somehow, but right now he was too tired to
think. However, hardly had he fallen asleep when the mayor of Madrid, Pedro
Rico, and another politician arrived and demanded to see him immediately.
Martínez Barrio drowsily came out half dressed.

''You are supposed to assume the duties of prime minister at six A.M.,'' said
the politician. ''But where? Pedro Rico and I have just come from the street. The
ministries are surrounded by hostile crowds. There has never been a more unpopular government. Armed civilians are patrolling all over Madrid.''

Martínez Barrio put on his jacket while observing the visitors with expression-
less eyes. Then he picked up the telephone and began to dial.

''Very well,'' he said with a touch of reproach, ''you'll see what I'm going to
do. War Ministry? Diego Martínez Barrio here. I wish to speak with Señor Minister of Justice Blasco Garson. . . . Manolo? I am no longer prime minister. . . . I can't head a government when the Popular Front rushes into the
street in opposition. . . I am just now going to inform the president of the republic that I resign.''

Martínez Barrio then replaced the receiver and there was silence. The last
chance had vanished.

3

As soon as Loyalist officers in the War Ministry learned that the Martínez Barrio
government had prematurely died and that General Miaja was no longer minister,

they began laying plans on their own for distributing arms to the people. According to Captain Miguel Palacios, a medical officer who had just joined the ministry staff, he telephoned several commanders in Madrid. Give out the weapons, Palacios ordered, with or without bolts. If necessary, the bolts would be taken from Montaña Barracks by force. Most of the commanders objected to Palacios's orders, thus immediately stamping themselves as rebels.

But one officer of unquestioned loyalty was Lieutenant Colonel Ernesto Carratelá, the socialist commander of the sapper regiment in Campamento.

"We're going to send some men and trucks over from the Casa del Pueblo to collect the rifles," Palacios told him.

Carratelá was pleased. For he suspected that most of the officers under his command favored the rebels and might try to seize the arms for themselves. Earlier he had ordered all suspicious personnel to go home in order to prevent a takeover. He had enough arms to supply several companies of militia, though few apparently had bolts.

When the civilians arrived, Carratelá greeted them and ordered an aide to have the rifles loaded onto the trucks. Suddenly a group of officers entered from the courtyard—the suspicious ones who had been ordered to go home.

"Are you going to give arms to these people?" one officer asked menacingly. "We don't want any arms to leave these barracks."

"Señores," Carratelá growled, "I am giving orders here."

"We've decided on what should be done," said the officer, ignoring the colonel's remark. "First of all, no arms can be handed over. We are ready to leave the barracks and occupy positions on the Manazanares bridges to crush any attack that might come from Madrid. Also, we demand that Lieutenant Colonel Alvarez Rementería take over command of the regiment."

Carratelá remained calm, knowing that Alvarez was unfriendly to the government, but apparently not that he headed the *junta* preparing the revolt in Madrid.

"Have you finished, señores?" the colonel said sarcastically. He then told a loyal captain: "Hand over four hundred rifles to these civilians. That's an order!"

"Traitor! Not one will leave here!" shouted a rebel officer.

"The rifles will go out, because I order it!" Carratelá exclaimed. "I'm commander of these barracks! Do you understand? You are deserters!"

Suddenly, a rebel officer fired about six bullets into Carratelá. The colonel collapsed, but then started crawling toward the door of his office. Several more shots rang out. And this time Carratelá did not move.

Campamento, like Montaña, was in rebel hands.

Later that morning, Christopher Lance, a lanky ginger-haired British engineer living in Madrid, awoke and thought this would be a fine day for fun.

"Too hot for church, old girl." he told his wife, Jinx. "Let's go off somewhere for a picnic."

But Jinx had reservations. "Not likely," she said, "that we shall run into any trouble, I suppose."

"Oh, Lord, no," Lance replied. "Everything's perfectly quiet."

It was almost always quiet on their street, Calle de Espalter, near the Paseo de la Castellana, where well-to-do Spaniards resided together with the smart international set. Whatever happened in the less exalted sections of Madrid, life went on here as usual, especially for the foreigners. Indeed, Lance and his wife had been living a gay, delightful life. Tennis, riding, sailing, parties, afternoon cocktails at the fashionable Embassy Bar on the Castellana—and picnics in the country.

Their crowd was mainly British, but included many Spaniards, mostly of the upper classes. Lance was particularly fond of the army officers he met at the exclusive Savoy Hotel nearby, enjoying their sense of humor and appreciating their high respect for Britain. Some had even attended school in England.

Lance, a warm, cheerful, gregarious man, also liked many of the lower-class Spaniards he met, not as cocktail companions, of course, but as people. He found the anarchists especially agreeable despite their tendency to shoot anyone who disagreed with them, often with a good-natured smile. They were all very fine people, he thought—when they didn't involve themselves in politics. Why weren't they like the lower classes back home? Peaceful, aware of their place. Why were they always going on strike here, and seizing land that didn't belong to them? Instead of going to church and thanking God for their blessings, they burned the church down. Nice people, to be sure, when they weren't full of hate and venom.

The day before, Lance had heard on the radio about the coup in Morocco and some risings in Spain itself. Just one more attempt by someone to seize power. Maybe this would end the strikes and the disorder and all the troublemaking, at least for a while. Once there had even been some shooting on the Castellana while he and his wife were in the Embassy Bar. Amusing incident, but still, a man had the right to drink his dry sherry in peace.

Not that Lance was especially addicted to peace. Despite his deceptively gentle face, with humorous eyes and a prominent nose set off by a small mustache, he had lived an adventurous, often violent, life. In World War I, he deserted his rear-echelon regiment to join another one bound for the front, where he won an award for bravery. After the war, he went to Russia and fought against the Bolsheviks until he was badly wounded. He then left for Chile on an engineering assignment, only to barely escape with his life after being caught in the middle of a revolt. Finally, he was sent to Spain to build bridges and railroads, and here, at last, he found peace. There were shootings and bombings, of course, but they didn't involve him. Actually, he rather missed the excitement of battle, though picnics could be fun, too.

On this sweltering morning of July 19, Lance gave his cook and chauffeur the day off and, with Jinx beside him and a basketful of tortillas, fruit, and wine in the back seat, set out for the Escorial, about thirty miles away at the foot of the Guadarramas. After they had driven a few miles without passing a single car, a group of armed civilians blocked the road and ordered the couple out. They were searched, then politely sent on their way. Lance joked about the incident but they were no longer in a holiday mood. So they stopped along the road short of the Escorial and had their lunch in isolated silence on a sun-baked patch of ground.

"What on earth is up and where the devil is everybody?" Lance finally said.

They gulped down their food and started back. Maybe they should have gone to church after all. Soon they were halted again—by a barrier of fallen trees and upturned carts. It had not been there before.

Suddenly, a group of men and women carrying rusty old rifles and red flags surrounded them. Lance knew from the men's red vests and black trousers that they were anarchists—the people he liked so much when they weren't shooting other people.

"Get out!" ordered one man.

When their money and personal belongings had been taken from them, the couple were shoved into a small house nearby and locked in a room. Their future seemed bleak, until one of their captors opened the door sometime later and smilingly addressed Lance:

"Comrade, I am glad to see that after all you are friends of the revolution."

"How did you find that out?"

The man pointed to a page in Lance's passport; it had a Soviet visa stamped on it. Lance, who had visited Russia, laughed heartily, until the man told him:

"The revolution has begun, comrade, and we shall need your motorcar for the cause."

Just when it looked as if they would be stranded in the country indefinitely, a squad of Assault Guards on motorcycles roared to a stop at the barrier. Lance explained his predicament to them, and within minutes the guards were escorting the couple back to Madrid. Soon they were all having drinks in Lance's apartment, and the party went on for hours.

Jolly nice people, thought Lance, *even if they did murder Calvo Sotelo.* They might as well enjoy themselves before Franco arrived—probably within a few days.

Late that same afternoon, Arturo Barea and his mistress, María, also returned to Madrid, arriving by train from their retreat in the pine forests of the Guadarramas. Barea's nerves were frayed. He and María had had another of their quarrels and he decided that if he couldn't find peace in the country he might as well go back to Madrid where he could at least be useful.

He had heard the news that Martínez Barrio had resigned and that another prime minister was in power—José Giral Pereira, a member of Asaña's Left Republican party. With the president reluctantly agreeing, Giral had approved the distribution of arms to the people and thus had socialist, Communist, and anarchist support. That morning, trucks had sped from the War Ministry to the Casa del Pueblo loaded with weapons for the socialist workers and others who could show trade union cards. The danger of surrendering to the rebels was now past, and Barea would once again seek to help the cause.

He returned to a city gone mad with joy, excitement, anger, hatred, and fear. Madrid seemed to be in the grip of a real revolution. Cars "requisitioned" by militiamen and splattered with roughly painted party and union emblems tore through the streets with armed men crouching on the running boards. Shots resounded everywhere as fifth columnists hiding behind windows and on roofs exchanged fire with youths who had barely learned how to pull the trigger.

Columns of smoke spiraled into the sky as church after church was set afire by crazed throngs persuaded that priests and other snipers were firing at them from the church towers. People raised the clenched fist and shouted, "Death to the Fascists!" as workers paraded through the streets, sometimes headed toward an armory to get arms, sometimes toward the nearest bar to demand free drinks in celebration of their coming victory over the rebels.

Barea hurriedly escorted María to her home, then hastened to his own, near the Plaza de Anton Martín. He found the streets leading to the plaza mobbed with people despite a dense smoke that enveloped them. The Church of San Nicolás was going up in flames. Suddenly there was a great shout as the dome, falling like a fiery meteor, crashed down inside the church walls and sent up a sparkling fountain of dust, ashes, and embers from the enormous cavity left in the roof. The people cheered wildly while firemen poured their jets on adjacent buildings to keep the fire from spreading.

Barea walked into a bar he often frequented and found the owner in near hysteria: "Arturo, Arturo, this is terrible, what's going to happen here? They've burned down San Nicolás and all the other churches in Madrid. San Cayetano, San Lorenzo, San Andrés, the Escuela Pía. . . ."

The Escuela Pía! His old school. He rushed out and saw the burning tower of San Cayetano topple to earth, barely missing some houses, and as he passed San Lorenzo he watched people dance and howl around it while flames licked at them. Then he came to the Escuela Pía and stared in anguish as it disintegrated in a swirl of smoke. Firemen and militiamen ran in and out trying to save what they could, and on one trip they carried out someone on an improvised stretcher—a withered old priest, deathly pale, with white hair and frightened eyes. Barea recognized him. It was his chemistry teacher.

Barea felt like weeping, but the tears would not come. "I saw flashes of my boyhood," he later wrote. "I had a sensation of the feel and the smell of things I had loved and things I had hated."

What had happened to the priceless manuscripts in the school library? To the magnificent collections in the physics and natural science departments?

He had to believe it was the fault of the priests and the Falangists, that they had fired at the people. He had to believe that his old teacher, though in his eighties and paralyzed, could not be guiltless. For only a people provoked and enraged would destroy such treasures. If the priests had given the militia the keys to the church instead of firing at them, this disaster would never have happened. He deplored the destruction. But he could not blame the destroyers.

Yet he agonized in the thought that those who burned churches to punish snipers might see a sniper on every roof. Would all of Madrid burn?

José Luis Sáenz Heredia hadn't slept at home for four nights. For he was certain they would be searching for him—the "reds," who, in the last few days, had killed Calvo Sotelo and countless others who opposed them. And besides, Sáenz had learned from one of the military conspirators that the revolt would soon begin. Now it *had* begun, and he felt like a hunted animal.

All afternoon he listened nervously as the sharp cracks of rifle fire mingled with the grinding gears of trucks that zoomed past his hideout on the ground floor of a building at the Puerta de Alcalá. Where the shots came from he didn't know. Suddenly he would hear a truck screeching to a halt in front of some building nearby and men cursing and women weeping as someone was dragged out and thrown into the vehicle, which whipped off again into the deadly distance. This scene was reenacted over and over, and soon, he was sure, they would find him.

And they would be merciless, for he was not simply a Falangist, but a first cousin of José Antonio Primo de Rivera, the founder and leader of the Falange movement. A member of a proud family that had given much to Spain, that had tried to save Spain from the reds, who would destroy its traditions and squander its wealth. He had felt his first thrill of pride when he was still a child in school. His teacher had been giving him zeroes on every examination, until one day in 1923. . . .

"Aren't you the nephew of General Primo de Rivera?" the teacher asked him.

"Yes," the boy replied.

"Then I shall give you the highest mark today, for your uncle has saved the country."

When Luis returned home in bewilderment he asked his mother what his uncle had done that day.

"He has made a *pronunciamiento*," she replied.

Sáenz harbored no hatred for those who might kill him. He knew and worked with many Marxists, and though he disagreed with them, he could understand their yearning for what they hoped would be a more just society. Too bad they didn't realize that Falangism would offer them exactly that. Anyway, Sáenz considered himself more an artist than a politician. By the age of twenty-five he had helped to direct three films, two of them under the famous actor and director Luis Buñuel. And though Buñuel was a Communist, the two had become fast friends and had agreed to disagree on their politics.

Sáenz had last seen Buñuel at the premiere of their film in April, the day before the Falangist funeral procession at which Lieutenant Castillo was accused of killing another cousin of José Antonio's. Sáenz had marched in this procession and he realized that day that the ideological breach could not be bridged even by the strong artistic communion he felt with Buñuel or the warm relationship he had with the studio employees. The mind had finally overcome the heart.

With the killing of Calvo Sotelo, Sáenz was an obvious target, and so he had gone into hiding. He must hide from his enemies, from his friends.

But now as a truck ground to a halt in front of his building he felt a strange sense of resignation, almost as if he were filming the climax of one of his comedies. He laughed to himself when he thought of the title of his last film: *Who Wants Me?*

The militiamen moved from room to room, their rifles underarm. After several minutes one emerged from the bathroom with a cartridge in his palm.

"I found this in the toilet tank," the man said.

Sáenz's friend, who was putting him up, argued that it must have been left there by the landlord, and he was away.

"Come on out in the hallway," the leader of the group ordered.

He cocked his rifle and was about to fire at Sáenz and his host when an officer from a nearby police station entered the building and shouted: "What are you doing?"

"They shot at us from this building," answered the militia chief.

"Do you have a search warrant?"

"No."

"Then you'll have to get one from the police station."

The leader left the building with the officer while the other militiamen locked the two prisoners in the apartment and guarded the door. Sáenz jumped from a window and raced down the street. He couldn't have written a better script.

Throughout the afternoon, Cipriano Mera, an inmate in Model Prison, listened hopefully to the pounding on the doors, which sounded like stampeding cattle. Hundreds of people had gathered in the Plaza de Moncloa in front of this huge modern building with long galleries shaped like the ribs of a fan. They demanded that all non-Fascist prisoners—political detainees and common criminals alike—be set free to join the "revolution." Mera and his companions added to the din by banging on the iron doors of their cells.

Mera was one of the most influential anarchists in Madrid, and many of the people congregated outside were fellow members of the anarchist-led National Confederation of Labor (CNT), which had recently ballooned into the city's biggest trade union. The CNT took orders from the Iberian Anarchist Federation (FAI), which embraced the most militant believers, including Mera. The demonstrators were angry and bitter, for the government was handing out weapons mainly to the socialists while ignoring them because it feared an anarchist revolution.

So, late that morning, CNT members from the workers' districts had converged on the quarter where shops sold sporting weapons. They rammed in the doors and swept the shelves clean. Once they were equipped with shotguns, hunting knives, cartridge belts, and knapsacks, they shouted "To the Model Prison!" and surged toward Moncloa to free Mera and the other prisoners.

Meanwhile, two anarchist leaders who had been liberated the previous day burst into the office of General Sebastián Pozas, the loyal inspector general of the Civil Guard, and demanded that he free all non-Fascist prisoners. When Pozas hesitated, one of the anarchists, Teodoro Mora, warned: "If within half an hour the prisoners are not out in the street, we, the workers, will break open the prison gates."

Pozas had no choice; the people had been armed. He gave the order.

At 6:00 P.M., the wardens flung open the gates of Model Prison, and Mera and other prisoners streamed out to be swallowed up by the joyous crowd. Mora hugged Mera and then then handed him a rifle. Mera gripped it like a child grasping a toy, sliding the bolt back and forth, inserting a magazine, clicking the bolt into place. As they climbed into a car, Mora said:

"Let's go to your home so you can embrace your family."

"Comrade Mora," Mera replied, "let's go to union headquarters instead. If this is a real revolution, the desire I might have to embrace my family is unimportant." Then, as he watched armed workers marching down the street, he asked: "Just who is making the revolution? I really don't understand it."

"Who is making it, Mera? The whole people, with the government at their head."

"You mean this government that until a few minutes ago was keeping me in jail?"

"Yes, comrade."

"Well, forgive me if I laugh a little. It's all a bit confusing."

Mera spoke acidly, for to him this was heresy. He was a true anarchist, who despised the present government as much as the preceding rightist ones. And he was just as repelled by communism, for its means were rooted in stifling bureaucracy and iron dictatorship.

But if all genuine anarchists agreed that government was evil, not all agreed on how to get rid of it. They were divided into two groups: *puritans* and *aliancistas*. The *puritans* did not want to collaborate with any group that refused to accept their doctrine. They favored "direct action," such as bank robberies and terrorism. The *aliancistas* were more pragmatic; they desired links with other trade unions and opposed violence.

Mera was a leading *puritan*. Before the ideal society crystallized, he would permit crimes—though not murder—if the criminal act furthered the cause and was sanctioned by the group. After all, anarchists didn't recognize government laws anyway. But let an anarchist commit a crime for selfish or "unjust" reasons and he would be severely punished, usually shot, though Mera apparently opposed this penalty. The problem was that in the chaotic period leading up to the revolt many pseudoanarchists—as well as Fascists and common criminals who infiltrated anarchist ranks—were committing "unjust" crimes. There were simply too many of these frauds to deal with adequately.

Cipriano Mera had led one of the anarchists' boldest moves to set the stage for revolution. As head of the CNT contruction workers in Madrid, he had helped to spark a strike that turned into a savage shooting match between the anarchists, who wanted to keep the strike going, and the socialists, who wished to end it. It was because of Mera's role in these disorders that the government arrested him several days before the revolt.

Now, with his release, he found that the government that had jailed him and that he had been trying to overthrow was suddenly his ally! Yet he would heed the decisions of the CNT central committee. Since his early years, he had been conditioned not to oppose the collective will of his fellow anarchists.

Born in 1897, the son of an impoverished garbage collector, he became a bricklayer as a boy. But though he never went to school, he learned to read by himself and was soon poring over sociological, literary, and philosophical works that few well-educated youths far older than he had ever ventured to read. He was especially drawn to the works of Bakunin, for this philosopher recognized garbage men and bricklayers as human beings and promised them a fair share of the world's goods.

In fact, Mera, despite his unusually nimble mind, never imagined himself as being anything but a bricklayer, and he would spend his off-hours organizing his fellow workers and teaching them to be humble, too. His idol was Buenaventura Durruti, a world-famous anarchist who led the national movement from Barcelona and had become a symbol of human liberation to anarchists everywhere.

Mera resembled a typical Spanish worker. He was called *El Viejo* (The Old Man), for his long face was lined and leathery, though he was not yet thirty. He had a tough jaw and rather flat nose, and he was gruff-mannered, uncommunicative, often sullen. But when he spoke of his dream, all the passion raging within him surged to the surface, transforming him into a dynamic leader, a man of granite and rough grace, whose every word struck home with the crack of a hammer.

But now it was time not for rhetoric but for revolution—with or without the government. . . .

Mera was welcomed with hugs at CNT headquarters, which, like the socialist Casa del Pueblo, was a madhouse full of people seeking arms, reporting for "battle," leaving on various missions. Shortly, Mera was given a mission of his own. With a group of men, he was to take over a palace on the Castellana that was reported to be a depository for Fascist arms.

When Mera and his group arrived at the palace they found no arms, but plenty of other things—chairs, vases, silverware—all being carried out by civilian looters. Mera was furious. He ordered the scavengers to drop their loot, and in his deep, commanding voice lectured them on the revolution. Its purpose was, he said, to eradicate the capitalist regime and create a more just society. Real revolutionaries were people with a social conscience who would never steal or destroy—except in the community's interest. Nor did revolution mean killing people, "not even a marquis."

Mera returned to CNT headquarters, disturbed by this vivid glimpse of human nature, which he was determined to alter. But he began to understand why the CNT committee was willing to work with the authorities. If the Fascists took over the government, they would snuff out the budding revolution. Therefore, the anarchists had to crush the Fascists before crushing the government. But the situation was not going too well. That day, Valladolid, Avila, Segovia, Burgos, Salamanca, Saragossa, and other cities had fallen to the rebels—though he was delighted that Barcelona, where fighting was heavy, was slipping under anarchist control.

Mera asked for a combat assignment. Certainly the rebels in Montaña, Campamento, and other barracks would rise up soon.

4

General Fanjul, still hiding in his brother-in-law's apartment, had managed to get little sleep on the night of July 18 as he tossed in bed listening for a knock on the door that never came. The revolt had started more than twenty-four hours earlier, and he not only lacked instructions but he didn't even know what his fellow conspirators were doing.

Finally—in midmorning—a knock. His sister-in-law cautiously opened the door and was relieved to see Luisa Aguado Cuadrillero, a plotter who was serving as Fanjul's messenger. She had come from General Villegas, the nominal head of the conspiracy in Madrid, with orders that Fanjul must seize First Division Headquarters immediately.

Fanjul was startled. Not unless he had an escort. Meanwhile, several officers arrived from Montaña Barracks. Fanjul was right, they said. They had already been to First Division Headquarters and, while General Miaja was no longer in command there, the other officers were afraid to support the revolt. It would be useless, perhaps fatal, for Fanjul to go there without an escort. But why not set up his own First Division Headquarters in Montaña instead? General Mola's troops would soon be arriving from the north to relieve the Madrid garrison. And if he were delayed, the men in Montaña could sally into the streets and take over key points in the city—if they acted before the government armed all the mobs. Anyway, most of the rifles in the hands of the people had no bolts, since about forty-five thousand of them were still stored in Montaña. Would he come?

Fanjul gladly agreed and the visitors departed, promising to return for him before noon. Shortly, the general saw from his balcony a car parked nearby and a man standing by it waving a handkerchief. Dressed in civilian clothes to avoid being noticed, Fanjul rushed downstairs to the car. He felt exhilarated. At last he was needed. No matter what happened, nothing could be worse than the last few days of helpless isolation. As he greeted the waiting officers, he said with almost pathetic appreciation:

"Señores, I'm entirely at your disposal."

Under a broiling afternoon sun, General Fanjul, now in uniform, stood before his men in the vast main courtyard of Montaña Barracks and told them in an emotional greeting that in the coming battle they must "win or die." All, it seemed, silently agreed. But they did *not* agree on which side must "win or die." For within the walls of this great fortress, with its three endless rows of windows and balconies, its squat buildings, and its broad plazas, the two worlds of Spain were trapped together.

Since the great majority of soldiers based here were on summer leave, only some eight thousand, including fifty officers, remained. All but two or three of the officers supported the revolt. However, most of the soldiers, including practically all noncommissioned officers, appeared to back the government, and their leader, Captain Santiago Martínez Vicente, was actively recruiting more.

Immediately after Fanjul's talk, a number of sergeants suddenly became too "ill" to fight. These men, Captain Martínez, and all other suspected foes were then stripped of their arms and locked in their quarters.

Among the most ardent supporters of the rising were forty-two cadets who had voluntarily hastened back to Montaña from their summer vacation. One of these cadets was José de la Cruz Presa, whose father was Loyalist General Manuel de la Cruz Boullosa, Miaja's undersecretary of war in the short-lived Martínez Barrio government. Shocked that his son had entered the barracks to fight for the enemy, the father telephoned Colonel Serra, whom Fanjul later replaced, and pleaded with him to send the youth home. The cadet would have to make his own decision, Serra replied. And so the boy did. He decided to "share the fate of his comrades."

But there was no split loyalty in Fanjul's family. His two sons, both officers, had also entered Montaña. When the youngest, twenty-one-year-old Juan Manuel, walked into his father's office the general, relates the son, was astonished.

"What are you doing here?" he asked.

"I've come to fight beside you, sir."

Juan Manuel could see the agony in his father's eyes. The whole family must now "win or die." After a moment of silence, filled with fear and pride, the father said abruptly: "Well then, back to your duties!" And Juan Manuel saluted and left.

About 4:00 P.M., responding to the general's call, young Falangists began streaming into Montaña, either daring to climb the main ramp or sneaking through side gates. When they had given the password to the sentries and set foot in the main courtyard they felt they had reached paradise. They had been certain that militiamen were carefully watching all the entrances and had half expected to be mowed down. But they had managed to infiltrate—with the secret connivance of an Assault Guard commander who wanted to hedge his bet on a Loyalist victory.

Some one hundred and eighty Falangists came pouring in within an hour or two, though a few were either turned away at the point of a gun or were wounded trying to get in. One of those who had rushed to this fortress was Felipe Gómez Acebo. Like his fellows, he was dumbfounded by this sudden last-minute order when all had been eagerly awaiting the call since the revolt started on the previous morning. Some had even slept the night on benches across the street.

Gómez Acebo was determined to break out with his comrades and attack First Division Headquarters, the radio station, the War Ministry, and other key points in the city. But why had there been a delay just when the militiamen were being armed? Had someone betrayed them?

Soon Gómez Acebo and the other newcomers were transformed into soldiers, with rifles and ill-fitting uniforms. They formed a motley contingent, virtually without training, just like the militiamen they were facing. But all they had to do, they were told, was to aim and pull the trigger—at the proper time. And when was that? Gómez Acebo wanted to know. When would they break out?

General Fanjul asked the same question as he sat in his office waiting for Mola's troops to reinforce his own. He had already drawn up a proclamation that described how the city was to be run when he took it over, including rules for censoring the press, playing patriotic music on the radio, and court-martialing those "who have not felt deeply in their souls the sacred stimulus of the defense of Spain." Fanjul couldn't wait any longer. He planned to attack as soon as his forces could mesh their actions with the moves of other units in Madrid.

But nobody was moving.

As the self-proclaimed commander of the First Division, he had ordered divisional headquarters to report immediately to Montaña. But the division staff was too confused and uncertain to do anything. Some members favored the rebels, some did not, and most were afraid of being killed if they obeyed Fanjul.

So they stayed where they were.

He had sent envoys to win over officers in the Presidential Guard and the Assault Guard.

But they returned empty-handed.

He had ordered a rebel officer at Cuatro Vientos Air Base, adjacent to Campamento, to seize the base for the insurgents, an especially urgent task since Getafe Air Base was already in government hands.

But this officer also failed.

Most important of all, he had ordered Lieutenant Colonel Alvarez Rementería, who had taken command of Campamento after Colonel Carratelá was killed, to head toward central Madrid with his sappers' unit and two batteries of horse artillery.

But all he got was an unexpected phone call some minutes later from General García de la Herrán, who had also gone to Campamento.

"What are you doing there?" asked Fanjul, who still didn't know that García was the new commander of the Madrid rising.

García couldn't do much. The commander of his horse artillery wouldn't budge. But if necessary García would order an attack himself. He would phone details later. However, Fanjul's telephone went dead before García could call again. Montaña was cut off from the world and the men inside were slowly being ringed by armed "thugs" screaming for their blood.

General Mola had told Fanjul in Pamplona that at H-hour the situation in Madrid would find its solution. Now, as H-hour neared, the solution could only be death—unless Mola's forces swooped down from the north in time to save them.

"To Madrid! To Madrid!"

The cadenced cry resounded through Pamplona with all the passion and fervor usually reserved for San Fermín. The people of Navarre, however, were now stimulated not by the scent of animal blood but by the smell of human blood. Bands blasted out militant rhythms, red and yellow monarchist flags decorated almost every balcony, religious medallions glittered on almost every chest.

"To Madrid! To Madrid!"

"And be sure to bring us Azaña!" shouted one woman.

It was 5:00 P.M., July 19, about the time General Fanjul found that Montaña was isolated. More than twelve hundred men were lined up in neat ranks on the esplanade before General Mola's Sixth Division barracks, ready to advance on Madrid, while wives, mothers, sisters, grandparents, and children stood nearby shouting words of encouragement. When Mola appeared and saluted the soldiers, their joy exploded into near hysteria.

The general's eyes glowed and his rigid features crinkled in a smile. He felt that he was not leading just a *pronunciamiento* but a genuine popular movement. The "traitors" on the other side claimed the people supported them, but who could feel the electricity of this moment and deny that the people were with the army?

Amid the euphoria, it was easy to forget that Navarre was not representative of Spain. No region in the country so longed for a return to medieval glories, to the days of the Crusades when Christ was King and Spain was truly Catholic under monarchs who would never have permitted the political and moral chaos bred by the modern "evils" of democracy and communism. Things would have been different, it felt, if Prince Don Carlos had been crowned king back in 1833.

In that year, as King Fernando VII lay dying, he ordered that his baby daughter, Isabel, succeed him, rejecting the claim of his brother, Carlos, that *he* was the rightful heir since he was next in the male line. With Fernando's death, Carlos called upon his supporters to forcibly place him on the throne, and the first bloody Carlist war broke out, followed by two others, in 1868 and 1872. The Carlists, led by the soldiers of Navarre, failed in each attempt, but they had never conceded defeat. And Carlism became a symbol of the longing for past grandeur.

Now, in the army rebellion, the Navarrans saw a new opportunity for achieving their sacred goal, though Mola had refused to commit himself to place the Carlist pretender on the throne when the government was finally crushed. A pure military dictatorship, under Church guidance, they felt, was still preferable to the present "Marxist," "anti-Catholic" regime.

The *Requetés*, as the Carlist militia called themselves, had for months been secretly training for this moment. Now they were flocking to Mola's banner, wearing red berets and green armlets marked with a red cross. In many families all the men volunteered, sometimes from son to grandfather. And since even the farm workers insisted on fighting, there was hardly anyone left to harvest the fields—a minor matter, with God calling for a new crusade. In one family, the father and two sons joined the crusade, but a third was reluctant; that is, until the mother refused to serve him meals because of his "cowardice." Finally, when fourteen- and fifteen-year-old children tried to enlist, Mola announced on the radio that for the time being he didn't need any more volunteers.

About five hundred *Requetés* would be sent to Madrid in the first contingent, with as many army conscripts—whom Mola didn't entirely trust—and two hundred blue-shirted, largely untrained Falangists. The Falangists deplored the feudalistic, fanatically religious mentality of the *Requetés*, but found common ground in their extreme nationalism and desire for authoritarian rule. Colonel Francisco García Escámez, one of Mola's best and most devoted officers, would command the combined force.

Escámez was to capture Guadalajara, just north of Madrid, and swing into the capital from the west while troops from other rebel-held towns converged on it through the Guadarrama passes. All these forces would have to move swiftly, Mola realized, since he had heard that the government was giving the people guns and threatening the conspirators with extinction. Originally, the "liberators" were to smash into Madrid on the next day, July 20. In some northern towns, however, the rebels were bogged down by fierce resistance and could not reach the capital for at least another two or three days. But could the besieged troops there hold out that long?

After Mola had spoken to his men they marched to waiting buses and trucks while the people swept in to embrace them and pin more medallions on their chests. And as the vehicles chugged off, the soldiers could hear their kin singing Navarran songs into the distance.

"To Madrid! To Madrid! For God and for Spain!"

The bristling exchange of fire between rebels and militiamen that kept all Madrid up on the night of July 19 sounded like full-scale war to occupants of the National Palace, for its ancient acoustics amplified every distant shot into what seemed to be an explosion in the next room. All the presidential guards, aides, and servants, and President Azaña himself were on edge, wondering if Fascists within the Palace were not shooting.

There was reason for concern. Two days earlier, the captain commanding the palace guard had pulled a pistol when his superior tried to replace him. The captain was finally overpowered by the Loyalist soldiers, but who could vouch for the loyalty of other officers in the guard? Besides, some of Azaña's servants had relatives living in the palace who had earlier been exposed as Fascists and were arrested.

In this depressing, almost surrealistic atmosphere, the president welcomed his guest at about 11:30 P.M. with little vitality and almost without voice. The guest was Captain Orad de la Torre, the artillery officer who had collected some rifles at Artillery Park. Earlier this day, he had been called back to the park to help repair two ancient 75-mm. Schneider cannons that he was to haul to Campamento. The government feared that the rebel artillery there would be brought into the heart of the city for an attack, and so the two Schneider cannons were to help Loyalist battalions capture that base in the morning.

But Orad de la Torre was more apprehensive about Montaña Barracks. Not only were the enemy forces there already in the heart of Madrid, but the bolts for most of the rifles in Madrid were there, too. The people must break in immediately—before the rebels broke out. And before Mola's troops arrived to help them. Moreover, Colonel Gil, the commander of Artillery Park, agreed that the militia storming Montaña should get the cannons.

Orad de la Torre had come to the palace to explain to Azaña how these guns could soften up Montaña for the kill. The president listened with a look of gloom and resignation. The first shell fired by the cannons, wherever they were aimed, would signal the start of the civil war he so dreaded; the beginning of a fratricidal massacre that would know no bounds. He had tried desperately to avoid such a catastrophe. When Martínez Barrio had said he was quitting as prime minister, Azaña pleaded with him to change his mind, arguing that no new premier could resist the growing demand for arming the people. He must try once more to reason with the military. But Azaña's plea had been in vain.

And so he had chosen José Giral Pereira to replace Martínez Barrio and, with heavy heart, told him to arm the people. Only a few hours earlier, he had even ordered him to ask Premier Léon Blum of France for military aid to carry on the inevitable civil war. Giral had wired Blum: SURPRISED BY A DANGEROUS MILI-TARY COUP. BEG OF YOU TO HELP US IMMEDIATELY WITH ARMS AND AIRCRAFT. FRATERNALLY YOURS GIRAL.

Certainly Blum would agree. He, too, was the leader of a recently elected Popular Front government living in the shadow of fascism. He surely realized that a rebel victory in neighboring Spain would advance Hitler's goal of isolating and eventually crushing France.

But before French arms arrived, the people had to save Madrid or the government would be dead and the military supreme in Spain. The revolutionaries, though dangerous, were still more acceptable to Azaña than the reactionaries. They wanted change that was far too drastic, but at least they wanted change. If any group had to make a mess of Spain, he preferred that the underprivileged have the opportunity—or at least have the chance to fight for that opportunity. Yet he despaired at the appalling price the country would have to pay.

Now, the president's pessimism gave way for the moment to Orad de la Torre's optimism. The captain saw his cannons as symbols not of death but of rebirth. Their blast would herald the beginning of a new era, a new life for Spain. Had not the storming of the Bastille changed the course of French history? Montaña Barracks would be Spain's Bastille.

The guns would go to Montaña.

"Don't worry, Señor President," the captain assured Azaña. "We shall capture Montaña. And as for Campamento, I was there some hours ago and I saw many people behind the trees. They are also ready to attack."

At about 1:00 A.M., July 20, the meeting ended and Orad de la Torre returned to Artillery Park to begin the odyssey that would help set the tone for a momentous struggle between men envenomed by the past and others terrified of the future.

5

Shortly before dawn, Orad de la Torre seemed to be the most popular man in Madrid. And his delight in this role was reflected in his dark eyes gleaming in the moonlight, in the cocky tilt of his officer's cap over one side of his lean face.

"Follow me!" he cried from the cabin of the first of three beer trucks that sluggishly crawled through the streets of Madrid, past the Prado Museum and then along Calle Alcalá. Two of the vehicles carried huge cannons and the third, hundreds of shells.

The people followed Orad de la Torre like the Pied Piper's rats. Armed with knives and shovels or, if they were lucky, with pistols, shotguns, and rifles, they virtually surrounded the trucks, which could barely move. Finally, at Puerta del Sol, the vehicles, adrift in an ocean of flesh, jerked to a halt and Orad de la Torre climbed out on the running board and shouted:

"People of Madrid! To Montaña Barracks!"

The people roared, and the trucks started edging through the waves again as hundreds and hundreds more joined the multitude, pouring out of houses along the way, streaming from the side streets. They tried to climb into the vehicles to touch the cannons, to examine and admire them. They argued over how many rebels one shell could kill. They sang the "Internationale" and cried, "Death to the Fascists!" Cannons! The people had cannons! Now they were invincible. Now they could change Spain, the world. Orad de la Torre was leading, he felt sure, one of the greatest triumphal marches in Spanish history.

A little before 7:00 A.M., the trucks finally reached Plaza de España, and the caravan merged with the great crowd already gathered there. As Orad de la Torre jumped to the street he was immediately embraced by Assault Guard Lieutenant Moreno, who, at gunpoint, had taken most of the rifles from Artillery Park shortly before the captain arrived to get some. Then a swarm of joyous, screaming men and women descended upon the guns like vultures on a carcass. Jesus had assumed the form of an artilleryman.

Orad de la Torre had seldom before paid much attention to the Cervantes monument in the center of the square: bronze statues of Don Quixote on a horse and Sancho Panza on an ass. But now he reveled in the sight. Don Quixote extended an arm precisely in the direction of Montaña Barracks several hundred yards away—even though he did seem to be giving the Fascist salute!

Silhouetted against the bright morning sky, stark and ugly on the crest of a hill, Montaña Barracks stood as a monstrous, mocking challenge to men who wanted to smash the world into rubble and start anew. It was a vast walled seventy-six year-old fortress embracing three different barracks—for infantry, sapper, and communications troops. These reddish buildings with gray stonework overlooked to the east the public gardens of Calle de Ferraz, to the west the Northern Railway Station, and to the north the broad Paseo de Rosales, which stretched into open country.

About twenty thousand people—men, women and even some children—lay sprawled, weapons in hand, behind trees and benches in the gardens, behind barricades of sandbags, mattresses, and paving stones on the streets. They crouched on the balconies and roofs of neighboring houses, some manning machine guns. There were socialists, anarchists, Communists, Assault Guards, loyal army officers, citizens who were simply curious or wanted to be a part of history, and even a small number of carefully selected Civil Guards, the traditional protectors of the Right, whose black tricorn hats amid the multitude would perhaps demoralize the defenders.

The attackers were supposedly under the overall command of a Civil Guard officer, but most had no intention of taking orders from anybody, for this was a very personal battle for each. An almost festive atmosphere permeated the whole area, and cafés nearby were crammed with *Madrileños* who, between sips of coffee, craned their necks to see the spectacular show.

Captain Orad de la Torre arrived with his cannons after the curtain had gone up. The soldiers inside Montaña, firing from the stone parapet extending along its long front, had already killed or wounded many people as they exuberantly dashed across adjacent streets or poked from behind a tree. But the sight of corpses did not dampen the holiday mood, for this was the ultimate carnival, and the prize for hitting the bull's eye was not a stuffed doll but a bloated body. One's own death or the death of a comrade had been reduced to the price of bad luck at a shooting gallery. What was man's life when man's dream was at stake?

Anyone with a weapon that worked was firing back at the fortress, warming up for the moment of supreme vengeance on those who had for centuries grown fat and powerful at the expense of the people. And the unlucky ones without guns or bolts waited impatiently to loot the armories within or to grab the weapon of a fallen comrade. The Loyalists were supported by four armored cars—and a streetcar!

As the trolley ground into nearby Plaza de Oriente, its bell clanging to clear people from the track, some workers stopped it and one of them cried to the motorman:

"Hey, you, where the hell do you think you're going?"

"Where do you think number thirty-one goes, you idiot? I'll be glad to take you to Argüelles—if you can afford the ride!"

"Don't you see what's going on, idiot? We're attacking Montaña Barracks."

"Yeah, I see. So what? What do you want me to do? Shoot with the streetcar?"

But the trolley was soon converted into a barricade, and the motorman, getting hold of a rifle, began to fire from one of the windows.

As machine-gun bullets from Montaña sprayed the streets, Arturo Barea ran into the gardens and threw himself behind a tree.

"Why the devil was I here—and without any kind of weapon?" he would ask himself later. "I knew perfectly well that it was sheer useless folly. But how could I be anywhere else?"

Still, why behind *this* tree, together with two men who were making a cruel joke of the revolution? Montaña was completely hidden behind a screen of trees, yet one man was blindly firing a giant old pistol at it, making a noise that frightened Barea out of his wits. The man's comrade then demanded that he be given a shot at the invisible target.

"No, I won't. It's my revolver."

"Let me have a shot, by your mother!"

"No . . . If they bump me off the revolver is yours; if not, you can go to hell."

When the second man playfully threatened his armed friend with a knife, he gave him the pistol.

"Here you are, but hold tight, it kicks."

"D'you think I'm an idiot?"

"Go on, get it over!"

Another blind shot into the trees.

How could the war be won with such children? Yet . . . did one have to hit the target to make his point? The idea was to fire, fire, fire. Kill the foe if possible, but the simple act of shooting soothed the soul. It was a declaration of freedom from the past, an affirmation of faith in the future.

Over the crackle of gunfire, loudspeakers installed on balconies bellowed emotional pleas. The soldiers were discharged, a voice boomed, so they did not have to obey the orders of their officers. Their loyalty was to the republic.

"Today you can go to your homes to embrace your mothers, your sisters, your fiancées. Greetings, comrade soldiers!"

Another voice then sounded: "Cease fire! Cease fire!"

This order, directed to the crowd, was barely audible over the din, but was passed from mouth to mouth. An Assault Guard officer in a blue *mono* was standing on a sandbag barricade near the Plaza de España shouting while enemy bullets flew around him. It was Lieutenant Moreno.

"Cease fire!" he cried. "We are going to send somebody to ask them to surrender, to persuade them that they are alone and have no reason to fight the government and the people."

Nobody paid attention. It was a waste of time, this surrender business. Better to kill them all. But the people finally obeyed, and soon firing from both sides faded into eerie silence.

Moreno then jumped down behind the barricade and gave final orders to a young worker who had volunteered to enter Montaña on a peace mission. Major Hidalgo de Cisneros had brought instructions from the War Ministry to make a final request for surrender. The time seemed ripe. The leaflets dropped by planes earlier and the pleas on the loudspeaker, as well as the sight of the besieging thousands, had probably demoralized the defenders.

Francisco Carmona Martínez listened carefully, happy to play so important a role but frighteningly aware that he might not return alive.

"Good luck," said Moreno.

And Carmona, carrying a white rag on a stick and followed by two comrades, began marching toward the main entrance of the enemy citadel. As the three men advanced, tensely watched by thousands of eyes, about the only sound that could be heard was their footsteps. The peace messengers climbed the ramp toward one of the gates, then halted when a sergeant and several soldiers emerged and asked them:

"Who are you? Who has sent you?"

"I wish to speak with your commander in chief," replied Carmona. "I represent the military and civilian forces surrounding the barracks. Do you wish to know my name?"

"It's not necessary," the sergeant answered. "Come in, but only you."

Carmona entered and furtively exchanged glances with the soldiers, as if they were trying to look into each other's minds. The rebels were smoothly shaven and immaculate in their well-pressed uniforms, and he was unshaven and disheveled in his dirty overalls. They were completely alien to him, except for the fierce pride and unreasoned *machismo* that made it easy for people on both sides to face death and dispense it. The external contrasts could not hide the common soul—a melancholy thought for one bearing a message demanding surrender.

Carmona was searched and blindfolded, then led through several corridors. Shortly, the blindfold was removed and he found himself in a dimly lit room facing a group of people gathered around a tall, corpulent, gray-mustached officer—Colonel Serra.

General Fanjul had apparently felt it beneath his dignity to receive personally a delegate of the enemy, especially a civilian, and so had given his deputy the task. Meanwhile, Fanjul, though aware of his critical situation, was still hopeful that his forces would be rescued, if not by Mola's men then by García de Herrán's horse artillery. Perhaps, he told his aides, the sounds of distant battle indicated that García was already on the way.

It was this mood of momentary optimism that Carmona confronted as he faced Colonel Serra.

"Well, what do you want?" Serra asked.

"I have come to you with orders from the government," Carmona said. "You must surrender within ten minutes. The barracks are surrounded by large, heavily armed forces. . . . I appeal to you to avoid spilling more blood."

Carmona paused, disturbed by the serene expression on the colonel's face. There was no sign that he had been intimidated. Serra replied quietly, ignoring Carmona's remarks:

"Since you're here, I'm going to ask you a favor. You have come as the bearer of a flag of truce, and so you are being respected, despite your civilian status. In a few minutes, a truck will leave the barracks to bring back a supply of bread. I give you my word as an officer that we officers won't taste this bread. As you know, we have many soldiers here. They should not be deprived of their ration. . . . We soldiers love the people, more than some leaders who deceive them, who incite them against us as if we were their enemies. Do me this favor— we'll be grateful to you."

"So you're not surrendering?" Carmona said.

"Exactly! Inform those who sent you that we shall resist as long as a single man remains alive. We shall not be the first to fire, but if your people do we shall reply fittingly. If necessary, we shall kill ourselves like men. We would prefer to die with honor than to live without honor. Embrace the señores commanders, my companions, for me, even though we may have to kill each other."

"I recognize your courage," Carmona replied, "but I hope you realize that you are going to drag these soldiers to a useless death, a sacrifice . . ."

The colonel gestured for him to stop, then shook hands with him. The meeting had ended. Carmona was led to the front gate, this time without a blindfold. He felt ill. How many Spaniards would die within hours?

"Comrades!" cried Captain Orad de la Torre as he stood in the Plaza de España shouting for silence. "We are going to fire the first shell in memory of Captain Faraudo, who died gloriously for the republic."

Then, addressing his assistants, he pointed to the gardens and said: "As soon as I've fired you're to carry the cannon over there as quickly as you can, do you understand? We've got to make them believe that we've got plenty of guns."

After a pause, he cried: "First cannon—fire!"

A great rumble shook the whole area and the fighters were stupefied. Then they burst into hysterical cheers and hugged one another and raised the clenched fist and waved their rifles in the air. The people had spoken with a thunderous voice.

Again Orad de la Torre demanded silence: "We are offering the second discharge to the memory of the heroic Lieutenant Castillo, assassinated by the enemies of the people. Second cannon—fire!"

The mob was even noisier this time. Rifles fired wildly and machine guns rattled furiously. Then dozens of men carried the cannons some distance away.

"This third discharge should make them surrender," said Orad de la Torre to another officer, correcting the elevation of one of the guns. "They'll think we have a complete battery. Each gun is to fire at maximum speed. The loaders must keep feeding the shells as fast as possible."

The guns spat shell after shell, each fired before the echo of the preceding one had dissipated. Finally, when there was a pause as the guns were carried elsewhere and the dust cleared over Montaña, the people could see smoke rising from the buildings, tongues of fire poking out of broken windows.

Then again: "Load! Fire! Load! Fire!"

The barracks vanished once more in billowing black, gray, and red clouds punctured by thousands of bullets from every direction.

Suddenly, there was a buzz in the sky, and the people stopped firing long enough to look up. A silvery speck sailed through the blue.

"It's ours!" someone cried.

But a wave of fear rippled through the crowd. Was it really "ours"? In a mo-

ment, they knew. The plane swooped down over the barracks and dropped its
bombload. The people again roared with delight, and some recklessly stood up
and threw their hats into the air—only to be cut down by machine-gun bullets or
mortar shrapnel in the midst of ecstasy.

Then a third cannon, a 155-mm. gun, arrived and also went into action, while
the plane returned twice more with lethal messages. By now, many of the people
had become more daring and, behind the screen of smoke, rushed toward the barracks, throwing themselves to the ground every few yards.

At about 10:00 A.M., a strange silence suddenly settled over the scene of carnage. Then the shout:

"Surrender! White flag!"

A large white rag was fluttering from a second-floor balcony. There was a
great babble of comment. Were they really surrendering or was this a trick? An
Assault Guard cried:

"Forward! *Viva la República!*"

And everybody's mind was made up. Amid screams and cheers, a great current of humanity surged after the Assault Guard as men and women abandoned
the trees and barricades and found themselves sucked into the massive flood.
Among those swept along was Arturo Barea, who later reported:

"I could see the stone stairways in the center of the parapet . . . they were
black with tightly packed people. On the terrace above a dense mass of bodies
blocked the exit."

Suddenly, a burst of machine-gun fire cut the air. The Assault Guard who was
leading the pack, waving his rifle in triumph, fell dead with a bullethole in his
head. Others just behind him also dropped silently. The survivors telescoped
against each other and halted for one stunned moment, then tried to scatter.

"Back! Back! It's a trap!"

Barea couldn't believe what was happening. He was standing in the middle of
the street on a lovely sunny morning and people were falling dead all around
him. As he ran for cover, "the barracks spouted metal from its windows. Mor-
tars sounded . . . with a dry crack. It lasted some minutes, while the wave of
cries was more frightful than ever."

Hundreds of casualties littered the area as if struck down by some supernatural
force.

"They'll pay for that trick!" someone yelled.

But the attackers had not been tricked. An aerial bomb had blown a hole in the
quarters where Captain Martínez Vicente, the Loyalist agitator, had been locked
up, and he frantically rushed from post to post, while walls caved in and smoke
choked almost every building, haranguing the soldiers: It was madness to defend
against such superior forces. Why die for a lost cause—a cause they didn't believe in anyway? A whispering campaign began, and soon most of the men were

ready to surrender. They then sabotaged the mortar shells and, without telling the rebel commanders, put up a white flag to signal the besiegers that a mutiny was breaking out inside. They failed to realize that the crowd would see the flag as a sign of surrender.

At about this time, General Fanjul, lying feverishly on a cot, his face and beard bloodied from a head wound, considered a desperate plan. Most of his men would burst out through the rear gates firing grenades, with some remaining behind to protect the bolts—just in case Mola's troops managed to storm the city in time.

Colonel Serra, who had been wounded in the arm, called a meeting of the rebel officers and, in the midst of a barrage, told them: "It's impossible to go on like this indefinitely. We have no arms to compare with those of the enemy. I can see fear on our soldiers' faces. If we don't succeed in making a sally tonight, we'll have to surrender. . . . It's certain they'll kill the general and me, and perhaps some other commanding officers. But the others will be able to save themselves."

A moment of silent anguish followed, then one officer replied: "My colonel, after so many hours of fighting and the heavy losses we have inflicted on the enemy, none of us can possibly be saved if they capture us alive. Anyway, there is no one who will surrender the barracks voluntarily."

Serra smiled. Yes, the officer was right. The barracks would fall with the defenders in them—unless they could hold out till nightfall and escape in the darkness. And when the meeting ended, Serra personally visited many of the posts trying to bolster the morale of his men. But most now sided with the enemy. At one post, several soldiers aimed rifles at him: Either surrender to the people or die! they ordered. Someone then ran to get Captain Alejandro Sánchez Cabesuda, one of the few passive republican-leaning officers in Montaña, who had become a kind of mediator between the two sides. Sánchez was especially fond of Serra. He rushed to the scene.

"What is it you fellows want?" he casually asked the men who were about to kill the colonel.

"*Viva la República!* " one of them cried. "We want the flag of the regiment taken down and the regiment to surrender!"

Sánchez went and lowered the flag and gave it to the soldiers. They cried again, "*Viva la República!*" and, without demanding more, let Serra go free as a mark of respect for Sánchez.

But the rebellion inside Montaña snowballed rapidly. In spite of the disaster that followed the raising of the first white flag, some soldiers climbed to the roofs and began waving others, while shouting that they were loyal. Then, hoping to make sure the rebels wouldn't mow down the advancing crowd again, they started firing from the rear on the insurgents manning the parapets and the windows.

Despite the shelling, the bombing, and the internal rebellion, the Falangists fought as if they expected to win. One of them had only one arm, but he continued to fire a pistol, loading it with his teeth. Another cripple, a hunchback, also refused to stop shooting. So did Felipe Gómez Acebo, who lay by a window overlooking the Paseo de Rosales and the great plain beyond, and picked off foes on nearby balconies and roofs. Every time he pulled the trigger he felt he had scored a stunning blow for his cause. His faith was as infinite as the scrubby countryside he searched in the distance, hoping to see Mola's relief forces, bugles blowing, racing to the rescue.

But it was too late.

At about noon, scores of people dashed from cover toward the walls of the fortress where they found refuge out of the line of enemy fire. Soon, hundreds, then thousands, rushed forward after them, ignoring the sporadic machine-gun fire that cut wide swaths in their ranks. One man, a miner, moved in a crouch along the wall toward the front gate and threw a stick of dynamite under it. There was a great explosion, and the gate and a machine-gun position next to it suddenly disappeared in a giant mushroom of rubble and dust.

"Inside! Follow me, everybody!"

A young socialist deputy screamed out the invitation as he leaped over the rubble into Montaña Barracks. Behind him, a solid mass of bodies poured through the jagged opening in the wall. Arturo Barea found himself part of the mass, as if grafted to the flesh of the world's sufferers. He was elated and horrified at the same time. He thrilled to the victory of the people; he froze at the hatred in their eyes.

But there was only a smile in the eyes of Enrique Castro Delgado, the young Communist leader who wrote for *Mundo Obrero* and would now form a militia regiment. Castro didn't hate anyone, or at least he would not admit he did. As a good Communist he couldn't afford such emotional luxury. He had to be practical. He neither hated nor loved, but only obeyed. As the people around him savagely vented their rage on every foe, Castro remembered the conversation he had with his friend, Luis Sendín, on the day of Calvo Sotelo's funeral. He recalled the formula they had discussed: to kill, to kill, and to keep on killing until forced to stop from sheer fatigue. Then to construct socialism on the mountain of bones that remained.

These people who were shoving, pushing, lurching ahead to make sure they would get their share of blood and loot—they were fools, the Spaniards of Goya and Garcia Lorca, who killed for revenge and even for the sheer joy of killing. Not him. Castro would kill because he was ordered to; because it was the formula. And his loot would be the minds of these fools. Yet, though Castro didn't like to think of himself as a traditional Spaniard, he clearly felt a certain personal sat-

isfaction as he saw haughty men in neat uniforms topple over, cut down by the
"riffraff" they disdained. Was this not just repayment for the cruel treatment
they had inflicted on him when he had been a soldier?

As the mob burst into the courtyard, General Fanjul ran to the rear of the compound, for if the civilians caught him, he knew, they would tear him to pieces.
He would give himself up instead to the more disciplined Assault Guards at the
rear entrances. He had no choice. But first he sent a messenger to find his son,
Juan Manuel. Soon his son arrived, and Fanjul explained to him what he had to
do.

"But, papa," said Juan Manuel, "they will shoot you."

The general smiled. He would never make it back for dinner with his friends
come next San Fermín. He seemed almost relieved. Isn't this what he had expected? At least it was over.

"Naturally, son," he replied. "When someone wins, the other loses. But
maybe you can bluff your way out. May God be with you."

Fanjul then embraced his son and walked toward a rear gate with several other
officers. But on the way, Captain Martínez Vicente and some of his followers,
who shortly before had been the rebels' prisoners, captured them and turned
them over to invading Assault Guards. The new prisoners were then led through
the hostile crowd to a waiting bus that would take them to Model Prison. Among
those accompanying the general was his eldest son, José Ignacio.

Juan Manuel, meanwhile, removed his jacket and managed to leave the barracks posing as a common soldier, but on the street someone recognized him and
shot him in the leg. Several Assault Guards reached him before more bullets did
and drove him to a hospital where a compassionate doctor hid him from militia
patrols that came to drag him out.

The people stampeding through the main entrance into the central courtyard at
first shot soldiers indiscriminately, even many Loyalists, while they cried out,
"Brothers! Brothers!" As they feverishly thrust forward, fusing with other
groups that had smashed in or climbed the walls at other points, there was scant
time to determine who was on which side. How could one tell a true brother from
an impostor? Many of the officers and Falangists had, like young Fanjul, discard-
ed their jackets and insignias so they would resemble common conscripts.

"We'll show you who they are," cried several soldiers.

But before they could, a machine gun raked the courtyard, mowing down dozens of invaders. A lone corporal was firing it from a high gallery, and when he
finally ran out of ammunition he knelt by his gun and held it in his arms as he
might a baby, until the survivors reached him. Then a powerful militiaman lifted
him up and yelling "Here he comes!" hurled him into the courtyard where he
landed with a heavy thud.

Enraged by the new massacre, the mob now sought blood more avidly than
arms.

Eusebio Muñoz, as a member of the CNT defense committee, was no stranger to violence, but he was sickened now.

"The people," he told the author, "moved like a mad sea, sweeping over everything in their path. Men and women who had been kind, peaceful citizens were suddenly converted into wild animals. I didn't want to join in the slaughter, but I realized that if I remained passive my friends might kill me, thinking I was too soft on the enemy. Almost unconsciously I picked up a Mauser, but instead of shooting anybody I walked out. I was looking for a fight, not a massacre."

According to rebel Corporal Luis de Rivera Zapata (now a colonel), some invaders even castrated the dead and gouged out their eyes. He saw one woman knife dead men in the chest. Though Rivera had been wounded in the legs by shrapnel from an aerial bomb, he remained at his post in the main courtyard and ordered his squad to fire into the crowd as it stormed in. Some of his men did, but about half started running toward the mob with clenched fists, shouting "*Viva la República.*" An enemy bullet then struck Rivera in the stomach and suddenly he saw a militiaman standing over him about to strike him with a rifle butt.

When he regained consciousness in a hospital sometime later, a comrade told him that the Assault Guards had saved his life. Later, his nurses helped him to slip to freedom.

Even after the mobs had broken into the center of the compound, Felipe Gómez Acebo continued firing from his post. Not a shadow on the glaring plain, and the only bugle blowing screeched the victory song of the enemy. At last he realized it was all over. Jacketless, he strode toward the courtyard, almost certain the invaders would shoot him. But though he walked right into their midst, they ignored him as they squabbled over who should get the rifles of the soldiers they had already killed. When he passed the engineering building, he heard one man telling the others:

"Do you hear those shots inside? Don't go in there. They're killing themselves. It'll save us bullets."

Suddenly, some militiamen grabbed Gómez Acebo and charged that he was an officer, pointing to his boots. But before they could shoot him, one of the men stepped in front of him and put up his hand. Gómez Acebo recognized him—an old schoolmate.

"He's all right," the man said. "I know him. I'll guarantee him."

When the group had dispersed, the man told Gómez Acebo to rush to a certain bar nearby. The owner was a friend of his and would protect him. They shook hands, and the Falangist walked out the front gate a free man—but disturbed by the thought that he might have fired at his old comrade if he had seen him during the battle, and even rejoiced that one more Loyalist was dead.

At the same time, the people outside the engineering building entered and smashed down the locked door to the flag room. Inside they found twenty officers sprawled in their own blood. According to Nationalist accounts, these officers had been ordered to fall into line by their leader, Roca de Togores, and while they were standing erect, as if at a parade, Roca commanded each of them to aim his pistol at his head or heart. Then he uttered his last words:

"Señores officers. *Arriba, España!* Ready! Fire!"

When the Loyalists broke in, Nationalist survivors say, they riddled the officers with bullets and stabbed them with knives, thus killing those who were still alive.

"Two shrews, together with several looters," according to one rebel account, "searched the corpses. They took their wallets, watches, rings, pulling them forcibly from their fingers."

In another room, say the Nationalists, other officers, including Colonel Serra, were being held prisoner by Captain Martínez Vicente, who had earlier captured General Fanjul. Some in Martínez's group demanded that all the rebel officers be killed on the spot, but the captain disagreed. Three executions would be enough, he said. And he selected Colonel Serra and two others to die.

Serra objected: "I am the only guilty one. Only I deserve death."

Then another officer who had not been selected, Major Mateo Castillo, shouted: "Why don't you pick me, you bastard? I have the right to die, too!"

Castillo's parents, who had been living in the compound, had earlier been killed by a shell.

By now, no one could control the civilians. They pounced on the prisoners, dragged them all into the courtyard, and shoved them against a wall. And while the crowd applauded and screamed as if at a bullfight, one of the few undisciplined Assault Guards, sitting behind a machine gun, mowed down the officers.

"Comrades," he cried when he had finished, "this is the justice of the people!"

Enrique Castro had rounded up some officers and Falangists in a large hall where every breath of fear seemed to echo in the silence. He walked past the line of prisoners, and when he came to the hunchback, ordered:

"Stretch yourself out!"

"I can't."

Castro looked, he later wrote, at "that shrunken head between the shoulders and those sad eyes; and that oblong face and those long arms. . . . He seemed to be sinking into himself."

"Take them out in files and stand them together by that wall," Castro ordered his men. "Let them face the wall. Hurry Up!"

As the group moved into the courtyard toward the wall, the hunchback left the file and walked over to Castro, holding out a note.

"Would you please give this to my mother?"

The two men stared at each other.

"Move on!"

"Give it to her . . . please!''

"Move on!''

Someone violently pushed the hunchback and he stumbled ahead as if drunk. Then a man in the file began singing the Falangist song "Cara al Sol'' and all the prisoners joined in. A shot, and "the hunchback straightened up as if he wanted to convert himself into a giant before falling forever. Then many shots, mingled with voices of courage and pride, of mysticism and fear. And more shots. Then silence . . . and solitude.''

Later, Castro would reflect on the scene:

"Slowly, with a curious and professional look [I] began to stroll amidst the corpses, to look at the grimaces, to measure the fury or the fear in the eyes that had not closed. And to watch the flies that were flying and landing nervously, as if they were surprised by that gigantic banquet they could never have imagined.''

Castro at last had to admit that he felt tired.

A famous leftist sculptor, Emiliano Barral, stood on his knees calmly sketching a rebel corpse, and a newspaper photographer coolly snapped pictures of people being slaughtered. But suddenly the photographer recovered his human feelings. He ran to an Assault Guard crying:

"Don't you see what's happening? Why don't you do something?''

"Do something?'' replied the guard with a gesture of futility. "What can I do?''

But one Civil Guard was trying to do something. He shouted:

"Nobody has given the order to kill! These people have surrendered. Their life is sacred!''

A cry came back, like an echo from the depths of the tortured Spanish soul: "Nothing is sacred anymore!''

But before militiamen shot down one group of men, they did permit a captured priest to take the prisoners' confessions. He cried out before falling:

"May God pardon us and . . . you, too.''

Finally, about 70 percent of the rebel officers and cadets and 30 percent of the Falangists lay dead, among them cadet José de la Cruz Presa, son of Loyalist General de la Cruz Boullosa, who had tried to persuade the youth to leave Montaña before the battle. The mob's lust for blood now gave way to a passion for arms.

The Assault Guards had already taken the bolts and most of the ammunition, but the militiamen ransacked every building looking for weapons, while dragging off whatever else they could find—clothes, tablecloths, curtains, rugs. One man threw rifles from an upstairs window to his comrades below, while others invaded the arms depot. Hundreds of black boxes were carried out of the depot and soon thousands of people were brandishing long-barreled Astra pistols.

As Arturo Barea left Montaña, he glimpsed into the officers' mess and saw dead officers "lying there in wild disorder, some with their arms flung across the table, some on the ground, some over the windowsills." On the esplanade he stepped over countless more bodies.

The people had won a great victory.

6

While thousands were storming Montaña Barracks, thousands more were trying to smash into Campamento, many of them led by Cipriano Mera, the anarchist bricklayer, who had rushed there before dawn with some of his comrades in a large "requisitioned" automobile. About fifteen hundred men were defending that stronghold, with the aggressive General García de la Herrán in command.

García had frenziedly tried to call General Fanjul again after their phone conversation had been cut the day before, but to no avail. Thus, unable to coordinate breakout plans with Fanjul, García found it impossible to help the general, especially after Loyalist planes bombed Campamento, further convincing the horse artillery commander that he should not send his men and guns to Montaña.

Now it was too late, anyway; Montaña had fallen and Campamento was surrounded by blindly attacking mobs. To Mera and the others, the attack seemed almost like a harmless game as they moved forward in a leisurely manner, all bunched up, everyone his own commander. Not a bullet zipped past them. But then, as they drew nearer, the enemy suddenly opened up and raked them with missiles at point-blank range. Scores fell and the rest raced back in shock.

Again Mera and his comrades forged ahead, but this time with greater wisdom. They spread out and were ready to drop to the ground when the enemy started firing. More casualties, but now they did not retreat. Again and again they attacked, each time inching closer. Then, shortly after noon, hundreds more joined in, coming triumphantly from Montaña.

Inside Campamento, General García and his deputy, Lieutenant Colonel Alvarez Rementería, the *junta* leader, had heard of Montaña's fall on the radio. And they knew that the news would swiftly spread and take the heart out of their men, already demoralized by the conflicts within the barracks, the steady advance of the enemy, and the constant bombing.

"How does the situation look to you, Alberto?" an officer asked Alvarez.

"Bad, very bad. I always told you we would be left to fight alone, and I was not mistaken. They've hung white flags in the horse artillery regiment and the other barracks."

The battle was lost, he admitted, but General García must be saved.

"This man's fate is to be the victim of others' weakness. He must be taken out of here whatever happens. We can't permit those scoundrels to assassinate him. We'll defend ourselves until the last moment."

Alvarez called a meeting of the officers and told García: "General, your life must be saved. It is precious to everybody. You shouldn't let yourself be killed here, because Spain needs you. Eusebio and Roman will try to get you out in the car."

Then, turning to the other officers, he said: "And since very little can now be done, save yourselves if you can."

But nobody moved.

"Colonel," said one officer, "if I have to blow my brains out to prove that I know how to fulfill my duty, I'm ready to do it right now."

General García's eyes shone with pride and gratitude. "I'm going to die in the street," he said. Then, shaking each officer's hand, he added: "I'll be seeing you, señores."

The general left and walked calmly toward the gate leading to the street. He strode past the guardroom, which was already in enemy hands, and no one tried to stop him. Then someone exclaimed:

"Here's the general! He's the most guilty of all."

There was a shot, and García raised his hands to his heart and stammered as he fell: "Oh, mother!"

Within minutes, almost all the other officers also lay dead as the mobs swarmed through Campamento.

Amid the delirium, Mera scanned the fields dotted with corpses. Many of the dead were anarchists who had never used arms before and knew nothing about fighting a war. Militarism, with its discipline, its ranks, its utter disregard for the individual, was to them one of society's worst evils. It was a philosophy, a system, entirely alien to anarchism. His men sprawled out there on the fields had died bravely, as anarchists, not as soldiers.

But there were so many. . . .

7

With the fall of Montaña and Campamento, all Madrid, that afternoon of July 20, became a grotesque circus in which people died alongside those who danced. Barracks after barracks surrendered to the Loyalists, often after new demonstrations of courage and new massacres by both sides. Captain Palacios, the former medical officer now working at the War Ministry, raced in his car through a hail of machine-gun bullets fired from the tower of the Basilica of Atocha to enter nearby Maria Cristina Barracks, where he tried to talk his old friend, rebel commander Colonel Tulio López, into giving up.

"Aren't you ashamed of what you've done?" asked Palacios like a parent scolding a child.

"Miguel," Tulio López responded evasively, "tell me as a friend. How close are Mola's troops?"

"Never mind Mola!" replied Palacios. "As a friend I ask you to stop this bloodshed!"

At that moment, the barracks were bombed. While smoke drifted through the window, the colonel walked out to the gate and hung a white flag over it. Palacios hinted that he should try to escape. But Tulio López gave himself up to the Assault Guards, though he knew death awaited him.

The end of organized resistance in Madrid marked the beginning of a sniper campaign that made almost every street a battleground. Rightists fired from church steeples, roofs, balconies, shooting at anyone with working clothes or dropping grenades into crowds. The Loyalists captured Circulo de Bellas Artes only after a bloody struggle, and reoccupied the Casa del Pueblo, which had been under fire from a neighboring convent, only after the convent collapsed into rubble.

When automobiles blasted through the streets gunning down militia patrols, the militia were ordered: "Comrades. Look out for cars with the license plates Madrid 46738, Madrid 32566, Madrid 42524, Madrid 31653, San Sebastián 21345, Barcelona 39184. . . . "

"Comrade, what do you think I am?" roared one militiaman. "An adding machine?"

But each car was hunted down.

At this moment of victory, even the random shooting could not keep the people off the street. If they weren't firing at snipers or dragging suspects out of houses, they were embracing each other, screaming their slogans, cramming into the bars and cafés, where drinks were on the house—if the bartender was not to brand himself as a rebel suspect.

The most crowded place of all was the Puerta del Sol, where thousands of people gathered to show off their trophies—helmets, bayonets, swords, binoculars, guns of all kinds. When government officials strutted out on the balcony of the Ministry of Interior and raised the clenched fist, the crowd burst into the "Internationale" and the Spanish national anthem, wildly clapping their hands in rhythm.

Suddenly, shots pierced the air. The people tried to run but they were so sandwiched together they could hardly move. Then an Assault Guard shouted:

"Lie down, everybody!"

Without thinking, everybody obeyed, forming a quilt of human bodies that completely covered the great square. Then another order:

"Cover your heads!"

With their bare hands? Was this a joke? They now realized that the "quilt" was one huge target for the snipers firing furiously from buildings overlooking the plaza. When someone shouted, "Run!" the people jumped up and trampled over each other trying to find cover. But bullets seemed to whiz from every building, every direction, and the doorways were already packed.

Finally, militiamen and Assault Guards, who poured out of Pontejos Barracks to the rescue, rooted the snipers from their hiding places and order was restored, while ambulances came to pick up the dead and wounded. The people then resumed their celebration as if nothing had happened.

Madrid's terror and intoxication had begun.

Indeed, only too vividly for Christopher Lance, the British engineer, as he, like most occupants of the luxury buildings on Calle de Espalter, pressed his face to the window. He saw gangs of men and "wild-haired" women racing down the street, waving knives, guns, and red flags. When they opened a fusillade, the faces suddenly disappeared from the windows and blinds were pulled down. Lance was about to close his shutters as well—until he saw a woman across the street shot dead while doing so. Bullets crashed through the windows, and he shouted to his wife:

"Down on your tummy, Jinx."

When the street was finally calm again, Jinx and her maid went out with shopping baskets to store up on food and fuel—while they were still able to move about. But every store was being ransacked by ruffians whom no one would dare challenge. The two terrified women returned home with virtually empty baskets.

Meanwhile, Lance went to his office on the Paseo del Prado and found that most of the Spanish employees had not come.

"If the Navarros don't turn up again," asked an assistant, "can you carry on?"

"No need to get the wind up," Lance replied. "It will soon be over."

"Not this time, I'm afraid. That is, not unless the army can get a quick victory."

Lance returned home, wondering what he should do now. How could he carry on his business when the people refused to listen to reason and leave the government in the hands of the educated, patriotic men with long experience in governing?

"Do you remember that dapper little royalist at the Savoy, Colonel Pinilla?" he said to Jinx. "Do you remember his telling me confidentially that there was going to be a showdown soon? By Jove, he was right!"

* * *

Captain Orad de la Torre was pale and had deep circles under his eyes. This morning he had been euphoric. Not only were the people at last rising against their exploiters, but he was playing a major role in this historic drama. Yet now, after the great triumph, he felt depressed. His melancholy had set in when the battle of Montaña had ended and he had walked through the ruins observing the grisly results of his marksmanship, of the struggle for liberty to which he was so fiercely dedicated.

Then came news about his brother and nephew—killed together at Campamento by a shell. A shell like one of the hundred and eighty he had fired himself that morning. And now, in the evening, he was at the morgue with his sister, Rosa, trying to find and identify the bodies. Once more he was breathing in the stench of the dead—people who had followed him to Montaña that morning; who had fought by his side; who had tried to kill him.

Finally, he and Rosa found their kin, the boy and his father. The youth was only fifteen but his face, now resembling white marble, made him look like twelve, a teenager who had hardly lived, yet had learned there was something more important than life.

There were others moving between the two rows of corpses, as they searched for a son, brother, sister, father, husband, sweetheart. One young woman walked up to Rosa and asked:

"Excuse me, but do you know where I can find those who fought at Montaña Barracks?"

Rosa pointed: "Over there. You'll find many . . . "

The woman, noting Orad de la Torre's blue *mono,* said falteringly:

"I mean . . . the others."

"They are all reunited here."

She was looking for her brother, said the girl, then added in a lowered voice so Orad le la Torre wouldn't hear: "A Falangist."

Moved by the girl's desperation, Rosa offered to accompany her. The captain, who had overheard the woman, wanted to say that he would go, too, but somehow it didn't seem right. His shell might have killed her brother.

"Go with her, Rosa," he said. "I'll wait for you outside."

And he went to the entrance and watched several men pile unpainted coffins into a truck—unidentified bodies that would be buried in a mass grave, rebels and Loyalists together.

The two women walked among the bodies when suddenly Rosa's companion stopped in front of the corpse of a young man, his hair still neatly combed, his chest pierced by three tiny holes. She bent down and gently kissed his forehead. Then the two women clung to each other and wept.

As they walked out arm in arm, Orad le la Torre was still watching the coffins being loaded on the truck.

* * *

Ten rifles, one submachine gun, about two hundred cartridges, some helmets—a discouraging haul. But this booty was all that members of the Unified Marxist Workers party (POUM) could scrounge from Montaña Barracks where they had been vastly outnumbered by other leftist groups. And nobody was more disappointed than Hippolyte Etchebéhère, who had to remain out of the battle because he didn't have a weapon.

His intense brown eyes set in a long sullen face reflected his revolutionary resolve. He and his attractive wife, Mika, had only joined POUM the previous day after arriving from Paris to fight in the anti-Fascist ranks. Hippo was the more extreme of the two. Born in Argentina of a middle-class Basque family, he had turned radical in 1919 after seeing Buenos Aires police mow down striking metalworkers, and some years later took off for Europe with Mika, a fellow Argentinian, to help kindle world upheaval.

Both were followers of Leon Trotsky, and felt at home with POUM since the party leaned toward Trotskyism. The couple had abandoned Stalinism when they went to Berlin in 1932 to help the Communists take power there—only to see their German comrades collapse almost without a struggle before the Nazi hordes. Stalin, they felt, wanted power simply for power's sake and used the Communist parties of other countries for his own selfish ends. Unlike Trotsky, he wasn't interested in immediate world revolution.

Spain, however, would not be like Germany. Here there was a real chance to spark a proletarian revolt that would burn its way into every country, for the workers' organizations were powerful and absolutely committed to victory or death. As they themselves were. Hippo, especially, savored the revolutionary atmosphere of Madrid. Mika had occasional doubts.

"Hippo," she had asked that day as they passed a church in flames, "do you think that burning a church is a revolutionary act?"

"Yes," he replied, "and I don't advise you to tell these men, as you are thinking, that there are works of art inside that should not be destroyed. Too bad about the works of art! The Church has always served the rich against the poor in Spain; it has always been an arm of oppression. Let them burn their churches!"

Hippo could hardly wait to fight, not because any party ordered him to but because his conscience did. Unlike the Communist party, POUM did not seek to own one's soul. There were no rules handed down by a supreme master; the party was knit together simply by a common faith. Anybody could join, and almost anybody did—including a number of young prostitutes. Mika had detested the whores in Paris, who used to make obscene remarks to her whenever she passed them. But these girls seemed completely dedicated to the cause.

The trouble was that while POUM had considerable power in Barcelona, it had almost none in Madrid. The Communist party was much stronger here and intimidated many prospective members, and besides, POUM had no real leaders or even members with military training. Now, as Hippo looked over the pathetic pile of "spoils" from Montaña, he saw the opportunity he had been seeking.

"Do you at least know how to use these arms?" he asked his new comrades.

They suddenly viewed him with suspicion. Was he making fun of them? Was he just trying to get a rifle for himself? When he saw their reaction, Hippo smiled and added:

"I'm not asking you to give me a rifle. I'd only like to teach you how to use these weapons. Take them into the next room."

Their hostility vanished and they picked up the arms. Mika did not try to follow them. She understood this was a men's affair, that her comrades, Spaniards who prided themselves on their ability to fight, would never forgive her if she watched while they displayed their ignorance and awkwardness.

Hippo, she knew, was becoming their leader, and would soon be commanding a small militia army of his own. But how little it would have to fight with; and it might have a two-front battle on its hands. For the Communist party was also forming militia units, and Stalin would undoubtedly back them—as long as they served his interests. And one of his chief interests at the moment was not revolution but the destruction of Trotskyism everywhere.

Enrique Castro Delgado was one Communist who had no doubt about Stalin's desire to communize Spain. Nor any qualms about Stalin's formula. As Castro thought about the dead and the flies swarming over them that morning in Montaña, he actually smiled and felt content. After the capture of Montaña, Communist party leaders had congratulated him for his role.

"Comrade Castro," Dolores Ibarruri said, "the party is proud of you. You . . . are an example for the whole party. We expect you to continue the good work."

It was not clear whether *La Pasionaria* was praising simply Castro's leadership and military astuteness in the attack on Montaña, or his ruthless killing of the prisoners as well; despite her sharp tongue, she had never seemed disposed to cold-blooded murder.

"And now, Castro," she said, "take this pistol, a present from the party. We are certain it is being placed in good hands."

Castro took the pistol, and all the leaders shook his hand. He would have the rank of major and be the first commander of a new Fifth Regiment, which the Communists would run. Hopefully, this regiment would become the nucleus of a Popular Front army that would win the war—and guarantee party domination of the postwar government. It was the job Castro had coveted.

Within hours, he set up Fifth Regiment headquarters in the Convent of Franco Rodriguez. The brick buildings in the compound, including the church, were turned into offices and barracks, and the large courtyard became a training ground. He would build an army, Castro vowed, "capable of applying the formula every day, every hour, every minute.'' He calculated that if the formula were applied on a scale one hundred thousand times that of Montaña, he would reach his goal. And he tried to imagine the corpses and the flies he had seen multiplied by a hundred thousand.

Castro gathered his officers in one of the rooms and discussed the formula with them:

''Comrades . . . only by winning this war shall we be able to achieve the revolution, socialism, to be another Soviet Republic. . . . You know, comrades, that to fight a war, an army is needed. That means we shall have to create an army, and as fast as possible. . . . But in order to create this army, many men have to be recruited . . . and taught to kill in such a way that killing becomes an art. Is that clear?''

''Yes!''

''This army will be our army. Listen carefully, our army. But only we will know that. For the others it will be the army of the Popular Front. We, the Communists, shall lead it, but we must appear before everybody . . . as fighters of the Popular Front. Is that clear?''

''Yes!''

''First, we shall set up groups of five men . . . who will start at nightfall to search for the Fascists. Second, a recruiting campaign has to be started in every quarter. We need thousands of men . . . of all tendencies, because this is the Popular Front army.''

And Castro smiled.

But he was not smiling later that night when the five-man patrols he had sent out returned with Fascist suspects. He was appalled by their lack of ''enthusiasm'' for this assignment. He called the patrol leaders together and told them:

''I find myself with men who are reluctant, with men who seem to be ashamed of this night work that requires them to enter homes and drag men out or kill them if they don't want to leave. . . . Comrades, this is a deadly struggle. The side that kills more men more quickly will win . . . Today the most important thing is to learn to kill, to know how to kill, not to grow tired of killing. A comrade can be pardoned for many things, many, but there's one thing he can't be pardoned for: not knowing how to kill, not wanting to kill.''

Then Castro sent his men to the barracks to sleep. Sleep well, he said, and with a clear conscience.

That evening of July 20, President Azaña held a reception for his palace aides. He greeted them with a brooding smile. Madrid's victory, he knew, had been forged with hands dripping Spanish blood; a victory that was not his anyway. The trade unions—the socialist UGT and the anarchist CNT—were now the real masters of republican Spain. And the most effective fighting arm of the socialists was the Socialist Youth, whose leader, Santiago Carrillo, was quietly serving the Communists.

Thus, the extreme leftist militia was now largely responsible for law and order, and the horrors of Montaña seemed an example of what this militia considered justice. Even while Azaña sat at a writing desk drinking coffee and sadly exchanging witticisms with his guests, shouts continued to resound throughout the city. Not mainly from snipers now, but from militiamen who were wildly shooting civilian suspects, and from the firing squads of two extremist officers who were trying captured rebel fighters in summary courts set up in the Casa del Campo and executing them on the spot.

And while the leftist revolution was spreading, so was the rightist uprising. True, Madrid remained republican, thwarting plans for a quick coup, and Barcelona also stayed loyal, after anarchist-led forces there crushed rebel troops. Valencia and most other major cities, too, were still with the government. Furthermore, the rebels suffered a tremendous blow when General Sanjurjo, on his way from Lisbon to Burgos to head a new Nationalist regime, was killed in a plane crash.

But battles were still raging everywhere, and wherever the rebels were in control they were slaughtering members of the Popular Front as a matter of official policy. General Gonzalo Queipo de Llano, the conqueror of Seville, had ordered the shooting of thousands—almost anyone who had voted for the Popular Front. And General Mola, *El Director* of the revolt, fully agreed with this order. On July 19, he told a meeting of mayors near Pamplona:

"It is necessary to spread an atmosphere of terror. We have to create the impression of mastery. . . . Anyone who is overtly or secretly a supporter of the Popular Front must be shot."

Azaña's coffee was bitter.

CHAPTER 3

Stalemate

1

By the morning of July 21, the roads leading from Madrid to the Guadarrama Mountains were jammed with trucks, limousines, buses, rattletrap cars, bicycles. Madrid's militia had already won a stunning victory over the rebels. Overnight, they had forged themselves into a popular army, however shoddy and undisciplined, and ravaged the forces that had hoped to hold out until General Mola's troops rescued them.

But what could be the decisive battle was still to come. Mola was closing in. If his men could smash through the two vital passes at Alto de León to the northwest and at Somosierra to the north, they would almost certainly sweep across the plains into the city and capture it even without the help of the rebels within. And so the cry was, "To the Sierra!" as thousands of Loyalists rushed to the mountains to choke off the enemy at the passes.

Not all the fighters, however, stayed very long. Antonio Gómez, a member of the socialist UGT, had been wheedled into driving three anarchist friends to the front. They had commandeered a car, but did not know how to drive it.

"To the Sierra!" cried the anarchists.

But first, why not stop for a few drinks? So Gómez waited outside in the car while his friends staggered from bar to bar ordering free liquor. Finally, the men were ready to fight. When they reached the foothills of the Guadarramas, however, one of them ordered Gómez to return to Madrid.

"Somebody's got to stay behind and protect the city!" the man argued.

Gómez then stopped at a checkpoint, got out, and quietly told the guards: "These people don't want to fight. I'm wasting gas. Maybe if you talked with them . . ."

A guard ordered the men toward the front, but after the car chugged along for a while the three anarchists demanded that Gómez stop again. It was late and they were drunk and they wanted to sleep right there in the car. In the middle of the night, all were startled out of their sleep. One of the men had accidentally fired through the roof of the vehicle—the only time any of them had pulled the trigger all day. Some hours later, they were on their way again to the Guadarramas, but hardly had they moved into the hills when someone observed: "There are no rebels here. Let's go back to Madrid."

So Gómez turned around and headed back, leaving his friends off at the nearest bar. The men were in a fighting mood. God help the bartender who refused them a free drink!

If some Loyalists preferred to fight in the bars, most chose to do it in the mountains. By dawn, July 22, the town of Gaudarrama was overflowing with about three thousand Loyalist fighters—militiamen, Assault Guards, Civil Guards, and army conscripts. Later they were joined by soldiers from the garrison at Wad Rab in Madrid, which had been uncommitted until *La Pasionaria* and a Communist militia leader, Enrique Lister, roused them to fight the rebels. Shrewdly, the two Communists had gone to the barracks and promised the men, who were mainly peasants, that they would get their own land after the republicans won.

Soon, together with Dolores and Lister, the soldiers were off for Guadarrama. When they arrived, the two Communists rushed to local headquarters, where they found the Loyalist officers in a small lamplit room bent over military maps. A new infantry regiment had come?

"Let them spend the night in the plaza," said one officer. "We'll see about them tomorrow."

La Pasionaria was furious, she relates.

"I don't know anything about the science of war," was her reply, "but I have a very strong impression that if we leave those men there, not one will remain alive to wake up tomorrow. Don't you think it would be better to take them to the front tonight so that if the enemy decides to attack tomorrow, he'll find a surprise—a trained and organized military regiment?"

"We're not familiar with the road to the mountains and don't have any guides."

The mayor of Guadarrama intervened: "I can show you the way to go without being seen by the enemy."

"Then discuss it with the chief of the regiment."

The two Communist leaders began to suspect the officers of "treason." And there did seem to be reason for distrusting some of them. A few, indeed, had already bolted to the enemy as soon as they had the chance.

The most notable renegade was Colonel Juan Carrascosa Rovellat, who had headed the communications regiment at El Pardo Barracks in Madrid. After Montaña fell, he was ready, he told his superiors, to take his regiment across the Guadarramas and capture Segovia from the rebels. At dawn, July 21, his men, including the son of socialist leader Largo Caballero, piled into trucks and, while they cried "Death to the Fascists!" and raised the clenched fist, the convoy sped through Madrid toward the mountains.

Near the Alto de León Pass, militiamen, with no reason to suspect betrayal, helped clear the path of obstacles so the trucks could pass. And soon the vehicles were bumping down the other side of the mountain into rebel territory—where Carrascosa grandly turned the regiment over to Mola's men. Largo Caballero's son and other soldiers who refused to switch sides were taken prisoner, while those who became turncoats were now among the insurgents atop the Alto de León ready to swarm down on Madrid.

But standing in their way were the Loyalists in Guadarrama, who were preparing to attack the summit in the morning. Militiamen had already shot about fifteen members of the Fascist "welcoming committee," including the baker and the tobacconist and his wife. Now, the enemy must be dislodged from the peaks.

Ramón Sender, a famous writer who had joined the militia, was in the long column that was ready to go. Lorries stood in the middle of the road loaded with men and artillery while other fighters sat by the roadside under the sun. All were impatient as they awaited the order to move. It didn't come.

Sender and his comrades were enraged. Why didn't the commander give the order? Suddenly, there was a shot in their midst. Probably some militiaman firing casually in his frustration, thought Sender. He turned around and saw an elderly officer stagger and collapse, his pistol falling at his feet. Someone picked it up and cried:

"It's Colonel Castillo!"

Colonel Enrique Castillo was to command this operation. He and his two sons had joined the Loyalists, though they were torn between their oath to the government and their friendship with brother officers on the rebel side. And the colonel's agony had been all the greater because he knew the militiamen distrusted them, as they did all professional officers. So Castillo solved his dilemma with a bullet in the brain.

"If all the officers who don't understand the people's cause followed his example," said one militiaman to Sender, "we would save a lot of cartridges."

Four hours of waiting, but still no go-ahead signal. Suddenly, the enemy on the summit struck first—with a barrage of shells that shook the town as if demons had entered its soul. So this was why the men had been waiting! Sender and the others could smell betrayal. First, their commander commits suicide, then the enemy attacks. All doubts evaporated. They had been tricked into loitering until the rebels could set up their artillery for this massive bombardment.

Sender tried to hide in the town hall, but it was already crammed with Assault and Civil Guards and so he stayed outside, pressing close to a stone pillar. Between volleys, men leaped from their shelters onto the trucks that could still operate, and the convoy crazily lurched up the hill leading to Alto de León. No one was in command. Nobody had any plan. The militia would simply blast its way to the enemy-held summit.

"Let's go up, comrades! We'll get rid of these cannons with our bare hands!"

Sender felt oddly elated. All around him mutilated bodies lay hugging, almost lovingly it seemed, the smoldering earth that would now claim them. Bits and pieces of trucks and guns were strewn everywhere. Houses had become powdered skeletons. Why should he expect to escape unscathed from the carnage? But at least he would fall fighting and not clinging to a pillar. The truck in front of his own overturned, and he heard the men scattered on the road laughing. Were they laughing at themselves or at death? Were they brave or simply incapable of weighing a situation seriously? Even a Spaniard could not fully understand the enigmatic Spanish character.

With the road blocked by the overturned truck, everyone jumped from the other vehicles and ran into the woods on both sides of the road.

"Up! Let's get them!"

Waves of crouching, crawling men inched their way ahead, bush to bush, tree to tree. They were all that stood between the invisible enemy and Madrid.

"And the command? Where was the command?" Sender once more asked himself. "Why were we there without leaders? . . . Perhaps military technical knowledge is not given to the rank and file if they are not mechanized soldiers . . . but only masons or peasants."

Sender looked around at his comrades.

"I saw that two of them were dead, although they were still upright and advancing. . . . The face is losing its expression, the glance its vivacity, for that is the first to die. Through the dead eyes we see the desolation within. . . . Perhaps I was dead, too."

Finally, the firing grew so heavy that even the walking dead could move no farther. . . .

"Don't go away, comrades. Don't go down to the town. We'll bring you what you need."

Two young girls who had climbed up to them like wingless angels were pleading.

"At least stay here until dark! An inspector has come from the War Ministry, and they are going to change the officers and send artillery."

The girls, dressed in *mono* overalls, their hair tied back with red ribbons, promised to return with cartridges and food. But one of them was killed before she could come back—though her spirit sparked a fire within the men.

Sender and his fellows edged forward again. Some reached the top. And others—the Civil Guards—went over the top, suddenly turning around and firing on their "comrades," while shouting "*Arriba; España!*"

The Loyalists held, and Mola's men were never able to move beyond the peaks they controlled until the war ended.

2

Cipriano Mera, on the morning of July 22, raced with his anarchist followers and some Assault and Civil Guards toward the nearby rebel-held towns of Alcalá de Henares and Guadalajara, northeast of Madrid. A column from Pamplona, he knew, was heading toward Guadalajara, where it would try to link up with the local defenders and push into Madrid while other rebel forces broke through the Guadarrama passes farther north.

Although an army colonel was supposed to lead the Loyalist contingent, the anarchists would take orders only from Mera. And his orders were to advance relentlessly. He not only had to beat Mola's force to Guadalajara, but he could hardly wait to settle a personal score. When he had once been jailed in that town, the warden had treated him cruelly. Now he would release all the prisoners still held there and deal with the man who had made him suffer.

About 9:00 A.M., the caravan smashed its way through Alcalá and, after capturing it, rolled on toward Guadalajara. It halted near the Henares River, and the men jumped off the trucks and ran toward the bridge leading into the town. But a machine gun sputtered a welcome. Casualties grew still further when a friendly plane mistakenly dropped bombs on them while all they could do was shake their fists at the sky. Despite losing many comrades, Mera and his men coiled for a new suicide strike. Wait, wait! pleaded the colonel in charge. Reinforcements would come. Why die unnecessarily?

While they were arguing, reinforcements did arrive, and the militiamen began racing across the bridge again, only to be mowed down once more. Without bothering to consult the colonel, Mera then led a group of men downstream and they waded across in water up to their necks. Then they darted from house to house until they found the machine gun. Soon it was silenced. The rest of the attackers then poured across the bridge, and the rebels who were not killed fled. Mera, the antimilitarist amateur, was already proving his gift as a military commander.

He now moved cautiously toward the center of town, hugging the walls, when suddenly he met an unarmed civilian. The two men stared at each other and the civilian turned pasty. It was Mera's former jailer! He was sorry, muttered the warden. He had only been doing his duty. Could he help it if he was a jailer? He trembled at what seemed his inevitable fate. Mera was silent for a moment, then replied disdainfully:

"You have nothing to fear from me! But from the others—yes!"

Some of his comrades had also been in the Guadalajara jail.

Mera escorted the warden past the long file of men behind him. Some raised their rifles. But they wouldn't dare kill anyone under Mera's protection. When the jailer was out of danger, Mera returned and, after setting free the prisoners still in jail, went into town with his comrades to celebrate. He had scored an important victory over the rebels—and himself.

A few hours after Guadalajara fell, fresh fighters rushed in from Madrid to stop Mola's Pamplona force before it could try to recapture the town. These new combatants would thrust onward to Sigüenza, where they would block the way to the rebel troops. And the Trotskyite POUM militia, led by Hippo Etchebéhère, would spearhead the drive.

Shortly, Hippo's men and other fighters steamrollered into Sigüenza, crushing the local rebels before Mola's troops arrived. Mika, Hippo's wife, who helped the doctor in the rear, was exposed to the horrors of war for the first time and was shocked when she saw men with great open wounds, some still writhing with life, some dead. She could no longer view them simply as revolutionaries or Fascists, leftists or rightists, but as human beings, reacting in the same way to pain, staring with equal innocence in death. Hate had still not penetrated her. She was a revolutionary, but could a better world really be built in a graveyard? Was there no moral link between means and ends? Though she pondered these questions, she would not reveal her doubts to Hippo.

Even victory did not bring an end to the killing, for Hippo had warned his men that looters would be executed.

"We are revolutionary militiamen, not a band of thieves," he said.

And when one man, Manuel, ignored the warning, he was "tried" and shot.

"We slept on the ground, on mattresses, side by side, and held each other's hand," Mika would later recall. "But we were never more apart, with Hippo locked in his world of war, tense as a bow, and I uneasy in this strange world of combatants so unlike the revolutionaries of my principles, haunted by the fear of Hippo's death."

She whispered to him, appealing to his idealistic instincts:

"Do not get killed, dear. You are valuable, indispensable . . . the most knowledgeable about the revolution. One can be brave without being rash."

"No, here in Spain, one must be rash if people are to obey you. Only physical courage counts in the scale of values. The leader must march in front, and not lower his head when the bullets whistle by.''

"And be killed.''

"Yes, perhaps be killed. . . . But let's not speak anymore about that. I have trust in my star, so don't torment yourself. This struggle that we sought in Germany, that we have waited for with our hearts and our clenched fists, we have found it. We must lead it with joy.''

"Good, let's speak no more about it. Let's change the subject. . . . I cannot believe that you ordered Manuel to be shot, as I've heard.''

"I did not order Manuel shot. He was condemned by the revolutionary tribunal. . . . He spent his time prowling and plundering. He ignored warnings. . . . He was shot. We had to make an example of him. We are in a civil war.''

Death had become so simple, so normal.

Before going to bed, Mika had bandaged Hippo's feet, which had turned black after the day's battle. She asked him why they were black. It seemed a sinister sign.

"What's the difference?'' he replied. "Have you become superstitious? What about your principles?''

But a strange fear gripped her, and she kept repeating to herself: "He must not die, not die, not die!''

Early in the morning, Hippo and his men were ready to attack the troops from Pamplona, which had just barreled into the nearby town of Atienza. Mika held her husband tightly and pleaded:

"My love, take care of yourself. Cover yourself well. It is very cold.''

Soon, as the sun rose, Mika could hear shooting and explosions in the distance. She imagined Hippo and his men running toward the village, firing and throwing grenades. Minutes passed, hours, it seemed. No one was returning, not even the wounded. Then a group of men came into view, the leader dragging his rifle, wiping tears from his cheeks.

"What misfortune, my God,'' he lamented. "What horrible misfortune. They have killed him. They have killed the chief.''

"It's not true,'' another cried. "Shut up! He's only wounded. He'll be brought back here.''

But the man who was weeping lay his head on Mika's shoulder and insisted: "He is dead, dead. We no longer have a leader.''

Mika quietly repeated with him: "Dead, dead, he is dead.''

And inside of her some voice said: "I must die also. I should be dead already. I must not survive him by a moment.''

Mika did not weep, but she trembled so violently that she could barely grasp the large pistol someone handed her—Hippo's pistol. And then a woman fighter who had seen Hippo die gave her a handkerchief stained with blood from his lips.

"I swear to you that he did not suffer," she said. "He lay like a tree struck down by lightning, smiling, his eyes wide open."

Mika caressed the pistol, and she heard Hippo saying: "What are you doing to our principles? You can think about your little individual destiny after the revolution, if you are still alive. This is not the time to die for one's self."

And soon the POUM militia had a new leader.

Colonel García Escámez had been plagued with problems ever since he left Pamplona on July 19 with the cheers of Navarre turning simple duty into a divine mission. His men should have reached Guadalajara within twenty-four hours and then surged into Madrid, while merging with other rebel forces battering through the Guadarrama passes. And he might have done so if he had not stopped to polish off Loyalist defenders in several towns along the way.

Finally, he ran headlong into Hippo Etchebéhère's determined force. But that wasn't all that brought his convoy skidding to a halt. A courier caught up with Escámez and gave him a message from Mola: Guadalajara had fallen into enemy hands and Escámez's force was not powerful enough to recapture it. He must double back, loop around to the west, and crash through Somosierra Pass, which was east of Alto de León and the second big mountain gateway to Madrid. Rebel troops from Burgos already at the pass were being pushed back by the Loyalists.

Somosierra Pass had changed hands several times since July 18. First, Loyalist peasants had dug in there; then a group of monarchists and Falangists forced them to retreat. On July 21, new government troops wildy counterattacked. And the wildest were those fighting under a militia chief, Valentin González, known as *El Campesino* ("The Peasant"), though he was actually a road contractor. *El Campesino's* tough face was dramatically embellished with a thick black beard and reflected the brutality that had characterized his life.

Born into a poor family in Estremadura, one of Spain's most backward regions, he became an anarchist like his father and at the age of sixteen killed four Civil Guards during a coal strike. He fled to the hills where he turned to banditry, then was captured and sent to Morocco to fight the Moors. But the first man he killed was his own sergeant—for slapping him. He then met an officer who converted him to communism, and he soon deserted to the Moors, helping them slay his own countrymen. He eventually returned to Madrid and was now a Communist commander.

El Campesino didn't follow any rules of war—especially after learning that the rebels had killed his wife, three children, father, and sister. He automatically shot all prisoners, and even some of his own men if they proved cowardly. Once, in his usual uncouth language, he lectured a would-be deserter on courage, then announced he would shoot him. He struck the man with his fist while firing into the air, and the victim, on regaining consciousness, was amazed to find that he was still alive. This soldier became a courageous fighter, as did most of *El Campesino's* men, who feared his wrath more than enemy bullets.

In one battle, *El Campesino* suffered a head wound and was sent to the hospital, but he refused to stay there. After two days, he was back in Somosierra, his head swathed in a huge bandage. Thinking that anyone with such a bandage must have a serious wound, the militiamen could hardly believe that he returned. The legend of *El Campesino* spread and even the Communist party could no longer control his actions or lust for publicity.

Now, his men, together with other groups, attacked the enemy and regained the peaks of Somosierra. A stronger rebel force then tried to storm the height again, but was thrown back with heavy losses. It was after this setback that Mola ordered Colonel García Escámez to reinforce the retreating troops and try once more to capture the pass.

On July 25, the rebels, now strengthened by Escámez's force, suicidally charged up the mountains, much as the Loyalists had done at Alto de León. One company managed to crawl up behind the enemy lines, and the government troops found themselves surrounded. *El Campesino* and other defenders finally broke through the steel ring around the peak but at a huge cost. And so by afternoon the rebels were again perched on the summit and controlled the pass.

But this victory did little to comfort Escámez and his men as they gazed down longingly upon what seemed like an almost defenseless Madrid. Not only did government planes hit them hard, but in the prolonged fighting they had almost run out of ammunition. Mola ordered Escámez after he had reached the summit:

"Not another shot! I only have twenty-six thousand cartridges for the entire north army."

And before Escámez could get more, the Loyalists had dug in deeply on a line below the peaks and it was too late to push them back.

CHAPTER 4

Nonintervention

1

General Mola was an excellent actor. He smiled and spoke cheerfully, even joking at times, and he went calmly for his usual evening walks. He also seemed utterly confident when he set up a Committee of National Defense in Burgos on July 24, with General Miguel Cabanellas, the commander of Saragossa, as figurehead president. Within a week, he predicted to the press after he had moved to Burgos, this new "government" would be ruling from Madrid.

Only Mola's closest aides knew of his despair in these last days of July. Although the rebels now controlled about half of Spain, their hold was tenuous in many places, and Madrid, the key to the whole rebellion, was lost, at least for the time being. His plans had hinged on speed, on storming into Madrid and ending the war quickly. And it had dismally failed. The rebels inside the city had been wiped out, and those trying to get inside, via Alto de León, Somosierra, and Guadalajara, had been stopped or beaten with heavy casualties. He had also lost Toledo, a vital town south of Madrid, though the rebels had locked themselves in the huge Alcázar there and were refusing to surrender.

What was more, Mola's supply of weapons and ammunition was rapidly dwindling while the Loyalists in Madrid had more than fifty thousand rifles, three artillery regiments, and most of the air force planes. And the "rabble" were growing stronger every day as they gained battlefield experience; they were already forming organized battalions. All they needed was an army with some discipline to completely dominate Mola's own forces. Especially since his men were most-

115

ly amateurs—however brave and eager—or conscripts who could not be trusted. If he weren't fighting equally untrained anarchists and trade unionists rather than real soldiers, the Guadarrama passes might serve more as Loyalist gateways to the rebel north than as rebel gateways to the Loyalist south.

As Mola sat forlornly at his desk, one commander after another called, pleading: "Aircraft! We must have aircraft immediately!"

"Yes, yes," he replied to each, "I'm giving orders now to send a squadron."

He had a total of twelve planes!

After hanging up, he would exchange a sad glance with his aide and tell him: "I can't help resorting to pitiful lies. What am I going to tell them?"

To compensate in part for the shortage of weapons and supplies, the general had to improvise. Aerial bombs were made from artillery shells, antiaircraft guns from ordinary 75-mm. cannons. Sometimes empty shells were issued to the troops; the noise would at least help to keep up their morale. And when there were no more army boots, rubber sandals were given out instead. Even surgical instruments were in short supply, and many amputations had to be carried out with straight razors. Nearly desperate, Mola considered withdrawing his soldiers from the Guadarramas altogether to a more defensible line along the Duero River farther north.

Meanwhile, he heard, France had agreed to fill the government arsenals with arms. The French newspaper *Le Jour* revealed that Premier Blum had promised to supply Prime Minister Giral with twenty bombers, fifty machine guns, and eight 75-mm. guns, as well as rifles, bombs, and ammunition.

Mola did not know yet that the order had been cancelled. At Britain's request, Blum had flown to London on July 23 and was greeted apprehensively by Foreign Minister Anthony Eden at the Claridge's Hotel:

"Are you going to send arms to the Spanish republic?" Eden asked.

"Yes," Blum replied.

"It is your affair," said Eden, "but I ask you one thing. Be prudent."

He made it clear what he meant by prudent. Britain had committed itself to aid France if a third country, presumably Germany, attacked it. But if Blum helped the Spanish government against the rebels, thus giving Hitler an excuse to invade France, Britain would not feel obliged to keep its pledge. In short, London was not ready for war and opposed any policy that might lead to a general European conflict. And besides, the ruling Conservatives in Britain feared that the Communists might control a victorious Spanish government—a possibility even more dire to some of them than a Fascist triumph.

Blum was caught in a political vise. He deeply sympathized with the Loyalists, but could he jeopardize France's security? True, a Fascist Spain would be a danger; France would have a potential enemy on three borders. But even more dangerous, he felt, was the prospect of fighting a war without Britain's help. At the same time, he could not ignore the rightist uproar at home over the promises he had made to the Spanish government. Blum had to tread carefully.

So he decided on a compromise: All the European powers—Germany, Italy, Britain, Russia, Portugal, as well as France—should vow nonintervention. If neither side received aid, the Loyalists stood a good chance of winning in the long run. For as Indalecio Prieto, the moderate Spanish socialist leader, had broadcast on July 24:

"Are they [the rebels] mad? Where are they going? Don't they see that the means for achieving victory are in our hands: money, industrial equipment, the navy, the air force, the matériel, the men? . . . If the uprising could not triumph quickly as the result of surprise, it is fatally condemned to failure."

On July 25, Blum returned to Paris and reversed his policy. He would halt aid to the Spanish government—though quietly permitting André Malraux, the writer and adventurer, to smuggle out some planes. Perhaps the other powers would then also agree to stay out of the struggle.

But French aid or not, Mola now looked to General Franco to save the cause. Franco had been unable to send his Moors and foreign legionnaires from Morocco; the Loyalist navy was blocking the way and he didn't have transport planes. Somehow, Franco had to get his troops across in the next few days and attack Madrid from the south—or the war would be lost.

"It is obvious," Mola told an aide as he leafed through some discouraging reports, "that it is Franco who will decide the war. If he doesn't give a push down there . . ."

To give himself this push, Franco was frantically appealing to Hitler and Mussolini for help. As soon as the revolt broke out, he had sent an emissary to Rome to ask for planes, heavy artillery, and fifty thousand rifles. Mussolini agreed.

"And there will be a man," the Duce said, "with every rifle and a crew with every gun."

A rebel victory, he reasoned, would at once eliminate the danger of a Communist takeover in Spain and, if a general war broke out, help to keep the British out of the Mediterranean and the French army in North Africa out of France. The Italian dictator changed his mind about sending regular troops only when Marshal Pietro Badoglio, the hero of Italy's Ethiopian victory, warned him that such a move might spark a general war—which Italy was not ready for.

"If you go into the Spanish adventure," Badoglio told him frankly, "please do not expect me to come in at the last minute and save the situation. I am one hundred percent against it."

Mussolini backed down, at least temporarily, though he would send "volunteers" later in the war. Now, he gave Franco only equipment and technicians—secretly. The world first learned this when, on July 29, an Italian bomber made a forced landing in French Morocco en route to Spanish Morocco.

Franco also sent emissaries to Germany, and with equal success. The Germans, like the Italians, recognized the risks of a general war, but were also willing to take them. Hitler wanted the rebels to win for the same reasons Mussolini did, and for other reasons as well. He was worried about a mutual security pact

France and Russia had signed in 1935 calling for each to aid the other if either were attacked by a third country. But with Spain Fascist, France would be caught in a geographical nutcracker and would be less willing to attack Germany if the Führer decided to invade Russia. Furthermore, Hitler felt, by keeping the war going in Spain, he would distract Allied attention from his arms buildup, while a rebel victory would guarantee an uninterrupted flow of Spanish iron ore and other vital minerals needed for this buildup. Finally, Spain could be an excellent testing ground for new German weapons.

Within days, twenty Junker bombers, six Heinkel fighters, and several transport aircraft and cargo boats, together with crewmen, technicians, and advisers, secretly landed in Spanish Morocco. And on July 29, Franco's first troops set foot in rebel-controlled Seville.

Thus, in early August, while Germany and Italy pumped into Spanish Morocco all the aid Franco thought he needed to cross the Mediterranean and smash into Madrid, France allowed only a trickle of arms to flow to the Loyalists, and Britain shut the valve altogether. The United States, for its part, was so dedicated to isolation that it even refused to join the nonintervention committee that France was organizing to stop all leaks.

Mola had no longer to perform an act. He began to enjoy his evening walks again. In a few days, Franco's troops rolling in from the south would fuse with his own in the north, and Madrid would collapse.

There was only one real problem now—Russia. Would Stalin react to the German and Italian arms shipments by sending aid of his own to the Loyalists?

After several days of war, Spanish Communist leaders met secretly with some of Stalin's top international agents to discuss this question.

"We have won great victories," boasted José Díaz, secretary-general of the party. "We have most of the territory, most of the people, the main raw materials, the most important industrial centers, most of the war factories, and all the naval units."

Jesús Hernández, the party's chief propagandist, scrutinized the listeners around the table—Dolores Ibarruri, the other party chiefs, the Comintern delegates, including Italian Communist leader Palmiro Togliatti and French Communist leader Jacques Duclos. But Hernández's eyes focused mainly, he writes, on Togliatti and Duclos, two of Stalin's most trusted servants. For would they have come to Madrid if they didn't have an important message from Moscow?

While Díaz talked, Hernández sought some hint of the message in their gestures, their mood. But in vain. Togliatti, suave and intellectual, casually cleaned his fingernails with cigarette paper, and the roly-poly Duclos indifferently scrawled notes.

The Comintern was Stalin's international tool for ensuring that the Communists throughout the world kept in step with Soviet foreign policy. Before Hitler rose to power in 1933, it tried to incite them to agitate and revolt in all non-Communist countries and to fight socialist rivals. But with Hitler posing a mortal threat to Russia, Stalin shifted gears. He decided to woo the democratic nations, especially France and Britain, hoping they would help him in case the Nazis attacked.

The Comintern thus began pushing for Popular Front governments—moderate leftist coalitions like those in France and Spain—that would enjoy Communist support even though the Communists might at first carry little political weight. The idea now was *not* to trigger Communist revolutions that would frighten the democracies, but to set up governments that would side with Russia in a crisis.

With unblushing cynicism, the Spanish Communists dutifully donned their masks. They no longer used in public incendiary expressions like "revolution" or "dictatorship of the proletariat." They demanded "parliamentary democracy," land for the peasants, aid for small businessmen. They spoke of Lincoln more often than Lenin as an example of a "liberator." And now, with the civil war spreading, they were, as Enrique Castro explained to his officers, building a new Popular Front army—under quiet Communist domination.

The appealing blend of anti-Fascist militancy, technical efficiency, and political moderation had already begun to send party membership soaring, and many solid middle-class citizens looked to the Stalinists as a shield against the revolution that anarchists, Trotskyites, and extreme-left socialists were trying to spark. Stalin could now see himself reaping a double benefit from the party's political masquerade. Not only would the democracies be more inclined to unite with Russia against the German menace but the Communist party might be able to control the republican government behind the scenes. And this would guarantee that Spain would serve Soviet foreign policy at whatever sacrifice.

The question now disturbing Jesús Hernández and some of his more independent-minded comrades was: Would Stalin help them to crush the German- and Italian-supplied rebels even at the risk of alienating the democracies—a victory the republic had to win if the party was to eventually set up a Soviet Spain?

Díaz, a weak, rather innocuous man, a convenient counterpoise to the party's real leader, the fiery *La Pasionaria*, droned on about Loyalist successes, until finally he broached this question.

"These initial results," he said, "can be compromised . . . if we do not get the war matériel we need from abroad."

When another Spaniard pointed out that Britain, France, and the United States would not help the government, Hernández cut in: "But the USSR can send us arms without delay."

The answer finally came.

"Little by little, Comrade Hernández," said Duclos. "Things aren't that simple. The USSR must take into account the position of the democratic powers. . . . If France and Britain have decided not to help you, it's because they fear war with Germany. If the USSR, by aiding the Spanish republic, loosens its links with these powers, she can be dangerously isolated."

"The fact is," insisted Hernández, "that our government is the legitimate government of Spain. . . . It is a member of the League of Nations. The principles of the League state clearly the right of each government to acquire arms necessary for its defense."

"That is a formal right," Togliatti interrupted. "But in real life, things are different."

"When the time comes to apply international laws," added Duclos, "each country thinks of its own interests and nothing else."

"[This argument] means appeasement, concessions," Hernández replied. "It can lead to a denial of our own international principles."

"Our principles have today the value that . . . the USSR gives them!" Duclos exclaimed.

"I don't agree," Hernández responded dryly.

There was a tense silence. Not agree with Stalin? Not agree that Spanish interests were subordinate to Soviet interests?

Apparently among the silent was Dolores Ibarruri. Russia had given her the strength to survive, the will to fight, the ability to believe. To doubt Russia would be to doubt herself; to deny there was hope for the men in the world's dungeons and bunkhouses.

Finally, Togliatti said: "The USSR must guard its security, the apple of its eye. Any careless action can break the present stalemate and set off a war in the east. Hernández's error is understandable. He has lost sight of reality and sees his country's socialist duties with the heart, not with the mind."

The meeting ended, and Hernández was bitterly disillusioned. Spain's life was at stake, and so was the party's, and Stalin offered aid "little by little." He was acting like any nationalist bourgeois leader!

Actually, Stalin had already decided to give the republic money and food, "gifts" from Russian workers and Comintern front organizations around the world. He couldn't appear as if he were betraying the Spanish workers, especially at a time when he was executing thousands of Trotskyites and other suspected dissidents at home. Perhaps later he might even send some arms and men—volunteers from *other* countries—if they were needed to keep the conflict going and Hitler mired in Spain. Meanwhile, Russia would both mobilize for a war and maneuver for a nonaggression treaty with Germany. Hopefully, France and Britain might still intervene in Spain and thereby involve themselves in a war with the Fascist nations. Russia could then stand aside and be the arbiter—and the inheritor of a ravaged Europe. And even if the democracies stayed out of the war, they might be so frightened by a Nazi threat in Spain that they would tighten mutual defense ties with Russia.

The point, therefore, was not to help the Loyalists win quickly and arouse Western fears of a Communist menace but to ensure that they lost slowly. Russia had to buy time—with Spanish blood.

And the best marketplace was Madrid.

PART II

The Revolution

CHAPTER 5

Terror

1

"How are you tonight, Señor Castanys?" asked the owner of Marichu's, a fine Basque restaurant that still had enough good food to satisfy the gourmet. "I'm sorry you must wait, but I am forced to take care of the militia first. However, if the señorita doesn't mind, you can eat in the little back room."

As Jaime Castanys and Janet Riesenfeld walked to the room, the militiamen smiled, annoying Castanys.

"It's probably your hat," he said sourly. "Nobody wears a hat here anymore. . . . I haven't [even] got a necktie on. It's all so childish. If I wear a necktie I'm an enemy of the government; if I don't I'm their friend. Naturally everyone's going to walk around without one."

When they sat down, Castanys's mood changed.

"Do you realize," he asked, "that this is the first meal we've had together since Mexico?"

Janet, a beautiful dark-haired American dancer, had just arrived in Madrid from New York, sneaking across the French border by posing as a newspaper correspondent for a U.S. agency in collusion with its real representative. After a hectic trip and numerous interrogations, she had managed to join Castanys, her Spanish fiancé.

They had first met in Hollywood, where Janet's father, Hugo Riesenfeld, was a famous orchestra conductor. Castanys, a reserved sensitive aristocrat from Bar-

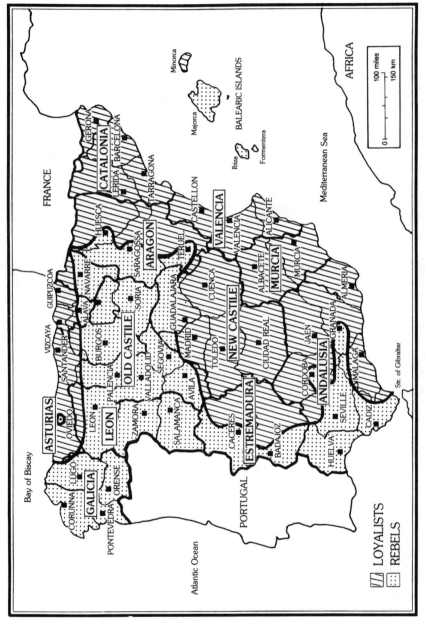

DIVIDED SPAIN—AUGUST 1936

celona, was tall and dark with heavy brows and sensuous lips. He had won a contest as the "handsomest man in Spain" and went to Hollywood with a film contract, although he was never given a role. Janet was only fifteen, Jaime, twenty, but they wanted to marry. Her parents disapproved and sent her off to finishing school, while he returned to Spain. Two years later, she married another man, but by the time she was twenty-one, divorce proceedings had begun.

Janet had never forgotten Jaime, and six years after they parted they met again in Mexico City, where she was on tour as a dancer and he on business as the head of a tourist agency in Madrid. With their love rekindled, they agreed to marry as soon as her divorce was final. Then, shortly before the revolt broke out, Jaime was called back to Spain.

"I'm a little afraid to leave you this time," he said as the train pulled out.

He shouldn't worry, Janet replied, for she would be with him soon. But shortly, she received a mysterious cable from him:

DARLING DELAY DEPARTURE FOR FEW MONTHS.

Janet ignored the wire and decided to leave immediately. Not only was she eager to see Jaime again but she had arranged for a performance in Madrid as a partner of one of Spain's best dancers, Miguel Albeicin. En route, the war broke out.

Now they were together again—but for how long?

"They won't make you go to the front, will they?" she asked.

"Is that what's worrying you, *mimo*? It shouldn't. This will all be over in a few weeks, before they even get to that. [The rebels] have been planning and getting ready for months. Don't you remember, I cabled you not to come? . . . Still, I'm glad you did. . . . You'll simply stay inside if there is any actual fighting when they enter Madrid."

Janet was puzzled. How could Jaime be so sure "they" would? From the little she had seen so far, it seemed clear the rebels would have to crush not only a people in arms but a spirit on fire.

Constancia de la Mora finally overruled her husband, Major Hidalgo de Cisneros, who wanted her to stay home. Cisneros had become acting air force chief after the commander had been captured and killed by the rebels. And Constancia could no longer bear doing nothing but wait for his hurried phone calls assuring her that he was safe. So she left for the Casa del Pueblo and arrived breathlessly after barely escaping sniper bullets. Pushing her way through the sweaty milling crowds, she asked a UGT official for a job. Sorry, she was told. She had no union card, and the union wasn't taking any chances on outsiders.

Constancia, however, was not discouraged. She began thinking of the children victimized by the war. Children like the little boy who many years ago had contemptuously muddied her new plaid skirt while she had been strolling down the Castellana with her governess; like the girls in the poor children's school who had eyed her resentfully when she had given them candy bars as a ritual offering of charity. Now the nuns in the convent schools had fled in panic. But what had happened to the children? She went with several women friends to the Ministry of Justice to find out, and an official who dealt with the protection of minors answered her question.

"I don't know what we can do," he replied in desperation. "We have plenty of empty buildings and hundreds of abandoned children, and nobody . . . to take care of them."

Later that day, the women stepped out of a car in front of an old walled convent and, on entering, found the place a mess, with the remains of the nuns' last meal still on their plates, dust coating every ancient piece of furniture, cockroaches scurrying through every room. The women set to work sweeping the rooms, cleaning the chimney, washing the dishes, scraping the pans. And that night fifty little girls were brought from another convent where they had been abandoned. They were scrawny and frightened and wore dirty dresses, having hardly eaten or washed for a week.

Constancia wanted to cry, but it was no time for sentimentality.

"We hope you are going to be happy here with us," she said. "And there is no need to talk in such low voices, because we are not afraid to hear you talking or laughing. Oh, we hope you will soon laugh and play! We have a lovely garden, you know! And more children will come tomorrow."

One child asked timidly: "Are we to live here forever now?"

"Then it is not true what the sisters said," another murmured.

"Don't tell her what the sisters said. Don't tell her!"

But others did. The militiamen would rape them!

Once reassured of their safety, they sat down for a dinner of salad and rice pudding, which none had ever tasted before. Recalling her own silent convent days, Constancia encouraged them to talk during the meal. Then to the bath. But one four-year-old screamed out when Constancia started to undress her: "It is a sin against modesty!"

When bodies had been scrubbed and heads deloused, the children were sent to bed. They were too shy to speak to each other. Soon, Constancia's own nine-year-old daughter, Luli, arrived from the country and taught them how to play games and sing folk songs.

To Constancia, this was why the people were fighting. To create a Spain where all children would sing and play—a Spain of joy and justice . . .

2

When Christopher Lance walked into his office the day after Montaña Barracks fell, he was stunned to see one of his clerks sitting at his desk.

"What are you doing in my chair?" he demanded.

The clerk coolly replied: "The workers have formed a committee and we are now in complete charge of the business. I naturally hope that I shall have your cooperation."

Lance wanted to grab the clerk and throw him out of the office, but he saw the need for discretion. After all, life in Madrid was cheap these days. Then other members of the committee, all old employees, strutted in and Lance now realized that the revolution had indeed come. Perhaps he could bluff his way back into authority.

"Get out of my chair!" he ordered the clerk.

Apparently conditioned by the past, the clerk quietly obeyed. Lance then sat down and a worker politely asked him to teach them how to run the business.

"It's not as easy as that," Lance replied. "The first thing you have got to realize is that at the back of the business is finance, and you will not be able to monkey about with foreign capital. . . . I have no intention of telling you anything about the works. I shall continue to carry on. You may go now."

The employees left, their revolutionary spirit crushed—for the moment. Shortly, the clerk returned, calmly removed a pistol from his pocket, and demanded that Lance make out a check to him for 150 British pounds. This time Lance didn't argue.

Madrid was in the throes of anarchy and revolution. Workers' committees immediately seized private firms, factories, and tenements. And since most foreign concerns were incorporated under Spanish law they could be confiscated, as Lance, who represented a British company, soon found out. Often, the workers took over only after rightist owners fled in fear, and thus helped to save the business from shutting its doors at a time when the economy was already crumbling. But even more often they simply grabbed control so they could share the profits among themselves, while the owners sometimes worked under them as common employees, feeling this would be safer than to go into hiding. Soon the unions were even running beauty parlors, shoe repair shops, and many small stores.

The Communists, socialists, and anarchists raced madly for the choice businesses and properties, and the winner would immediately paste up a banner on the front door staking his claim. Office buildings and luxury hotels would house a party's headquarters, restaurant, and courtroom, where a *cheka* (people's court) meted out vigilante justice to "enemies of the republic." The various groups also scrambled to control public services and utilities. And there was hardly a car left running loose on the road that had not been "requisitioned."

Stripped of all real power, the bourgeois government not only stood silently by but also snatched what it could of the enemy's wealth. It funneled the bank accounts of suspected rebels into the war chest and even blasted open safety-deposit vaults to help fill it up. More important, the government seized the largest industries and within days transformed a city of bureaucrats, clerks, and construction workers into an industrial center second only to Barcelona. Almost every kind of war matériel would soon roll off the new crudely installed assembly lines.

While instant socialism may have saved Madrid—and all republican Spain— from instant economic collapse, its by-product was a built-in chaos that swiftly burgeoned into terror and banditry. Soon, militiamen were using vouchers instead of guns for extortion. Each trade union and party gave its members War Ministry–endorsed vouchers that they could use to "buy" gifts for their families and girl friends and dine each day at a communal café or restaurant without having to pay a peseta. And tipping was taboo under the new proletarian rules. Although the vouchers could supposedly be redeemed when the war was over, no one really expected to pay or be paid, and a proprietor could not refuse to accept one—if he yearned for a long life. In fact, some "customers" just filled their shopping bags with goods and walked out without leaving a voucher.

The anarchists were perhaps the most honorable of the thieves. Any who violated their moral code, which required them to deposit all appropriated wealth and goods at their headquarters, were dealt with summarily.

The Communists were the most pragmatic. Stalin had ordered them to seek the confidence of the petty bourgeoisie, so they took over only those shops and industries owned by known far-rightists or abandoned by fearful owners. They became the "protector" of the small businessman, whose support they wanted.

And they pressured the trade unions and parties to transfer all their seized property to the government. In this way, industry, owned by the state, would manufacture war goods more efficiently, and the Communists could more easily control the economy when they eventually took power.

But the anarchists, abhorring all government, fiercely resisted nationalization of the seized property. The trade unions, they felt, should run all enterprises and the government none. That would be a step closer toward the anarchist millennium. Besides, the anarchists had no desire to help clear the path to power for the Communists.

Meanwhile, as the leftists battered each other in a race to run the revolution, Madrid reeled in the joyous stupor of a city gone wild with proletarian power. Militiamen dressed in their *monos* swarmed from the front into the fashionable areas where they filled the once chic cafés and bars and lounged on street corners in the company of girl friends and prostitutes, while cars asplash with slogans and union initials raced through the boulevards, their horns screaming triumphantly.

Not even the most fastidious middle- or upper-class gentleman would dare be seen wearing a necktie or a hat, or even a new suit, while women ripped up their red petticoats and draped the cloth over their balconies, either out of patriotism or panic. And though movies and bullfights still drew huge crowds, tennis courts were nearly deserted, since the leftists viewed tennis as mainly a bourgeois pastime.

So pleasant had Loyalist life become away from the front that many militia-men decided to stay away. Thus, militia leaders would send men periodically into the drinking establishments to drag out the deserters, or at least to relieve them of the gun they had been boasting had wiped out a Fascist battalion.

Luckier were those "heroes" who really did wipe out Fascists, or mere suspects—behind the lines.

3

In a garden off the Paseo de la Castellana, a big arched sign illuminated with gaily colored lights could be seen from blocks away at night and perhaps be mistaken for the entrance to a cabaret. But the bulbs formed the words, "García Atadell Brigade." Here, in an old palace, Agapito García Atadell, a typographer and highly respected member of the Socialist party, carried on his vital work. He was one of the government's chief secret investigators, whose job was to root out snipers and traitors, give them a fair trial, and carry out sentences. The Loyalist press lionized him: He was one of the keepers of Madrid's security, a super-policeman of the people, and a sterling example of republican justice. He was the answer to the illegal *chekas*.

Since the normal tribunals with their suspect bourgeois judges had ceased to operate after the revolt, more than twenty-five makeshift courts, the *chekas*, had suddenly mushroomed. Each party and trade union held trials in its own *cheka*, acting on its own authority. The results could be seen every morning in the Casa de Campo or along some lonely roadside where riddled bodies lay rotting under the sun. The victims had been taken for a *paseo* (ride), it was said.

According to rebel survivors of the summary trials, the Communists were the cruelest wardens and judges, often employing torture to extort confessions. And the communist newspaper *Mundo Obrero* encouraged them by calling for the "extermination" of all traitors.

The anarchists, on the other hand, were regarded as relatively fair and humane. But since they were not under discipline, as were the Communists, their conduct varied according to the individual. The genuine anarchists opposed casual murder, and the anarchist federation, the FAI, denounced publicly the "monstrous acts" committed by men disguised as anarchists or by Fascists posing as militiamen. When the anarchists did kill, they often did so with a sympathetic smile, as if to say: "I really don't relish doing this, but I hope you understand it's for the good of society."

But all these groups were motivated by fear of the sniper and the saboteur, who continued to puncture the inflated pleasures of a new life without law or constraint. Many also agreed that the fewer ''Fascists'' around, the better. And they were often helped to render justice—or injustice—by denouncers poisoned with jealousy or greed. Thus, former Interior Minister Salazar Alonzo, who had joined the Falange shortly before the revolt, was denounced by his wife, whom he had left for another woman. Alonzo was arrested and, after a quick trial, executed.

Many suspects were dispatched without the benefit of even a quick trial, most often in an area called the Pradera de Isidro. Hundreds of Madrileños, including women and children, came here each day in a gay mood to watch as victims were brought in trucks and shot down against a brick wall. One of the most famous victims was General Eduardo López Ochoa, who had been confined in a military hospital. The workers blamed him for crushing the Asturian miners' revolt in 1934 and murdering thousands in the aftermath, though he had apparently tried to avoid unnecessary bloodshed.

Knowing López Ochoa was in danger, the government sent Assault Guards to transfer him in an ambulance from the hospital to a safer place. But a mob captured the vehicle, took him to Pradera, and executed him. They then decapitated his corpse and paraded his impaled head in the streets.

Fascist women were often shown no more mercy than the men. Militiamen arrested twenty-seven-year-old Josefina de Aramburu, a leading Falangist, and after a *cheka* trial that night took her to Chaumartín Cemetery to be shot. But when the squad leader, a young Communist bookseller, ordered his men to fire, they refused.

''We just cannot kill a woman,'' said one member.

The leader himself then took Josefina to his car and drove to the Plaza de España, where he stopped and told her: ''My orders are to execute you but my men cannot bring themselves to do it. So get out and run.''

The terrified girl jumped out of the car and started dashing down the street. But after a few steps she collapsed with a bullet in her head—the first woman to be taken ''for a ride.''

Some Fascists were more fortunate. Felipe Gómez Acebo, the Falangist who had been captured in Montaña Barracks and then freed by a militiaman he had known from school, was arrested again shortly afterward. He was hauled off to a *cheka* and condemned to die that night. But before he was taken from the jail, the warden, who was related to Gómez Acebo's girl friend, passed by and recognized him. Gómez Acebo was saved again.

Another prisoner was not so lucky but at least died with some satisfaction. As the car driving him to the execution site stopped at a militia checkpost, he suddenly shouted, ''*Arriba, España!*'' and the guards, thinking they were about to be attacked, emptied their machine guns into the vehicle, killing not only the condemned man but his escorts as well.

One rightist pulled an even more dazzling trick—and lived. He was visiting his Loyalist fiancée and her family when the militia knocked on the door. He quietly left his hosts, locked the door of a back room from the outside, then climbed out of a window and edged his way along a ledge to the window of the locked room. He entered, stuffed a handkerchief in his mouth, and tied himself to a chair. When the militia broke in they found the man and "released" him.

"I am a militant of the Popular Front," he gasped, "and they've been keeping me prisoner."

The militiamen shot the whole family, and the rightist was free to seek another fiancée.

Arturo Barea was sickened by the wanton killing.

"This was the scum of the city," he was to write. "They would not fight. They would not carry through a revolution. But they would rob, destroy, and kill for pleasure. That carrion had to be swept away before it infected everything."

Barea tried to reassure himself that the infection was a natural if despicable phenomenon of war, that his people were not lost. Then, one night, he heard a chilling confession in the bar he frequented.

"What a night—I'm exhausted! I've accounted for eleven."

A neighboring doorkeeper was standing against the bar, a rifle beside him. He described how he and some comrades had "got rid of more than a hundred this time."

Barea had known this man since he was a child. He was honest, good, kind.

"But, Sebastián . . . who dragged . . . you into this?"

"Nobody."

"Then why are you doing it?"

"Well, someone has to."

Sebastián then confessed that he had once belonged to a Catholic organization, and he had to prove to his fellow workers that he wasn't a traitor. It was better to kill than be killed.

Sebastián shook his head slowly and added: "The worst of it is, you know, that I'm beginning to like it."

President Azaña and other government leaders were aghast at such crimes, but they were helpless to stop them. Almost all loyal military men, Assault Guards, and Civil Guards were desperately needed at the front, and the few left in the city, as well as the regular police, were terrified of the militia.

"The leftist revolution," Azaña would later write, "began without the assistance of the republican government, which neither could or wanted to assist it. The revolutionary extremism spread before the eyes of the amazed ministers. In view of this violent turn, the cabinet . . . was deprived of the means to thwart or suppress the criminal actions. The government lacked the necessary armed forces. . . . And if such troops had been available, I am certain that their involvement would have risked a second civil war."

The government tried to make a deal with the militia. According to Gregorio

Gallego, a leading anarchist, Police Chief Manuel Muñoz urgently called him
and another anarchist to his office.

"I know you're opposed to the arbitrary executions and house searches," Muñoz said. "We must end with the Pradera and I want you to help me. For you are
the only ones with enough strength. . . . I swear to you that the government
cannot sleep, and for me it's a nightmare."

The killings were abominable, the anarchists agreed, but they couldn't fight
their own comrades. They would be placing themselves in danger. No, it was the
duty of the government to stop the crimes.

And the government tried to do its duty—with the help of Agapito García Atadell.

The García Atadell Brigade was the most illustrious of several "official" *chekas*
the government set up in the hope of restoring justice in Madrid. García Atadell
seemed the right person for such a job. Not only was he intelligent, humble, and
unquestionably loyal but he had the complete trust of such important men as Indalecio Prieto, the moderate socialist leader, who constantly implored the people
to be humane to suspected enemies.

For all his humility, García Atadell persuaded his high-placed friends to publi-
cize his *cheka* so that the people would know that it was legal and demand that
the illegal ones shut up shop. He helped things along by installing his bulb-lit
sign and emphasizing to all visitors that he was running no slipshod backroom
kangaroo court. He decorated the reception room with attractive secretaries who
sat at their desks wearing low-necked, brightly colored dresses—a cheerfully
welcome sight to those concerned about rough revolutionary justice. And García
Atadell himself was always polite to his prisoners.

Soon even the foreign press was lauding him for his efficiency and fairness.
Louis Delaprée, the correspondent of *Paris Soir* known for his brilliant reporting
of the war, wrote:

"Señor García Atadell . . . has laid his hands on a vast center of espionage. . . . The affair has impassioned everybody, and the overly imaginative
who suspect plots everywhere are triumphantly saying: 'I told you that we are
surrounded by the ears and eyes of the enemy.'"

Delaprée had never gotten past the reception room; neither, apparently, had
García Atadell's political backers. For in the other rooms the militiamen were
less polite than their leader. They cursed and beat the prisoners before throwing
them into the garage in the garden and keeping them locked up in filth and darkness, sometimes for days without food. A prisoner might then be brought to
García Atadell, who would reprimand his men.

"You never notified me of this prisoner's arrival," he would say. "I didn't
know he had been in the 'garden' so long. You must be more considerate, comrades, more considerate."

García Atadell would then let the prisoner order any food he desired. After a good meal, the man sat before the tribunal and was judged—and almost invariably dragged off to the outskirts of town to be shot. For though the government wanted to execute only proven spies, snipers, saboteurs, plotters, and persons actively aiding them, García Atadell and his men asked only one question: Did the defendant sympathize with the rebels? And since García Atadell mainly went after the rich, he assumed the rich did, if only to keep their wealth. He thus marked after almost every defendant's name the letter ''L'' followed by a period. In case anybody checked too closely, an ''L'' could be said to stand for ''liberated'' —though the period was the code mark for death.

García Atadell usually knew the approximate size of the prisoner's bankroll as well as his political and religious ideas since this data was leaked to him by the socialist Union of Madrid Doorkeepers, which closely watched all tenants of buildings its members guarded. Maids were also very helpful. And in the name of the government, he confiscated the property of the condemned. But the illicit tribunals were also raking in expropriated wealth, which went to the parties and the trade unions, or was sometimes pocketed by members of the tribunal. García Atadell was furious. How could the government stand for such illegal seizures? This was simple theft!

True, his superiors agreed. But the government needed time to steer the wayward ship of justice. After all, not everyone was as honest as García Atadell.

4

José Luis Sáenz Heredia, the film director and cousin of José Antonio's, had been living in terror ever since he escaped from the militia by leaping out of a window. He ran to the home of José Antonio's father, where he stayed for several days, then hid with his uncle and sister in the house of some friends. Soon the friends, fearful for their own lives, politely suggested they go elsewhere.

But Sáenz had nowhere else to go. So he lived on the street dressed in the shabby clothes of a vagabond, surviving on bread, sleeping on the sidewalk or on chairs in refreshment kiosks. Finally, a friend recognized him and invited him to stay at his home. Sáenz sneaked in when the doorkeeper was away and had a bed to sleep in for several days. However, with the militia searching every house, this friend, too, could no longer keep him.

Sáenz was desperate. There was only one thing to do. He returned to his film studio and threw himself on the mercy of his former employees, who had formed a committee that now supervised the studio, keeping it open though no films were being made. They were shocked to see him.

"Why have you come here?" one of them asked.

"We have worked together for four years," Sáenz replied. "Not as Communists, anarchists, or Falangists, but as friends and colleagues. You should know by now whether I'm a good man or an evil man. If I must be shot, I prefer that you shoot me. But if you don't think that I deserve to be shot, then it's your obligation to protect me."

The men were stunned. Sáenz had posed a difficult dilemma for them. Falangists were being executed simply for being Falangists; that was the law of revolution. And it was easy to obey this law when the victim was a stranger, a symbol of the past and all they hated. But here was a man who had treated them fairly and kindly, a man they knew was not evil, whatever his politics. Should they kill him like the others?

Committee members gathered in the projection room to decide while the director nervously waited outside. After half an hour, the men came to him, looking grim. Sáenz expected the worst.

"We've decided to protect you," said the committee leader, a homely little carpenter known as Sinistro. "You may live here. But there are two conditions: You can't go into the street or use the telephone."

So Sáenz happily moved into an office furnished with little more than a mattress. A cousin of José Antonio's living under the protection of Communists, socialists, and anarchists!

Most of the men went to the front during the day and returned at night, when they would sit on a studio set and hash over the day's fighting. Sáenz would join them and listen to stories of how they killed rebels by the dozen. And while they talked they shared their food, wine, and cigarettes with him. Sáenz began to feel he was two people, a schizophrenic character out of some dimly conceived script he might someday write—if he survived. He loved his cousin, José Antonio, and was almost religiously a Falangist; yet he loved these men, too, simple persons who believed in their own ideologies with equal fervor, men of huge heart even though they killed with little mercy.

He wanted to repay them in some small way. Thus, violating his vow not to use the telephone, he called his uncle's servant to ask him to bring some money. But the servant wasn't home, so he left his number. He then phoned his sister and she sent him one hundred pesetas by messenger. With this money, Sáenz bought quantities of tobacco and wine at a bar across the street and that night distributed the gifts to his protectors. They were joyous—and surprised.

"Where did you get the money?" one asked.

"Oh, don't worry, I'm rich as hell," Sáenz replied airily.

Then one evening the servant returned his call.

"Is there anything I can do for you?" he asked.

"No, never mind," Sáenz replied. "Everything's been taken care of."

But the servant insisted on seeing him, and Sáenz slammed the receiver. A half hour later, a truckload of militiamen arrived and seized him. The servant, Sáenz suddenly realized, must have been talking to him at gunpoint.

His friends were furious when he told them he had used the phone.

"What a stupid thing to do," said Sinistro.

"I agree," Sáenz replied. "But I felt I owed you something."

The two men embraced and Sinistro went with him to the *cheka*. Sáenz was thrown into a cell with several other prisoners, one of whom turned pale. It was the servant.

That night, two militiamen entered the cell and turned a flashlight on each prisoner. Sáenz was suddenly blinded.

"No, not this one," grunted the man standing over him. "That one."

"Come with us and take your jacket," the other intruder ordered the prisoner.

Sáenz knew the signs. If a prisoner was told to take his jacket, he would not be returning. Soon they would come for him. And this time the ending would be no surprise.

Father Florindo de Miguel, dressed in rumpled layman's clothing, embraced his dear old friend. Miguel had just come to Madrid from León and was visiting Eladio Ruiz de los Paños, who had studied with him in the Toledo Seminary but had long since left the clergy. Ruiz invited Miguel to move in with him, but the priest was hesitant, though he had no place to stay.

The "reds" were arresting and killing priests, as well as anyone who dared hide them. And Miguel didn't want to endanger the household. Besides, Ruiz's small apartment was already packed with a dozen members of his family. All of them, however, insisted that he stay. What an honor to have a priest in their home as the great landowners did. And so, with slight pangs of guilt, Father Miguel slept that night in the best room in the house.

But he did not sleep well, nor did most clergymen or nuns in hiding. For no group was more victimized by the revolution than the clerics, though the few who were known to side with the poor against their masters were safe. And Loyalist fury grew when reports streamed in from rebel zones indicating that the Church condoned and even supported Franco's program for mass murder.

While thousands of workers were being executed, all but a few priests looked on silently, simply offering, with little success, to send them off to heaven with the last sacraments—as if their slaughter was not the Church's business. Some priests fought in the rebel ranks. One who had been hiding in a tree in the Guadarramas picked off a number of militiamen before he dropped to the ground himself, pierced by a Loyalist bullet. Others were accused of firing from church steeples—a charge seldom proved but reflecting the popular distrust of clerics.

Father Zafra, whose real name was Juan Galán Bermejo, became famous for the atrocities he committed as a chaplain in the foreign legion. When Zafra found a man hidden in a confessional booth in the Badajoz Cathedral, he shot him on the spot. In another town he discovered four men and a wounded woman in a cave, and later reportedly boasted: ''I made them dig a grave and buried them alive to teach this breed a lesson.''

Many Loyalists, in turn, sought vengeance for the ''betrayal.'' While the government seized all clerical property it could find, the masses burned down churches and imprisoned and usually shot clergymen who did not sympathize with them. Even laymen who simply belonged to a Catholic organization or had gone to church regularly were suspect. For who but a Fascist could be so devoted to the Church?

Symbolizing Loyalist rage was the transformed statue of the Christ Child of San José. The figure now wore red trousers and blue suspenders, with cartridges stuck in the belt, and grasped a pistol in one hand while holding aloft a red banner in the other. It was mocking the ''Fascist'' Church that was seen as mocking God.

Father Miguel did not consider himself a Fascist. Nor, apparently, did he consider the Church even partly responsible for its tragic plight. The people had simply been misled by evil power-hungry men. And now he had to hide from them because they wanted to kill him for reasons he couldn't understand.

But though he had restless nights, he was always up before dawn to prepare for Mass in the dining room, attended by the whole household. There were no ornaments, only an improvised altar and a crystal cup serving as the calix. No matter. What a joyous feeling to kneel and converse with the Lord in the midst of the holocaust. But then, one morning during prayer, the doorbell rang.

''Everyone quiet,'' Ruiz whispered. ''I'll see who it is.''

Father Miguel rose, seized by the same panic that gripped all of them, and got ready to swallow the eucharistic bread. There were cautious steps toward the front door, then Ruiz's voice and a moment of silence. Footsteps again, and Ruiz returned—alone.

''It was only the milkman,'' he said, smiling.

Miguel was now adamant. He must move out or the whole family might suffer because of him. So he went to look for a room in a boardinghouse when suddenly, as he walked along the street, he heard a familiar voice.

''It's been a long time. What have you been doing?''

Miguel looked around and to his delight saw another old school chum.

''Antonio!''

The two men hugged. And when Miguel told his friend about his situation, Antonio answered: ''Come to my house. There you won't bother anyone because there are only Manuela and I . . . and the two kids.''

Miguel was touched. Like Eladio, Antonio would risk his life to help him out. Since Antonio insisted, Miguel moved into his house the next day.

Again, one morning, the doorbell rang. Miguel, who was in his room reading, heard voices and thought that Antonio's wife was talking with some neighbors. But then, gradually, the tone of the conversation sharpened. Uneasily, he climbed out of bed and looked through a transom into the dining room. The militia!

How could he escape? His room led to the hall, and since the militiamen were inside the apartment he would try to sneak down the stairs. He opened the door and managed to reach the stairway without being seen. Then joy turned to despair. He had left a bag in the room with his documents in it, and while they showed he was a "lawyer" they also indicated his birthplace. The "reds" would certainly check with the authorities there and learn he was a priest.

He must go back for the documents, Miguel painfully decided. The militiamen, however, saw him before he could return.

"Who is this?" asked one of them. "What's this man doing here?"

Before Antonio or his wife could speak, Miguel coolly replied: "I'm a friend of Antonio's. The war caught me here and I can't go home. I'm a lawyer and I live in León. I'll show you my documents."

He produced the papers and handed them to the *responsable*. The man scrutinized them carefully.

"All right," he said, "but how do I know this card is yours, that you didn't find it in the street? Where did you study?"

"Here, in Madrid."

"Then you must know someone from the leftist side who will vouch for you and tell me you are the Florindo de Miguel on this card."

"Of course. I could call fifty," Miguel replied confidently.

He then telephoned a friend who belonged to a trade union. A few minutes later, a car drew up in front of the house. When the friend, Julio, entered, the militia chief immediately explained the situation. Julio said:

"Yes, yes. This is Florindo de Miguel, lawyer."

"You'll vouch for him?"

"Certainly. He's coming with me right now."

The two men left, and as they reached the street they heard Antonio's wife and children crying and pleading. Antonio tried to calm them:

"I'll be back soon. Don't worry. I haven't done anything wrong."

But the family continued to wail pitifully.

"Poor Antonio," Miguel lamented. "He was so good to me. Julio, can't you do something for him?"

"No, nothing." said Julio. "I was lucky to be able to do something for you."

"Then let's wait for him at the door. I want to say good-bye to him, perhaps forever. At least with a look, I want to say good-bye, wish him good luck."

"Don't be stupid!" Julio exclaimed. "You'll lose everything. You don't realize the danger."

And he pushed the priest toward the car. Miguel climbed in, feeling faint.

"You're right," he said. "Let's go. It's better. I don't want to see the militia take him away. Take me to the home of my friend Ruiz de los Paños."

And Miguel prayed for Antonio.

Paradoxically, the atheistic communists, despite their reputation for hardheartedness, were often more tolerant of the clergy than most leftists—precisely because they were atheistic. For unlike the others, they did not feel that the Church had betrayed God since, to them, there was no God to betray. Thus they tended to judge clerics less on an emotional basis than the anti-Church believers did.

Dolores Ibarruri, who had viewed religion as a sham ever since childhood and was capable of cruelty if her cause required it, claims to have pitied the nuns, who now found themselves in desperate straits. Some had even been killed. She went with a comrade to visit a religious community that they had learned was hiding in a particular building.

"Forgive us for intruding," Dolores said as they entered. "We've come to help you. . . . Although it may sound vain, I'm sure you've all heard of me and . . . that from all the stories you've heard of how evil I am, you all think I'm the devil himself. But please be calm, nothing will happen to you. I'm *La Pasionaria.*"

The nuns gasped.

"You're under the protection of the Fifth Regiment," Dolores said, "which means that no one will dare harm you. However, I would like to propose that you all work, do something useful, that you help us in some way that won't conflict with your religious sentiments."

The mother superior replied: "We could work in the hospitals caring for the sick and wounded."

"I'm sorry, sister, but you can't work in the hospitals. The wounded soldiers wouldn't accept it."

"Then we can look after the children."

"Not that either, because they wouldn't trust you with their children."

"Well, what can we do then?"

"You can make clothes, little jackets, bonnets, and shoes for evacuated children, for the orphans and the abandoned children, right here in this house. We'll come to pick up the clothes and help you get all the material you need so you won't have to go and walk around the city."

La Pasionaria startled the sisters when she offered to bring them religious statues and crucifixes as well. But the next day, she came with the material *and* the religious articles.

"God bless you!" said the mother superior.

La Pasionaria apparently was almost as shocked as she had been when, as a

child, she watched other nuns dress a scarecrow in purple velvet robes to look
like the Virgin.

5

Within days after the revolt began, Christopher Lance was virtually running the
British embassy. The ambassador, like many of his colleagues, had gone to the
cooler resort town of San Sebastián just before the rising and left the embassy in
the hands of a meek bureaucratic vice-consul. Lance, with some difficulty, persuaded this young diplomat to let all Britons move in until they could be evacuated, promising to "run the whole show." And he kept his promise. After staying
for some time in the building, almost six hundred Britons, including his wife,
Jinx, were off to Valencia, where a ship had anchored to take them home.

In mid-August the British government, which had been waiting for the rebel
forces to enter Madrid before sending an important diplomat there, finally realized that the city wasn't about to fall and dispatched a chargé d'affaires. G.A.D.
Ogilvie-Forbes was a cheerful, modest, plump man who liked to play the bag-
pipes when he was alone, and was scrupulously unbiased in his relations with the
Spanish government, though he was Catholic and well informed about the atrocities in Madrid.

Forbes appointed Lance an honorary consul, but Lance continued to go to his
office daily. He was determined to keep the business alive, though not quite sure
he could keep himself alive, with the workers' committee constantly plotting
against him. However, making prudent use of his diplomatic status, he also kept
busy extricating his Spanish friends from danger. Since his own embassy, because of its neutral policy, could not give asylum to them, he hid them elsewhere. He brought them food and news of their families, and buried their pistols
in Retiro Park, for any suspect caught with a weapon was automatically shot.

One day in late August, Lance went to comfort the family of a seventeen-year-
old boy, Manolo, who had been arrested. He would do everything possible,
Lance promised, to find the youth and get him released. And he actually managed to persuade Police Chief Muñoz, whose friendship he had cultivated, to free
the boy.

But soon afterward, someone came from the nearby village of Paracuellos del
Jarama to see the family and told a lurid tale of bodies being buried there the previous night. He thought that he saw Manolo's among them. Lance immediately
investigated.

With a description of the boy, he drove through the barren rocky countryside to the village, hardly more than a cluster of stone hovels. In the eerie silence, he stopped his car and saw an old wrinkled peasant with suspicious eyes. But the man's suspicion seemed to wane when he saw the British flag on the car.

Had there been any shooting around there? Lance asked casually.

"Oh, yes, I helped to dig the grave. I was ordered to do so by the young men, señor."

They walked through some parched fields and came to a long mound of earth—the mass graves.

Lance then described young Manolo. Had the peasant seen him? The man thought he had.

"Show me where the shooting took place."

They moved to a nearby road rimmed by a long ditch. The excavated earth formed a kind of wall behind the ditch, and the wall was laced with tiny holes—bullet holes.

Dazed by the horror, Lance sped back to Madrid and stammered out to Manolo's family the tragic news. When they broke down, he almost did, too. He had been a soldier and had seen many comrades die, but this was not war. It was cold-blooded murder. He couldn't stand by and do nothing. If he was powerless to help the victims, at least he could help their families. And so he looked for other missing loved ones, searching the morgues, the parks, the roads—and the police photo archives.

As a "convenience" for relatives, the police photographed every corpse found, and there was constant hysteria at police headquarters as mothers, wives, sons, daughters, shuffled through the appalling pictures of people with half their faces shot away—usually from a *coup de grace* in the head—and finally recognized the person they were seeking. Lance could at least spare some people this agony by looking through the files himself.

One night, on a tip, he drove along the Burgos road a few miles outside Madrid and turned down a narrow lane. Suddenly his headlights revealed a straggly line of men standing along a ditch opposite several persons pointing guns at them. Those with the weapons, caught in the glare, swiftly turned toward a truck on the road as if they were trying to repair it. Lance stopped alongside the lorry and gave the clenched fist salute.

"*Salud,* comrades," he said cheerily. "Do you want any help?"

"No, comrade," replied one. "We can fix it."

Lance then continued on. And when he had gone some distance, he heard the rattle of automatic weapons. Shortly, he drove back, and there lay the corpses.

In the next days he saw hundreds more as he searched for people whose families had learned of his activities and came to him for help. Finally, he decided that identifying dead men was not enough. He had to save the live ones.

The lucky live ones crowded into the foreign missions—though not into the

American embassy, which was even more afraid than the British embassy of compromising its neutrality. These refugees were mainly aristocrats, well-known rightists, and people with money. Some diplomats, often without their government's knowledge, demanded stiff "entry fees," and Cubans especially were believed to have fattened their bankrolls from this business.

Life in these embassies was often a social microcosm of that in Spain, even though most occupants were from the upper class. The titled and the rich inhabited the best rooms, ate the best food, and did the least work, while the lower stratas lived in the cellars, cleaned up the building, and consumed the less appetizing dishes. Thus, discontent and even hatred divided the people who were hiding from a common enemy. But in their cramped prisonlike world, there were marriages, births, and even a divorce—ironically, under republican law. (The divorce was annulled after Franco came to power.)

Although the militiamen were constantly threatening to invade the missions and grab their foes, the government respected the right of diplomatic asylum and was actually pleased there were places presumably beyond the reach of its own executioners. It even let some embassies evacuate refugees from Spain.

But the militiamen found ways of trapping people seeking asylum. One way was to set up a "Siamese embassy," complete with ambassador and secretaries, even though Spain had no relations with Siam. Soon, refugees piled in, cramming every corner and paying a high price for the privilege. Each day a truck would come to take them to a waiting ship in Alicante. Only it never got farther than an execution site where the voyage ended.

Once militiamen played on a mother's greed to lure her son to death. She came to see the youth, Pepito Canalejas, at the Cuban embassy, and other refugees overheard her telling him:

"They have taken two thousand pesetas and won't return it until you give them some details on declarations you made to them."

"It's a trap, mama," the son replied. "They only want to capture me."

"But you must leave. I cannot lose that money."

Canalejas responded, his voice trembling: "I warn you, mama, if I leave I shall die."

"A coward, that's what you are," screamed his mother. "You won't leave because you are afraid. Your father was an important man, but when he went out in the street he never had an escort."

"And he was assassinated!"

"Coward! Coward!"

Pepito Canalejas left the embassy and was shot.

The tension felt by the refugees was often shared by their diplomatic protectors. The Belgian counselor even reported to his government that Communists and anarchists were in command of Madrid. Washington grew so worried about this message that it queried its own embassy in Madrid about it. The ranking

American diplomat in the embassy, Eric Wendelin, cabled back that the report was "too strong and is likewise contradictory," adding:

"Communists and socialists are supporting government, which, in my opinion, is stronger now than two weeks ago. Government is making serious effort to impose discipline [on] militia forces with considerable apparent success."

Wendelin sent this message on August 22. He might not have sent it the following day . . .

Some threatened *Madrileños*, unable to find a suitable hiding place, volunteered to stay in government prisons. Oddly, it was not always easy to get an "accommodation," with about seven thousands suspects packing them. Sometimes, to relieve the situation, the militia would simply dispose of people before they reached jail. On the night of August 12, a train loaded with some seven hundred prisoners was steaming by the Vallecas quarter of Madrid when militiamen flagged it down.

"We'll take care of these people," the leader told the guards on the train. "All the prisons and the jails are already full, and there is no need to feed them at the people's expense."

The prisoners were ordered out of the train, lined up, and shot down by three machine guns.

Jails thus had their attractions, and the most "attractive" one in town was Model Prison, which was often called the Palace of the Moncloa, since it was like a palace among prisons, with its large cells and good plumbing. Some of the top politicians and soldiers in the country had at one time or another plotted revolutions and *pronunciamientos* while gazing through its barred windows. However, after the revolt conditions were less comfortable: About two thousand prisoners were jammed in, often seven to a cell, and the food was barely edible. Still, one could sleep at night without listening for the fatal knock on the door, since the prison was run not by the militia but by professional personnel. And though some prisoners were executed they were at least given trials with a semblance of decorum and justice.

General Fanjul was among the inmates sentenced to death. He was executed on August 17 after marrying his courier, Luisa Aguado Cuadrillero, only hours earlier in his death cell. Luisa buried more than one loved one. While she attended Fanjul's funeral with her son by a previous marriage and the general's executor, militiamen shot the men dead as they stood by the grave. But the general's son, José Ignacio Fanjul, and other rebel prisoners in the Model were hopeful they would survive. The government had made an example of the elder Fanjul for his resistance in Montaña Barracks and didn't seem eager to spill more blood than necessary.

However, news from the southern battlefront then started drifting into Madrid. Franco's Moors and foreign legionnaires, debarking in Seville every few hours from new German air transports, were pushing toward the capital. And the untrained, poorly armed Loyalist defenders were scurrying in panic before his fighter planes and tanks. After a fierce battle at Badajoz, near the Portuguese border, the rebels smashed into the town, rounded up about two thousand people in the bullring, and machine-gunned them in the greatest mass slaughter of the war to date.

Reports of the massacre drove home to the Loyalists in Madrid what Franco planned to do with them—helped by rebels inside the city, later known as the fifth column. Fear and suspicion grew. And the most dangerous men were locked up in Model Prison.

To make sure these prisoners would not attempt a breakout—and to set the stage for a ''Badajoz'' of their own—militiamen stormed in and, without government authorization, began searching the cells for arms, but found none. Next, they opened the cells of the common criminals, including many revolutionaries accused of murder and robbery, and let them run wild.

''Give us freedom!'' these prisoners demanded.

And if they didn't get it, they warned the wardens, they would kill all the Fascists in the prison—which was exactly what some guards and militiamen were encouraging them to do. Many of these criminals were released after promising to fight at the front; but some, who weren't, protested by setting fire to the prison bakery woodshed. The agitators for massacre had their ''provocation.'' The Fascists, they cried, had burned their mattresses, hoping to escape in the confusion.

As smoke curled into the summer sky and remained motionless in the warm air, guards in the plot, perched on neighboring rooftops behind machine guns, suddenly began riddling rebel suspects who were taking their daily exercise in the prison courtyard. Then, after dark, when firemen had quenched the fire, the militiamen herded the survivors into a huge basement. The prisoners, dressed in pajamas, squatted on the ground watching a disheveled young man as he hunched over a table nearby and thumbed through some files by the light of two candles. In the flickering glow scores of figures stood around the man like orange-masked phantoms in a nightmare, while their victims from that afternoon lay grotesquely along the walls.

The question was: Who and how many more would die that night?

Word that the political prisoners were trying to break out spread almost as fast as the fire in the woodshed. And the reaction was violent. Maddened by Badajoz, people flocked to the prison from all over Madrid in cars, trucks, and on foot, and soon thousands surrounded the smoking structure.

''Let's kill all the prisoners!'' went the cry.

And the ring of humanity tightened around the prison as sirens wailed and guns sputtered. Five square blocks were cordoned off, and it looked like Montaña all over again—only this time the enemy was unarmed.

The diplomatic corps warned Prime Minister Giral: All foreign missions would leave Madrid if any more prisoners were killed and would urge their governments to intervene. Moderate socialist leader Indalecio Prieto rushed to the scene and over a loudspeaker begged the mob to go home. Did they want the world to call them savages? But the people would not listen and even threatened him. As he climbed into his car he cried: "Today we have lost the war!"

Other political leaders came and appealed to the crowd. They would set up a special tribunal, they promised, to try all Fascists taking part in the "mutiny." But the demonstrators demanded blood *now*. And so did many of the militia leaders inside the prison, who continued to haggle over the death list while the terrified prisoners sat listening. The "judges" shuffled through the files on the candlelit table, selecting well-known names at random. But this was murder, someone argued. Perhaps, another answered with cruel logic, but wasn't it better to murder some than to let the mob kill all?

The shooting began before the list was completed. Names were called out, and militiamen dragged the victims to a cellar, one by one. Melquiades Alvarez González, a staunch if maverick republican and dean of the Madrid Law College, and José Martínez de Velasco, a moderately rightist politician, pleaded for mercy, vehemently denying they were Fascists. But in vain. Julio Ruiz de Aldo, a Falangist leader, arrogantly swore at his executioners, blurting insults even as they snapped their bolts.

Among others who died were Fernando Primo de Rivera, the brother of Falangist leader José Antonio; General Rafael Villegas, the nominal leader of the abortive Madrid revolt that ended with Montaña; José Ignacio Fanjul, the elder son of General Fanjul; and Pedro Durruti, a Falangist and brother of Buenaventura Durruti, the most important Spanish anarchist. When told that Pedro had resisted fiercely before being shot, Durruti commented coldly: "Well, at least he died like a man."

Shots echoed through the prison all night long while militiamen continued to rummage through the files for more and more names they recognized or thought had an aristocratic ring. Finally, after dawn, the last two victims, a young prisoner and an old one, were being led to their death when a guard insulted the youth, provoking him to strike his tormentor. The militiaman stumbled, then without uttering a word fired a deadly burst from his submachine gun. Meanwhile, the old man clung to a wall, pale and trembling, and wailed a prayer. The same escort turned his gun on him and shouted: "You, too, stupid! The sooner we finish, the better!"

Another volley, and the victim moaned as his body writhed on the floor. A *coup de grace* was apparently the final shot of the long night. According to Juan Llarch, an anarchist writer, about seventy bodies in all littered the courtyard and cellars.

"An August afternoon in Madrid," President Azaña summed up in his diary. "I'm watching . . . from the window: a cloud of smoke, signs of disquiet,

news of the fire in the prison . . . a sad night . . . desolation. At 7:00 A.M.,
Giral reads to me on the phone the decree creating popular tribunals. 'This way
we'll save thousands of lives,' he exclaims. Nightmare . . . pain for the republic . . . fathomless sadness. In the afternoon, tears of the . . . president."

After the last murders, the crowd, finally pacified, melted away. Those lucky
enough to have tickets to the great benefit bullfight to be held that afternoon, August 23, were perhaps the most content. While Azaña wept, they would see still
more blood flow—even if the victims would be mere bulls.

"Sunday I awoke with a feeling of excitement," Janet Riesenfeld would recall.
"There was a full day ahead. A concert, lunch at Jaime's *pension*, a bullfight,
dinner—all with him."

Janet found life in wartime Madrid exciting indeed. She had moved into a
charming little apartment and, through her famous gypsy dancing partner, Miguel Albeicin, had met some of Spain's finest artists. With the war raging, she was
not dancing for money but for all kinds of benefits to raise funds for the republican cause. Although she had arrived knowing almost nothing about Spanish politics and history, Miguel and other republican friends had soon transformed her
into an enthusiastic "Loyalist." She did some of her finest dancing right in her
apartment where, at impromptu parties, she and Miguel would click their heels
and their castanets almost all night to the ecstatic shouts of "Olé! Olé!" from
people leaning out of windows overlooking the courtyards.

But whenever Jaime Castanys was free she would be with him, enjoying the
throb and vigor of a Madrid that couldn't imagine itself seriously endangered.
The war had come close enough to add spice and even romance to life here—for
those on the right side—but not close enough yet to stir fear.

Yet Janet often found Castanys in a morose mood. Although he came to some
of her parties and joined in the "Olés," he seemed out of place in the wartime
revolutionary atmosphere of the city, so full of the bustle of men going off to the
front, of wives rushing to the factories, of galas and rallies and parades and "special" bullfights. And he was constantly criticizing the government and provoking
her to defend it. But it was probably more his Catalan prejudice, she thought,
than any sympathy he might harbor for the rebels.

The people of Catalonia, the cultural center of Spain, had always felt disdain
for Madrid as a city of rather uncouth bureaucrats, and resented being under its
rule. And Catalan aristocrats were the least intrigued of all by this metropolis. Janet had learned something of their arrogance when she arrived in Barcelona, the
Catalan capital, on her way to Madrid and called on Jaime's family. She was not
even invited in! Jaime would dare marry an American, a creature even more
primitive than a *Madrileño*?

On this sunny Sunday morning, however, Jaime seemed to be the gay relaxed
person she had known in Mexico, as he thrust a huge bouquet of *claveles*—red

carnations—into her arms. They strolled along the Paseo de la Castellana and up a tree-shaded lane to a little café near the concert hall. The streets and the café were strangely empty. Most *Madrileños* apparently were either too tired, too shocked, or too afraid to go out after the night of terror in Model Prison.

"Madrid is still asleep, recovering from Saturday night," Castanys said, without mentioning what happened on Saturday night.

This was not a time for ideological arguments.

"Miguel's invited us to the bullfight this afternoon," Janet said.

"I'm afraid I can't go, Janet."

She begged him to change his mind.

"I can't. Something very important has come up."

They attended the morning concert and afterwards he abruptly left her. Janet then went to the bullfight with Miguel and his friends, wondering what was important enough to make Jaime abandon her on this beautiful Sunday afternoon.

After the Model Prison murders, the government tried its best to stamp out the *cheka* terror. Watchmen were forbidden to carry keys to houses and apartments so they could not let armed bands in. Police and militiamen were forbidden to make searches without special passes. And "illegal" *chekas* were forbidden to operate, with the promised popular tribunals set up in their place. Members of all Popular Front parties, the CNT, and the old judiciary sat in each jury.

These safeguards, however, did little to quell the terror. For one thing, the professional jurors hesitated to question militia charges against accused people, fearing they would also be suspected. Thus the new tribunals, like the old, executed many victims unjustly—now, ironically, with official approval. Meanwhile, Garcia Atadell kept his bulb-lit sign up, competing for blood and money with these other legal courts, and most illegal *chekas* refused to shut down. So, despite all the new laws, Madrid remained a lawless city.

This did not bode well for José Luis Sáenz Heredia, the film director, who was still languishing in an "illegal" *cheka* jail awaiting trial. Finally, after almost two weeks, his turn came.

"Are you a Falangist?" a militiaman asked.

"No," Sáenz lied.

"But you are the cousin of the head of the Falange. You must be one."

"Why?" replied Sáenz with studied coolness. "Just because we're related doesn't mean we think alike. We're two different people. He's a lawyer. I'm an artist. I've always associated with workers and never had anything to do with politics."

"You're lying. We have your record."

This wasn't true, Sáenz knew. All the Falangist files had been destroyed.

"But you can't have it," he said, "because there is no record."

The time had come for a decision. Sáenz, sweating and murmuring a prayer to himself, was reconciled to death. How could a red court be expected to acquit a cousin of José Antonio's? But the *responsable* said: "You are free."

Sáenz nearly choked on his prayer. He stumbled out into the sun and ran all the way to his studio, about a mile away. Breathlessly, he looked around for the workers. He found Sinistro, the carpenter, and the two men hugged each other and wept.

Sáenz would later learn that both his workers and Luis Buñuel, the Communist film director he had worked for, had intervened in his favor. It would be a crime, they said, to kill so decent a man. The heart had for once triumphed over the mind.

6

Loyalist Madrid's heart was hardened by a growing fear that conspirators, or fifth columnists, were plotting day and night to seize the city from within, or at least smooth the way for the forces of Mola and Franco. There was still no unified resistance movement in Madrid, but many rightists were working for the rebels independently. Thus, the enemy seemed to know in advance almost every move on the government's military chessboard and was usually able to checkmate it.

So suspicious were some militiamen that they took almost any electrical device they found for a radio. While they were ransacking the room of one man, they saw a set of earphones attached to an alarm clock.

"Aha! A radio set!" exclaimed one militiaman.

"No," the building superintendent explained, "the man is deaf and fixed that so that he could hear his clock."

"I tell you that's a radio," shouted the militiaman. "And when I say something, don't you deny it!"

"As you please," replied the superintendent. "You can call it a piano if you like."

The deaf man was dragged out and executed.

Yet dozens of real fifth columnists were found with radio sets in their rooms. Others chipped away at public morale and helped rebel supporters to survive and escape. They spread false rumors that Franco would be in Madrid "tomorrow." They paid storekeepers high prices for certain foods so the poorer classes couldn't buy them. Falangists disguised as workers seduced young female trade union members so they would reveal the whereabouts of their fathers' military units. Rightist doctors made out false documents certifying that young men were unfit for military duty.

The man in charge of milk distribution arranged for the wives of his rightist friends to be ''pregnant'' so they would receive larger rations of the scarce milk supply—at the expense of Loyalist consumers. The head of the War Ministry's Purchasing Committee, responsible for obtaining quartermaster supplies, gave jobs to rebel supporters and helped hundreds escape to enemy lines in the committee's cars. And since almost anyone could join the anarchist CNT, many rebels infiltrated it and carried CNT membership cards for protection, while at least one group put a CNT banner on an empty house that it used as a hiding place.

But the most frightening sign of enemy activity was still the sporadic sniper fire and the sudden machine-gun bursts from phantom cars. One day, Janet Riesenfeld was relaxing in an open-air café while nearby some children made designs on the sidewalk with colored clay, each depicting a scene of Loyalist triumph—a militiaman shooting a rebel or perhaps stamping on a swastika-marked serpent. She was watching one little boy at work when suddenly there was a shot, and the child collapsed, screaming. Then two more shots and two other wounded children.

Militiamen at the tables dashed after the sniper and gunned him down. And when the ambulance had come and taken the children away, the atmosphere returned to normal and people ordered more *vino*. If the aim of the sniper was to sow panic, he had failed.

Such violence gradually faded after militiamen began searching every house, apartment, and shop suspected of harboring Fascists. Nevertheless, the militia squads could not possibly root out all the snipers or rebel gangs. During one unusual battle in the East Cemetery, Falangists and anarchists killed each other off to the last man. When the gravediggers arrived, they were startled to find that all the dead were wearing the black and red anarchist neck scarf, since the Falangists had disguised themselves as anarchists.

This created a dilemma. Who should be buried in the Catholic part of the cemetery, and who in the civil? It was decided that those with genteel faces and smooth hands would be laid to rest in the Catholic area, and those with rougher features, in the civil zone.

Though Christopher Lance was determined to play the Scarlet Pimpernel, he had no idea how he could save people condemned to die in some bullet-raked ditch. Finally, he found his first clue. Young Manolo, who was killed in Paracuellos, had actually been discharged from prison only hours before his death—as the chief of police had promised Lance. However, when the boy stepped out of the prison gate, militiamen grabbed him and threw him into a truck.

This kidnap technique, Lance discovered, was common practice. Sometimes the militiamen themselves ordered a prisoner to be set free—so that they could take him "for a ride." Some wardens at Model Prison, in fact, had secretly gone to the British embassy to reveal how prisoners were being illegally seized. And they could not stop these kidnappings because the killers connived with some prison guards, as they had in the massacre after the woodshed fire.

What he must do now, Lance reasoned, was to learn in advance of a prisoner's pending release so that he could save him from Manolo's fate. But where could he find an informer? He suddenly remembered a young man, Carlos, at police headquarters, who appeared to oppose the *paseos*. When he bluntly asked Carlos if he would furnish him the names of inmates about to be discharged, the man gladly agreed.

Shortly, toward the end of August, Carlos gave Lance the name of one. Lance drove up to the jail in an embassy car, breezily walked in, and said to the desk clerk:

"Good morning, comrade, I am Captain Lance, attaché at the British embassy. I've come to take Rodríguez away. There has been an order for his release."

The clerk conferred with the warden, who confirmed that Rodríguez was to be released, and soon a white-faced man with a package under his arm emerged from the cell area.

"Come along, Rodríguez!" Lance called to him.

And the two men walked out the front door and climbed into Lance's car.

"I am from the British embassy," said Lance. "I am going to take you to safety. Tell me quickly the address of a friend who will be willing to shelter you. *Not* your own home."

"It's a trap," replied Rodríguez fearfully.

But he finally placed his trust in Lance, who drove him to a friend's house.

Lance then went to see Ogilvie-Forbes, the chargé d'affaires, who, though delighted, warned him: "Take care you don't get that big nose of yours into trouble."

"If I do, I shall know you are there to bail me out."

"I couldn't bail you out, my dear fellow, if you got bumped off."

As he sipped a whisky, Lance was already thinking of how he could bail others out before they were "bumped off."

Father Florindo de Miguel also vowed to save people—their souls if not their lives. And he would do this even at the risk of his own life. He made this decision following a new tragedy. After Antonio's arrest, Miguel had gone back to live with the family of Eladio Ruiz de los Paños once again, only to see Ruiz, too, dragged off to jail. A group of Communists picked him up as he stepped outside, and then searched the house. They might have arrested Miguel as well if Ruiz's wife had not called in an anarchist neighbor who vouched for everybody in the apartment.

Miguel could hardly bear this new blow. Antonio and now Eladio had been taken, and he was still free, though he should have been the first to be sacrificed. He had even refused to hear Eladio's confession simply because he, as a priest from outside, didn't have the authority of the Madrid diocese. Now Eladio might die without confession. Never again would he refuse such a request.

Miguel moved out of Ruiz's house and, still posing as a lawyer, rented a room in a boardinghouse—where he found himself in the midst of the enemy. In fact, living there were several militiamen from his hometown of Belvis! He listened in frozen silence at the dinner table as they boasted how they had executed townsmen who turned out to be Miguel's own relatives! What was more dangerous: staying in or going out? He decided to go out.

As he strolled by the National Library on the Paseo de la Castellana, he had an idea. He would spend every day in the library, poring over books in some obscure corner. Nobody would find him there. And so he followed this plan daily, until one day he stopped by to see a friend. Would he mind hearing confessions from a certain family? the friend asked.

Miguel immediately agreed, and was soon hearing confessions not only from that family but from neighbors in the same building. By the time he left, it was too late to go to the library.

The next day, he resumed his normal schedule but found the library closed. He asked an old man sitting on a bench nearby if he knew the reason.

"But don't you know what happened?" the man replied, looking at him strangely. "Yesterday at five they closed the doors and arrested everyone who was inside, from the director on down. And everybody who was there reading. They took eight truckloads of people."

The man lowered his voice and added: "Apparently it was an espionage center for the Fascists."

Miguel was silent. Yesterday at five! While, by chance, he was hearing confessions! God had saved him.

Janet Riesenfeld was furious. For the third time in a week, Jaime Castanys was breaking a date. There was always something keeping them apart. Either he was busy or she was dancing at some benefit gala for the Loyalist troops.

"Darling, I beg you to understand," he pleaded over the phone.

"I have tried to understand," Janet replied, "but frankly I can't. After all, I know you're not rushed with business."

Actually, with the war raging, Castanys's tourist agency was doing no business at all.

"I've told you. It's very important. . . . What are you going to do?"

Janet recalled that a few days earlier she had met a man called Villatora at her newspaper agency office—a leading member of the press militia made up of war correspondents who doubled as combatants and government officials. He had taken her to a rehearsal of a play and invited her to join him and his friends any evening at Café Brazil.

"I think I'll go to the Café Brazil," Janet now told Castanys, who knew of her meeting with Villatora. "Villatora has asked me to join him and the other correspondents there."

"You know that I don't want you to see him. The less you become involved with Spaniards these days the better. . . . All I ask is that you please stay at home this evening. I insist on it.''

But Janet was not about to take orders, especially after being so casually stood up. So she went to the café, a favorite meeting place for artists, writers, reporters, police agents, and prostitutes. Villatora introduced Janet to other Spanish reporters, including one called José María, a tall man with striking green eyes who seemed to be the center of attention. Janet found the atmosphere stimulating as the men exchanged battlefield anecdotes and spoke of the bright new future they envisioned. Was there really a war going on? All of them seemed so relaxed, so calm. They might have been rehashing the results of the latest soccer match.

Suddenly there was a crash. Someone screamed, and the men jumped up with pistols drawn, overturning the tables and rushing to the door.

''What was it?'' Janet asked Villatora after several moments.

''A waiter dropped a wine glass.''

The thin veneer of normalcy had peeled away, and Janet glimpsed the real Madrid, the raw nerve of tension beneath.

Hardly had her new friends caught their breath when a light flashed in the sky.

''A parachute flare!'' Villatora cried. ''They're trying to find a target.''

There was a great explosion nearby, then a moment of silence. Then panic again as women in the café sobbed hysterically.

''Put out the lights!'' someone shouted.

Another blast, and a fading buzz overhead. It was over. The lights went on, and Janet felt dazed. On this night of August 27, the first enemy bombs had fallen on Madrid, exploding near the War Ministry but miraculously hurting no one.

Shortly, Castanys rushed in and ran to Janet.

''Are you all right, darling?'' he asked. ''I thought I would find you here when I couldn't reach you at home. I was frantic.''

But when he saw she was safe, he suddenly grew resentful.

''Let me take you home now,'' he said.

Villatora asked him to join the group, but he curtly declined. Then Janet, in embarrassment, left with him. When they were alone, Castanys angrily burst out:

''I told you not to go out tonight. I told you I didn't want you to be with these people. You haven't the slightest idea of what is going on here. Now please do as I say—don't see any of them again.''

She was too tired to talk about it now, Janet said. What a fascinating evening—except for the bombs.

They hardly noticed the summer snow on the streets—leaflets dropped by the bombers:

'PEOPLE OF MADRID, YOU ARE WARNED THAT THE STRONGER YOUR OBSTINA-CY, THE TOUGHER OUR ACTION WILL BE.'

The warning was underlined.

7

"San Fran-cis-co, open your golden gate . . ."

The rhythmic notes of this popular American song tinkled gaily in the hot summer air as a grinning Moorish soldier furiously worked the pedals of an old player piano in the ruins of the village café. In his delight, he ignored the staccato machine-gun bursts coming from the street. He simply pedaled faster and faster as if trying to drown out the crackle in the background. Almost deafened by the bizarre cacophony of sounds, John Whitaker of the New York *Herald-Tribune* watched from the café as six hundred people collapsed like puppets with their strings cut.

A little earlier, rebel officers had herded these prisoners along the street and given them cigarettes. Then the machine guns were suddenly set up and began firing as the unsuspecting villagers were taking their first puffs.

"The whole six hundred men seemed to tremble in one convulsion," Whitaker later wrote, "as those in front, speechless with horror, rocked back on their heels, the color draining from their faces, their eyes opening wide with terror."

Before the song was finished, all lay sprawled in their blood.

This scene was reenacted in almost every town and village along the route of Franco's advance from Seville toward Madrid. And the general and his commanders did not weep as Azaña and some of his ministers did over the murder of enemy prisoners. They ordered it.

There were tactical reasons for doing so. After the slaughter in the Badajoz bullring, Colonel Yagüe, now the commander of Franco's forces, explained to reporter Whitaker:

"Of course, we shot them. What do you expect? Was I supposed to take four thousand reds with me as my column advanced, racing against time? Was I expected to turn them loose in my rear and let them make Badajoz red again?"

Antonio Bahamonde, a top aide of General Queipo de Llano, the rebel commander in Seville, further commented after he broke under the deluge of blood and fled abroad: "[The rebel leaders] knew very well that only by the force of terror . . . would they be able to dominate the people. . . . It is terror in the guise of order, and the order is the order of the cemetery."

But there were also philosophical reasons for the rebel massacres. A Franco press officer told Whitaker:

"We've got to kill and kill and kill, you understand. . . . You know what's wrong with Spain? Modern plumbing! In healthier times—I mean healthier times spiritually, you understand—plague and pestilence used to slaughter the Spanish masses. Held them down to proper proportions, you understand. Now with modern sewage disposal and the like, they multiply too fast. They're like animals, you understand, and you can't expect them not to be infected with the virus of Bolshevism. After all, rats and lice carry the plague."

How to rid the nation of these human rats and lice?

"It's our program, you understand, to exterminate a third of the male population of Spain. That will clean up the country and rid us of the proletariat. It's sound economically, too. Never have any more unemployment in Spain, you understand."

General Queipo de Llano put it less elegantly in a broadcast:

"The common people are swine. They must be killed like swine! . . . We do not want to be bothered again in our lifetime by Bolsheviks. These seducers of the people must be made to feel the pangs of hell before they die. . . . Spain must again be made a country fit for *caballeros* ("gentlemen") to live in."

In another broadcast, Queipo seemed to define what he meant by *caballero*. "The reds' women," he said, "have . . . learned that our soldiers are real men and not castrated militiamen."

So many Loyalist corpses littered the roads that General Mola himself grew disgusted. He thus ordered that victims be shot only in courtyards, fields, and cemeteries. The roads should remain clean.

Even a Nazi adviser to Franco, Captain Roldan von Strunk, protested the mass killings, and apparently not just for esthetic reasons. But Franco simply replied: "Why, this sort of thing can't be true—you've got your facts wrong, Captain Strunk."

Bahamonde, the renegade rebel officer, concluded that the rebels were incomparably more brutal than the Loyalists, for their murders were "organized and directed by the authorities," while the militia killings were largely committed by men "running wild without authority."

Whichever side was more brutal, Franco's men—at least the Moors and foreign legionnaires—were clearly more efficient. For they were seasoned professional killers who sought to murder almost an entire class systematically, under discipline and without passion. When the main slaughter was over, the less experienced Falangists and *Requetés* remained in the conquered areas to finish off many of those who had slipped through the dragnet of the front-line fighters.

The Moors, primitive Moroccan tribesmen, did not look like first-class soldiers as they lounged in the gutters, dressed in flowing robes, called *chilabas,* or in baggy tan trousers and shirt with a red fez or tightly wound turban on their heads. Nor were they highly motivated by ideological ideals: They didn't have the faintest idea why the Spaniards were killing each other. They fought because they were paid fifteen dollars a month, often in worthless old German marks, which they considered a fortune; because their tribal chief, paid off by Franco, ordered them to; and because they loved a battle.

But as they were cultural innocents, they could be trained like animals. Neither fear nor doubt diluted their discipline on the battlefield, and they hardly knew the meaning of the word "retreat." They also developed deep, doglike attachments to their masters, the Spanish officers, and were often ready to die for them. These masters, in turn, threw them a cherished bone: the traditional right of the Moorish warrior to loot, murder, and rape.

When the Moors had fought for their tribal chiefs against the Spanish army only a few years earlier and exercised this right, the same Spanish officers had called them savages who deserved to be exterminated. Now they were encouraging, even ordering, these savages to exterminate fellow Spaniards. Ironically, more than four hundred years after being thrown out of Spain by the great nationalist queen, Isabella the Catholic, the Moors had returned as heroes of a Spanish nationalist movement—because there were so few Spaniards who would fight for it.

Just as ironic, the Spanish foreign legion, made up almost entirely of Spaniards, was now fighting alongside the Moors against other Spaniards. Only some years earlier, the legionnaires and the Moors had been slaughtering, torturing, and mutilating each other in the Moroccan War, and countless photos were snapped after each battle showing a legionnaire holding a decapitated head or a bagful of ears.

Like the Moors, who were no longer fighting for their own land, the legionnaires fought for the money and the sheer love of war. But they were not innocents. Most were desperados, social misfits, glory seekers, adventurers, people who wanted to disappear and even to die. And many did, sometimes at the hands of their own commanders, who could shoot them without trial for desertion, cowardice, or other offenses. The legionnaires were losers who felt they had nothing more to lose. And although they understood, if vaguely, why Spaniards were killing Spaniards, they didn't care. They had fled from society because it rejected their simplistic concepts of survival, and its problems did not greatly concern them.

Their society was the legion, cut off from the world and its realities. The legion had given them a home, trusted comrades, good food, anonymity, a twisted self-respect, and an outlet for their steaming frustrations—all that a loser could want. So they fought not for Spain, not for Franco, but for the legion, which just happened to be under Franco's command. And they fought to the death because the best thing about life was this chance to risk it. Being cruel to themselves, they were barbaric to the enemy—not because they hated him but because this was an easy way to express their contempt for civilization, a final happy, bloody blow at the phantoms eating at their souls. And since killing had become so important a stimulant for them, they had turned it into a grotesque form of art.

Conversely, the Loyalist executioners—"uncontrollable" criminals and ruthless extremists with more stomach for rear-echelon butchery than front-line battle, men driven by greedy personal motives or burning social grievances—were sloppy and capricious in their homicide. They let many "guilty" people slip past them while shooting others for no reason at all.

Franco was contemptuous of these killers, so cowardly—and amateurish. Soon his own barbarians would blast into Madrid and make it a city fit for gentlemen.

CHAPTER 6

Desperation

1

After the fall of Badajoz, the day of purification seemed almost at hand. Franco's troops had already linked up with Mola's southwest of Madrid, and tons of German and Italian war matériel piled up in Africa were flowing to the soldiers of the arms-starved northern army. Still, Franco could not ignore the bravery of many of those Loyalists who preferred killing at the front rather than in the rear.

They had fought so tenaciously at Badajoz that only a handful of legionnaires in the unit lived to break in, though there were enough left to knife the defenders to death and then machine-gun the rest. But while the militiamen were brave in street fighting when the battle was man to man, they were less so in the open field. There, as bombs and shells rained down on them, they would, in their helplessness, scurry into some village to seek safety inside the stone houses. Bombers would then leisurely drop their loads, burying hundreds of fighters under heaps of scorched rubble.

And the southern road to Madrid led through open fields almost all the way.

The northern road through the Guadarramas might also soon be clear, it seemed, as Mola's men, carrying their shiny new arms from Franco, got set for another onslaught on Madrid. The two generals would crush the city in a nutcracker. Mola had had a far rougher time than Franco up to now. Aside from the lack of arms, he had no professional fighters to match the Moors or legionnaires, no

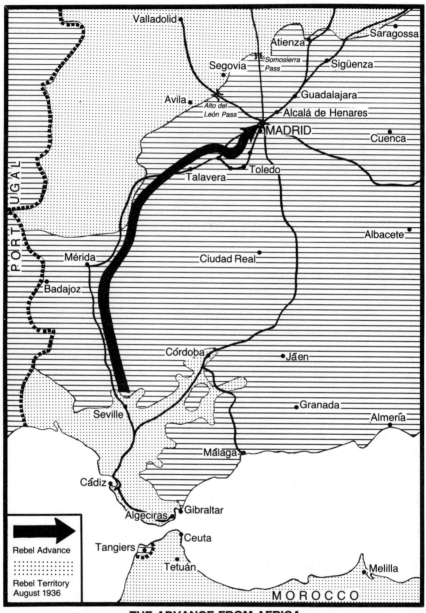

THE ADVANCE FROM AFRICA

open fields to bomb and strafe. In the mountains, a small group of Loyalists could hold off an army of attackers. But Mola shared one advantage with Franco: fighting an enemy with little discipline or military knowledge.

In the Guadarramas, however, the Loyalists did not run desperately to the nearest village for cover; they sauntered leisurely to the nearest village—and sometimes to Madrid—for a beer.

This was the plague afflicting Cipriano Mera's anarchist group. One time, it attacked enemy forces threatening the Lozoya reservoir, Madrid's precious water supply, and courageously fought them off while suffering great casualties. But hardly had the survivors reached the reservoir when they turned around and headed back to their base in a nearby village.

The commander of the anarchist column in the area was astonished when he saw Mera and his men.

"Why are you coming back, my sons, abandoning your terrain?" Lieutenant Colonel del Rosal, a trusted professional officer, asked delicately, with due respect for their distrust of command.

"Don't be angry," Mera replied as he might to his father, "we're all willing to return there when you order it."

"But my sons, don't you realize that your effort has turned out to be futile? You must do what you are ordered to do, and not whatever strikes your fancy. . . . Once you have conquered the terrain you must seize the pickax and shovel and build barricades to protect yourselves from enemy bullets."

"But, Comrade del Rosal," said Mera, "don't you see that if we amuse ourselves by digging ditches and building barricades we'll spend Christmas here? We're from the FAI and don't need barricades. For us the question is to always go forward."

Del Rosal responded: "So always go forward! But please, never backwards."

Reluctantly, Mera's battalion trudged back to the reservoir and began digging in. But then some of his men decided they must go to Madrid for a while, arguing that they had to replace their torn clothes or their worn-out hemp shoes.

"Is it necessary to wear a tuxedo to shoot?" Mera asked.

And finally, against all anarchist principles, he threatened to use force if they tried to leave their posts. He was crestfallen, writing later:

"I asked myself . . . why the men did not exercise the self-discipline which our convictions imposed upon us, why . . . they abused the liberty they enjoyed."

Why so many had to die in the name of this liberty—and would die in even greater numbers now that Mola was ready to attack with his new arms.

"To the Somosierra . . . as fast as you can," Enrique Castro Delgado ordered his driver.

Mola was on the move, and Castro's crack Fifth Regiment, the core of the

Guadarrama defense system, would have to hold the peaks or Madrid might be crushed in a pincers.

Castro already had a pile of problems. And at the top of the heap was *La Pasionaria*, who had praised him so highly after the fall of Montaña Barracks. Here he was trying to build the Fifth Regiment into a model of military efficiency, the perfect kernel of a new Communist-run republican army, and Dolores kept interfering with his plans. In his view, she was nothing more than a demagogue.

One day she had summoned him to her office and, while large portraits of Lenin and Stalin scowled down at him, said: "Comrade, the Political Bureau considers this the time to organize a powerful feminine movement. . . . We feel it necessary to create women's companies."

Castro was incredulous.

"I assume they're to be formed only for auxiliary functions."

"No. . . . It's necessary to put an end to the notion that a woman is a second-class human being."

"I don't understand."

"It doesn't matter . . . just organize the companies!"

A few weeks after Castro had done so, a medical captain reported to him that in less than a month over two hundred militiamen had been infected with venereal diseases. Castro was furious—especially when he learned that the militiawomen were responsible. The next day he ordered them to report to the regimental clinic. About 70 percent were found to be infected. Castro wanted to shoot them.

Instead he went to see Dolores, whose face hardened when he showed her the medical report.

"It's a trick," she said.

"It's a disease," Castro replied.

They stared at each other with mutual disdain.

"Why do you prefer the whores to the combatants?" Castro asked.

Then he walked out, slamming the door behind him, and ordered the women's companies dissolved.

Now he had another problem. The Communists controlled the Fifth Regiment, but not all of his officers were Communists. Thus, some could not be entirely trusted, and one of them was Major Miguel Gallo, a professional officer and a good Catholic.

Castro's car stopped in front of Gallo's headquarters in the Somosierra, and as he greeted the major he noted the religious medallion suspended from his neck.

"What's happening?" Castro asked.

"Mola's forces are approaching . . . the peasants have informed us that they're coming in trucks . . . and wearing red berets . . . and carrying standards of the Virgin and saints . . ."

And Gallo looked down at his own medallion.

Castro was disturbed by Gallo's doubts and scruples. He should perhaps be killed, but he was too popular with his men. It would be better to persuade him.

"Listen, you can tell me," Castro said. "You can tell me it's a crime to kill those who . . . believe in God. I understand your distress, Gallo. But think of Spain, of our Spain. . . . Spain cannot go on being casinos and hunting grounds."

Castro laughed inwardly and ordered: "Command, Gallo! Place your men on the mountains dominating the highway. Order them not to open fire until the entire enemy column has penetrated into our pincers. Order them at that moment to attack like savages . . . even though it hurts you, Comrade Gallo."

The two walked to the crest of the hill and saw trucks zigzagging up the road. Soon, two Loyalist machine guns opened fire, followed by rifle shots and grenade explosions, and the trucks lurched to a halt. Their occupants jumped out, only to be mowed down, and within minutes it was all over. Shortly, a motley file of prisoners, with their hands raised, were brought to Castro and Gallo. They were all sent to rear headquarters for interrogation—except three dressed in black coats and red berets.

"Priests?" Castro asked.

"Soldiers of Christ the King!" replied one.

"And the commandment 'Thou shalt not kill'?"

"It lacks reality today . . . Today it is not a matter of fulfilling the commandments of God . . . It is a question of God continuing to live in the soul of a people."

"But here it is not a question of God. The question is whether the republic will live or die!"

Glancing at Gallo, Castro went on: "I'd pardon you if you were only priests mingling with the combatants in order to save their souls . . . for we have nothing against God. But it turns out you're soldiers of Christ the King, who have forgotten the commandment 'Thou shalt not kill,' who carry pistols in your belts."

As he gave a sign to one of his men to cock his pistol, Castro added: "You can shout as much as you like and whatever you like. And if God listens to you, good for you."

"*Viva Cristo Rey!*"

There was a shot, and the priest who had spoken collapsed. As his two colleagues lowered their heads and prayed, Castro threw two pickaxes and two shovels in front of them and ordered:

"Bury him! We don't want to touch him with our sinful hands."

The two priests dug a grave and lowered their dead comrade into it. And when he had been buried, Castro told the others they could leave. He then looked at Gallo and said:

"War is war!"

Gallo turned and walked away.

Soon afterward, a lieutenant colonel rushed into Major Gallo's headquarters. He bitterly condemned the killing of the priest and ordered Gallo to withdraw his troops to the village of Buitrago. Castro intervened:

"Look around you. Hundreds of eyes are thinking in what part of your body they should put a bullet."

The militiamen slowly closed in.

"But a counterattack will follow," the lieutenant colonel argued.

"So what?"

"We'll be defeated. And the road to Madrid will be open. You'll pull back to Buitrago!"

The circle of militiamen tightened and they began to shout:

"Coward!" "Bastard!" "Is Franco giving you the order to withdraw?"

"I've been a socialist for thirty years," the lieutenant colonel cried.

"We're not withdrawing!"

And as the furious officer started to leave, some militiamen grabbed him, and one of them yelled: "We're going to hang this bastard."

Castro, prodded by Gallo, ordered: "Take him to Buitrago."

When the men ignored him, Castro drew his pistol and approached them.

"Back! Back!" he shouted, his eyes ablaze.

And he led the officer to his car.

When several men aimed weapons at the vehicle, Castro climbed in and shouted out the window: "The commander of the Fifth Regiment is speaking to you. Fire if you want to!"

And the car raced off to Buitrago. When it arrived, Castro gave orders to some approaching militiamen, apparently anarchists.

"Lock him up in the church. Place a guard. Take him out at night and send him to Madrid. And hand him over to the Socialist party. He isn't a traitor; he's a fool."

Shortly, a friend of the lieutenant colonel, fearing for the man's life, asked Castro to let *him* take the captive officer to Madrid. Just then, there were several shots.

"It's already too late!" Castro replied.

2

Prime Minister Giral was determined to end the killing within Loyalist ranks, and to do this, he realized, he had to build a professional army, disciplined and well

General Emilio Mola.
SERVICIO HISTORICO MILITAR

Colonel José Moscardo, Colonel José Varela, and General Francisco
Franco after victory at Alcázar. SERVICIO HISTORICO MILITAR

José Antonio Primo de Rivera. SERVICIO HISTORICO MILITAR

Colonel Juan de Yagüe. SERVICIO HISTORICO MILITAR

General Joaquin Fanjul. JUAN MANUEL FANJUL

José Calvo Sotelo. SERVICIO
HISTORICO MILITAR

Lieutenant José Castillo.
CAMBIO 16

President Manuel Azaña.
BRANDEIS U. LIBRARY

Prime Minister Francisco Largo
Caballero (center). SERVICIO HISTORICO MILITAR

Prime Minister Diego Martinez Barrio. CAMBIO 16

Prime Minister Santiago Casares Quiroga. SERVICIO HISTORICO MILITAR

Indalecio Prieto. CAMBIO 16

Major Vicente Rojo (standing) and
General José Miaja. ANGEL ROJO

Major Ignacio Hidalgo de Cisneros.
CAMBIO 16

André Malraux. SERVICIO HISTORICO
MILITAR

Captain Urbano Orad de la Torre.
URBANO ORAD DE LA TORRE

Dolores Ibarruri ''La Pasionaria.'' BRANDEIS U. LIBRARY

Enrique Castro Delgado. CAMBIO 16

Santiago Carrillo. CAMBIO 16

''El Campesino.'' SERVICIO HISTORICO
MILITAR

General Emilio Kléber. SERVICIO
HISTORICO MILITAR

Buenaventura Durruti. SERVICIO
HISTORICO MILITAR

Mikhail Koltsov (behind rifleman). CAMBIO 16

Cipriano Mera. CAMBIO 16

Major Miguel Palacios.
MIGUEL PALACIOS

Janet Riesenfeld. D'GAGGERI

Militiamen head for Guadarramas.
LA ACTUALIDAD ESPAÑOLA

Suspected Fifth Columnist
arrested. LA ACTUALIDAD
ESPAÑOLA

International Brigade arrives in Madrid. LA ACTUALIDAD ESPAÑOLA

Loyalists defend Casa de Campo.
BRANDEIS U. LIBRARY

Loyalists attack in University City. BRANDEIS U. LIBRARY

Madrileños take refuge in subway during bombing. SERVICIO HISTORICO MILITAR

Refugees live on Madrid street.
SERVICIO HISTORICO MILITAR

Refugees flee bombs in Madrid. BRANDEIS U. LIBRARY

Moors move to front. LA ACTUALIDAD ESPAÑOLA

Rebels attack toward Madrid. LA ACTUALIDAD ESPAÑOLA

equipped. He hardly looked like a man who could perform such a colossal task. Unlike the masses he nominally led, he was neat and clean-shaven and even wore a starched collar. He had a meek face with dark pouches under his bespectacled eyes and could far more easily be imagined behind the counter of the pharmacy he had owned than in the prime minister's chair, expecially at a time of war and revolution. And, in fact, he did not hold any of the levers of power. He did not even have a general staff to help him, simply a war minister who personally gave orders over the phone to his battalion and column commanders—if they bothered to listen to him.

Yet Giral struggled valiantly to change things. In the last days of July, he called up two years of conscripts, but either they were already fighting in the militia or just ignored the call. And who was there to force them into service? Giral then tried to form "volunteer battalions" which would be merged into a "volunteer army," but ran into an ideological wall. Socialist labor leader Largo Caballero demanded that the new army remain a jumble of autonomous militia groups "in keeping with the revolution."

The Communists were practically alone in backing Giral's plan. How could the Loyalists win the war with a scramble of independent units? How could their party come to power unless it controlled these units? It could only manipulate a united army. And it would. For it had the best officers, the shrewdest politicians, and links with Stalin, who held the key to the armory needed for victory. Still, the Communists were careful not to antagonize Caballero, since they planned to use him.

"No one," the Communist *Mundo Obrero* double-talked, "could think of creating anything that runs counter to our glorious popular militia. [We must simply] complement and reinforce the popular army."

And by the end of August, Stalin sent agents to help the republic do exactly that, though not so it could win the war and convert itself into a soviet state as the Spanish Communists planned. Stalin simply wanted to keep Franco busy fighting for Madrid and Hitler busy helping him—too busy to march into Russia.

An officer studying a map in Giral's office looked up at the short, bespectacled visitor with the reddish face and wavy hair. He winked and said:

"French?"

"No, Russian."

The officer smiled, dismissing the answer as a joke.

A short time later, a girl at a newsstand asked the man the same question, and laughed when she received the same reply. Several militiamen then saw the man in a café and, raising their cognac glasses, cried: "Long live our faithful friend, France!"

Well, what was the use?

"*Merci*," the man replied.

But he *was* Russian. Mikhail Koltsov had arrived in Madrid in late August as a correspondent for *Pravda*, the Soviet Union's leading newspaper. But he was also one of the Kremlin's top agents, who reported directly to Stalin, using the code name Miguel Martínez.

Koltsov had come to Spain with other Russians—police agents, advisers, diplomats. Ambassador Marcel Rosenberg, who had been deputy secretary of the League of Nations, was the chief of mission, though he was only a decorative figure. Besides Koltsov, the three most powerful Russians coming at this time were General Vladimir Goriev, the main military adviser; Arthur Stashevsky, who remained in Barcelona as the Soviet trade envoy; and Alexander Orlov, an NKVD (secret police) officer.

They came so quietly that people refused to believe they were Russian. And Koltsov only admitted he was because he was in Madrid officially as a journalist. The last thing Stalin wanted the world to know was that the Soviet Union was meddling in Spain. Why provoke the Germans into possibly attacking Russia, or the French into breaking their alliance with that country?

Some days before the Soviet mission arrived, Russian officials had met secretly in Odessa with three Spanish dignitaries. They needed arms, the Spaniards pleaded, and they would pay in gold. A deal was struck. But to conceal it, Stalin issued a decree on August 28 (published three days later) forbidding "the export, reexport or transit to Spain of all kinds of arms, munitions, war matériel, airplanes, and warships."

Stalin would join Léon Blum's nonintervention committee to cover his intervention, as Hitler and Mussolini would join to cover theirs.

Meanwhile, Koltsov and the other Russian agents sidled in to help communize the Loyalist army and turn it into an instrument of Soviet foreign policy. Spanish Communists had laid the groundwork with their Fifth Regiment. Now the Russians, helped by their Spanish comrades, would gradually direct war policy—but as subtly as possible. They couldn't step too hard on the toes of the non-Communist republican officials for fear the squeals might give them away.

And Koltsov, especially, was not a man to step on toes. He could sometimes be arrogant, but he was charming, human, brilliant, and extremely complex. An important figure in Soviet literary circles, he seemed torn between the conflicting demands of his loyalty to Stalin and his conscience. He believed in the ideology but apparently not in the terror. Spaniards instinctively liked him since they sensed that he was, like them, seething with inner discord beneath a veneer of passionate commitment. Did he know what Stalin's strategy was in Spain? This is not clear, but it seems he suspected betrayal and tried to influence his master to help the Loyalists win the war as swiftly as possible.

General Goriev, too, had a way with Spaniards, the few he allowed himself to meet. Deceptively the picture of an English gentleman, he was tall with blue eyes and, at forty-four, slightly gray; like Koltsov, he hid his tension under a cool exterior. Goriev, also known as Jan Berzin, was an aristocrat who fought with the Bolsheviks against the czar's armies and emerged with a chestful of medals. He then crushed a revolt in Kronstadt in 1921, led an abortive coup in Germany two years later, and brought Sinkiang, Chinese Turkestan, into the Communist fold in 1932. After serving as chief of military intelligence, he left for Spain—to see that no one won too quickly.

But Goriev, rather unsophisticated politically, may have been less aware of how he was being used than Koltsov appears to have been.

"The essential thing," he told Communist propagandist Jesús Hernández, who had asked him about Soviet aid, "is to win the arms race against the Fascists. . . . Be calm. The 'House' [Moscow] has already informed us that our planes will arrive in several days."

NKVD leaders, in fact, had met on September 14 to arrange for shipments which Orlov, their representative in Spain, would distribute.

"But," said Hernández skeptically, "the attitude of France and Britain and the nonintervention projects will make it difficult for the USSR to send us arms."

"There will be a way to arrange this. If there is none we'll invent one."

Hernández then went to Koltsov and asked: "Do you know when the arms will arrive?"

"How would I know?" the Russian replied. "Logically, they should be here already."

He sounded as impatient as the Spanish were.

Hernández and non-Communist republican leaders, too, were impressed with Koltsov and Goriev. They were different from Stalin's usual servants. They actually seemed to care whether Spain lived or died.

And they knew that if the Russian arms, especially the aircraft, did not arrive soon, it would almost certainly die, despite the frantic effort of a few Spanish and foreign pilots to delay this fate with some old flying machines.

Major Hidalgo de Cisneros bitterly reproached himself. He had made a disastrous misjudgment, and now his planes had practically vanished from the skies. The Loyalists, he thought, would crush the revolt within days, weeks at most, and so he had acted as if each day could be decisive. He sent out his tired pilots and their antiquated planes hour after hour to bomb and strafe. It seemed logical, especially since the enemy had almost no air defenses.

But suddenly his slow fifteen-year-old Breguets without nose guns were facing modern Italian Fiats, and soon he had practically no pilots, planes, gasoline, or spare parts. Yet what was left was in the air. One pilot even refused to rest between sorties. When the revolt broke out, Sergeant Urtubi had been in Morocco and was forced to fight for the rebels, who had few experienced flyers. But since they mistrusted him, a Falangist captain sat behind him on each flight with a pistol cocked.

One day, Urtubi abruptly turned around and with his own pistol fired a whole magazine into his guardian, then, just as the plane was about to crash, returned to the controls and flew on to Madrid. The next day he was in another aircraft on a mission against the rebels.

But the Loyalists needed more than a few overworked pilots like Urtubi to fight off the advancing enemy. And no Russian planes had arrived yet. So the French leftist novelist, André Malraux, decided to help out. . . .

"Will he be much longer?" asked Louis Fischer, an American Communist writer who had stopped off in Paris to visit Malraux on his way to Spain. "What is he doing in there?"

Malraux's wife replied that he was at his desk phoning: "He's buying tanks."

Malraux also bought planes—thirty Potez 540s and ten Bloch 200s, as well as a few Breguets. Some of these old aircraft could hardly fly, but the Spanish government was glad to put up the money for them. And by early August, Malraux, an amateur flyer with almost no knowledge of bombing or navigation, was in Madrid, a gold-braided *coronel* in command of an international air squadron.

Thin, taut, with a forelock falling over one eye, Malraux reveled in the role of liberator. As an archaeologist in the Far East, he had spent more time pleading the causes of native Indo-Chinese before indifferent French colonial officials than digging in the ruins. He so exasperated these officials that they charged him with stealing some of his archaeological finds, and he was only freed from jail after a court appeal in France. He then went to China, where he defended the unstable Kuomintang government as minister of propaganda, and in the next few years, when he wasn't writing world-acclaimed novels, he was combing southern Asia and the Arabian desert for treasures of the past.

But he cared more about the politics of the future. Four days after the Spanish Civil War broke out, he called a public meeting in Paris's Palais du Sport and asked: "Who will come to Spain with me to start a Loyalist air force?"

Malraux hired pilots, gunners, and ground technicians, paying each a monthly salary of $1500 plus bonuses. They were a mixture of idealists, adventurers, and neurotics. And one joined to get combat experience as well as to fight the Fascists. He was Yehezkel Piekar, a Palestinian Jew who had served as a bodyguard of Zionist leader David Ben-Gurion and fought for the Jewish underground, the Haganah, which was battling the Arabs in the Holy Land.

When Piekar went to see Malraux in Paris, the Frenchman immediately offered him a contract, though the young man had only fifteen hours of solo flying. Malraux did not even ask for documents.

"But maybe I'm a Fascist," Piekar said. "You don't know me."

"If you're a Jew," Malraux replied, "you're not a Fascist. I have never met a Jewish Fascist."

Soon Piekar and the others were attacking the rebel forces tramping toward Madrid, with Malraux invariably in the lead bomber. After the rebel victory at

Badajoz, the squadron desperately tried to halt the enemy's northward march. On one flight near the village of Medellín, Malraux sighted a long enemy convoy crawling north. And so did the French reporter Louis Delaprée, who had gone along.

"The airmen saw not men, but insects," Delaprée would write. "The order was given to disperse them. They did more; they annihilated them. In the middle of the road, a lorry had stopped. The driver, his head slumped over the wheel, seemed to be asleep. The cargo of this exhausted driver was no ordinary cargo, but twenty dead men hit by the same burst."

The other lorries stopped and "seemed stuck in the road like flies on a strip of flypaper," as Malraux himself was to describe the scene. And the convoy was destroyed.

But except for a few attacks like this, Malraux's ancient planes could be of little more than nuisance value and, when meeting German and Italian fighters, were able to escape only by sheer luck; planes that did return safely were often riddled with bullet holes. Yet the squadron was an important morale booster for the Loyalists. An international force was helping them!

The Hotel Gran Vía, squadron headquarters, became the meeting place for some of the world's literary giants, including Ernest Hemingway, John Dos Passos, Ilya Ehrenburg, Arthur Koëstler, and Rafael Alberti, as well as Malraux, who was usually the center of attention. For all were intrigued not only by his brilliant conversation, but by his brash transformation into the "savior" of Madrid.

Not every Loyalist, however, appreciated his contribution. Major Hidalgo de Cisneros deplored it, claiming the squadron was "more a burden than a help." He was especially resentful that some rowdy mercenaries spent more time in the bar than in the air, while his own men were in constant combat. Besides, Malraux was getting all the publicity.

Nevertheless, though Malraux and Piekar survived, within a few weeks most of the original flyers were casualties and most of the planes twisted wreckage— monuments to a few hours, even minutes, of grace for Madrid, the possible difference between seizure and salvation.

Enrique Castro Delgado barely had time to rejoice over his quick victory at Somosierra when he had a new worry. Franco's troops in the south had been temporarily paralyzed by the shattering air assault of André Malraux's squadron near Medellín, but they regrouped and stormed into Talavera de la Reina in the Tagus Valley, the last important town before Madrid. Castro's men in that area had to recapture it or Madrid would be in mortal danger. However, they had panicked in the retreat and lost their fighting heart. The men of his model Fifth Regiment! Castro would personally turn them into fighters again.

He drove to their camp in the Tagus Valley and was furious when he saw militiamen milling around with no leaders in sight. Finally, in local headquarters, he found Major Ricardo Burillo, the Communist sector commander, a renegade aristocrat with a distinguished bearing that made him look strangely out of place amid the stubble-faced proletariat. Even now, as he lay fast asleep on a mattress, he was wearing pajamas, almost unheard-of garb in the republican army. When Castro awakened him, Burillo was startled.

"What brings you here, Major Castro?"

"The situation, major. It's difficult in my view. Could you tell me why?"

"Castro, Talavera is lost. There is no direction . . . no army . . . and no combativeness, though you must, for political reasons, speak every day about the militiamen's heroism. The militiamen are good, magnificent men but not soldiers. And simple men don't get accustomed to war easily, to killing or to dying. They have a fear in the soul, the fear of being encircled. And it's enough for them to see a group of Moors on one of the flanks to utter screams that scare thousands of men: 'The Moors!' And . . . they run and run . . . until they drop in a ditch from fatigue. Look at the men. In their faces you'll find the reason for everything."

As they went out, Castro did look in their faces. Burillo was right . . . but Castro would change the "reason for everything."

Suddenly, the hills in the distance seemed to undulate with life. The Moors! Militiamen jumped out of ditches. Engines started up.

"Comrades!" cried Castro. "I need thirty volunteers. Only thirty. And two machine guns! I don't intend to send you to death, but to prevent death from encircling all of us."

A pause. A group of Communists came to him, then, several carrying two machine guns. Castro set up the guns some distance apart, facing the fleeing mob, and he stood between them. He would motion to the men to halt. If they disobeyed, the volunteers would fire above their heads while others would hurl hand grenades to "make an impression."

"But if you see that they keep running, shoot into their midst," he ordered. "It's a painful price. Let's go, comrades! It's the party now that commands."

Castro raised his arms, signaling for the men to stop, but they ignored him, trampling those who fell. Machine guns then sputtered bullets and hand grenades exploded while Castro kept shouting in vain. Then more bursts, and several militiamen dropped to the ground. Finally, the human flood slowed down and trickled to a halt. Castro drew his pistol and moved slowly toward his men, stopping about fifteen yards away. "Comrades! Are you crazy?" he cried. "Nobody is attacking you from behind. Stop for a moment and look behind you. It's the fear provoked by some son of a bitch, by the shout 'We're cut off!' A fantasy!"

The Moors had apparently withdrawn.

The militiamen finally calmed down and Castro let most of them rest, forming two parallel defense lines with the others, each guarded by trusted Communists who would make sure that no one would run again. When reinforcements arrived, these men must try to recapture Talavera. In their faces Castro still saw fear, defeat, shame.

Yet they were all that blocked the road to Madrid.

On the evening of September 3, Mikhail Koltsov, the *Pravda* correspondent, stopped in at the socialist Casa del Pueblo to get the latest news. The atmosphere was heated. Franco had taken Talavera and apparently opened the southern road to Madrid. Mola was now well armed and threatened the Loyalists from the north. The rebels had seized strategic Irun on the French border . . . and Loyalist Spain had an almost powerless government.

Prime Minister Giral tried to act vigorously, but he was still a petty bourgeois pharmacist who could not win the confidence of the masses. True, he served to reassure the Western democracies that the republican government was moderate, middle class, and worthy of their aid. But the time for deception was over. There had to be a popular emergency regime representing all Loyalist forces, one strong enough to build a new defense system, purge the administration, and ruthlessly control the economy. And all this had to be done overnight—before the rebels could smash into Madrid.

But who would run the new government? Loyalist leaders fought each other over this question almost as passionately as they were fighting the rebels. Moderate socialist Indalecio Prieto wanted Giral to stay in his post but to bring socialists and Communists into his cabinet. No, responded revolutionary socialist leader Largo Caballero; the masses loved only him. The Communists alone wanted no real change, for they could more easily manipulate Giral than they could the ambitious Caballero. And they could do it best from outside the government.

But it soon became clear that Largo Caballero was right: Most workers did love only him. President Azaña saw no choice. Would Caballero take the post?

Yes, the socialist leader replied—if the Communists joined his cabinet. With Franco so near, why shouldn't they share the responsibility for a possible disaster?

Why *should* they? asked the Communists. Better to pick up the pieces *after* the disaster.

Stalin disagreed. There was no time for political intrigue. He didn't want any "pieces"; he wanted Madrid to hold. And the greater the Communist influence on government policy, the greater the chance of holding.

So the Communists changed their minds, and Caballero agreed to take over, hoping eventually to lure the anarchists into his cabinet as well, despite their hatred for all government. Then there would be no one left to pick up the pieces; all would topple or triumph together.

Now Koltsov entered Caballero's small office and found the prospective ministers sitting around on sofas waiting for a telephone call from the palace. Caballero had gone there to present his cabinet choices to Azaña and was to phone as soon as the president had approved them. There was just a chance he would not. Azaña was a bourgeois republican who had always vigorously opposed revolution. Now he was being asked to give his blessing to a revolutionary government!

Caballero's future colleagues smoked in silence, reflective, nervous, more resigned than rapturous. Despite Caballero's strong grip on the masses, few of these men believed he was a good leader. Yet they realized that it was precisely this grip that made him the only man who could weld Loyalist Spain into one great fighting machine. Only he, it seemed, could save Madrid.

Caballero, sixty-seven, was short, stocky, and balding, a brusque man, stubborn and intolerant of anyone who didn't agree with him. He was an activist, not a thinker. Born into a poor Madrid family, he started working at the age of seven and became an accomplished bookbinder, ropemaker, and bricklayer. He was elected secretary-general of the UGT in 1917, and was soon sentenced to life imprisonment for antigovernment activity. But he was shortly released and later served under the rightist dictator General Primo de Rivera, considering him an improvement over past leaders. After serving as minister in the first republican government, he was jailed in 1934 by the succeeding rightist regime for taking part in the Asturian revolt.

Behind bars, Caballero read Marx and other Communist literature for the first time, and he walked out a year later a newborn extremist who demanded a "dictatorship of the proletariat." The Communists, then weak, saw in him the perfect pawn for catapulting them into power. They desperately tried to merge the Socialist and Communist parties under their control, flattering Caballero with the title "Spanish Lenin" and promising to support his policies. But he resisted.

For while he may have been a revolutionary, he was also a nationalist and never trusted Russia or the Spanish Communist intriguers. Though vain, he was simple, honest, and naïve with little understanding of the ideological dogmas he constantly repeated and sincerely accepted—until experience shattered one illusion after another. Like most Spaniards, he was ready to switch views rather than cling to burst illusions, and to fight with equal verve for his new cause.

But his beliefs were often seasoned with opportunism and *machismo*. A new centrally commanded army? Never? That would mean just another military caste—this one run by the Communists. Even barricades and trenches were out. The idea was to attack, attack. Not to hide like cowards.

And so the men sitting in his office were worried. Yet they felt that Caballero could do less harm as the government's leader than as its main critic. For, saddled with the responsibility, he would have to be pragmatic, as they were in accepting him as their chief.

Waiting for the call from the palace was a mixed breed of politicians, with moderates heading only the minor ministries. There were five bourgeois republicans, three right-wing socialists, three left-wing socialists (including Caballero), and two Communists. One of the key figures, socialist Julio Alvarez del Vayo, who would be foreign minister, was a suave intellectual and well-known journalist. He had close ties to both Caballero and the Communists and was thought by some to be a secret Communist. Another was Jesús Hernández, the Communist propaganda specialist picked to lead the Ministry of Education. And Juan Negrín, a deceptively mild-mannered socialist professor who was appointed finance minister, would be a man of destiny.

But perhaps the most important choice of all, and certainly the most blubbery, was the moderate socialist leader Prieto, who had a pale triple-chinned face with droopy piggish eyes that were among the most observant in Spain. He told Koltsov exactly what he thought of the fellow socialist he would work for: "a fool who wants to be considered shrewd, a cold bureaucrat who plays the role of a mad fanatic, a schemer who pretends to be a methodical bureaucrat . . . a man capable of spoiling everything and everybody."

Actually, President Azaña had wanted Prieto to be prime minister before the revolt, but Caballero's supporters, the mass of laborers, blocked the appointment, preferring almost anybody to their hero's bitter competitor. Yet Prieto, a wealthy publisher of bourgeois origin who had made his money as a merchant, might have been the only man who could have staved off the civil war. Ramon Serrano Suñer, Franco's brother-in-law, who was later his foreign minister, told the author that the rightists' fear of Caballero helped to spark the revolt.

"But if Prieto had become prime minister, there would have been no revolt and no civil war. For we trusted him despite his leftist beliefs."

Prieto was, in fact, the power behind the Giral government, though he was not a member. And while he detested Caballero, he was prepared to serve under him, even in the secondary position of minister of navy and air force.

The telephone rang. It was Caballero calling from the palace; the president had invited the new government to present itself. The politicians rushed to the cars parked outside and were embraced by the militiamen guarding the front door. At last a government of the people!

Koltsov raced off to file a story to *Pravda*. And to let Stalin know that Madrid might still hold out a little longer—if Caballero acted swiftly to recapture Talavera.

"I'm General Asensio."

A tall, urbane, smartly uniformed officer stepped out of his car and introduced himself to Enrique Castro Delgado and Major Burillo. General José Asensio Torrado had just come from the Guadarrama front, where, under his supreme command, the militia had stood firm against all attacks.

A veteran of the Moroccan wars, he was considered by military experts one of the best regular army officers the Loyalists had. But he was an officer who didn't mix in politics, obeyed his superiors whoever they were, and expected strict obedience from his own subordinates—an unpopular attitude in an army of undisciplined revolutionary militiamen. The Communists, especially, hated him because they could not control him, though even Koltsov recognized his military prowess. Asensio stood in the way of the Communist plan to slowly grab the levers of military authority.

But Largo Caballero, for all his damning of the "military caste," saw in Asensio the best chance for holding Madrid. And so his first act on coming to power was to promote him to general and rush him to the Talavera zone as commander of the central front, together with seven thousand additional troops. Now Asensio had come to retake Talavera.

As Castro greeted him, he searched his eyes for some clue to his character, wondering how to handle him. But the general immediately gazed through his binoculars at the defense positions and said: "These lines are shit, Major Burillo."

"That's all we have," Burillo replied.

"But as I arrived here I saw hundreds of men lying under the trees."

Castro then intervened: "They are men sick with fatigue and fear. They must be allowed to rest. Unless, general, you come with fresh forces."

Asensio was furious.

"Fresh forces?" he exclaimed. "What these bastards need is a kick in the ass that will make them get up."

He drew his pistol and added: "You'll see how I'll make these bastards fight!"

Castro saw how his men were watching this newcomer. "General, listen to me for a moment."

"I only want to tell you, Major Castro," Asensio responded, "that I'm the commander here. I! . . . Do you hear me well? The commander."

At that moment a man started running toward them, and Asensio mistakenly thought he had panicked, though he was actually coming to Castro with a message. Clutching his pistol, Asensio growled:

"You're going to see, major, how this son of a bitch stops running!"

As Asensio began moving toward the messenger, Castro stepped between them and said: "Be careful, general! We have many generals. Too many."

Asensio stared at Castro.

"Go away, major," he said.

"General," said Castro, "look behind you. Don't be afraid. Turn around, please."

Asensio turned and saw several pistols and rifles aimed at him. He lowered his own weapon.

"All right, major," he said, "you may leave!"

"I'm waiting for reinforcements. My men do not obey anyone unless I tell them to. And I want . . . to tell them that you are the front commander. That they should obey you."

Asensio then stalked off to his headquarters, and Castro went to meet the reinforcements. He admonished the commanders:

"Beware of General Asensio. Obey him! But only if you think the order is right. Only as long as he treats you like men, not like animals. I think he hates militiamen. I also have the impression that he is a morphine addict or a cynic. Or a scoundrel!"

And a general hardly capable of recapturing Talavera.

French reporter Louis Delaprée relaxed with a group of militiamen in a small olive grove in the Tagus Valley, about three miles from Talavera. It was 6:00 A.M., September 9, and they had slept little, though they would soon assault Talavera once more. General Asensio ordered his nine thousand men, including the militias of Castro and Mera, to attack again and again. And now, feeling more secure because of their great numbers, they did, with much heroism.

But Yagüe's troops clung to Talavera and threatened to outflank the militiamen. Still, Asensio would not give up—not with Madrid in dire peril. On this warm morning, his men would thrust forward another time. And Delaprée was with them, risking his life as usual, though his conservative pro-Franco newspaper, *Paris Soir*, often did not publish his articles because they showed the Loyalists in a human, sympathetic light.

As he joined a militia officer for breakfast, he saw two books in the man's knapsack squeezed in between a loaf of bread and a package of cheese. One, Delaprée noticed, was a collection of poems by Gongora, the other, a beginner's book on Marxism.

"Between this deliciously beautiful poetry and this desperate catechism," Delaprée wrote that day, "my new comrade found himself in perfect balance, marvelously at ease, alert and gay."

After breakfast, the officer read aloud some of the poems, but was soon interrupted by shell bursts nearby. The enemy was counterattacking.

Putting his books back in his knapsack, the man ran off with the rest of his group to meet the foe. All day long, the fighting went on, and finally the rebels were forced back across the Tagus River into Talavera. At Asensio's headquarters, the general, sitting at a table full of maps and beer bottles, told Delaprée:

"Tomorrow, we shall renew the offensive. We shall not permit them one day of rest."

But as the rebels once more threatened to cut off his force, sweeping them with aerial and tank fire, Asensio watched with agony as the men who had fought so well in the past few days suddenly panicked once again and surged to the rear right past his headquarters.

Delaprée was leaving when an officer came up to him and asked: "Are you the French journalist who was with Lieutenant González Pardo this morning?"

"I don't know anybody by that name."

"Ah! I thought . . . he left this for you."

And the officer handed him two small books.

Delaprée immediately recognized them.

"Yes, that's me. Where is the lieutenant?"

"He's dead . . . three bullets in the stomach. He asked me to give you these books if we could find you."

Tears came to Delaprée's eyes.

"Farewell, my friend," he would later write. "I knew you for only an hour, a poor little hour of human life, but I shall never forget you and your books, depositories of your dreams. Your memory shall always be with me. I shall see you always, one finger raised, as you recited Gongora's most beautiful sonnet, which was less precious, though, than the throbbing of your generous heart. Good-bye, my friend."

And Delaprée drove off to Madrid—which now, it seemed, Franco could take at his leisure.

3

In Madrid, life went on as usual; few *Madrileños* were aware that the door to the city had been unlatched. Although there were occasional light bombing raids, people still crowded the cafés, where militiamen continued to brag about victories never won. The atmosphere remained brisk, even exciting; the enemy would never reach Madrid, especially now that Largo Caballero, a warrior of the people, was running things.

And he had, in fact, already performed wonders in his first days in office—setting up a general staff, coordinating military actions, purging the army and the bureaucracy of Fascists and incompetents. As his ministers had hoped, responsibility was transforming their revolutionary leader into a pragmatist.

Since the people were happier and more confident than ever, why shatter their illusions? So the government tightened its censorship of all news from the front, hiding the truth from the *Madrileños* while it waited for a miracle. After all, Soviet arms were on the way and could change everything—if they arrived before the rebels did.

To help shield the people from reality, "information specialists" were snatched into service. One of them was Arturo Barea, who had been looking for a way to further aid the republic. Since he knew French well and at least read English he suddenly found himself a Foreign Ministry press officer, censoring the reports of foreign correspondents. He had to be at the Telefónica from midnight to 8:00 A.M., but he rather liked the hours, for he had an excuse not to be with his wife at night, and not to be with his mistress in the afternoon, when he slept.

But psychologically his job was disturbing. He was ordered to cut out anything that did not indicate the Loyalists were winning, and the correspondents coming from the front tried by every means to get the facts through, using slang, obscure language, and insinuations. Barea was thus constantly scanning the dictionary for double meanings and blue-penciling line after line. The reporters were furious, and so was Barea—not only at them for their glib assurance that Madrid would soon fall but at himself for simply wiping out a dreaded reality with a stroke of the pencil. He was faced night after night with the terrible truth, however cleverly disguised. And the truth was difficult to live with.

Besides, militiamen were drifting into town embittered and self-pitying, and the facts were gradually leaking out anyway. All somebody had to do was to count the civilian dead in the city morgue. The number always grew with danger, and it was now growing daily . . .

As Janet Riesenfeld was about to descend into the Diego de León subway station with her friend Villatora, she glanced up at an enormous red-brick building next to it and asked him what it was.

"It used to be one of the largest Jesuit schools in Madrid," the militiaman replied. "Now it's . . . a prison."

"There's something else. I hear a great many shots around here at night," Janet pursued. "Sometimes it wakes me up about five in the morning. It sounds like a volley from a firing squad, and then there's a pause, and directly afterwards one sharp shot."

"It *is* a firing squad," Villatora replied casually, "and that one shot is the *coup de grace*. What you hear probably comes from this very prison."

They silently went into the subway station and waited for a train. Villatora was taking Janet to visit wounded Loyalist soldiers in a hospital.

She could still hear the young girl in her building screaming: "They're taking him! They're taking him!"

They had come for her father, a minor post office official whom somebody denounced, and he never came back. Perhaps they had taken him to that red-brick building.

When Janet and Villatora sat down in the subway car, she asked: "Have you ever witnessed an execution?"

"Many," he answered coldly. "I have no pity, no emotion as far as these people are concerned. You see, in each prisoner I don't see a man but an agent of a fierce, destructive force. In each one that falls I see the saving of not one but many hundreds of our people."

At one subway stop a middle-aged woman and two young boys entered and sat down opposite them. They were shabbily dressed and carried old suitcases. As they rose to get off a few stations farther on, Villatora suddenly pulled at Janet's arm and they followed. Then Villatora rushed after the woman and the boys and led them into a small control room on the platform. After several minutes, he emerged alone.

"What's happened?" Janet asked.

"The bags that those three were carrying," he replied, "are full of munitions . . . The labels caught my eye. They came from the most expensive hotels of Seville, San Sebastian, and Nice. The poverty of their dress didn't go with these signs of wealth."

"What are you going to do with them?"

"The militia will take care of them."

Yes, the woman and the boys were the enemy. They were carrying guns to kill people like her friend Villatora. But she preferred not to think about it. That evening she would be seeing Jaime and she hoped there wouldn't be another argument. She wanted to sleep well—right through the shooting at five in the morning.

Father Florinda de Miguel no longer had to worry about where to hide during the day. After militiamen had shut down the National Library, charging it was a meeting place for Fascists, he spent almost all his time secretly taking confessions. One day a nun asked him if he would take that of a dying old woman. There was, however, a problem. The woman had two red sons who lived with her! The mother, explained the nun, had shocked them when she asked for a priest.

"Mother, you're delirious," one replied. "Don't think about such things. You're not as sick as you imagine. You'll see. I'll call the doctor."

"Don't call anybody!" the mother replied. "I don't need a doctor for my body. I need a doctor for my soul."

Day after day, mother and sons argued over the needs of her soul. The lives of the sons might even be endangered if they agreed. "Treason" was a loosely used word in those days. Finally, the mother said: "I'm going to die. I don't mind dying, but I do mind dying like a dog. Children, you are leaving me to die like a dog."

The sons could no longer refuse. They contacted the nun, who knew their mother, and she sent Father Miguel to see the dying woman. She wept with happiness as she confessed to him and he gave her communion. Then, while he administered extreme unction, the sons entered, rather sheepishly. As the priest was about to leave, they shook his hand.

"Thank you, father," they said. "Thank you very much."

Then, one of them asked: "Tell me, father, aren't you afraid of doing this? It's very dangerous!"

"What can I tell you?" Miguel replied. "Yes and no . . . It's hard to explain. But don't you think that the happiness I brought your mother—and you, too—is worth exposing oneself to danger? And don't think this is an unusual case. As a matter of fact, I hardly do anything else.''

Miguel smiled, and the youths did, too.

José Luis Sáenz de Heredia, José Antonio's cousin, did not feel safe even after a *cheka* had set him free. He stayed on at his film studio under the protective wing of his employees, but his name was too well known. Other militiamen, he was sure, would come for him, and this time they might kill him without a trial. He must escape to the rebel side.

So Sáenz went to the Cuban consulate with two Cuban friends who agreed to swear that he was a citizen of Cuba, and he asked to be "repatriated." He was given a passport and on September 23 boarded a train for Alicante with about twenty genuine Cubans, as well as his brother, Rafael, and several other Falangists who had also managed to scrounge passports. At Alicante the group was to board a British warship that was evacuating foreigners from Spain.

Shortly before the train pulled out, three militiamen entered the cabin where Sáenz and the other Falangists were sitting.

"Which of you is the cousin of the Fascist José Antonio?" one of them asked, waving a pistol.

Sáenz tried to remain calm. Had someone recognized him? When all the suspects insisted they were Cubans, the militiaman shouted: "We know that one of you is his cousin. Someone here is named Sáenz de Heredia."

The militiamen carefully checked the passports, all of them with false names. In frustration, they picked a passenger at random and accused him of being their man, but he pointed to the name embroidered on his shirt and the initials engraved on his ring to show that he was not.

"Well, one of you is a liar," snapped the *responsable*, "and I'm going to bring someone who can identify which one of you is Sáenz de Heredia."

And the militiamen left, stationing a guard at the cabin door. The train would depart in ten minutes. Sáenz stared at his watch like a man counting the ticks of a time bomb. Finally the guard disappeared and the train chugged forward.

However, Sáenz's ordeal was not over yet. Often the militiamen sent word ahead to the next station to check on passengers, a railroad attendant told him. The train shortly jerked to a halt and people got on and off . . . but no militiamen.

Alicante at last. A British naval officer and some sailors were at the station to meet the Cubans and take them to a hotel. The group slept there that night and the next morning lined up in a warehouse at the port, where several militiamen questioned each person. Only then was one permitted to go to the wharf, where a motorboat was waiting to take the passengers to the warship.

It was Sáenz's turn for questioning.

"Do you know Cuba?" a militiaman asked him.

"No."

"Strange, you're a Cuban."

"I was born in Cuba but I came to Spain when I was very small."

Sáenz had calculated that if he replied yes they might ask him questions about Cuba he could not answer.

"Have you ever been arrested?"

"Me? Never!"

The interrogator replied: "Don't get upset. It's not necessarily a bad thing to have been in prison. I was there for five years. It can be an honor."

"Yes, but one that I never had."

Sáenz was finally told to pass to the wharf. Safe at last! But then came his brother's turn. On the wharf Sáenz could hear him.

Yes, Rafael said, he had been arrested.

He had heard what the militiaman had told his brother and so assumed he gave the right answer. But they would not let him pass and ordered him to stand aside.

"Why?" Rafael asked.

"Do you see this empty magazine cartridge?" a militiaman replied. "Last night I emptied it into somebody's guts on the wharf. So you'd better shut up!"

Rafael sidled to a grilled window and whispered to his brother outside: "They're going to kill me."

And he removed his ring and gave it to José for their mother.

Meanwhile, all the passengers had boarded the boat except Sáenz and his brother.

"Hurry!" the British officer by the boat called out. "We can't wait any longer."

"Wait! Wait!" Sáenz pleaded. "Maybe they'll still let him go!"

The militiamen called Rafael for further questioning.

"Why were you arrested?"

"Because I struck someone who was bothering my girl friend."

They stared at him, as if trying to read his mind.

"All right, you may pass," said the *responsable*.

José, listening at the window, was elated.

"But first leave a contribution for our cause."

"I don't have any money," said Rafael.

A militiaman searched him and found some coins.

"What's this?"

"Someone must have slipped them into my pocket. But you're welcome to them."

Should they let him go? The militiamen now argued, while the British officer called to José that unless he came instantly the boat would leave without him. And he started up the engine.

Seconds later, Sáenz and his brother leaped aboard, and the motorboat zoomed through the waves.

A great ending, thought the film director.

4

While the disaster at Talavera stirred the vengeful Loyalist firing squads to seek more victims in Madrid, it stirred the Loyalist leaders to seek a safer place for the gold stored in the capital. Spain's $700 million gold reserve, the world's fourth largest, was hidden a hundred feet underground in the Bank of Spain. The vaults holding the bullion had virtually impregnable steel doors, accessible only from stairways leading into concrete wells, which could be flooded in an emergency.

But what if the rebels captured Madrid? They would have the whole glittering treasure anyway, and the government would have nothing to go arms shopping with. Loyalist leaders had already promised to pay Russia in gold for the war matériel it was now shipping to them. Somehow, the gold must be saved, even if Madrid couldn't be.

As the government anxiously pondered this question, so did the anarchists. The Communists, they felt, had grown too influential, and that was one reason the government had already cheated the anarchists out of their rightful share of weapons. And when Soviet arms arrived, they would probably get none at all. Yet even the few arms they did have could not all be used at the front. Some had to be cached away for the inevitable clash with the Communists when this civil war was over, or perhaps even before. For certainly the Communists were planning to wipe them out, just as the Bolsheviks, when they took power, had annihilated the Russian anarchists.

How could they get enough arms to fight the Fascists now and the Communists later? Buenaventura Durruti, Spain's top anarchist leader, felt his movement's survival depended on the answer. His men couldn't fail now, not after winning more power than any anarchist movement in history. They had become the virtual masters of Catalonia when they crushed the rightist forces in Barcelona in the first days of the war. And they followed up with victory after victory as they thrust westward into the region of Aragon toward Saragossa, though they were now bogged down almost at its gates because they didn't have enough arms and ammunition.

At the same time, Durruti carried the revolution with him, collectivizing every village and industry he plucked along the way—to the rage of the Communists. Had not Moscow instructed them to make sure the republic won the confidence of the bourgeoisie both at home and abroad? Besides, the anarchists were preempting the party's plan for a postwar upheaval of its own.

But the Communists needn't have fretted so. For like Durruti's war, his revolution was also now in trouble. The economies of the collectivized areas were crumbling since there was no expertise, raw materials, or money to pay the workers and the peasants. And the situation grew worse when some villages tore up their money and began a barter system in a disastrous economic experiment.

It seemed clear: In order to fight the war and push the revolution, the anarchists needed gold.

At the beginning of September, an anarchist delegate, Diego Abado de Santillán, went on a mission to Madrid.

Could Catalonia have sizable credits for building up "war industries"? he asked Prime Minister Giral.

No, replied Giral, the government didn't have the money.

Actually, Giral had no desire to nurture anarchist revolution. Nor the separatist ambitions of Catalan leaders, who had practically declared their region's independence.

Well, then, Santillán slyly suggested, wouldn't it be a good idea to transfer the gold reserve to Catalonia? The gold would be much safer there than in Madrid.

The meeting ended abruptly.

But Durruti's dream of gold did not. And he knew how to handle the politicians.

"There is only one way to deal with them," he told Santillán and García Oliver, the second most important anarchist. "The way we've always used. It is for the people to decide on how to use the gold."

Durruti then made a proposal. Why not simply steal the gold in the Bank of Spain? His comrades were aghast. Just walk in and leave with $700 million worth of gold? The idea was fantastic! Yet Durruti spoke as if he were suggesting an ordinary holdup of the kind he had staged so often to finance the anarchist movement.

Durruti was born forty years earlier into an impoverished family in León. His uncle founded the first workers' movement there and led a long strike that authorities finally crushed, turning Buenaventura into a bitter unyielding rebel before he was twelve. After a few years of elementary schooling, he worked as a metallurgist and joined the anarchists because they demanded instant revolution. His two brothers, Manuel as well as Pedro, also leaned toward the extreme—but the opposite extreme. While Loyalists were to kill Pedro in the Model Prison massacre, fellow Falangists would kill Manuel for failing a test of loyalty. Possibly he refused to betray his anarchist brother.

With his dynamism and electric personality, Buenaventura soon emerged as vice-president of an anarchist union in San Sebastian. Then, as a kind of proletarian Robin Hood, he launched a campaign of robbery and violence to fund and foment the revolution, hatching many of his plots during his frequent sojourns in jail.

In 1923, he and his men broke into a bank, barely escaping with the loot after a shoot-out with Civil Guards. Even after he was arrested and imprisoned, he was suspected of helping to plan the murder of the archbishop of Saragossa, who was shot by anarchist comrades that year because he symbolized "reactionary" thinking. The following year, Durruti failed in an attempt to kill King Alfonso XIII, the most important rightist symbol of all, while the monarch was visiting Paris. He spent the next few years roaming Latin America, where he became known as the "Gorilla" after a spree of terror in four countries. He robbed banks, subway stations, bus drivers, and a hospital, and allegedly killed a policeman.

Durruti returned home when the republic was born in 1931, and was welcomed as a hero by his comrades. He began using his large accumulated "earnings" to ready his movement for revolution, keeping not a peseta for himself. Practically all he owned was the pistol he carried and the clothes he wore; he was seldom seen without the same worn leather jacket and peaked leather cap. Like his ardent follower Cipriano Mera, he was a dreamer. But he would kill more easily than his disciple, for he was even more impatient, and saw little distinction between dream and reality. One merely blended into the other.

It was this simple naïveté that appealed to all who met him—except, of course, bank guards on duty at the wrong time. And his rugged appearance enhanced the magnetic image. He was tall with a powerful, hairy body, curly black hair, penetrating dark eyes, a swarthy complexion, and an intimate good-humored smile that could disarm his worst enemy. If his fellow anarchists worshiped him, most other Spaniards esteemed him, seeing in him an undiluted mix of *machismo* and idealism—though some were a bit disillusioned when they visited his modest home and found him peeling potatoes or helping his wife with the housework. And if he spilled a little blood occasionally, well, he did it for what he considered a worthy cause, however utopian. Indeed, some people thought him "oversentimental" for refusing to let his men kill prisoners or to engage in *paseo* murders.

And no one doubted his courage. Since the war began, he had lost many men because he stubbornly insisted on self-discipline rather than the barracks-room discipline that violated his anarchist scruples. But he had lost no battles, though he had to halt before Saragossa. His men would follow him anywhere. And those who wouldn't were stripped of their weapons, as well as their clothes—which "belonged to the people"—and sent back home in their underwear.

But most of his men remained fully clothed; for they believed his prophecy that military victory would mean an anarchist society. When one journalist suggested to him that even if the anarchists came out on top they would simply inherit a pile of ruins, Durruti replied:

"We have lived in miserable shacks, in caves. We will know how to adjust for a while to a situation familiar to us. But don't forget that we also know how to build . . . So why doubt our ability to rebuild a new world? . . . We know that we will inherit only ruins. The bourgeoisie in its last hour can leave us nothing but ruins, but a new world will open before us. Here in our hearts, at this minute, this world is being born.''

So impatient was Durruti that he was constantly ordering attacks whether militarily wise or not. When the Russian writer Ilya Ehrenberg visited him, he could hardly believe why the anarchist was about to launch one of his assaults.

''It's not a question of strategy,'' Durruti admitted. ''Yesterday, a child of twelve who escaped from Fascist territory asked us: 'Why don't you attack? In my village, everybody is surprised. Is Durruti also afraid?' Do you understand? When a child asks such a question, it's all the people who are asking it. So we must attack. The strategy is secondary.''

Ehrenberg stared at Durruti and thought: *You also are a child.*

Now Durruti was grinning innocently and suggesting that he and his comrades grab the blocks he wanted to play with—blocks of gold!

And he was so persuasive that his two comrades, Oliver and Santillán, agreed. Durruti had always accomplished the impossible, and if he said the impossible was possible that was good enough for them. Durruti immediately drew up a plan. A freight train secretly carrying a thousand trusted men would leave Barcelona for Madrid, with the agreement of CNT railway officials. On arrival, the men on the train, joined by three thousand members of an anarchist column fighting in Madrid, would storm the Bank of Spain and haul the gold to the freight cars, which would speed back to Barcelona. No one but the three plotters were to know about the plan until it was under way—not even fellow members of the CNT national committee.

In mid-September, Durruti, wishing to remain anonymous in Madrid, flew there in one of André Malraux's planes together with the Frenchman, who had no idea what his passenger was up to. Durruti met Santillán in the capital and was delighted to hear that all arrangements had been made. Now he would learn about the bank vault layout and alarm system.

And on the night of October 1, he would make the most monumental heist in history. If Franco—or the Communists—didn't upset his plans.

Major Hidalgo de Cisneros had unofficially headed the republican air force almost since the start of the war, but under the Caballero government his headache became official. He had always been close to the new minister of the navy and air force, Indalecio Prieto, and Prieto lost no time in making the appointment. Cisneros's headache soon grew worse as Franco's German and Italian planes swept the skies over the road to Madrid almost without challenge.

Even Urtubi, the brave pilot who had killed his Falangist guard and flown to the Loyalist side, was no longer around. He had several narrow escapes. Once he parachuted from his burning plane behind rebel lines, but stole some peasant clothes and a donkey and bluffed his way back into the Loyalist zone carrying a load of straw. Though Cisneros was joyous, he was so short of pilots that he sent him up in another plane that same day, only to have him parachute out once more, this time, fortunately, over Loyalist territory.

Finally Urtubi's luck ran out. While on a reconnaissance mission, he was attacked by a squadron of Fiats and when he had shot down one and run out of ammunition, he deliberately rammed another. Both planes fell, but only the Italian pilot survived—to tell of his adversary's heroic deed.

And André Malraux's international squadron, which was still getting all the headlines abroad, only made Cisneros's head throb more. The Russian technicians agreed that the squadron was useless, in fact, dangerous because it was full of reactionary Trotskyites. When the Russians asked the Palestinian Jewish flyer, Yehezkel Piekar, to reveal the names of squadron members, Malraux ordered Piekar to refuse. Had he come to help Spain win its freedom only to have some of his men assassinated for their political beliefs?

There were also the anarchists. They kept trying to take over Cisneros's air force by undermining discipline and spreading distrust of the professional officers. They were nothing more than a "type of fifth column," Cisneros later wrote.

He had complained to Prieto, but the minister was helpless. Caballero, Prieto said, would not antagonize any of his forces, and that was that. Only the Communists tried to help the air force chief. It was terrible, they agreed, that the ministry would do nothing to relieve his headache. They understood his problems. They were also the best airmen and the most efficient administrators. And they showed the most spirit. If all Loyalists were like the Communists, Cisneros was sure, Madrid would not be in danger and the government would win a quick victory. Who cared about the intricacies of ideology at this critical moment? All that mattered was winning the war.

And so, one evening at dinner with Prieto, Cisneros casually sprang the news: He had joined the Communist party! Prieto turned pale and "looked as if he were suffering a stroke," according to Cisneros. Without saying a word, the minister lifted his ponderous body from his chair and waddled out of the room. Cisneros was upset. So what if he had become a Communist? He only wanted to be part of a superior fighting machine that could best defend Madrid and the nation—like thousands of other Spaniards, including most of his own fliers, who would never have dreamed of joining the party in normal times. Besides, weren't the Communists calling for democracy? Every day, every minute, they were demanding it. Prieto was simply prejudiced.

Cisneros was afraid his wife, Constancia, would be shocked, too. She stood solidly with the people, the great oppressed masses, but she did come from an elite family. Psychologically, his final leap and all that it implied might be too much for her. So he would not tell her, for a while anyway.

Constancia, meanwhile, had also joined the party, and essentially for the same reason: the Communists were more dedicated, more determined than others. But she, too, kept this a secret as long as she could. Her husband, after all, was an aristocrat and might not understand. Even though the fate of Madrid was in the balance.

Enrique Castro Delgado was driving to the Ministry of Agriculture, but couldn't imagine why he had been summoned there. The minister, Vicente Uribe, was one of the two Communists in the Caballero cabinet, but he had little to do with the Fifth Regiment. Things were not going well, and Castro was in a surly mood. As he had feared, General Asensio failed to recover Talavera, and his own Fifth Regiment was in trouble. Communist party publicity had given his fighters an inflated image: They were all supermen, invincible. True, they were better soldiers than most militiamen. Yet they, too, had run at Talavera.

The publicity had worked wonders. New members were flocking to the party and its power was growing in the government, but if the Fifth Regiment could not hold Madrid, all the political gains might be lost overnight. For the party's deceit would be clear.

Shortly, Castro was facing Uribe in the minister's large office. Uribe had a sullen look, and Castro felt uneasy. After staring at the ceiling for a moment, the minister turned to his guest and said: "The Political Bureau [of the party] has appointed you director of agrarian reform. This morning your appointment was published in the *Official Gazette.*"

"No!" Castro exclaimed.

"Yes, Castro."

"Is that a punishment?"

"It's a promotion."

"And the Fifth Regiment?"

"It's on the move. It can get along without you. But now we need to win over the peasants . . . and the Political Bureau thought of you."

Castro felt like crying. He thought to himself: *You've won, Dolores. You've won. Now the Fifth Regiment will be your toy.*

No matter. He would win, too. He would turn the peasants into Communists— or kill every one of them.

But what would happen to Madrid? Without him, the city might be finished, and Spain afterward. And then all the peasants would be lost to the party anyway.

5

After General Asensio had failed to recapture Talavera in early September, General Yagüe decided to let his exhausted men rest while he reorganized his forces for the final drive on Madrid. However, he did the Loyalists a much greater favor than he did his own troops. For if the rebels had kept hammering, the panicky militiamen might have run all the way to Madrid or beyond. But Yagüe had also given *them* a chance to rest and reorganize. And so when he resumed his attack, he was surprised to find that with their backs to Madrid, their homes, and their families, they had regained their fighting mood. They had built trenches and now they stayed in them. The telescoped battlefield experience of the past few weeks was finally making soldiers out of militiamen.

Thus, instead of racing over an open road to Madrid, Yagüe's men stumbled from trench to trench at the rate of only about three miles a day. Finally, on September 21, they marched into the townlet of Maqueda. And there the rebel leaders were faced with one of the most critical dilemmas of the war. Maqueda was a crossroads: One road led straight to Madrid, the other to Toledo, south of Madrid. Which road should they take?

Madrid! Yagüe insisted. He would not repeat the mistake he made by halting at Talavera. Give the Loyalists no rest. The rebels must not gamble now, with the big prize—and his own glorious place in history—all but won. Franco, however, was skeptical. Madrid would fall regardless. He agreed with the German diplomat in Madrid, Hans Voelckers, who had reported to Berlin that the capital could not withstand a siege. It had no foodstocks, antiaircraft artillery, or line of defense, even trenches, while the militiamen were poorly armed, poorly led, and inexperienced. Madrid was there to take!

Franco was furious with Yagüe for damaging the rebel image by taking so long to march from Talavera to Maqueda. And now his own personal image was at stake. The whole world was waiting to see if he would answer the cries for help from the rebel force trapped in Toledo's Alcázar since July. Led by Colonel José Moscardó, commandant of the Toledo Military Academy, about thirteen hundred soldiers, Civil Guards, and Falangists had been holding off hordes of militiamen who had been relentlessly attacking this ancient fortress. And adding to the drama, seven hundred women and children, including a hundred hostages from Loyalist families, were huddled in its dank cellars.

Living mainly on the meat of horses and mules they slaughtered, the rebels had made headlines around the world for their stubborn stand. Especially after a reported telephone conversation in late July between Moscardó and his twenty-four-year-old son, who had been captured elsewhere.

"What is happening, my boy?"

"Nothing. They say they will shoot me if the Alcázar does not surrender."

"If it is true, command your soul to God, shout *Viva España*, and die like a hero. Good-bye, my son, a last kiss."

"Good-bye father, a very big kiss."

Although the Loyalists had warned the colonel they would shoot his son within ten minutes if the Alcázar did not surrender, they did not do so, though the youth was executed with others sometime later in reprisal for an air raid.

Moscardó had become a symbol of rebel courage and rectitude as he continued to defy the Loyalist besiegers, who didn't have the artillery, air support, or professional officers needed to smash through the thick walls.

Major Vicente Rojo, who would later play a vital role in the defense of Madrid, had walked into the Alcázar blindfolded during a truce and pleaded with Moscardó to change his mind, but the colonel refused, simply asking that a priest be sent to "satisfy the spiritual needs" of the defenders. The next day, a Loyalist priest came and urged Moscardó to evacuate the women and children at least. The answer was still "No!"

Now, with Maqueda captured, the Loyalists were desperately trying to take the Alcázar before Franco could relieve it—if he chose to. Caballero himself visited the scene, demanding that the fortress be seized within twenty-four hours. So more bombs were thrown, more guns fired, but the only result was a premature birth inside the fortress. Still, victory seemed closer for the frenzied Loyalists as rebel ammunition ran low and hardly more than one horse remained for food.

On the day Maqueda fell, Franco met with Mola and other colleagues in Salamanca to make two historic choices: the man to lead the whole rebel army, and the road to take from Maqueda.

Who would be the generalissimo—Mola or Franco? Mola had organized the revolt, while Franco had come in only at the last minute. But Mola was realistic. He knew that Franco was more popular with the troops because of his reckless bravery, and was better known abroad because of his drive on Madrid. And he wasn't as ambitious as Franco. Let him run the army. After the war, it could be decided who would run the country. And so, in a spirit of magnanimity, Mola himself suggested that Franco be the generalissimo. Everyone agreed, and Franco humbly accepted. His plan had worked out perfectly. He had assumed almost none of the risk, yet would have all the power.

He now decided to take the road to Toledo, though he would send a small force directly toward Madrid.

The rebel air force chief, General Alfredo Kindelán, says he asked him: "Do you know, my general, that Toledo may cost you Madrid?"

"Yes, I know," Franco replied. "I've thought a lot about the consequences of my decision. What would you do?"

"I would go to Toledo even though by doing so I might jeopardize our chances of taking Madrid."

"That's what I've decided," said Franco. "Because spiritual factors weigh heavily in all wars and especially in civil wars. For this reason, we must impress the enemy with the fact that whatever we attempt, we can carry out without their being able to stop us. . . . I hope a week's delay on the march on Madrid won't produce the consequences you foresee. But even if it did, I wouldn't give up the chance to take Toledo and free the heroic defenders of the Alcázar."

And besides, why be satisfied with the modest role of generalissimo? Now was the moment of destiny. As the savior of the Alcázar he would be the *caudillo*, the chief. He would then enter Madrid with the power of a king.

The decision was thus made—even as the Loyalist forces, after losing Maqueda, were fleeing once more along the road to the capital.

A great ear-splitting blast shook the Alcázar on the morning of September 17—more than a dozen tons of exploding dynamite. But as the swirl of smoke and dirt dissolved into cobwebs of dust, the red and gold royal flag was still there fluttering atop the ruins.

Toward dusk, there were new explosions, but this time the shells landed in the Loyalists' lap! Franco's men had arrived. A group of militiamen rushed to the headquarters of their commander, Lieutenant Colonel Burillo. What was happening? they shouted.

"What do you mean?" Burillo calmly asked.

"Perhaps you don't hear? Fascist artillery is shelling us."

"Of course. So what? We'll defend ourselves."

"Oh, no we won't. We're not willing to be cannon fodder. Apparently the government doesn't want to help us. Unless you can put an end to the Fascist shelling in fifteen minutes, we're leaving the town. Find yourself other fools."

The militiamen were as good as their word. In about fifteen minutes they were dashing toward Madrid, littering the roads with their weapons and equipment so they could move faster. The great stampede had begun. Men, women, and children, some with their meager belongings piled on donkeys, ran through the narrow streets into the open country behind the militia. They stopped to catch their breath only when they reached the hilltops overlooking Toledo, while peasants, still hardly aware there was a world beyond their village, calmly worked in the fields and threshed their wheat. By the morning of September 28, practically the only Loyalists left in Toledo were the scores of wounded in San Juan Hospital who could not be moved.

The attacking Moors and legionnaires, now under the command of Colonel José Varela, who had replaced Yagüe, first raced for the Alcázar and freed Colonel Moscardó and his rebel companions, though apparently no hostage came out alive. They then stormed into the hospital and either bayoneted the wounded or blew them up with grenades as they lay helplessly in their beds. And when Father Muiño, custodian of the treasures in the Toledo Cathedral, begged the invading troops on his knees to have mercy on the patients, the killers reportedly cut off his arms and murdered him, too.

Franco rushed to the scene of liberation and smiled as cameras clicked while he hugged the thin, pale, bearded figure of Colonel Moscardó. Was this moment not worth a delayed conquest of Madrid? Was it not a good thing to let the world see that he placed human values above military strategy? He was looking ahead, far ahead.

Meanwhile, the militiamen staggering northward along the dusty Toledo road were looking ahead only to the embrace of Madrid, where they could lose themselves in the multitude, remember their principles, and forget their shame.

Three days after the fall of Toledo, on September 30, the Loyalists had their own "Alcázar"—the magnificent cathedral of Sigüenza. About sixty miles northeast of Madrid, Sigüenza was the town that Hippolyte Etchebéhère and his Trotskyite-leaning POUM followers had helped to capture in late July shortly before he was killed. Hippo's wife, Mika, had then taken command of the group and it bitterly fought off rebel attacks on this town for almost two months.

Colonel García Escámez's troops kept trying again and again to smash into Madrid via Sigüenza from the north at the same time Varela's troops were rolling in from the south, but the colonel found Mika and her comrades as tough a barrier as they had been when Hippo was alive.

By September 30, the Sigüenza Cathedral was teeming with militiamen, together with many wives and children of local Popular Front officials; they refused to surrender despite near starvation and constant shelling and bombing. Meanwhile, Mika and her small band of POUM fighters were battling the enemy in Sigüenza's streets and from their fortresslike headquarters building—until October 8. On that day, a massive enemy air attack shattered the building, killing and wounding many of Mika's fighters.

"To the street! It's finished! We're leaving!" Mika cried as the walls began to cave in.

The survivors, carrying the lightly wounded but forced to leave behind the more serious cases, stumbled over the rubble to the cathedral where they joined more than seven hundred desperate people. They found themselves trapped in the debris of a gold and marble prison amid saintly statues—many dismembered, some still erect—staring at the human wreckage with eyes of cold compassion. A mother with an infant in her arms accosted Mika and begged her to find milk for the child. The militiamen had taken all there was for themselves, she cried, and Mika must make them give some to her.

"Why me?"

"Because you are a leader. You command. Have pity!"

Pity? Could a commander who sent people to their death have pity? Besides, the wounded had more right to the milk than the baby did.

Mika went to see a young injured comrade, Chata, who lay in a room with other casualties. Her leg was badly mangled and infected and only immediate amputation could save her, but there was no doctor, no medicine, not even aspirin.

"I have two things to ask of you," Chata groaned, "one for you, one for me. Get away, save yourself, and if you escape, return to your country and ask for aid." Then the girl pulled Mika close to her and whispered with fevered lips:

"As for me, before leaving ask someone to kill me. I don't want the Fascists to kick me to death."

"Don't be romantic," Mika replied. "You are not dying, and the Fascists have not yet taken the cathedral. Reinforcements will come to liberate us at any moment."

Mika's assurance cloaked her pessimism and sense of guilt. She could have ordered a retreat before the enemy surrounded Sigüenza. But then there had been hope. Madrid had sent word that it was rushing two thousand fighters to the town, that the defenders must hold until they arrived or the whole northern front would be demoralized and collapse, and this would mean certain death for Madrid. So Mika had held, until finally forced to take shelter in the cathedral.

Reinforcements? It was evident now that there weren't even enough men to hold the line south of Madrid. Who cared about Sigüenza at this critical time? So what was the purpose of staying? Honor, said some of her comrades. Wasn't that why the enemy refused to give up the Alcázar? Should not the Loyalists show the same spirit? But the Alcázar defenders, said others, had reason to hope until the end that they would be liberated, while Loyalists holding out in the cathedral would be committing suicide. But Mika decided to stay, even as shells crashed through the ancient walls of the cathedral, blinding her with the dust of hallowed masonry. Many others, mainly the anarchists, tried to escape in the dark through the enemy lines, while some who remained were killed.

After several days the shelling suddenly stopped and a cry broke the silence: "Don't fire! Don't fire!"

A man waving a white flag ran toward the front door of the cathedral. He had been a prisoner of García Escámez's, and the rebel commander was sending him here with a message.

"They've killed our wounded in the hospital," the man gasped. "When their officers went away, there was no one left alive, and it wasn't Moors but Spaniards. When my nephew was wounded by a bomb this morning I carried him to the hospital on my back, and now he is dead like the others."

"Quick, tell us your message!" a militia leader interrupted.

"They demand the surrender of the cathedral tomorrow morning before nine o'clock. The men must leave without weapons and with their arms raised. If you accept these conditions your lives will be spared, the commander said."

The man stared at Mika.

"Aren't you the woman who commanded in the POUM house? . . . Don't give yourself up—they're looking for you everywhere. They're asking everybody about you."

"What do they know about me?"

"Many things. They found . . . a pile of papers that you wrote on our war. . . . If you fall into their hands you will suffer a horrible death."

Mika suddenly realized that when she had fled POUM headquarters she left her battle diary under the mattress of her bed.

The militiamen told the messenger that they wanted the surrender terms in writing, hoping to gain time this way. Mika, feeling she must now try to escape, met with her group. Some would go with her. Some would fight to the end; maybe, by some miracle, reinforcements would rescue them after all. Those who made it to freedom would plead with Madrid to rush aid to them. Mika looked at Hippo's watch, which she always carried with her, but she did not see the time. She saw only him. If he were alive, he would have saved Sigüenza. He would have formed an iron army that would have won the battle. How could she have presumed to replace him? Would he be running now, even from certain death? Before leaving, Mika went to visit Chata once more, and the girl gave her an envelope to deliver to her mother in Madrid. Inside was a photo taken at her communion.

"You are a believer, Chata?"

"I don't believe in the priests, but the Virgin is another thing. Tell my mother. . . . Invent something so that she will have hope of seeing me again."

In the darkness, Mika and several comrades climbed a rear wall in the courtyard of the cathedral and under heavy machine-gun fire crept through the enemy lines. What would happen to Chata, to the rest of the wounded, to the civilians— the women and children? To her own fighters, who had learned from Hippo that suicide was more honorable than flight?

Except for one youth, Mika and her group reached safety. Those left behind would die.

6

Despite the rout at the Alcázar the Loyalist leaders felt enormous relief when Franco chose to attack Toledo before Madrid, for if he had not, the Moors and legionnaires might now be raging through the streets of the capital instead. The Loyalists in Madrid had an extra week or more to prepare for the final showdown. Not every man, however, used the borrowed time profitably.

Agapito García Atadell, the commander of the Atadell Brigade, decided that he had killed enough rich spies and traitors in his garish but fashionable slaughterhouse. His bag of booty was already bursting. He had better get out of Madrid before Franco got in or he'd never have the chance to live like his victims had before they died. So, loaded down with his loot, he quietly left for the seaport of Alicante and sailed to France, where he boarded a ship headed for Cuba.

A new world suddenly opened to him. Aboard the ship he was a figure of grandeur—buying drinks for all the passengers, leaving the waiters huge tips, throwing lavish parties—until the vessel unexpectedly stopped over in the rebel-controlled Canary Islands. Customs officials detained him by chance and finally realized who he was. In prison, García Atadell apparently did, too. He underwent a mystical religious conversion.

"I am no longer a socialist," he wrote his friend Indalecio Prieto. "I will die a Catholic."

And so he did. Just before he was garroted to death he cried: "Long Live Christ the King!"

If García Atadell had lived he might have become a priest—and spelled out the words with light bulbs.

With Toledo lost, another Loyalist also thought about smuggling valuables out of Madrid—not a bagful of jewels but a bankful of gold. The thought of the Fascists or the Communists getting their hands on the gold in the Bank of Spain gave Buenaventura Durruti nightmares. But Durruti was now ready to carry out the sensational heist he had meticulously planned. And even if Franco eventually captured Madrid, the anarchists, with so much gold to buy arms, could hold out indefinitely in Catalonia and eventually retake the capital and all Spain.

Just hours before Durruti was to give the signal, however, his colleague Santillán suddenly had doubts. Without telling Durruti, who he knew would bitterly object, he leaked the plot to other CNT national committee members. They were horrified. Steal the national gold reserve? That would surely mean civil war between Catalonia and the rest of Loyalist Spain—in the middle of the civil war they were already fighting. They demanded that the robbery be canceled.

Durruti was furious, and he cursed Santillán as a coward and a traitor, but he could not brazenly defy the order. The gold would have assured the victory of anarchist revolution. Now the last chance may have slipped by, for with Soviet arms the Communists, so weak at the start of the war, would have all the power, and they would use it to destroy the anarchists if they could. What Durruti did not know then was that even if his men had managed to reach the vaults they would have found no gold.

The Communists had beaten them to it! . . .

"You have an important mission to fulfill, comrade," said José Díaz, secretary-general of the Communist party.

El Campesino, the barbaric Communist commander, smiled through his black beard, realizing that the mission must be important for Díaz to come personally all the way to the Guadarrama front to see him. He was pleased that the party recognized his exceptional merit as a commander.

"I am ready to carry out whatever the party orders me to do," *El Campesino* replied.

"You will be responsible," Díaz went on, "for transporting the gold in the Bank of Spain from Madrid to Cartagena. You will oversee the operation of removing the gold from the bank and take charge of whatever else must be done."

The militia leader was surprised, he later said. He had apparently been expecting a combat assignment.

"Will I have to use arms?" he asked.

"No, we've prepared the operation well. Everyone involved in it is a follower."

Later that day, September 14, *El Campesino* and his men were standing in the basement of the Bank of Spain opening the gigantic vaults. They saw an awesome sight: 7800 cases of glittering treasure neatly stacked up. Enough gold coins and bars to buy all the planes, tanks, cannons, and rifles they needed, with enough left over to finance a revolution when the war ended—unless Russia had other plans.

While his men lugged the cases to the street and piled them into thirty-five trucks, *El Campesino* checked off an inventory list. The removal, he would say later, "was done in an atmosphere of the deepest mystery and it had all the characteristics of a robbery."

When the trucks were loaded, they raced off and stopped some blocks away, where red flags were placed on them to indicate "explosives" and new drivers took over, thinking they were transporting volatile chemicals. At South Station the gold was reloaded on freight cars and a few hours later arrived in Cartagena, the bustling naval base in southeastern Spain where most of the republican fleet was anchored and could stand sentinel. Trucks then carried the gold to a cave nearby and guards remained on duty around the clock, not dreaming that the wealth of centuries had been placed in their custody.

This remarkable "robbery," unlike the one Durruti had planned, had the government as its accomplice, at least Prime Minister Largo Caballero and Finance Minister Negrín. Frightened by the Loyalist defeat at Talavera, as Durruti had been, the two leaders agreed the government had to move the gold out of Madrid swiftly or risk losing it—and the war. So, a day earlier, on September 13, they persuaded the cabinet to authorize the transfer of the treasure "to a safe place," without saying where.

However, according to *El Campesino*, only the Communists carried out the operation, "several of them dressed in the uniform of Assault Guards," and even the bank director, a loyal non-Communist republican, was deliberately delayed at a meeting until the gold was gone.

Why were the Communists chosen to play so vital a role in the drama? Apparently because only they could be trusted to keep the secret of where the gold might ultimately go—Russia. It is unclear whether Caballero and Negrín decided definitely before the gold left Madrid to ship it to Russia, but it appears they tried to make sure the secret would be kept if they did.

Arthur Stashevsky, the Soviet commercial adviser, had been working on the republican leaders for some time. He tried "to gather into Soviet hands the control of the finances of the republic," according to Colonel Krivitsky, the Soviet intelligence chief in Europe. And when the gold was endangered, Stashevsky had a logical argument: Only Russia could be relied on never to turn it over to Franco. And besides, had not the republican government promised to pay for Soviet arms in gold anyway?

What's more, the gold could not remain long in Cartagena, for if the Loyalists didn't send it out of the country soon Franco might learn where it was. And then he and his German and Italian friends would stop at nothing to grab it.

While Spanish Communists knowing the secret of the gold now dreamed of endless shiploads of Soviet weapons being unloaded into their arms, they set out to create a Communist-dominated army that could make the best use of these weapons—during and after the civil war. And Franco's time-consuming attack on Toledo gave them a few extra days to bring Caballero around. The prime minister must give up his "primitive" ideas. He could not defend Madrid with scattered militia forces and without trenches and barricades. This was not the time for revolution or *machismo* but for facing the facts.

The Russian advisers, Goriev and Koltsov, appeared to share the dream of their Spanish comrades, whether or not they were fully aware of Stalin's broader aims in Spain. They and their fellow-traveling colleague, Foreign Minister del Vayo, pleaded with Caballero to form a "real" army. Even the influential American Communist, Louis Fischer, joined in the pleas. Fischer wrote Caballero a letter bluntly condemning his defense policies, and the prime minister invited him to his office for a talk. Caballero, looking old and tired, said: "You ask why we have not built trenches. Do you know that . . . more than two months ago we sent to Barcelona for shovels and haven't received them yet? You suggest barbed wire for entrenchments. Have we got barbed wire? . . . Don't think this job is so easy."

"But that's unbelievable," Fischer replied. "Spades and wire are not munitions. If you can't get those how can you hope to buy rifles and other weapons?"

"Rifles? We received eighteen thousand from Mexico, the only country that has helped us. And now we have whole squads fishing them out of the Tagus and hunting for them in the fields where the men fleeing from Toledo threw them."

And what about building concrete trenches and dugouts?

"You try to deal with our trade unions," Caballero wearily responded. "Their representatives were here this afternoon. They came to make demands on me!"

"But *you* should be making demands on *them*. Besides, you are the leader of the Spanish trade union movement. Surely they will listen to you if you ask them to construct fortifications instead of subways. If you have tools and materials for villas you have tools and materials for dugouts and trenches."

"That is more complicated than you suppose. If the socialist trade unions obey the government the . . . CNT will conduct propaganda against the socialists and try to attract their members. This is Spain."

Yes, this was Spain, and Caballero was Spanish. Nevertheless, the Communists managed to make him move. All militia units would be "militarized," he decreed, on September 28, the night Toledo fell. They would be reorganized into three-thousand-man "mixed brigades," each composed of three or four battalions plus auxiliary units. But this would not be just another professional army, and to make sure, the prime minister set up a corps of army commissars headed by Alvarez del Vayo. The Communists were delighted. The commissars were supposed to instill the "republican" spirit in the men, raise their morale, do the job of chaplains in most armies, as well as check on the loyalty of the professional officers. But without consulting Caballero, Alvarez del Vayo chose mostly Communist commissars to run the corps, and they subtly preached that the "best republican was a Communist."

Only the anarchists still refused to give up their independent militia units. Accept military discipline? Never! Give the Communists a chance to control and destroy them? Never! Actually, it would be weeks and months before a real republican army would start to take shape.

But almost immediately workers, whatever their ideology, stopped building subways and villas and began constructing dugouts and trenches, if they weren't busy fighting. The only people in the Madrid region who still clung to their traditional work habits were the peasants, many of whom had never visited the city. And who cared what happened on another planet?

Enrique Castro Delgado, the new director of the Agrarian Reform Institute, stared directly into the eyes of the official dealing with credits for peasants and asked: "What credits am I authorized by the law to approve?"

"Credits up to twenty-five thousand pesetas."

"And if they need more?"

"You cannot give it to them, señor. . . . The law is the law."

Castro rose from his chair and shouted: "Listen to me! For me the law does not exist. For me only two aims exist: to carry out agrarian reform and ensure agricultural production in order to feed the people and the army. On everything else, señor, I shit! . . . . If I can't sign credits exceeding twenty-five thousand pesetas, and they solicit a credit of fifty thousand, you—listen carefully—will make two requests of twenty-five thousand pesetas each!"

"I won't be able . . ."

"You'll do it . . . or if you don't, tomorrow I'll drag you out to the highway and riddle your body with bullets. Do you still refuse to obey my orders?"

"I'll do it."

Castro smiled as the official hurried out of his office.

Within days, every peasant who wanted credits to buy land of his own and the tools to work it would get the money, no matter how much chaos such huge loans created. Castro's real aim was to break the traditional hold of the socialists over the rural areas and make the peasants a pawn of the Communist party. Then all peasants not absolutely needed to produce food for the Loyalists would repay the loans with their lives, if necessary—on the front line. The Communists had to build a barrier of flesh to keep the Fascists from taking Madrid and all Spain. And Castro would help to build it.

He explained to his assistant, Morayta, who was also a Communist: "The most important thing . . . is that the peasants say: 'Only since the Communists came have we been getting land and money.' The other things don't matter to me. This money . . . its only value is that we can win the peasants with it."

"Is that agrarian reform or bribery, Castro?"

"What do I care? The means are not important. Only the end is, Comrade Morayta!"

Shortly, five of Castro's spies arrived after investigating the work and private life of the socialist in charge of the agrarian reform teams that worked in the villages—and kept the peasants loyal to the Socialist party. Armed with the report, Castro called in this man and said:

"I've summoned you to tell you the following: From this moment on the agrarian reform teams are dissolved. . . . You'll hand over the cars, the credentials, the premises, and whatever they contain."

"Anything else?"

"That seems little to you?"

"It seems impossible to me. Aside from being an agricultural expert and functionary of the institute, I represent the Federation of Agricultural Workers. I think this will make you understand that I can't carry out your orders."

Castro got up and approached him menacingly, while his five agents closed in.

"You're neither an agricultural expert nor a functionary of the institute nor a representative of the Federation of Agricultural Workers," he roared. "You're simply a thief! . . . A miserable thief!"

The socialist now rose and replied: "And you're a scoundrel and an *agent provocateur*. . . . I won't leave here."

"You'll resign!"

And Castro then asked one of his men to read aloud the report they had prepared: The socialist had sold the peasants' produce on the black market. He used the institute's gasoline for his own private purposes. He lived like a rich man, with two cars. He had a mistress, though he was married. . . .

"Now sit down and write your resignation saying you prefer to fight in the heroic ranks of our militias," Castro ordered. "And sign it. Then go away. I'm warning you that if you try to rebel against my decision you'll be exposing yourself to death on the highway, while looking at the stars."

The chief agent then prodded the socialist with a pistol barrel, and the man bent over Castro's desk and wrote out his resignation.

"I've signed only under duress," he said bitterly.

"Try not to tell anybody," Castro replied.

But the socialist did. And a few hours later Castro learned that all employees of the institute were meeting to decide on what to do about him. He immediately rushed to the meeting hall and sat down in the last row, listening to his underlings call him a dictator who was ruling at the point of a gun. They all agreed to write a resolution asking the prime minister to dismiss him.

Castro then rose and walked slowly to the rostrum, silently scanned the audience, and began sputtering figures of land distribution achieved under republican and socialist control, showing there had hardly been any agrarian reform since the birth of the republic.

"When I came here," he said, "you were a bunch of loafers who needed between fifteen and twenty days to approve a credit request. Now that request in handled in three days. . . . I oblige you to work, even resorting to threat? I don't deny it. But you're only obliged to work, while there are tens of thousands of men who are being obliged to die."

After pausing for effect, he added: "You may send the government whatever you like . . . but I want you to know that within eight days all men under thirty years of age will join the army 'voluntarily,' except the experts who have to continue their work here. The female personnel will take a proficiency examination, and those who fail will be dismissed. . . . Also, I am going to ask the tribunals to investigate certain functionaries."

Then he looked at the men who were writing the resolution and said: "And now, gentlemen, finish the document . . . and let's wait and see where the rope will break."

Castro then marched out. He had won. And peasants came to him every day in their dirty corduroys and offered him bitter homemade cigarettes in gratitude for his generosity. The Communists were good. They were kind. And to protect their land and money, yes, many agreed, they would fight the Fascists, who would take it all away from them.

Later, Castro would write: "The agrarian revolution has already become a fact. . . . Now it is they, those new owners, who have to fight and die to defend it . . . and to bring us, step by step, toward the power . . . that the republicans think is the republic, but which will be ours, ours, imbeciles, ours!"

And so, with Castro's cynical help, a barrier of flesh was rising around Madrid, though it was reinforced with little of the steel needed to keep out an enemy armed with modern weapons—and helped by a dedicated fifth column.

Janet Riesenfeld could hardly believe she was in Madrid. She was visiting Jaime Castanys's *pension* for the first time, but it was more like a private home. Around the dinner table, covered with a lace tablecloth and set with silver and crystal goblets, sat men in dark suits and black ties and women in black silk gowns, their brooches and rings sparkling. While the maid quietly placed before them gourmet dishes apparently purchased on the black market, they talked about the theater, music, literature. The war? It didn't exist. Everyday life—and death? No one seemed to care.

Was this all a dream? Was she suddenly living in the past with ghosts? Jaime came from an elite family and had little in common with the masses, she knew, but how could he bear such insufferable friends?

When the demitasse had been served, the maid whispered to Castanys that someone had come to see him. He excused himself, then returned after a few minutes and took Janet with him. In the hall, he introduced her to a middle-aged woman.

"Janet," Castanys said, "I've just been talking with Señora Lázaro. . . . I think it would be a very good idea for her to come and live with you and be your companion . . . I've told her that I know you'll agree with me, so she'll come to your house tomorrow morning."

Janet was shocked and said nothing. When the woman had left, Castanys explained: "I know what you're going to say, darling. But . . . she is completely alone, her husband and brothers are fighting at the front, and now she has no money. . . . She's not well and her health is breaking down."

Janet's fury gradually turned into sympathy. Well, all right, she would give it a try.

When the dinner party ended, Castanys left with Janet to escort her home. Suddenly they heard a shot nearby and saw a militiaman lying on the street. Janet started to run toward him, but Castanys pulled her away. Enraged, she cried:

"We should have gone back!"

"Don't be stupid."

"He was hurt!"

"He was dead—couldn't you see him?"

"He might have only been wounded."

"For heaven's sake, Janet, can't you see the danger you would expose yourself to? Do you want to end up in prison—or worse? . . . They won't be able to find out who fired the shot. They'll use anyone they find there."

When they arrived at Janet's apartment they found her two militia friends, Villatora and José María, waiting for them. Her maid had let them in.

Of all the nights for them to visit her—when she was with Jaime! There was a cold silence, and Janet, to cover up her embarrassment, spoke the first words that came to mind: They had seen a militiaman shot. She immediately realized her mistake.

"Well, what did you do?" asked Villatora. "Was he dead?"

Another silence.

"Was he dead?" Villatora repeated.

José María saw that Janet was uneasy.

"Of course he was dead," he said. "They seldom miss their targets."

But Villatora persisted, asking Castanys: "Are you sure he was dead? Did they find out who did it?"

"I don't know."

"Why don't you know?"

"We didn't go back."

Villatora glanced at José María and they got up and walked to the door. As they were about to leave, Villatora warned Janet:

"You'd better be careful. These days it's not so safe to be with a man like that."

The visitor came from an old aristocratic family and had impeccable bank references, and so he managed to arrange a meeting with the war minister of an Eastern European country.

"I have come here," he said, "to buy a number of war planes from your government. . . . We are in the market for at least fifty machines at Your Excellency's price. . . . We believe that your country has a stake in keeping the Fascist powers out of the Mediterranean."

The minister said quietly: "I request you to leave my office at once. . . . I am the war minister; I am not a merchant. Good day, sir."

The visitor left discouraged. He was a voluntary agent of Stalin's man, Krivitsky, and he really believed he owed it to humanity to succeed. He would try again the next day. But within hours, a top banker came to see him at his hotel. Was it true there were some people who were interested in buying planes? Soon an agreement was reached, and the agent assured the banker that on behalf of the "Chinese government"—a convenient cover party—the papers would be in perfect order.

Within days, a Norwegian ship loaded with fifty pursuit planes and bombers was sailing for Alicante—only to find Franco's German and Italian vessels blocking the way. The captain then switched course toward Barcelona, but was forbidden to anchor there by a Russian agent aboard the ship, for the anarchists controlled Barcelona, and there would be no Communist arms for them or for anyone who didn't play Stalin's game. The ship chopped back and forth across the Mediterranean before finally slipping through the blockade at Alicante.

Other vessels sailed into Spain at about the same time, in mid-October, also carrying war goods—planes, tanks, armored cars, cannons, rifles. Some of the matériel, like the fifty aircraft bought in Eastern Europe, was purchased by a chain of Soviet-controlled import and export firms set up with false fronts in Paris, London, and other leading European cities. The rest came straight from the Soviet Union on ships using phony names and papers. In all, about a hundred

planes and an equal number of tanks were among the items that would be unloaded in Spanish ports during the next months, fewer actually than Loyalist leaders
had expected.

Russia had first hinted it might send military aid at a meeting of the nonintervention committee on October 7. Italian aircraft had flown Franco's troops to
Spain, the Soviet delegate charged, and if such aid did not cease, Moscow would
feel free to intervene, too. This threat triggered a tempest. The Russian charge
was a lie, ranted the Germans and Italians. The Russian threat would escalate
chances of an international war, warned the French and the British.

Stalin grew worried. Everybody, including the enemy, knew about the shipments already on the way to the Loyalists, just as everybody knew about those to
the rebels. And it was just as well. What propaganda gains could Russia—and,
incidentally, the Spanish Communists—make if Soviet generosity were not a
topic of conversation? But to openly admit to such generosity could be perilous.

Thus, on October 16, at the very moment the first Russian arms were being unloaded in Spanish ports, a Soviet official was adamantly denying that his country
was giving such aid. He told the Moscow correspondent of the New York *Times*:
"The Soviet has given its word that it will not intervene in Spain and the Soviet
has always lived up to its word."

Why provoke Hitler by publicizing the aid, even if he knew about it anyway?
Eventually, he would get the signal: Stalin wanted a deal with him. And why
provoke Blum and risk losing even the security of the Russo-French pact? Stalin
couldn't afford to gamble. Save Madrid, yes. But quietly, subtly, safely—and
temporarily.

"The arrival of the first Soviet arms gives us an essential element of propaganda," Palmiro Togliatti declared at a meeting with Spanish Communist leaders.

The Spaniards were less impressed.

"Perhaps we should make a little less noise about such a small shipment,"
suggested one sarcastically.

Turning to Jesús Hernández, now the minister of education, Togliatti asked
dryly: "Do you also think that the USSR can forget its duty to international soli-
darity?"

"I don't think anything," replied Hernández, with obvious doubt.

"Nobody must doubt Comrade Stalin," said one of Togliatti's Comintern colleagues.

And thousands of young men from all over the world did not. . . .

"The war sure is getting serious—that's the last packet of Camels in Barcelona."

Keith Scott Watson was enjoying his stay in Spain, at least so far. It certainly
beat the dull life back in England. He was dining at Café Catalan with his beautiful new girl friend, Rosita, and everyone was treating him like a hero. Tall,

myopic, flaxen-haired with a sardonic expression and a slight lisp, Keith was one of the thousands of youths from many countries who had answered the call to rescue democracy in Spain.

Stalin needed International Brigades to help drag out the civil war, and especially the coming crucial battle for Madrid, which could determine how long the war would last. Aside from a few hundred advisers and technicians, he would send no Russians, for such intervention would be too blatant, though he encouraged exiled foreign Communists living in his country to go, if only to get rid of them.

The Comintern, which ran the worldwide recruiting campaign, ordered every Communist party to sign up a certain number of volunteers—not only trusted Communists but liberals and idealists who would give the campaign a "democratic look." Trotskyites and others with anti-Stalinist tendencies were weeded out, though some were able to infiltrate. There were also adventurers, fugitives, social misfits, people who might otherwise have joined Franco's foreign legion.

Actually, about 60 percent of the volunteers were Communists, but Watson was not one of them. He was a liberal—with a taste for adventure. And besides, what the hell, he had always wanted to see Spain. Once in Barcelona, he was assigned to a British machine-gun squad, which was to head soon for Albacete, the secret new base of the International Brigades.

As Watson and Rosita drank, ate, and chatted, an American sitting at the next table invited them to join him and his friend. The two men introduced themselves: James Minifie of the New York *Herald-Tribune* and Louis Delaprée of *Paris Soir*. They were visiting Barcelona but would shortly be returning to the Madrid front. Delaprée especially was eager to get back. He felt almost at home in the trenches where he had met such men as the soldier who had been killed after reading him poetry between shell bursts.

Watson talked about the war with the two reporters until Rosita, feeling neglected, called the waiter over and requested a deck of cards.

"What do we do now, play poker?" asked Minifie.

Rosita shuffled the cards and Keith cut them, wondering whether their two companions thought they were a couple of confidence tricksters. Rosita placed the cards in three piles and kept turning them face up.

"I see you have much love," she told Watson. "When you have found it, you will lose it always."

Then, after cutting more cards, she predicted: "You will not do that for which you came here—there is a coach with a fair woman and with it is death."

Rosita looked disturbed, though Watson did not seem to take the prediction seriously.

Delaprée then asked: "Will the comrade try my destiny?"

Rosita resented his amused look, admonishing him: "You must be serious. The cards cannot lie."

After Delaprée had cut the cards she looked at them and then at him, apparently feeling uncomfortable.

"Here is a journey . . . a large city, death is all around it . . . you must not leave it," she warned him. "From the air there is death for your honor!"

Minifie laughed. "Cheery little soul! Tell me what awful end I have waiting for *me*."

"No, *hombre*," Rosita replied with irritation. "It is not a good thing to laugh at the cards."

And everybody ordered more drinks.

The telephone rang in the War Ministry and the caller asked to speak with Prime Minister Largo Caballero, who was also war minister.

"And who are you?" asked an undersecretary.

"Comrade José Pérez of the FAI in Valencia."

"He's very busy. What do you want to tell him?"

"That the situation is very grave and they're going to capture the town."

But this "news" from an unknown caller was not enough to bring Caballero to the phone. Comrade José Pérez was disappointed. His joke hadn't worked. The joke was that he was, in fact, General Varela pretending he was a "comrade." And that he was phoning not from Valencia but from the village of Illescas, halfway between Toledo and Madrid. But if his joke had failed, his attack had not though victory was taking longer than he had expected.

It seemed to be Talavera all over again. Flushed with their conquest of Toledo, the rebels lingered there for more than a week before lunging toward Madrid, giving the panicky enemy a new chance to regain breath and courage, regroup, and counterattack. But this time the fault lay at the top.

Franco, for one thing, was busy there posing for snapshots in the ruins of the Alcázar and, with his prestige at a peak, arranging for his entry into Madrid not simply as a conquering general but as the new head of state. Some of his supporters, including his influential brother Nicolás, decided to help him without consulting Mola and other generals, who had already agreed to make him generalissimo but preferred to choose political leaders after the war.

On September 28, the day the Alcázar fell, the rebel chiefs met again in Salamanca to approve a decree announcing Franco's promotion. When the decree was read, fury broke loose. Franco was named not only generalissimo but the chief of government as well. No! cried Mola and others. But after a bitter argument they had to go along. Franco was now, exactly as he had planned, the man of the hour in rebel Spain. So the decree was approved, and brother Nicolás raced to the printers with it—after changing a few words. Franco would now assume "all the powers of the Spanish state."

In effect, he would not be the chief of government but the head of state, the equivalent of a president or a king. Mola and his supporters were enraged. Franco had tricked them a second time. But once the decree was published nobody would dare quibble about the title of the hero of the Alcázar, and so he was installed on October 1. His political caution and quiet showmanship had finally yielded the ultimate prize. He would be the *caudillo*.

To placate Mola, Franco now named him his supreme field commander, and Mola, swallowing his bitterness, accepted this new chance to win eternal glory in Madrid. Varela would be his southern commander and the discredited Yagüe, Varela's deputy, though the two men despised each other.

But not only power intrigues held up the attack on Madrid. Mola had to worry about his northern fronts, too—in the Basque country, Asturias, Aragon—where Loyalist breakthroughs could lessen the pressure on Madrid. And he had to transfer troops and equipment from these fronts to give greater muscle to the final drive on the capital, though only a little might have been needed to take the city right after the rout in Toledo.

Finally, on October 7, the assault began. It was then that Mola boasted he would soon be having coffee in Café Molinero, even giving the exact deadline for his historic sip—October 12. His optimism seemed justified. Not only had the militiamen fled Toledo in disorder, but General Varela was one of the toughest, bravest, and most skillful officers in Spain.

A former sergeant, he had risen through the ranks with extraordinary feats in Morocco that twice won him the nation's highest military decoration. And he was driven by a hatred for the republic perhaps even more intense than that of Mola and Franco. He had been jailed for a year after taking part in General Sanjurjo's abortive revolt of 1932, then trained the *Requetés* of Navarra, whose ultrareactionary views he shared—the main reason why he clashed with Yagüe, who supported the Falange's more modern totalitarian philosophy. Varela was the ideal military man, cool, cruel, impeccably groomed down to his immaculate white gloves. He had even been seen with his medals pinned on the silk dressing gown he wore at night.

But it took him until October 17, ten days, to reach Illescas, while Mola's coffee turned cold in Madrid. And even then, Loyalist General Asensio managed to get his men to counterattack the next day, dragging many of them from Madrid in doubledecker buses while shooting some deserters. However, the Loyalists were soon on the run again when the rebels threatened to outflank them.

Meanwhile, another rebel force battered its way into San Martín de Valdeiglesias, thirty-five miles west of Madrid, and surrounded Loyalist troops led by anarchist Cipriano Mera. With tactical wizardry and sheer nerve, Mera managed to lead his trapped men to safety, but the rebels now threatened Madrid from three sides. Only the east remained open.

The front was so fluid that the Loyalists were not even sure where it was, so when Varela found the telephone in Illescas working, he thought it would be amusing to let Caballero know. Well, he would soon be seeing him in Madrid anyway.

On the top floor of the Soviet embassy in Madrid, a code clerk rushed into the office of General Orlov, the Soviet intelligence adviser, and handed him a radiogram.

"Just in from Moscow," the clerk said, "and here are the first lines: 'Absolutely secret. This must be coded by Schwed personally.'"

Orlov, whose code name was Schwed, quickly deciphered the rest of the message: "Arrange with Prime Minister Largo Caballero for shipment of the gold reserves of Spain to the Soviet Union. Use a Soviet steamer. Maintain utmost secrecy. If the Spaniards demand a receipt, refuse—I repeat, refuse. Say that a formal receipt will be issued in Moscow by the state bank. I hold you personally responsible for the operation. [signed] Ivan Vasilyevich."

The signature was Stalin's code name.

By early October, Finance Minister Negrín was desperately searching for a place to hide the gold, so he accepted the offer of Stashevsky, the Soviet commercial adviser, to send it to Russia, which would get most of it anyway in payment for arms. Stashevsky immediately informed Stalin, who then cabled his instructions to Orlov. The plotters told no one—except Indalecio Prieto. For he was minister of the navy and air force and his warships were needed, Orlov says, to escort the gold-laden Soviet vessels as far as Algiers. But Prieto later insisted that he learned about the shipment only by accident; he happened to visit Cartagena while the gold was being loaded on the four Soviet ships that would haul it to Russia. Anyway, the operation was so secret that even President Azaña was not consulted.

On the morning of October 22, six Spanish sailors entered the cave at Cartagena and carried out the treasure chests, hoisting them onto twenty army trucks, and for three moonless nights the vehicles shuttled between the cave and the port. During the day the sailors were locked in the cave, where they slept, ate sandwiches and peanuts, and played cards for peanuts.

During the third night German planes swooped down and unleashed bombs on the piers, hitting a Spanish freighter docked near the Russian ships. Panic ensued. Had Franco learned about the gold? The Spanish sailors and Soviet crews worked feverishly, and within hours all the gold was safely stashed away in the floating banks.

Now came the moment Orlov had dreaded: A Spanish treasury official asked him for a receipt. He replied casually:

"A receipt? But, comrade, I am not authorized to give one. Don't worry, my friend, it will be issued by the State Bank of the Soviet Union when everything is checked and weighed."

Most irregular! The official would have to call Madrid. But that was the last thing Orlov wanted. Couldn't a treasury agent be sent on each ship to carefully guard the gold? The official reluctantly agreed. Soon the ships were ploughing through the waves with their precious cargo toward the Ukrainian port of Odessa on the Black Sea.

When the gold arrived, Stalin was so overjoyed that he threw a lavish party for his top NKVD people and was heard to say: "They will never see their gold again, just as they do not see their own ears!"

Meanwhile, the four Spanish treasury agents were kept counting the gold for months—finally realizing that Stalin had no intention of letting them leave Russia, at least not until the end of the war. Neither the Russians nor the Spanish government leaders wanted word of the gold shipment leaked. The Spanish people, even the Loyalists, might not understand why their national treasure had vanished.

None, after all, could see his own ears.

7

President Azaña gazed despondently through the window of his office at the jumbled buildings, the towering steeples, the broad avenues, the green parks, and the distant mountain peaks. His beloved Madrid. It was October 16, and rebel troops were forging closer each day. And even Russian arms and foreign volunteers, he felt, could not stop them.

Azaña turned toward his three visitors, members of his Left Republican party, and lamented, his face paler than ever: "They'll enter Madrid, and they'll destroy everything—the palace, the Prado, everything. And they will take vengeance on the people. And before they do, the people will take *their* vengeance."

He recalled the murders at Model Prison. After that massacre he had wanted to resign, but his supporters urged him not to. Did he not personify the republic to the world and symbolize democracy to his people? Real moderates such as Indalecio Prieto pleaded with heartfelt sincerity, while the Communists begged in the interest of Soviet foreign policy. Azaña couldn't resist such pressure and agreed to remain, brooding and despairing in his golden cage.

Should Madrid perhaps be given up without a fight? he now asked his visitors. One of them, Regulo Martínez Sánchez, reminded him of a speech the president had made in November 1935, shortly before the election that carried the Popular Front to victory.

"A half million people came to hear you," Martínez Sánchez said, "and you

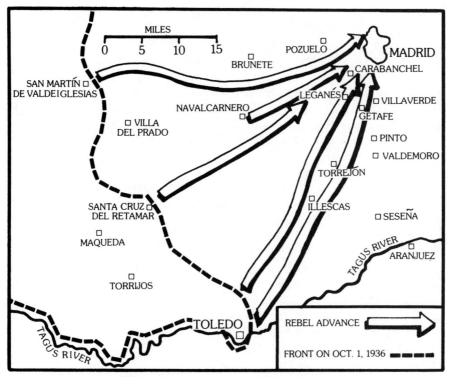

THE APPROACH TO MADRID

told them to fight and not to give up until they won. You made them fight and we won the elections. Now, when everything is at stake, shouldn't we also fight?''

Azaña reflected a moment. Yes, they must fight—even though they would probably lose. But should he remain in Madrid during the battle? The government, he said, had suggested he leave for Barcelona. It feared that Catalonia, which was largely in anarchist hands, would exploit the present chaos and try to break away from Spain, declaring its independence as most Catalans had always dreamed of doing. But with the president of the republic there, the people would be restrained. Anyway, if Madrid did fall and he were captured, Franco would surely execute him, and the republic would be gravely damaged.

His visitors agreed that he should leave, though the masses might misunderstand and think he was abandoning them. Why should he stay? He no longer had any power but was simply a prisoner of forces he could not control nor even understand. He was being slowly destroyed, together with the Spain he had so loftily led. The visitors saw before them a tragic figure, once proud and strong, whom they no longer recognized. For him the fight was over. He was already dead in spirit.

And so, on October 19, President Azaña quietly left Madrid. The government explained to the people that he was making a tour of the eastern fronts.

A few days later, on October 25, Christopher Lance also peered through a window overlooking Madrid, from his room in the British embassy, and tried to glimpse the green fields beyond the rooftops. The sun was beaming in a cloudless sky. And it was Sunday. Too bad his wife, Jinx, wasn't there to go on a picnic with him.

But Lance had more on his mind than a pleasant outing. Beyond those rooftops there might just be a path his threatened friends could tread into rebel territory. He had been vainly seeking one for weeks—and the closer Franco got to Madrid, the more frantic and bloodthirsty the murder gangs became.

Lance phoned William Hall, a British banker. Would he go with him for a picnic tea in Aranjuez, a garden town about thirty miles southeast of Madrid?

Soon they were on their way. They passed some militiamen digging a trench about nine miles from Aranjuez, then, as they drove on, saw another group running toward them in panic.

Where was the front line? Lance inquired.

But they seemed to know as little as he did.

Any Fascists on the road?

No.

Visibly relieved, the two roared off again.

Ahead, they saw still more men. But these looked like regular troops and they had a tank. Lance was surprised.

"Never knew the government had any tanks. Some real soldiers at last, Bill."

Suddenly there were shots. Their car had been hit.

"By God! They're Franco's party!" Lance cried, slamming on his brakes.

He had wanted to find a path into rebel territory so he could save the lives of his Spanish friends, and now he had found it—perhaps at the cost of his own life! The Englishmen leaped out of the car with their hands up, and Lance fell into a ditch on top of two dead militiamen.

Three officers walked up to them, and one, noting the British flag on the car, asked in English:

"What on earth are you doing here?"

"Actually, we're from Madrid and are on our way to have a nice little tea in Aranjuez. I hope you are not going to spoil the party."

They did. All climbed into the car, and Lance, at the wheel, was told the way to regimental headquarters.

"It's becoming quite a habit," one of the officers said. "You are the second lot today."

"Good heavens! Who were the others?"

"A bunch of journalists—American and British. At the very spot where we got you. In fact, the corpses you fell on were their escorts."

A few hours earlier, the car of Henry Gorrell of the United Press had also come under fire and he and his driver jumped into a ditch, but when the driver dashed back to the car Gorrell was afraid to follow him and was captured. Shortly, another car raced down the road, this one carrying James Minifie of the New York *Herald-Tribune,* who had just returned from Barcelona, Dennis Weaver of the London *News-Chronicle,* and their driver and escort. Guns spat bullets at them, too, bringing their car to a halt. The rebels shot the driver and escort on the spot and added the two reporters to their catch.

And now, two more Anglo-Saxons! Could they all be so stupid? Or were some of them spies? Headquarters would decide if any would be executed.

In Toledo, Lance and Hall were brought before a colonel.

"How very English of you!" he beamed. "Calmly driving out for a picnic in the middle of someone else's war! Tea indeed! Horrible stuff. Quite mad of you, you know."

He then telephoned General Varela and asked: "What shall I do with them, general? Shall I have them shot—or shall I invite them to dinner? . . . Very well, sir."

He smiled and told his captives: "The general says that you are to dine *first.*"

The next morning, the two Britons found themselves standing before a thin-faced, well-built little man in a soft leather jacket and black tie—General Varela himself. The general laughed at their story and told them that Franco personally wanted to see them in Salamanca, his new headquarters. Lance was impressed by Varela. A good-natured chap. But a little earlier the three reporters had also seen Varela and came away less enthralled.

The general had laughed then, too, saying: "I can't imagine how it is that you were not shot at once. Of course, there's time for that yet—if you do prove to be spies."

Weaver later wrote: "He laughed again. This was a tremendous joke. I thought of our two friends shot in the ditch . . . and detested the general."

Varela then assured the reporters: "Madrid will fall within twenty-four hours. And I . . . I am the general who will ride into the red citadel at the head of my troops."

But Franco, it seemed, was not so sure. The next night he met with Lance and Hall in the officers' mess in Salamanca and told them coldly:

"You are in a dangerous position here and you know the penalty for the kind of business you are on. However, I shall give you a chance. I shall instruct your escort to take you to Burgos, where you will see Señor Merry del Val, who will give you certain instructions."

Lance was furious. Here he had been helping Franco's friends in Madrid and the general was calling him a spy! They were driven to Burgos and there Merry del Val gave them Franco's orders—together with a list of about twenty persons.

"Those are some important friends who are hiding in Madrid," he said. "The generalissimo requires that you should give the word of an Englishman that you will return to Madrid and do everything you can to get them out."

The irony rekindled Lance's fury, for he was being blackmailed into doing something he had been trying to do anyway. He was in a dilemma. If he agreed, he might appear guilty; if he refused, he might be executed. One thing was certain: Once he made a promise, even under duress, he would feel obligated to keep it.

"All right," he finally said. "We are prepared to have a shot at it. But we can't promise any more than to do our best, and only for the reason that this is exactly the work I am trying to do in Madrid already. Not spying, señor, but helping to save your friends from the firing squad. You might tell the generalissimo that."

And the next morning, October 30, Lance and Hall were driven to the border town of Irun, where they walked across a bridge into France—some hours before the three captured reporters were to follow.

It seemed odd. Varela had boasted that he would be *in* Madrid within twenty-four hours, yet Franco wanted Lance to get twenty friends *out*? Why, if the rebel army was about to get in? Just to find a hole in the shifting front lines, as Lance had already learned, could take days, even weeks. And it might be impossible to help the man at the top of the list: Alvaro Martín Moreno, the son of Franco's chief of staff, Colonel Francisco Martín Moreno. For he was one of the most wanted of all rebel fugitives in Loyalist Spain.

Franco's logic was apparently based on information he had just learned. Taking Madrid might no longer be a simple matter of chasing a mob of panicky militiamen northward. Until now the chase had been too leisurely. Prime Minister Largo Caballero, with his usual indiscretion, had dramatically broadcast to the world on October 28, the evening of Franco's meeting with Lance:

"The time has come to deliver a death blow. . . . We have at our disposal a formidable mechanized army. We have tanks and powerful aircraft. Listen, comrades! At dawn, our artillery and armored trains will open fire. Immediately, our aircraft will attack. Tanks will advance on the enemy at his most vulnerable point."

Actually, Franco had learned earlier that Russian arms were on the way. On October 19 he had signaled Mola that "the imminent arrival of important reinforcements makes advisable the concentration of maximum force on the Madrid front to speed up the fall of the capital."

And now Caballero had confirmed that these "important reinforcements" were already at the front line poised to attack. Perhaps that was why the generalissimo had been in such ill humor and so anxious about his friends in Madrid.

His triumphal entry might be delayed a little more than twenty-four hours.

8

Ramón Sender, the writer-warrior, stood atop a small hill in the village of Valdemoro and excitedly watched thousands of men move toward the enemy, this time supported by more than plain guts. They had set out at dawn, October 29—just as Prime Minister Caballero had promised the night before, to the anger and chagrin of his commanders. Despite the warning, however, Franco was in for a surprise. Though he may have been disturbed by Caballero's threat, he apparently did not really expect a full-scale attack led by fifteen Soviet-operated T-26 Russian tanks and long-range artillery, while Russian planes commanded the skies.

Sender had proven himself such a gifted commander in the Guadarramas that he was not only promoted to captain but was named chief of staff of a newly formed brigade that, together with other forces, was now attacking. The brigade included the Fifth Regiment as well as other units, and its commander was Enrique Lister, who had earlier replaced Enrique Castro Delgado as head of the Fifth Regiment. Castro was still busy converting peasants to communism with the fervor of a missionary.

Largely under the quiet direction of Soviet General Goriev, the metamorphosis of the militia into an army had begun, and the men were ready for their first big test. They would surge east to capture the village of Seseña. Then on to Torrejón, north of Illescas on the Toledo–Madrid road. Varela's rebels were marching along the road toward Madrid, but Lister's brigade would try to cut them off.

As Sender observed the vastness and complexity of the operation, the anguish of past weeks melted into joy. Who could have imagined the Loyalists would be fighting back so soon with tanks and planes and men no longer terrified of enemy power? In the bright sunshine the whole world seemed aglow with new hope. Everything was going as planned—but where were the tanks? The infantry was supposed to stay only fifty to two hundred yards behind them, but couldn't keep up, and the heavily armored khaki monsters had vanished in the distance. . . .

The tanks had lumbered across the fields and didn't stop until they reached Seseña—not dallying even there. Why wasn't anyone shooting at them? the Russian operators wondered. And where was the Loyalist infantry? It wasn't following. Perhaps it had come from another direction and had already driven the enemy out. So the tanks entered the village and slithered down the main street of what looked like a ghost town.

The column ground into a small square surrounded by old stone houses, and there in the center huddled about two hundred infantrymen. At last their comrades! The Russian commander in the lead tank opened his turret and stood with the upper part of his torso protruding, ready to greet them. An officer approached and amiably asked him:

"Italian?"

The two men stared incredulously at each other. They were enemies! The Russian disappeared inside and slammed the turret shut. Immediately the tanks spurted fire from their guns and the whole square exploded in a swirl of smoke. Almost all the rebels lay dead, either blown to pieces or flattened under the treads of the tanks, which crashed through the cluster of men and lurched down the narrow streets knocking out cannons and machine guns. One man climbed out of his tank while under machine-gun fire just to pull down a monarchist flag fluttering atop a house.

Once out of the village, the tanks decimated a convoy of enemy troops rushing to the front line and smashed through two other villages, leaving more corpses and wreckage in their wake. Two tanks ripped all the way to Torrejón, the brigade's second objective, where they were knocked out by Molotov cocktails. A rebel officer who led the attack on these tanks, Luis Valero Barmejo, told the author that a Russian gunner in one of them kept firing even after both of his legs had been blown off.

However, since the Loyalist infantrymen were still nowhere in sight, the rest of the tanks turned around and headed back toward Seseña. The second trip through this village was a bit rougher than the first, for the enemy had had plenty of time to prepare a "welcome back" party. The Russians found themselves trapped in a labyrinth of tortuous lanes, with rebels in almost every stone house along the way lobbing grenades or Molotov cocktails at them. But the tanks fired point-blank into the structures, burying defenders under piles of debris, and finally blasted their way out of town, though leaving one more burning hulk behind.

Meanwhile, rebel planes showered the exhausted Loyalist infantrymen with bombs and machine-gun bullets, scattering them in confusion. Sender, back in the command post in Valdemoro, was shouting orders over the telephone to commanders who didn't know what was happening.

Where were the troops? The sector commander asked. Were they going to attack Torrejón? Sender was shocked.

"Our first objective is Seseña."

"Then you are not attacking Torrejón."

"Of course not. And it surprises me that you should ask that, as you issued the instructions for our brigade."

"Of course. But I ask you because forces coming from I don't know where are already going toward Torrejón."

"I can assure you that our brigade is going against Seseña."

Sender hung up, but shortly the same commander called again.

"Whose troops are those attacking Torrejón?"

"I don't know that anyone is attacking the village. But I'll inquire and let you know."

Suddenly, an aide rushed in and cried, pointing to the right flank: "What troops are those coming toward us from over there?"

Sender froze. They were his own, in full retreat! In a few minutes, his headquarters was seething with militiamen in disarray. Sender questioned one of the officers:

"Where is your company?"

The officer merely shrugged his shoulders.

"That is not an answer," Sender growled.

"But it is the only answer I can give you. We have not seen a single tank. Not a single shell fell in the village. Not an airplane arrived. [We were apparently expected] to take the town with a few hand grenades and bayonets, but we had many losses. And then, as if anything more were needed, the enemy airplanes arrived and scattered us."

As did a rain of artillery.

Sender couldn't understand. He had seen the tanks move off toward Seseña with his own eyes.

"What village have you been at?" he asked.

"Where we were meant to go. There."

And the officer pointed toward the horizon where Torrejón stood silhouetted in the distance against the sky.

Sender felt crushed. He silently walked away. Somehow he just couldn't tell these poor survivors that they weren't supposed to attack Torrejón until Seseña had been taken.

That they had attacked the wrong village and been hit by their own artillery!

Although the attack on Seseña and Torrejón was a great tactical disaster for the Loyalists, it was an even greater psychological triumph for them. For while the Loyalist press trumpeted the militiamen's glorious "capture" of the two villages, it conveniently ignored their frantic flight. Now the rebels were supposedly on the run, even as the Loyalists were still beating a panicky path toward Madrid.

"The enemy is no longer our superior in armament," the newspaper *El Socialista* boasted. "We now have absolute superiority over them in both men and armaments and . . . in our air forces. Therefore, from now on there will be no excuse for our militiamen, who must continue to advance. . . . [They] are now bound to recapture as soon as possible the ground abandoned to the enemy."

And while the Loyalists transformed defeat into "victory" the rebels turned victory into "defeat." General Mola, seeing that the Moorish horse was of little use against the Russian tank, nervously canceled a plan for a cavalry charge across the Jarama River, southeast of Madrid, aimed at cutting the road to Valencia and sealing off the capital. And Generalissimo Franco was even grimmer than he had been the night before the attack, when he had icily greeted Christopher Lance.

Franco's worst fears had materialized. Russian arms, even better than his own, had arrived in Madrid before he had. How could he now tell the world he was master of Spain? What he thought would be a mere romp a few days before could turn into a stalemate or even a retreat. Caution again dictated his action.

He must get more arms at once.

Hitler, equally concerned, agreed. The deceptive Russians had trampled on the nonintervention pact. But he would outtrample them—if Franco bowed to his demands. Like Stalin, the Führer had carefully measured his aid: not too little, not too much. Just enough to assure rebel victory over a militia horde that brandished only a few antiquated weapons. Unlike Stalin, however, Hitler was determined to win, if at minimum risk and cost. Since September Hitler had shipped to Franco fifty Krupp Mark I and IB tanks, growing numbers of Junker 52 bombers and Heinkel 51 fighter planes, and some antitank guns, along with advisers and technicians headed by Colonel Wilhelm von Thoma.

Yet, with all this new help, the rebels had moved toward Madrid as if on a holiday stroll, at least by German standards. And now the Loyalists had tanks and planes from Russia and would get more. If at Seseña the Loyalist infantry had kept pace with the tanks, or if the Russians had simply massed *all* their armor and blitzkrieged the rebel forces, Franco's whole army might have crumbled and the course of the war been reversed. Franco had been saved because the enemy was inept, but, in Hitler's view, so was Franco. Otherwise, he would have been in Madrid long ago.

Actually, Hitler had decided earlier, on October 23, to stuff rebel arsenals—conditionally. Italian Foreign Minister Galeazzo Ciano had come to him and said that Mussolini supported such a move, and the Führer quickly saw the chance to tighten his alliance with the Duce.

"In Spain," he said, "the Italians and the Germans have jointly dug the first trench against Bolshevism. . . . The Mediterranean is an Italian sea. And future change in the Mediterranean situation should be made in Italy's favor. Just as Germany should have freedom of action in the east and the Balkans."

Franco would get more equipment and instructors but no combat troops, Hitler stressed, as he didn't want to risk a European war "for which Germany was not prepared."

The Spanish conflict would, in fact, help the Führer prepare for such a war, since besides strengthening his bonds with Italy, a giant aid program in Spain would give him a testing ground for his equipment and technicians. So Franco would get the help he wanted—at a price. And he would pay it; he had no choice.

On October 30, the day after the Seseña scare, Hitler called in his foreign minister, Constantin Neurath, and gave him strict orders. Neurath rushed to radio Admiral Wilhelm Canaris, the Nazi intelligence chief, who was then in Spain: "In view of possible increased help for the reds, the German government does not consider the combat tactics of white [rebel] Spain, ground and air, promising of success. . . ."

Canaris had to tell Franco that if he didn't capture Madrid swiftly Germany and Italy could not recognize his government. And to succeed he would need powerful reinforcements, which Germany would be glad to supply *if* Franco:

1. placed *all* German arms, old and new, under a German commander responsible only to him and accepted this commander's advice on how to use them (the German force would be called the Condor Legion and would embrace about five thousand men at any one time);

2. fought the war more systematically and aggressively;

3. kept the Russians from using the harbors to land their supplies.

Canaris met with Franco and gave him Hitler's message. Would the generalissimo agree to the conditions? Both men knew the terms were humiliating. Franco would no longer be able to make independent military decisions. Neither, it is true, could Prime Minister Largo Caballero on the Loyalist side, but Russia exerted its control more subtly, and it all seemed honorable since the Spaniards were paying in gold. Hitler demanded no gold but absolute obedience. He would virtually guarantee victory in Madrid if Franco would trade in his pride. Franco briefly thought it over. Caution had served him well so far; misplaced pride could cancel the gains. This was certainly not the time to gamble.

He would pay the price.

Yet, Madrid probably could have been his for a pittance in the next hours if his men had simply chased the enemy, once more a frantic mob, through its virtually undefended gates. But while spared a fatal rebel attack, the city would pay for Franco's humiliation—starting that very day, October 30.

CHAPTER 7

Panic

1

Because of government censorship, many *Madrileños* learned of Toledo's fall only about a week after it happened, and they lived until then in a world of frenzied fantasy, far from the reality of the war raging around them. The revolution had joyously arrived, and the rebels, they were sure, never would. Why worry about them when the press spoke only of government victories? Life had been one wild, euphoric dream.

But with the news of Toledo, the dream began turning into a nightmare for the Loyalists and the nightmare into a dream for their captive rebel brothers, though some *Madrileños* yearned only for the peace of a clear-cut victory by either side. Press reports of the ''great triumph'' at Seseña slightly eased the growing panic, but more vivid than the headlines were the scenes of terror and flight that no propaganda could erase.

Madrid had become a huge, seething pressure cooker as about a half million refugees streamed in from neighboring villages before Franco's troops could kill, rape, and rob them. Ragged, weatherbeaten peasants plodded down the main streets leading donkeys that pulled wagons loaded with paraphernalia. One young boy proudly led a procession of several carts carrying his parents, grandparents, sisters, and brothers. A shepherd coaxed a herd of sheep along the Paseo de la Castellana while cows grazed amid cackling chickens in the parks, which had become vast, littered camping grounds for the homeless newcomers.

With the populace thus swollen by about 50 percent, food grew scarcer each day, except for black marketeers and their customers. The queues lengthened before the grocery stores, which offered, under a strict rationing system, little more than fresh fruit and vegetables, bread, Russian fish, and leftover jars of asparagus and boxes of corn flakes, which only Anglo-Saxons would eat here before the war. Meat? There were a few stray cats and dogs left, and occasionally there was a donkey killed by a bomb. The communal restaurants were practically the only ones still open, serving droves of militiamen and refugees, who paid with worthless government vouchers. The main problem was that the sole supply routes stretched from the east—the railway from Valencia and the road almost parallel with it. And trucks were often delayed because of the fuel shortage or were hijacked en route.

As hunger grew, so did desperation. The cafés no longer bristled with the gaiety of strutting self-proclaimed war heroes but catered to frightened people seeking assurances from friends that Franco could not enter Madrid. The *chekas* worked overtime trying to fill the morgues while there was still time. The wealthy not yet arrested were paying anybody with a car a fortune to get them away before the Loyalist holocaust reached its bloody peak. And many Loyalists were looking for comrades with cars to get *them* away before the rebel holocaust began.

Amid the fear and despair Prime Minister Largo Caballero remained silent, speaking only once, when he shouldn't have—warning the enemy of the attack that would take place on October 29. He was too afraid to confide in the people, too tired to rouse them to furious last-ditch battle, leaving this mainly to the Communists, who were driven by a mystical zeal and were ready to die for Stalin. Strong-arm squads dashed about recruiting citizens for service with gun or spade. A proclamation warned:

"The people of Madrid . . . must organize . . . to be prepared for something even so incredible as the capture of Madrid."

Banners were stretched across the alleys around the Puerta del Sol screaming *La Pasionaria's* steely pledge: *"No Pasarán!"*

Notices were plastered on the walls asking: "Men of Madrid! Will you allow your women to be raped by Moors?"

And *La Pasionaria* urged the women themselves: "Women of Madrid! Do not hinder your husbands from going to war. It is better to be the widow of a hero than the wife of a miserable coward."

She then led a parade of women through the streets, and they shouted to the men in the cafés: "Come out! Come out and fight for Madrid!"

Madrid's trial had only begun. Until October 30 there had been many air raids, but except for a few bombings in the downtown area the missiles hit mainly the workers' quarters in the suburbs and, however devastating, did not seriously interrupt city life. In fact, after the first few raids many people did not even bother to run to the subways or cellars when they heard the air raid sirens. And if they did, they sometimes brought along their gramophones and danced all night at impromptu parties.

Others would dash into the streets to gaze at the silvery enemy planes streaking through the sky. And if they were watching a movie they would not budge from their seats. Some were even angry that the sirens and antiaircraft guns drowned out the sound track. Finally, the government stopped using sirens as they frightened the *Madrileños* more than the threat of bombs, especially after the sirens went "crazy" one day. The sound detector kept signaling the approach of aircraft motors every few minutes and the sirens kept screeching—but no planes. What had gone wrong? Technicians dismantled the detector and found a bee whose buzz sounded exactly like that of a plane!

But if even sirens could not seriously shake Madrid's fantasy world, on October 30 something did. A dozen almost simultaneous explosions convulsed the center of the city, each on a street or in a square swarming with people, and the time was 5:00 P.M., the busiest shopping hour. At the Plaza de Colón, sixteen persons lay dead and sixty wounded. Near Calle de Luna most of the women standing in queues for milk or kindling wood were casualties. At the Plaza de Progreso, twelve children who had been playing were now doll-like corpses, joining in death seventy other youngsters killed in an air raid on the nearby town of Getafe that same afternoon. A socialist deputy described what he saw at the Puerta de Toledo: "There were dead everywhere. Limbs ripped off. I saw an old woman sitting upright on a bench. But she had no head."

Yet no one observed a plane or heard it buzz over the city. And no one could imagine a pilot so bad that he would miss every strategic target or so good that he would hit all the most compactly crowded zones, without a single bomb falling on a roof or in a courtyard. The bombs were dropped not from a plane, the outraged government believed, but from roofs or balconies.

Wherever they came from, this appeared to be the first deliberate attempt to escalate the panic in Madrid, force the city to its knees, and make Franco's own knee-bending before Hitler more bearable.

As Madrid helplessly awaited the mortal blow amid blazing banners, whining bombs, and rotting corpses, Janet Riesenfeld pondered her own future. Jaime Castanys had given her an ultimatum: She must choose between him and the cause she had embraced. She could never live in Jaime's world now, yet she could not imagine a world without him. Perhaps if she delayed her decision long enough the dilemma would simply evaporate. Or perhaps events would decide for her.

Janet arrived home one day to find two militiamen waiting for her. Her apartment was a mess. The floor was littered with clothes and household items and her bed had been torn apart.

"You know a woman called Amparo Lázaro?" one of the men asked.

"Yes."

"Through whom did you meet this woman?"

Evading the question, Janet said: "I'm sure if you ask Señora Lázaro she will tell you that I am in no way involved in whatever you may suspect her of."

"I'm sorry—that's impossible. Señora Lázaro was apprehended and shot this morning."

Janet was shocked. She remained silent when she was asked again who had introduced the woman to her. By answering, she was now sure, she would be sentencing Jaime to death.

Soon she was sitting in a small room in the police station awaiting further interrogation, and for three hours she was alone with the truth.

"I began to move about the room," Janet later wrote. "Why had he done it? . . . How little he must have thought of me! . . . Then I realized that Jaime had given me the answer he had requested. He had shown me . . . that for him there was something greater than our love, and that for me there might possibly be the same thing. And at that moment I felt only sympathy and pity for him. How much it must have cost him to do this!"

Janet was finally brought before a senior official.

Why had Lázaro been shot? she asked.

"For smuggling munitions to Franco's snipers," the man replied.

Then he repeated the question: Who had introduced her to the woman?

And again she refused to answer.

The official gave up, and Janet was taken back to the little room. Later that night the door opened and José María entered smiling. He drove her home.

The next morning Janet walked into Jaime's office.

"What's wrong?" he asked anxiously. "Where were you last night?"

When Janet coldly explained what had happened, he started toward her but she stepped back.

"Don't try to explain, Jaime," she said. "I know everything you're going to say: That you didn't think she would really get caught; that the American embassy would help me. That's all beside the point."

"Did the embassy have any difficulty getting you out?"

"The embassy had nothing to do with it. It was José María who saved me. But let's not waste time talking about that. You have to get away. They will surely come after you next!"

"How do you know? Did you mention my name in connection with Lázaro?"

When Janet denied she had, he said: "You think that José María may have?"

"If he did Jaime, he did it only to save me. You know very well José María could have made trouble for you long ago had he wanted to."

Her decision had been made for her, she said. She would return to the United

States. As she started to leave she turned and stammered: "Jaime, I'm so afraid for you."

He stared at her for a moment, then shook his head and said: "Don't worry about me. There's nothing anymore—nothing."

Even if Franco's troops, now almost at the gates of the city, arrived in time to save him, there would be nothing.

2

Franco's troops were now surging northeastward toward Madrid in an all-out drive to capture it before the new Russian arms could be effectively used against them. By November 2 the rebel line thus curved like a sickle from Brunete in the west to Pinto in the south, only twelve miles from the capital at some points. But if the high command was worried, the rebels in the field were not. They were sure that Madrid would be theirs within hours.

Captain Sifre Carbonel, who commanded a *tabor* ("battalion") of Moors, was especially confident. Luck was his companion. In all the fighting from Seville he had not even been scratched, though his *tabor* had been riddled with casualties. He had had to replace his officers two or three times, for so many had fallen. Why, he wondered, was he himself bulletproof?

In the battle for Brunete, west of Madrid, he felt so guilty that he decided to tempt fate. Wearing a conspicuous Moorish red fez and a blue *chilaba*, he stood up, a perfect target, and calmly peered through his binoculars while bullets zinged past him. He must prove to his men that he had not survived because of cowardice. Maybe if he was lucky he would be wounded just slightly—not seriously enough to take him out of the battle. Then he would be rid of his complex.

Carbonel's Moors, deeply attached to him, were dismayed.

"Captain, get down!" they cried.

But Carbonel ignored them—until they threw stones at him and he began to wonder if, ironically, he might end up in the hospital for wounds inflicted by his own men. So he finally got down. He had made his point.

"You are a saint like Franco," said one of his men. "The bullets respect you."

The Moors then kissed the hem of his *chilaba*. With a saint as a shield, nothing could stop them now from plowing into Madrid, where massive spoils were awaiting them.

When Brunete had fallen, another rebel officer who entered, Captain Carlos

Iniesta Cano of the foreign legion, found an abandoned Loyalist car and went for a ride with his comrade Lieutenant José de la Torre Pineiro. Since they drove away from Madrid, they did not expect to run into any trouble. But hardly had they gone five kilometers when they saw a group of armed men blocking the road—the enemy. The rebels had advanced so fast that, without realizing it, they left behind them many Loyalist troops. It was too late to turn around.

Iniesta pressed down on the brakes as about fifty men aimed guns at the two intruders.

"Out of the car!" a man yelled.

The two rebels obeyed and stood with their hands raised.

"Who are you?" Iniesta asked a tall militiaman who wore an anarchist insignia on his beret.

"Ninth Battalion of anti-Fascist militias," replied the man.

Iniesta, smiling to conceal his fear, put down his arms.

"Whew! You really frightened us," he said. "We thought you were Fascists."

The anarchist looked skeptical and began asking detailed questions about the captain's unit. Iniesta was ready with the answers. The day before, his men had found some documents in a small cloth bag left behind by the enemy that listed names of militia units and their commanders. He remembered many of these names and spouted them off. His captors were impressed. No enemy would have such knowledge. When Iniesta saw them lower their guns, he asked confidently:

"Who's the commander here?"

"I am, captain," said the tall militiaman, saluting with a clenched fist.

Iniesta frowned. "You don't know anything about the tactical situation. This is not the right place to be. You call yourself a commander?"

"I'm sorry, captain. But we're alone. The rest have run. Cowards. We're not professionals. If I've made a mistake, I'm sorry."

Just when the captain thought the game was won, a militiaman said: "Comrade Captain, you have a car and we have a wounded man."

Lieutenant Pineiro feigned indignation: "This is terrible. Largo Caballero is a real son of a bitch, abandoning you like this, not even helping you with the wounded."

Iniesta tried to hide his ire at this remark. Pineiro would only arouse suspicion by reviling the Loyalist leader. But the name-calling actually proved helpful. What rebel would dare say such a thing about Caballero in the company of Loyalists? These two men were obviously sincere.

"We must take the wounded man somewhere," said Iniesta.

"Where can we go safely?" the militiaman asked.

Iniesta thought swiftly. "Well, very near here is a little town—Brunete."

"Are you sure it's the safest place?"

"Yes, and it's only about five kilometers away."

The captain waited nervously for the reply. In the confusion of battle, did they know that Brunete was in rebel hands? If they did, his ruse might end—and so might his life.

After a moment, the men went to bring the wounded Loyalist to the car. The two rebels exchanged glances. They would not only get away, they'd go with a prisoner. But why just one? When the men had returned with the casualty, Iniesta said:

"As you know, this whole zone is surrounded by Fascists. It's very dangerous, and I have only a small pistol. We don't want to abandon the wounded man if we're attacked, and so we need protection. One of you come with us."

Everyone volunteered.

"We can carry only four. So only one more."

Pineiro then got in the back seat with the wounded man and a volunteer climbed in front next to Iniesta. As the car was about to drive off, someone cried: "Wait!"

Had the enemy known all along? Had they also been playing a game?

The tall man yelled through the car window: "We're in a bad position. And I'm only a corporal. We have no real commander. Would you send back a truck to take us to Brunete?"

"Sure, corporal."

"Don't forget. *Salud!*"

The car then sped toward Brunete, while the volunteer boasted of the heroic role he had played in the war. Iniesta encouraged him to talk, hoping he would be too preoccupied with his heroism to notice the Moors in the distance. Finally, Pineiro casually asked:

"Carlos, do you see those troops coming toward us?"

"Who are they, I wonder?" replied Iniesta.

"They look like Moors!" said Pineiro.

"You're right!" Iniesta exclaimed.

"Turn around! Turn around!" the Loyalist cried.

"I can't. There's no place to maneuver. Don't worry, I was in Morocco. I can speak their language. I'll salute them in Arabic and they won't know we're the enemy."

"No, it's too dangerous."

"It would be more dangerous to turn around."

Moments later the Moors were surrounding the car.

"Captain Iniesta!" said one, recognizing the driver.

The captain turned toward the Loyalist and growled: "You're a traitor. You told us to go to Brunete, and Franco is here."

"No, no, I'm a Communist!" replied the volunteer.

Iniesta laughed. The game was over.

"I'm a captain of the legion," he said. "Give me your rifle."

The Moors grabbed the two captives in the car and took them away. Then Iniesta sent some men in trucks to collect the other Loyalists farther up the road.

He didn't want to keep them waiting.

3

"Castro, new delegations of peasants want to see you."

Enrique Castro Delgado, the director of agrarian reform, looked up from his desk at his assistant Morayta and replied indifferently: "You receive them—and treat them well. Give them all they ask for. Say yes to everything."

The peasants must be given something to defend. They must be led with tenderness to the battlefield and into the Communist party. But let somebody else do it. There was only one thing on Castro's mind now.

"The battle is approaching," he said. "The battle for Madrid. The battle that must be won. Otherwise we've lost the war, despite what the politicians and military leaders say . . . Agrarian reform—it's all shit! Everything's shit except Madrid."

When Morayta had left, Castro gazed out of his office window at Retiro Park. It was November 4. In the late-autumn cold, the people were bundled up, walking swiftly, silently. They seemed to Castro to be searching their consciences. Should they fight and almost surely lose? Should they kill and almost certainly die?

At least they had a choice. Castro had none as he sat watching them, helpless to fight, helpless to kill. And yet he was a master of the "formula," the art of killing pitilessly, even passionately, for the cause. Yes, who cared about the stupid peasants at this critical moment? If Madrid and the war were lost, Spanish communism would be lost, too. For Madrid symbolized Communist power. And the Fifth Regiment, *his* Fifth Regiment, was the core of its defense. If it held, the party would win all the credit, and perhaps most of the people, *including* the peasants.

But could it hold under his successor, Enrique Lister, whom he considered a drunken fool? The news grew worse every hour. The day before, the Loyalists had flung fourteen thousand men, forty-eight Soviet tanks, and nine armored cars into coordinated flank attacks on the Toledo and Aranjuez roads in a great final surge to cut off the advancing rebels. They pushed into Torrejón, severing the Toledo road, but once again victory dissolved into defeat.

As soon as the tanks withdrew from Torrejón, the infantry feared that the enemy would surround them and retreated, too. And the Spanish crews that drove some of the tanks for the first time, after only ten days' training, hardly knew what they were doing. One man never learned to shift gears; another could not fire the tank gun because the safety catch was on. So all the Russian tanks and all the Russian advisers could not put the Loyalist army together again.

And while the enemy now closed in, Castro sat trapped in his luxurious office, dressed neatly in a suit, a spectator to the events he should be directing. His refined talent for killing was criminally going to waste.

Suddenly the telephone jolted him out of his bitter reverie. A Communist party official was calling:

"The Getafe front has collapsed! The Political Bureau orders you to leave immediately for the front. The panic of the militiamen must be overcome. They must be stopped!"

Castro ripped off his jacket, rolled up his shirt sleeves, and checked his pistol. Then he rushed to his waiting car and the chauffeur sped toward Getafe, only a few miles away on the Toledo road, and continued on until a ragged mob of men came into view. The car drew up to them and halted, and Castro climbed out. He saw in the men's faces the familiar fear, fury, grief, the terrible anguished look of defeat. And hunger, too, for the government had neglected to send them food. They stopped before him and he stared at them. Some were his former pupils.

"Tired?" Castro asked.

Nobody answered, and then several officers came up to him and said: "At your orders, major."

Castro looked into their eyes, wishing to insult as well as to embrace them.

"Sit down, comrades," he said. "Sit down and close your eyes. And breathe deeply. And think of how few kilometers you have to go. Think of what lies beyond those kilometers—your homes, your wives, your children. And after you've thought about this, do what you wish—run or stay!"

After leaving them alone to ponder for a few minutes, Castro returned and said: "Listen to me, comrades, officers, and militiamen . . . for you know well that I never lie. Our reserves are completing their training and in a few days will leave their bases for these front lines. Within a few days! Endless convoys of arms and ammunition are approaching Madrid. Your wives and children sleep without fear, thinking that you will stop the enemy. . . . We must resist several days more. . . . Can I trust you, comrades?"

"Yes!" the men shouted.

"Comrades, officers, listen! With the remaining men, reorganize your companies. It does not matter if they number forty or fifty men. At this moment, comrades, it is not the numbers that count, but courage, heroism. Anyone who does not obey is a traitor and will be exterminated in front of his former companions to serve as an example. It does not matter whether he is a militiaman or an officer! The thing is, comrades, that each meter the enemy advances should be costly to him in blood and time. . . . Quickly, comrades. *Viva* the Fifth Regiment!"

Artillery shells burst nearby, drowning out the notes of a Viennese waltz that trickled from a car radio. The enemy was near. But so were their families. The men obeyed, some jumping out of ambulances in which they had been hiding with the wounded.

Later that day José Diaz personally appealed to Castro: Would he return to the Fifth Regiment and help save Madrid?

Meanwhile, General Varela boasted to reporters in conquered Getafe: "You can announce to the world that Madrid will be captured this week."

And he rushed off to a meeting of the top command to help decide how to do it.

Despite Varela's optimistic forecast, he and the other rebel generals were still worried. How many Russian planes, tanks, and guns would they be facing? The Loyalists had failed to exploit their new weapons in the two big attacks they had launched so far, but they were learning and would probably fight better in the streets than they did on the roads and in the open fields. Planes and tanks could not possibly capture Madrid. Only men could, and the Loyalists outnumbered the rebels fifty thousand to twenty-five thousand. Also the rebels in the Guadarramas were unable to break through, while the promised new German equipment would not arrive for several days.

But though the rebel leaders assessed every danger, none really doubted they would capture Madrid. And the least doubtful of all was Mola. The city would not fight to the death, he was sure. How could men who had run like pursued animals in recent weeks suddenly stand up to the Moors and legionnaires, in the city or in the country? Varela, who had watched the enemy fight to the last man in such places as Badajoz, was less certain, whatever he told the press. Franco, as usual, was also cautious, and Yagüe was the least convinced of all that Madrid would easily fall. But their views differed only in degree. Would it take two days, three, four . . . ?

Mola had already given his troops orders on what to do when they seized the city. They would immediately free pro-rebel prisoners; arrest political suspects and throw them into concentration camps; confiscate all property of Loyalist organizations; punish those who would not help the "liberators"; and take no prisoners if they encountered armed groups. Franco himself ordered the men to destroy the reds and foreign volunteers found in the city, but warned them not to loot, rape, or patronize prostitutes until there were safeguards against venereal disease.

But if the rebel leaders agreed on what to do when they were in Madrid, they disagreed on how to *get* in, though in the first days of November the generals met frequently to weigh the alternatives.

Cut the road to Valencia east of Madrid and starve the capital into surrender? This would take too long. And besides, Franco wanted to keep the road open so the *Madrileños* could flee, leaving behind mainly his fifth column, which could then take over with less trouble. An attack from the southeast? Too dangerous, all agreed; they would have to fight their way through the workers' quarters of Villecas. That left a strike from the northwest or a direct frontal attack from the south.

A frontal attack, argued Mola. It was the shortest way, thus would take the shortest time. And time was vital, with Stalin pouring arms into Madrid, and Hitler and Mussolini eagerly awaiting its fall so they could recognize the Franco government. What's more, piercing Madrid's heart would force the demoralized, undisciplined reds to meet the attackers head-on, and in such a face-to-face battle Franco's more experienced troops would demolish them. The other routes, by contrast, would leave the rebels too vulnerable to flank attacks.

Two infantry columns should launch a diversionary attack on the southern suburb of Carabanchel, Mola advised, while three columns, the main force, moved west, then wheeled east through the wooded Casa de Campo, crossed the Manzanares River into University City, and swept into the Plaza de España. From there, they would fan out and slice through the city like the sharp edge of a knife.

Yagüe sharply protested: This was the most dangerous plan of all. The Casa de Campo was not only dotted with oak trees ideal for enemy ambushes, but was fortified with machine guns, concrete bunkers, mines, and barbed wire. The best way to steamroller into Madrid, Yagüe insisted, was from the northwest through the Puerta de Hierro and Cuatro Caminos. They were the most weakly defended quarters since the Loyalists probably did not expect the rebel southern army to pounce from the north.

But Franco and his German and Italian advisers backed Mola's plan, and so did Varela, though he feared that if the battle for the city took more than two or three days his relatively small force might flounder in a stormy urban sea. Like Mola, they were impatient, despite their lingering doubts. Why waste time with roundabout attacks? Head straight for the Plaza de España. Only five thousand men would form the spearhead, with the rest protecting the open flanks and serving as reserves.

Varela would unleash his two-column diversionary force on November 5. While wreaking havoc on Carabanchel, one column would march toward the Segovia Bridge, and another toward the Toledo Bridge farther south to make the Loyalists think this was the main attack. Then, on November 7, the three columns of the main force would sweep around to French Bridge in the north and storm through the Casa de Campo all the way to the Plaza de España.

November 7—a good day for the triumphal entry. What better way to celebrate the anniversary of the Russian Revolution?

Constancia de la Mora had not seen her husband, Air Force Commander Hidalgo de Cisneros, for two months. When she met him in his hotel room in Albacete, his new base, she could hardly recognize him. His prematurely gray hair had turned white, his face had grown thinner, his eyes had lost their sparkle.

Constancia had just come from Alicante, where she had transferred her orphanage when the rebels began bombing Madrid. The children she had found abandoned in a Madrid convent, hungry, unbathed, frightened, had been welcomed in Alicante by all the school children in the town and even a brass band.

Constancia was moved—and proud. She felt she had made a real contribution to the new Spain by turning the orphans into lively children who liked to romp and play and would, perhaps one day, help to lead the nation with compassion and a social conscience. But as the news from Madrid grew steadily worse, she began to wonder if that day would ever come. On November 5, with the rebels at the city's gates, Constancia drove to Albacete to see her husband—and to learn the truth.

Cisneros had good news, and his face, despite the lines, shone like a child's. Superior Russian fighter aircraft, nicknamed *Chatos* ["pug noses"] by the *Madrileños,* had arrived and already fought off German and Italian planes that had been bombing Madrid steadily for the past several days. So there was still hope for Madrid. For the Spain of Constancia's orphans.

"Connie," said Cisneros, "one country at least understands our fight."

And it was true; Russia understood. Madrid must hold—until Stalin decided he no longer needed it.

4

But in Madrid, on November 5, even some of Stalin's close collaborators doubted that Madrid could hold. Thus, Louis Fischer, the American Communist writer who had advised Prime Minister Largo Caballero how to prepare for the attack on the city, now needed some advice himself. Madrid seemed to be dying. Should he stay, Fischer wondered, and perhaps die with it? Panic had seized the city as the distant roar of cannon shook the earth and the deadly drone of aircraft split the sky. Terrified *Madrileños* tripped over one another rushing into the subway stations, no longer with their gramophones, though they emerged and cheered ecstatically when the new *Chatos* streaked out of nowhere to chase the enemy off.

Others marched toward the front with the bold stride of martyrs, women clinging to their men, while refugees poured in from the suburbs, many from Carabanchel on the last streetcars, their belongings piled on the roof. Most foreigners and many Spaniards had already packed their bags and scurried to Valencia, and those who neither fought nor fled wore the haunted look of people condemned to death.

And rebel propaganda fanned the fear. Burgos radio broadcast a program called "The Last Hours of Madrid," announcing the order of the victory parade that would pass before the War Ministry, the leaders of the military bands, and the places in Madrid where the Falange would be free to punish Loyalists. And Radio Lisbon even described how Generalissimo Franco had already "entered" Madrid on a white horse. Meanwhile, the rebels issued six-page stories to foreign correspondents on Madrid's fall, leaving blank spaces for the details. And waiting just outside the city to burst in with the first troops was a *Requeté* religious expedition from Seville, including priests and carpenters who would set up an altar in the Puerta del Sol for the celebration of Mass.

In the midst of the terror and the turmoil, Fischer went to the Palace Hotel, where the Russians were staying, but he found it almost deserted. Virtually the entire Soviet embassy staff had already left. Stalin did not want the enemy to identify his agents, much less capture them, and had ordered them to "stay out of artillery range." Finally, Fischer found Orlov, the NKVD chief.

What should he do? Fischer asked.

'Leave as soon as possible!" Orlov exclaimed. "There is no front. Madrid is the front."

Fischer walked down the Gran Vía pondering this advice. He wrote later: "I walked slowly. Was this the end? . . . Suppose Franco takes Madrid? . . . I did not feel like taking chances with Moors, foreign legionnaires, and rebels on a rampage."

As he passed the Hotel Gran Vía he looked through the window and saw André Malraux sitting in the lobby. Malraux had been in low spirits since losing most of his aircraft during the retreat from Toledo. When Fischer entered and asked about the current situation, the Frenchman replied, as if reciting a communiqué:

"The enemy is in Carabanchel."

"How do you know?"

"We bombed them there this morning."

What should he do?

"Get out quickly! Get a car. If you can't get one I'll fly you out of Madrid tomorrow morning. But first you'll have to go bombing with us."

Fischer decided to find a car.

"Get out quickly!"

Prime Minister Largo Caballero gave this same advice to his cabinet the next afternoon, November 6, at a meeting in the War Ministry while the windows rattled from the boom of artillery and the shrill tirades of frightened ministers. Actually he had wanted to move the government out of Madrid earlier, as the Communists had urged. But the anarchists would have accused him of treason for abandoning the *Madrileños*.

He had, indeed, thought of giving up the city without a fight, as suggested by his new undersecretary of war, General Asensio. Caballero had promoted Asensio and appointed General Pozas to replace him as central front commander to appease the Communists, who had made Asensio the scapegoat for all the militia failures. Even if the Loyalists could miraculously hold Madrid, why, Asensio argued, tie up tens of thousands of troops defending a city with little military value? Better to leave the capital, hem the rebels in, and counterattack with a strong reorganized army. And Caballero agreed.

As a professional military man, Asensio did not give much weight to the political and psychological importance of holding Madrid. And as a politician, Caballero preferred to withdraw from Madrid temporarily and return in a burst of glory rather than leave his forces to die in a massacre that might cripple the republic as well as his political career. But neither the Communists nor the anarchists would hear of this plan.

So Caballero felt the least he could do was to push the government out of Madrid—and this meant dealing with the anarchists. Just two days earlier, on November 4, he made peace with them, even persuading them to join his government. Now there were four anarchist ministers, and they would have to share responsibility for any future military or political failures and to accept government decisions, including one to leave town if the majority so voted.

The anarchists had been caught in an agonizing dilemma and had finally decided to flout the most basic tenet of their philosophy: Fight all government. They were now *in* the government. But could they have acted otherwise? They had to counter Communist influence or the Communists would quash them. Reflecting their pain, the new minister of health, anarchist Federica Montseny, reminisced later:

"How many reserves, doubts, how much anguish I had to overcome personally in accepting this post! For others, a governmental post could be the goal and the satisfaction of measureless ambitions. For me, it was nothing less than a break with an entire life's work . . . which itself derived from the life's work of my parents."

The civil war had compelled the anarchists to see things as they were, not as they wished they were. Montseny, the first female cabinet member in Spanish history, had even helped to persuade Durruti to take orders from the government. He must leave the front in Aragon, where the anarchists ruled, and come to Madrid with several thousand of his men.

Never, he replied.

But if he didn't, the Communists would control the capital, and perhaps even the country. Durruti had to rescue Madrid in order to rescue the anarchist revolution. No other anarchist had his prestige, his charisma, his reputation for courage. He must go!

Durruti debated with himself. Reality had already begun to pollute his ideological purity. To the horror of many anarchists, he had said over the radio, "We renounce everything except victory," and stressed the need for discipline with the "shocking" statement, "We are against this false freedom invoked by the cowards in order to flee." Such words clashed with his deepest convictions. And so did his reluctant decision to go to Madrid and place himself under the command of men he sensed would betray him and his followers.

Now, only two days after the anarchists had agreed to violate their creed by joining the government, they felt that Caballero was already betraying them— and the people of Madrid. No, the anarchist ministers shouted, the government must not move out of Madrid. It must not leave its citizens to be massacred by Franco. With Communists sitting there in the cabinet room, they could not say what troubled them just as much: that the Communist party, with its Soviet arms, would then control Madrid.

Caballero scoffed. The same militiamen who had been running since Talavera, he said, would be defending Madrid. Why should they be expected to stop running now? Besides, how could the government function in the middle of a battlefield, especially with a civil service probably riddled with fifth columnists? How could it coordinate the nation's forces when Madrid might be cut off from the rest of Spain and the world at any moment? And if the rebels captured the ministers, every country would recognize a Franco regime. However, if the government left and Madrid then fell—which was likely—the Loyalists could attack from outside as Asensio had advised in the first place.

While the ministers heatedly debated their fate, one motorcycle dispatch rider after another arrived from the front line with urgent messages: Rebel tanks were pushing through Carabanchel toward the Toledo Bridge leading into the metropolis . . . the airport and radio station at Quatro Vientos had fallen . . . the shell supply for the Loyalist guns was running out.

Caballero made it clear: Unless the cabinet agreed to move, he would resign. In the feverish atmosphere, everyone but the anarchists agreed that the government must leave, and they had to accept the decision.

The trouble was, some ministers pointed out, Caballero had waited too long. Now the people would call the government cowardly and their morale would plummet even further.

Caballero, said the Communist Uribe, should, before leaving, explain to them the reasons for the move. Nonsense, replied the prime minister. That would only spread more panic.

The ministers and their closest aides would drive that night to Valencia. They could call for their families later. Some preferred Barcelona, but they didn't argue. The important thing was that they were leaving Madrid.

And who would remain behind to command the forces in the city—and surrender it if necessary? Caballero had just the man. A man who impressed even Russian General Goriev, since he seemed the type who could be used: General Miaja.

That evening, Arturo Barea went to the Foreign Ministry as usual to get instructions from his boss, Rubio Hidalgo, on how to handle the reports of the foreign correspondents. Barea always found these meetings disagreeable. Rubio, who looked dramatically Machiavellian with his thin black mustache, his dark glasses, and his cynical smile, was, Barea felt, an opportunist with little knowledge of journalism or even the cause.

Rubio wiped the sweat off his bald head with a handkerchief and said: "Tonight the government is transferring to Valencia. Tomorrow Franco will enter Madrid."

Barea was stunned.

"We're going tomorrow, too," Rubio continued. "Of course, I'm referring to the permanent staff only. I hope—the government hopes, I should say—that you will remain at your post up to the last moment."

"Of course."

"That's good. . . . The government will move to Valencia tonight, but no one knows it yet. Written instructions will be left with General Miaja, so that he can negotiate the surrender with the least possible loss of blood. But he doesn't yet know it himself, and he won't know until after the government has gone. . . . It is absolutely necessary to keep the government's move a secret, otherwise a frightful panic would break out. So what you have to do is to go to the Telefónica, take over the service as usual, and not let a single reference through."

"What shall I do tomorrow, then?"

"As there will be nothing you can do, you will close the censorship when your shift is over, go home, and take care of your own skin, because nobody can tell what may happen."

Barea then went to the Telefónica, where the correspondents were frenziedly shouting over the telephone and clacking out stories between gulps of coffee and whiskey. He hated them for their political dispassion, their professional detachment. What was a matter of survival for the *Madrileños* was simply a "hot story" for them. They were cruel, callous, even traitors to humanity. He would wield his sword, the blue pencil, with special pleasure tonight. They would not get a word out about the government leaving and Madrid dying.

Only a few of these reporters cared for the cause, and one of them was William Forrest of the London *Daily Express*. For he was a Scottish Communist. But he was also a dedicated reporter and, having learned that the government was about to leave, was determined to scoop the world with this news. His censored report, of course, did not mention the evacuation. But by stringing together the first letters of each sentence the editors would read: "Gov't fled Valencia." He managed to telephone instructions on the code to the stenographer in his London office. But the editors didn't understand, and so the world, like Madrid, would not know until the next day.

Meanwhile, Barea worked through the shell-shocked night bitterly harboring the secret in his soul.

Earlier that day, General Miaja sat behind his desk drawing lines on a map of Madrid and studying the enemy's likely routes of advance. He was the commander of the Madrid area once again. Surprisingly, since after serving for a few hours as war minister on that momentous day of July 18, he hardly earned a reputation as the republic's most valuable general.

Sent to the Córdoba front, he was ordered to attack rebel strongholds there, but he refused. It would be madness, he argued, for his skimpy force to do this without reinforcements. But the War Ministry insisted. When would he enter Córdoba?

"Never!" Miaja succinctly replied.

He was then removed from his post and sent to command the Valencia garrison, but again he made demands. Caballero must give him greater power so he could control insubordinate militiamen. So once again he was relieved of his command, and this time left without a job. He must either be incompetent or disloyal, thought the government. But then, on October 28, it gave him back the Madrid command, though Miaja was not to learn until later just why his services had suddenly become so urgently needed.

As Miaja now gloomily analyzed the map, his adjutant entered.

"General," he said, "the war minister requests that you go immediately to his office."

A half hour later, at 2:00 P.M., Miaja was sitting with Caballero, wondering why he had been summoned—and why the minister's desk was so clean.

"What would happen, general," asked Caballero, "if the government left Madrid?"

"The government should have left earlier," Miaja replied with his usual bluntness. "I still believe it should leave . . . but I don't know what the consequences might be of a move that will certainly look like flight."

The people could be so demoralized that Franco might easily take the city, he added. But that was a risk that should be taken.

The government, Caballero replied, would probably leave that night and Miaja would be left in charge of the city. His orders? The general would receive them before the departure.

"I shall faithfully obey the government's orders and shall fulfill my duty until the last moment," Miaja said.

The general was pleased; he was being handed the key military command in the war. But he was also agitated; the government clearly expected him to be nothing more than a sacrificial offering to Franco. Caballero was acting in bad faith. . . .

It was then that Caballero, now acting as prime minister, asked his cabinet to approve the transfer to Valencia. And hardly had it done so when, at 6:45 P.M., he rushed down the marble staircase into the central courtyard and climbed into his car, which was already full of suitcases.

Meanwhile, General Asensio called in General Pozas, who had replaced him as commander of the central front, and General Miaja. Asensio merely handed each a sealed envelope marked: "Very confidential. Not to be opened until 6:00 A.M., November 7."

They must obey the instructions on the envelope, Asensio ordered. Then he, too, hurried to a car and headed for Valencia. Miaja and Pozas stared at each other. By 6:00 A.M. would either of them be alive? Would Madrid be alive? The two men agreed to disobey orders. Each ripped open his envelope and read the note inside. They looked up, confused. The envelopes had been wrongly addressed. They exchanged notes.

Miaja was to defend the city at "all costs" with the help of a *junta* made up of delegates from each Popular Front party. But if he was forced to retreat, he should form a new defense line at Cuenca, about halfway to Valencia. Pozas, whose headquarters was at Tarancón, some sixty miles southeast of the capital, would command the forces manning the new line, if one was needed.

The two generals were incredulous. Franco was storming Madrid and they were supposed to have waited about ten hours before knowing what to do. And if they had not opened the envelopes before Pozas left Madrid and had waited until 6:00 A.M. to do so, they wouldn't have known what their orders were even then since they could not have exchanged notes. Obviously, the government did not want to fight for the capital. All the Loyalist troops in Madrid, as well as the civilians, might thus have been slaughtered, either by Franco's rampaging army or by the fifth columnists awaiting their moment of revenge.

Miaja, with two aides, plodded through the deserted corridors of the War Ministry, glancing into brightly lit rooms in which files, official announcements, and half-filled coffee cups littered the tables. He walked through the open door of Caballero's office and plopped himself down behind the large desk.

"The third time!" he exclaimed, having served as war minister briefly in February 1936 and again in July.

Now, however, he was the master of Madrid. But a master without servants, other than his two personal aides. They were alone, it seemed, in an eerie, uninhabited world, with only the blasts of artillery nearby to remind them that there were other creatures still alive.

Miaja pushed a button on a switchboard to ring for an assistant. No response. He pushed another. Still no answer. Then he pressed all the buttons at once. Nothing happened. He removed his round glasses and nervously wiped them. There was no one in the ministry to help him, and the enemy was about to crash into the center of the city.

The chauffeured cars sped down the road to Valencia throughout the night without an obstacle in their path—until their headlights revealed men on both sides of the road aiming rifles at them. They screeched to a halt, and a man wearing a red and black neckerchief poked his head into each vehicle.

"Where are you going?"

"Special mission."

Everyone was going on a "special mission."

Anarchist militiamen had heard that the government was "deserting" the people and were not impressed with the high political status of the passengers.

"Gang of miserable cowards," one of them cried. "We should kill every one of you."

Prime Minister Largo Caballero and several other ministers who had left Madrid earlier had already gone by before this checkpoint was set up in Tarancón. But many other officials, including, ironically, one of the anarchist ministers, were caught in the ambush. All their arguments were in vain. And when one government dignitary shouted, "To hell with these madmen!" and ordered his driver to crash through the barrier, the anarchists chased the car on motorcycles and shot the fugitive dead.

The officials were herded into a house and their captors pondered what to do with them. Shortly, Cipriano Mera and Eduardo Val, secretary of the CNT national committee in Madrid, arrived and joined in the discussion. Should the prisoners be shot? Or perhaps sent to the front line? At first, Mera did not want to let them go, not even the anarchist minister. They had done a shameful thing by running at a moment when the people needed powerful, courageous leadership. But could *any* government give powerful, courageous leadership? Perhaps the flight was actually a blessing. The anarchists might never have another opportunity like this to fill a power vacuum in Madrid. To make a real revolution in the heart of the nation, or at least stop the Communists from taking over.

So Mera was not disappointed when Val said the prisoners should be freed, but replied, as if reluctant:

"In return, comrade Val, you must permit us to go to Madrid with a thousand men from my column."

Val agreed. And Mera envisioned final victory. In addition to his thousand men, Durruti would soon be marching into Madrid from Barcelona with several thousand more. Perhaps enough to deal with the Fascists now and the Communists later.

Mera thus sent the trembling government leaders on their way. Hopefully, they would never return to Madrid.

5

On this cold moonless night of November 6, Madrid lay like a helpless whale on the beach of oblivion. In the Casa de Campo, young and old alike breathlessly dug narrow, almost useless, trenches from tree to tree, pausing only to guzzle wine brought by people from neighboring houses. In the city center, the streets, dimly lit by blue-painted lamps, were deserted, except for an occasional militia patrol lurking in the shadows, or a frightened newsman rushing to the Telefónica to file a coded story on the imminent fall of the city.

In the embassies, rebel-sympathizing refugees joyously counted the minutes until their liberation, playing their "last" game of cards and plotting their first act of vengeance. In Loyalist homes, people anxiously sat by the radio grasping for even the most meager scrap of hope that a miracle was in the making. In the hospitals, wounded men, remembering Toledo, begged their attendants to poison them. In the Hotel Gran Vía, one of the few hotels still open, people sat in the gloomy lounge speaking softly so rebel spies could not hear them and jumping at every scrape of a chair or slam of a door. They tried to ignore the shrill voice of a young man pleading with a government official for a pass that would permit his Communist wife to leave Madrid before it was too late.

And in Carabanchel, where the cry *"Los Moros! Los Moros!"* resounded, feeding the city's terror, young men and women knelt on the streets behind makeshift barricades of stone and furniture while the unseen enemy ricocheted bullets off the walls of their homes and moved gradually toward Toledo Bridge, a short march from the Puerto del Sol. . . .

"Carlos, let's go to Toledo Bridge," said Enrique Castro Delgado to his political commissar, Carlos Contreras, an Italian Communist.

They left Fifth Regiment headquarters, jumped into a car, and raced toward the bridge. As they approached it and saw men running away, Castro and Carlos leaped out to stop them.

"Comrades," Carlos shouted, "Madrid is looking to you. The Fifth Regiment is looking to you. Democratic Spain is looking to you. The world is watching you, the world that yearns for the triumph of our revolution. . . . If anyone is tired, if he can't stand on his feet, or hold a rifle, let him say so . . . and another comrade will take his rifle."

Castro then climbed on a truck and cried: "Whoever cannot go on, let him take one step forward."

The men were silent, and all remained where they were.

"So comrades," said Castro, "to the battle positions!"

As the men started to return to the barricades, Castro saw nearby an artillery officer trying to pull his cannon to the rear. He rushed over to the officer and demanded:

"What are you doing comrade?"

"Saving the gun."

"If I ordered you to leave this gun here, to start firing point-blank, what would you do?"

"I wouldn't obey you. One cannot ask an artilleryman to act like a madman. Because that is madness."

"I'd have to kill you, comrade, if you disobeyed me. I know this is madness . . . but only wonderful madness can lift the spirit of the men who are fleeing. Do you understand me?"

"No, I don't want to understand you, major."

Castro then aimed his pistol at the officer.

"Lieutenant," he said, "I'm ordering you not to move the cannon. And I'm ordering you to fire."

The officer stared at Castro and knew that he was serious. He began blasting away.

"Fire, comrade lieutenant, fire! Look how they're retreating."

As Castro and Carlos drove back to headquarters, they knew the rebels would be back, that they would attack again and again. Their own exhausted, demoralized men had to hold for another forty-eight hours. The International Brigades had only begun to organize and train, but perhaps they would be here by then.

Later that night, Castro sent thirty volunteers in armored trucks into the battle. Bullets could easily pierce the armor, and the trucks would turn into coffins, he knew. But when the men at the front saw them they would be encouraged to fight, to die in their positions, too.

"It's a simple mathematical question," Castro bluntly told the volunteers. "Thirty men dead for thousands of men fighting. The result: Madrid is saved."

When they had left, José Díaz, the Communist party's secretary-general, called Castro to his office. Díaz was ill and in great pain as he lay on a sofa.

"The Political Bureau," he groaned, "has decided to move to Valencia. . . . You will be responsible to the party for military affairs."

Castro was delighted. Now no one would be watching over his shoulder—except *La Pasionaria*, who refused to leave.

On returning to his headquarters, he immediately began to exert his new authority, first turning his attention to the political prisoners filling the jails. In the first days of November, the government had debated long hours on what to do with these prisoners, for if Franco entered Madrid and released them he would have eight thousand more executioners to help him.

Reflecting the indecision was the division among the anarchists, as described by the anarchist leader Gregorio Gallego. Evacuate the prisoners immediately and form them into work battalions, some suggested. Use them as hostages, others said. Imprison them in official and strategic buildings to keep the rebels from bombing these places, still others advised.

The Communist attitude was also unclear. Koltsov writes, perhaps to cover up what happened, that since there weren't enough trucks or buses for a massive transfer at this late date, he wanted the inmates, in groups of about two hundred, to walk to prisons in the rear escorted by loyal peasants. At least the most dangerous could be evacuated, and any who escaped could be hunted down later.

" 'Liquidation,' in its broad sense," Gallego says, "was supported by few people. Those who did support it did so in a shameful manner, and later practiced it secretly."

Meanwhile, Largo Caballero ordered Interior Minister Angel Galarza to evacuate the prisoners, but in the chaos nothing was done.

Now, on the night of November 6, no one was in charge of the prison system. Almost all top law enforcement officials, including Galarza and Police Chief Muñoz, were in flight. Before departing, however, Muñoz, apparently under Galarza's instructions, left a signed order with his subordinates that authorized them to have any inmate released from prison.

This order would permit the police to carry out Koltsov's alleged scheme or any other evacuation plan. But it would also permit "shameful" men with access to the order to remove prisoners so they could murder them. This was probably not the intention of Muñoz, who had always tried, if ineffectually, to curb the *paseos*. But who was there now to keep order?

Indeed, on this night, before General Miaja could form a ruling *junta*, Madrid had no government at all. An ideal time for the unscrupulous to act as they wished. And General Mola had nourished their wish, and their fear, with a boast he made to the press some days earlier. Four columns, he said, were marching on Madrid (though a fifth would join them shortly afterwards).

"But, general," interrupted a British correspondent, "you have spoken of *five* columns."

"The fifth column is already in Madrid and operating successfully," replied Mola, coining an expression that would endure.

So with the government gone and Madrid left to die, why quibble about legal niceties? Castro didn't.

"I have ordered that the massacre begin," he told a security aide. "The fifth column of which Mola spoke must be wiped out without pity before it strikes." And he slyly added: "I have already told you that you have the right to make a mistake. There are times when you will find yourself faced with twenty people and you know that one of them is a traitor but you don't know which one. That is when you have one problem with your conscience and another with the party. Do you understand?"

The aide understood.

And the massacre began.

Felipe Gómez Acebo and his fellow inmates in Model Prison were churning with mixed emotions on this historic night. They exulted every time they heard the explosion of an artillery shell or an aerial bomb in the distance. Franco was pounding at the door of Madrid and might liberate them within hours.

But at the same time, the atmosphere in the prison seemed ominous. The guards were frightened and constantly conversing. Police and militia came and went in a kind of quiet panic. And the prisoners remembered that whenever Franco had bombed Madrid, men were "released"—so they could be killed by vengeful gangs waiting outside.

What would their jailkeepers do now with Franco so near?

Gómez Acebo sought solace in his incredible record of luck. When the militiamen at Montaña Barracks had been about to shoot him, an old schoolmate among them had saved him. When he had been arrested later and again seemed doomed, his girl friend's uncle, a police chief, came to his rescue. If only his luck could hold another day, perhaps another hour. Then he would be free at last after the months of suffering in a small crowded cell where he slept on a concrete floor crawling with lice.

Shortly after midnight, Gómez Acebo heard a commotion. A large group of police and militiamen arrived, and soon a voice ordered all inmates whose names were called to shout their cell numbers. These men would be transferred to another prison. Name after name echoed through the galleries. Then the clanging of cell doors slammed shut. Gómez Acebo wasn't deceived. Nobody was ordered to take a blanket, and he knew that meant one would not be needed.

Most of the men called were military officers who a few days earlier had refused the chance to join the Loyalist side; they were the most dangerous because they were trained fighters. In the courtyard their wrists were tied together with thin cord, then they were led to green double-decker buses that had often been used for holiday tours.

But this would be no holiday. About an hour later, the people of Paracuellos de Jarama, the village where Christopher Lance had found the graves of many men some week before, heard repeated volleys. Panic-stricken, they fled from their homes and spent the night in the fields. At dawn they would return home and be ordered to dig more graves.

Gómez Acebo's luck held. His name had not been called—yet.

6

In the ghostly emptiness of the War Ministry, General Miaja sat at his desk from 9:00 to 11:00 P.M. frantically calling the home of every staff officer he knew. But always, no answer. Finally, one man picked up the phone, listened to Miaja's plea for help, and hung up. Then the general's fortunes began to change, and some officers agreed to rush over. The government had not thought these men important enough to join the caravan to Valencia.

Miaja impatiently paced the floor as he waited for the officers to arrive. He was a man possessed, driven by a sacred mission born partly of pride, partly of mule-like obstinacy, partly of fear that the rebels would slaughter half of Madrid, with himself at the head of the list. Yet, he realized, there was almost nothing to stop them.

The whole top echelon of authority had vanished—ministers, civil officials, political leaders, labor chiefs, Russian advisers—and there was no central military command at all. He didn't know where the enemy was, or even where his own men were; they were all fighting their own little battles, with his tanks scurrying around from place to place serving as mobile artillery. Even his files were missing, since the government had taken them all. He *did* know that he had only 120,000 rounds of ammunition, unusable in many of his old rifles and hardly sufficient to last four hours, and that he had only enough cannon shells to last three hours.

Shortly, the garden of the ministry was bathed in shadows cast by headlights, and by 11:00 P.M. Miaja was holding his first meeting with his new general staff. He immediately chose Major Rojo as his chief of staff. Rojo, the officer who had entered the Alcázar and failed to persuade Colonel Moscardó to surrender, was only a junior officer but a brilliant one, and, like Miaja, he had a knack for selecting excellent subordinates. Some held higher rank than he but had such a deep respect for his ability that they did not resent being under his command. A bespectacled, patient, humorless man, Rojo was a puzzle to many of his colleagues for he was a fervent Catholic and a purely professional soldier without any ideological commitment. Why should he fight for the Loyalists? He gave the answer to Enrique Castro when asked: "Because I took an oath to the republic."

Miaja now ordered the officers to round up all the column commanders scattered along the front. An intensive search began, and in a short time all were gathered in the anteroom outside Miaja's office, convinced they would be organizing a "strategic retreat" from Madrid that night.

What else did military logic dictate? asked the professional officers.

To stay and fight, the militia leaders replied, though hardly expecting a conventional old soldier like Miaja to agree.

When the men entered Miaja's office, they were astonished to find their new commander smiling and confident.

"The government has left Madrid at the mercy of the enemy," Miaja said. "The moment has come to be men. Do you understand me? To be men! *Machos!*"

The word *machos* thundered through the room. After so many revolutionary slogans, this old Spanish expression, reminding them that they were all Spaniards whatever their politics, struck home with special impact. Miaja then exclaimed: "I want those who stay with me to know how to die!"

He stood up, walked a few steps, and spoke again: "If there is anyone here who is not capable of this, of dying, he had better say so now."

No one answered.

"Is there anyone?"

Silence.

Miaja sat down again, once more serene. "I congratulate you on your attitude, gentlemen. That's what I expected of you. See the general staff for orders. Good night and good luck."

The trade union leaders then marched in and were also shocked to find a ferocious man. He must have fifty thousand men in the front lines by dawn, Miaja roared, and it was up to the unions to see he had them.

"But, general," someone asked, "are there arms for them?"

Yes, there were arms, replied Miaja. The unions themselves were hoarding them. He did not say what they all knew: that the militia groups planned to use them later against one another. They must hand over all the arms, ammunition, and dynamite they were hiding, he demanded. And if there was still not enough, the men would have to use those of the dead. The hour of sacrifice had come and no one could retreat a single inch.

He repeated: They must be *machos*!

By 4:00 A. M., November 7, Miaja had set in motion one of the most massive and spontaneous popular risings in the history of any city. Militiamen canvassing every block for recruits hardly had to pull anyone out of bed, for frightened men suddenly became brave as they heard the artillery blasts and listened to the cries of their children. People set up war committees to transform every house into a fortress. Combat units gave up their independence and agreed to take orders from the general staff, though Miaja and Rojo weren't sure where to send them since they had almost no intelligence on the enemy. Within six hours the general had helped to turn a mob of beaten men into an army of iron-willed fighters.

The miracle was happening—Madrid was not lost yet. However, the president of Guatemala, for one, thought it was. He had already sent the Ministry of Communications a cable for Franco congratulating him on his great conquest. Many foreign correspondents, meanwhile, expected the generalissimo to walk into the Telefónica at any moment and change the censorship rules.

Arturo Barea, who remained on duty, was furious when someone tried to report the news that the rebels had crossed three bridges over the Manzanares and were fighting hand to hand with Loyalists in the courtyards of Model Prison. When he refused to let the report pass without official confirmation, one huge American reporter who had been drinking all evening grabbed him by the lapels and shook him violently. Franco was in town, the reporter growled, and the Loyalists had nothing more to say. Barea said nothing more. He simply drew his pistol and ordered two militiamen to keep the reporter under guard.

Would Franco really enter Madrid that morning of November 7? Miaja couldn't be sure. But he acted as if his nondescript army had already won. With complete calm, he lay down fully dressed on a cot and asked to be awakened in two hours, at 6:00 A.M.—the hour when he was supposed to learn what his mission was.

PART III

The Attack

CHAPTER 8

Resistance

1

The artillery barrage had stopped and the roll of drums now echoed through the cold dawn, mingling with the clatter of horses' hooves. In close formation, the Moorish cavalry pranced through the streets of Carabanchel toward Toledo Bridge and the center of Madrid. Young men and women crouching behind barricades or on the balconies of houses fired at the horsemen with old rifles and shotguns, and some toppled to the ground. But the rest forged ahead, without pausing, as if mesmerized by the rhythm of the drums, which grew louder and more terrifying every second.

"They're coming!" cried a militiaman behind the first barricade. "They won't stop."

"Reload your goddamn shotgun and keep shooting!" shouted another.

Several girls ran stooped along the barricade, encouraging the men: "Fire! Fire! Don't let them get us!"

The men continued to shoot as they listened to the drums of death. But the Moors kept coming. The frenzy in the trenches spread, while the women ran back and forth delivering ammunition and dragging away the wounded.

"Fire! Fire!"

But was it too late? Through the haze of war, they gazed into a whirlpool of billowing *chilabas* and horses' manes, hardly yards away. Suddenly, a motorcycle with a machine gun attached roared into the street, right in the path of the

THE BATTLE FOR MADRID

stampeding enemy. As the weapon rattled, the men on horses dropped to the street like fruit in a hurricane. The drums stopped beating, and the ranks broke, running into what seemed like an invisible wall. The horses turned around and galloped back, many without riders. The attack had failed.

But the militiamen were too exhausted to rejoice.

"I'm going to sleep," said one.

"No one sleeps here," a comrade replied. "Not until we win. Then you can sleep for thirty hours."

The enemy did not sleep either. Later that day, Moorish and legionnaire infantry struck jointly behind Italian armor.

"Tanks!"

The men climbed out of the trenches and began running to the rear, when suddenly two militia leaders jumped in front of them, raised their hands, and yelled: "Stop, comrades! Let's attack them!"

Their voices dissolved in a wild medley of screams, explosions, and grinding motors. But they kept shouting, and finally two words stuck in the thick grimy air: *"No pasaràn!"*

Some defenders halted . . . then others. The two leaders began moving toward the enemy, armed only with pistols.

"Everybody! Let's go!" one cried.

And the men, only seconds before pale with panic, lunged forward, side by side with women and even children. A raging half-armed mob, the people of Madrid, surged like a gathering surf toward the enemy. It was a strange battle— human flesh colliding with steel machines. Even as some fighters fell, others advanced like robots obeying some electrical impulse. They walked faster, then broke into a run, leaping over parapets, over shell holes and crevices, ignoring the missiles that were tearing great bloody gaps in their midst, throwing stones if they had no bullets.

While the mindless, maddened crowd pushed ahead, a young sailor, Emilio Coll, crouched behind some rubble beside the road. He had seen the Soviet film *The Sailors of Kronstadt*, which showed youngsters stopping czarist tanks in the Russian Revolution with a few handmade bombs, and now here were enemy tanks and he had a stick of dynamite! He puffed on a cigar and lit the fuse with it, and as the first tank lurched to within yards of him he dashed into the street and hurled the dynamite at the treads. There was a great explosion and the tank began to burn, forcing those behind it to turn around and crawl off, with the infantry tagging behind.

Once more, the Loyalists had held. And General Varela, in his rear headquarters, was filled with anxiety. He had laughed on learning that General Miaja was commanding the defense of Madrid.

"He's a poor old grandpa," he had said. "We'll beat him easily."

But now his old doubts returned.

Had he not warned Mola? The same men who could panic easily could fight courageously. They had stormed Montaña Barracks in the face of blistering machine-gun fire. They had fought fiercely in Badajoz. And now they were blindly attacking his tanks in Madrid. More artillery, he ordered. More tanks, more planes. His men must try again—and again.

And they did, gradually grinding their way over a carpet of corpses toward Toledo Bridge. The Loyalists grew desperate again and were about to blow up the bridge. But then, Eleuterio Cornejo, a seventeen-year-old-youth, emulated Émilio Coll, dynamiting the first tank and blocking the way to the others, while his comrades charged the enemy infantry with bayonets.

Toledo Bridge was saved.

Meanwhile, other rebel troops were edging toward Segovia Bridge farther north. If they crossed it, they would find themselves in front of the National Palace, Spain's traditional seat of power. Militiamen rushed to the bridge but Junkers dropped tons of bombs on them and the survivors scattered like fish when a stone is thrown into a pond. As the rebels were about to cross the bridge, a truck careened to a halt at the opposite end and, while a loudspeaker blared the "Internationale," *La Pasionaria* stepped out of the cabin. The music stopped and she cried:

"Come back! Come back! Across the bridge is the enemy. We must save Madrid!"

The men stopped running and began forming a circle around her. A huge circle of hundreds.

"No pasaràn!"

The men started running again, but this time toward the enemy across the bridge, screaming, firing, falling. And the rebels also ran—almost a mile to the rear.

Segovia Bridge was saved, too.

Major Tella, whose objective was Toledo Bridge, reported his difficulties in his column diary: "Besides a labyrinthlike system of trenches, each house has become a bulwark from which the enemy harasses with machine guns."

And Colonel Barrón; as he moved toward Segovia Bridge, recorded in his diary: "Our forces have to make their way through the interior of the houses, breaking partition walls, struggling with the enemy in all rooms of the houses they occupy, dislodging him with only a great effort."

General Varela could no longer afford to throw men into the cauldron consuming his troops in Carabanchel, which was a secondary target, anyway.

But in the Casa de Campo, where there were no houses to obstruct his advance, he was sure things would be different. The trouble was, Franco had ordered him to hold up a full-scale attack there for another day, until November 8. New German artillery had just arrived in Spain and the generalissimo, still cautious, preferred to wait until the guns could be brought up to the front lines before striking all-out. Another day lost.

Meanwhile, Varela's troops would probe the Casa de Campo to test resistance and set up a line as close as possible to the Manzanares River, from where his men could spring into the heart of Madrid the next day.

With mixed feelings, Colonel Yagüe watched through the early-morning fog as a company of legionnaires, led by Captain Iniesta Cano, dynamited parts of the stone wall encircling the Casa de Campo. (Iniesta was the man who had shrewdly posed as a Loyalist when he ran across some militiamen near Brunete and ended up capturing them.) If all went as well in the next two days, Yagüe's men would burst through the great park, cross the Manzanares, and sweep into University City and the Plaza de España. Then all Madrid would be at the rebels' mercy. Yagüe had opposed this route because of the intricate system of trenches and fortifications there. But he might have been wrong. So far, only the twittering of birds disturbed the morning silence.

Iniesta's troops entered the park and marched over a springy mat of yellow leaves that had fallen from the trees swaying in a brisk breeze. On warmer days, in better times, thousands of people had sat under these trees poking their hands into picnic baskets and pulling out a tortilla or a bottle of *vino*. But today there would be no picnic.

Suddenly, shots. In the gray mist, Iniesta's legionnaires and a unit of Moors that had marched in from different directions mistook each other for the enemy and bullets whizzed back and forth. When they realized their error, both groups ran on toward the river, darting from tree to tree. But soon there were more shots. The Loyalists had been alerted.

Yagüe raised his binoculars to his eyes. His men had been stopped by a curtain of bullets and mortar shells coming mainly from the fields to the west. The colonel watched in bewilderment as scores of his men collapsed on the damp earth. And Captain Iniesta Cano was in no position to trick the enemy this time.

Yagüe immediately assembled all three of his columns in the menaced area to foil the Loyalist counterattack, which threatened to wipe them all out. Just as he had warned Franco, Mola, and Varela. The Casa de Campo was a huge trap!

"Who is General Miaja?"

Enrique Castro Delgado had hardly heard of him. Miaja was an obscure general with an obscure record, and now he was leading the defense of Madrid at this critical moment. Let the people think they were fighting and dying for democracy. Let Miaja think so. But those who lived would live under communism. What was this battle all about if not to clear the way for a Soviet Spain? Men like General Asensio who didn't "trust" the Communists had to be discredited, thrown out. Would Miaja play the game, even if he didn't know the rules?

"I don't know anything about him," said Tomás, one of Castro's aides.

"Find out . . . his tendencies or his present political views, his military capacity."

"Yes . . . his weaknesses. . . . All men have them. Even St. Peter had them. Some are conceited, others are fond of women. Others are cowards or ambitious. . . . Certainly Miaja has some weakness . . . and it's very important to know it. . . . Depending on your report, we'll either destroy Miaja in a couple of days or convert him into a hero in our service."

Tomás left and returned shortly with his report. Miaja, he said, was a "lukewarm republican, mediocre officer, vain, and easily manageable if he can be made to believe he is the genius and soul of our resistance."

Castro was delighted. Just the kind of man the Communists needed to surrender Madrid—to them.

Miaja was thus greatly in demand. Only the day before, he had been just the kind of man the government needed to surrender Madrid to Franco. No one considered that he might be the kind of man who liked to play his own game.

Desperate reports from the front streamed into General Miaja's headquarters all day long.

"My men fall asleep with their rifles in their hands . . ."

"I have no more soldiers . . ."

"I have had eighty percent losses . . ."

"The enemy is twenty meters from my position . . ."

"I need orders to retire, or reinforcements . . ."

Where should his unit retreat to? asked one commander.

"To the cemetery!" replied Miaja.

How could there be reasoned answers when the battle itself was unreasonable? Reason demanded that the Loyalists withdraw from Madrid, but their leaders showed only contempt for this solution. Actually, the delirious cries for aid, they felt, were an encouraging sign. They proved the men were holding. Fighters in flight usually threw away their arms; they didn't ask for more. Rojo sent out squads to scour the barracks for weapons, the cafés for shirkers. Every bullet, gun, and man in Madrid had to be thrown into the struggle.

And more besides. Miaja badgered the supreme command in Valencia for reinforcements. Send the International Brigades, he pleaded. But they were just being formed, was the reply. Anyway, they were to attack the enemy's rear and cut him off in Madrid. When? When they were ready—within seven days.

Seven days! Why not seven years? The results would be the same. It would be almost impossible for Madrid to hold out without help for more than forty-eight hours, Miaja stressed. But the government was so sure that Madrid was doomed it was planning to send troops only to besiege the city *after* it fell, as General Asensio had originally planned. Miaja was furious. He needed the troops *now!*

And Stalin could see his point. He sensed that a miracle might happen afterall, and so did his advisers, who hurried back to Madrid that day even before they reached Valencia. The chances for a bloody, prolonged stalemate were growing, and the Russians apparently made it clear: "Their" International Brigades, as well as Spanish forces, should be rushed to Madrid.

The government relented.

Meanwhile, Mikhail Koltsov helped to recruit new commissars to inspire the troops and tighten discipline. Yet he himself, like some of the other Russian advisers, had dangerously ignored the discipline Stalin imposed on his agents, having embraced the Loyalist cause emotionally when he was to support it only pragmatically, while it served Soviet interests.

"First, raise the morale of the fighters," Koltsov ordered. "Not a step back. Encourage the commanders. Organize groups of dynamiters and antitankists. Create second and third lines. Build more barricades, and hold until our reserves come up to smash Franco."

Then Koltsov rushed off to telephone his hourly account of the battle to Moscow, which broadcast it as his countrymen marched through Red Square celebrating the anniversary of the Russian Revolution.

There was a parade in Madrid, too—three hundred women, led once more by *La Pasionaria,* shouting: "It is better to die on your feet than to live on your knees! Everyone to arms!"

Their cries clashed with the sound of radio appeals drifting out of almost every window: Make every house a fortress. Fill bottles with gasoline and cork them with cotton wool. Light them and fling at tanks and armored cars from rooftops and windows. Set up house committees in every dwelling to comb out fifth columnists. Build barricades, whatever one's age.

One woman would learn that day that her second son was killed; she had lost another in July. As before, she remained dry-eyed. She simply stared at her husband and said: "And you, my henpecked husband! What are you doing?"

The husband got up, put on his cap, and silently left—to die in the Casa de Campo.

Spaniards expected to die. The commissars had told them they would—raising their morale, as Koltsov had ordered, but in a curiously Spanish way: "You are going to die. There is no possibility that you will come back. But posterity, thankful, will remember you, and classify you among those who generously gave their lives so that Spain might live."

Yes, that was the way to die—as *machos.*

General Miaja, the "lukewarm republican" and "mediocre officer," had steeled Madrid for battle, and now he formed a civilian defense *junta* that would help him run the besieged city. He searched for prominent political personalities, but almost all had fled. So he picked twenty- to thirty-year-old leaders from the Popular Front political groups and trade unions. What a blessing that the government had left, he felt. No more feuding or fudging. The young leaders were flexible and strong-willed enough to put aside their differences and devote themselves completely to winning the battle.

Yet, Miaja never did like politics. And after listening to these new civilian leaders wrangle over every question he could hardly wait to get back to his military staff meetings where he could tell his deputies to keep quiet if they talked too much. But he didn't dare antagonize the politicians, for without their support his "people's" army would disintegrate. So he sat and whittled away at a wooden stick until finally he reminded the *junta* that Madrid was still in desperate straits.

"Everyone must make a gigantic effort. . . . I demand it!"

While the army fought Franco, the *junta* would fight the fifth column, but the indiscriminate *paseos* must end. The *junta* members agreed, among them United Socialist Youth leader Santiago Carrillo, who was in charge of public order.

Carrillo, at twenty-one, now had one of the most important—and most difficult—jobs in Spain. He was even more powerful than his socialist father, Wenceslao Carrillo, undersecretary of the interior, who had also chosen to remain in Madrid. For the young Carrillo had become a kind of police chief just when the fifth column was emerging in force to help Franco push into Madrid, and when some *Madrileños* were in a mood to wipe out every suspected rightist in the city, especially those in jail. And since many of his colleagues distrusted him, his job would be all the harder.

As head of the Socialist Youth, Santiago had several months earlier merged his group with the much smaller Communist youth group and then secretly placed the joint organization under the umbrella of the Communist party. Only the day before, on November 6, he had officially joined that party, taking with him about half the Socialist Youth members, and was thus viewed by the socialists as a man who had betrayed both his party and his own father. At the same time, as he had only just become a full-fledged Communist, the Communist party did not completely trust him either. And both the bourgeois republicans and the anarchists remembered him for a claim he had made in support of the deceptive Soviet line:

"We are not Marxist youth. We fight for a democratic parliamentary republic."

Outrageous insincerity, cried the republicans. Reformist quackery, charged the anarchists.

Whatever his ethics or ideology, Carrillo was a brilliant young man who had rapidly climbed the political ladder—if, ironically, with the help of his anti-Communist father. He was born into a poor Asturias family of metal workers, and while his father languished in jail charged with socialist agitation, Santiago went to a workers' class taught by a local street cleaner. But when he came to

Madrid, where his father rose in socialist labor ranks, he rose alongside him to be the Socialist Youth leader, and then it was he who was frequently in jail. Here he learned more than he ever had from the street cleaner, virtually memorizing Marx, Lenin, and Engels. When he left prison, he came out a dedicated Communist.

Even as he sat in his new post, fifth columnists laid ambushes for passersby from roofs and dropped grenades on traffic. Panic spread . . . but so did public fury. Militiamen dashed into buildings from where the missiles were fired, searched every room, and killed guilty and innocent alike. They even set one building on fire.

Meanwhile, in Model Prison the prisoners grimly awaited their fate, certain they would either be freed or slain that night. And, as on the previous one, militiamen came for prey. Felipe Gómez Acebo listened again as a guard shouted names, as the victims cried, "Here!" and were led off to oblivion.

Then . . . "Felipe Gómez Acebo!"

His name! In the brief pause that followed he could hear from the cell window the war whoops of the Moors. Gómez Acebo shouted:

"They took him last night!"

Silence. Then the guard went on reading other names.

Gómez Acebo had been saved again.

But nearly six hundred others were hauled away—a few to another jail outside town, but the rest to the villages of Torrejón de Ardoz or Paracuellos del Jarama. Once more, prisoners were lined up facing previously dug graves and were mowed down. And the villagers were again ordered to cover the bodies with dirt, apparently burying some of the wounded alive.

Santiago Carrillo could have had nothing to do with the murders committed the night before—which, in any event, Enrique Castro admitted he ordered. But as the chief of public order, was he responsible for the new assassinations? Carrillo claims he was not.

"I made the decision to move these prisoners," he says. "I couldn't allow these men to swell the ranks of the attackers, and neither could I put at their disposal an escort, which would have to be withdrawn from the front lines. Madrid might well fall from one minute to the next. . . . Where was I going to get an escort? . . . On the road . . . forces that we could not clearly identify took over the convoy and killed the prisoners, who were already out of my jurisdiction. . . . It was a military question. I did not intervene personally nor do I consider myself responsible in any way for the disappearance of those men."

But the killings would continue almost every night until early December. And Felipe Gómez Acebo would survive. Having been stricken off the list of prisoners, he was officially dead.

* * *

Major Mariano Trucharte stood in an anteroom of the War Ministry and demanded to see General Miaja, even though the general was dining with his commanders.

"Why don't you give me the message and I'll bring it to him," said the general's adjutant.

"I can't do that. It's secret."

"Well, I don't know whether he'll receive you."

"If he doesn't, I cannot be held responsible for the consequences. I have some
papers taken from the enemy."

Trucharte was commander of the hodge-podge of militiamen who had stopped
the first Italian tanks trying to push through Carabanchel to Toledo Bridge that
day. Émilio Coll, who threw the stick of dynamite that stopped the leading tank,
was one of his men. After the battle the victors had climbed into that tank and
found the crew dead. They searched the bodies and pulled from the tank commander's pocket a lengthy document, and Trucharte, after examining it, thought
it was urgent enough to bring to Miaja's personal attention.

But he had to settle for Major Rojo, who left Miaja's dinner table to collect the
document. As Rojo walked back, he glanced over it—and suddenly forgot about
his dinner. The document, marked "Operational Order Number 15," was General Varela's plan for capturing Madrid!.

Rojo showed it to Miaja and the general's puffy face lit up. What was it? The
other commanders were curious. Suppressing his own excitement, Rojo read the
document aloud in a calm voice, pausing every few sentences to make a notation
in the margin with a red or blue pencil. The men were stunned. Varela had laid
out almost every detail. What extraordinary luck—to learn the enemy's moves in
advance!

Gloom suddenly turned into jubilation. Despite the great victories that day, despite the refusal of a single unit to retreat, the commanders doubted that their
men could survive another day. How long could even the bravest soldier keep
fighting strictly on nerve? November 7 might be remembered as one of the most
glorious days in Spanish history, but would November 8 be one of the most tragic? The foreign press, uncensored during the first chaotic hours after the government's flight, had already reported that the rebels occupied the Gran Vía all the
way to the War Ministry.

The XI International Brigade had just arrived in Vallecas, at the eastern edge
of Madrid, but the supreme command in Valencia was apparently waiting to see
if Madrid could hold out without help for another day before assigning the foreign volunteers to a possibly suicidal mission. The *Madrileños* themselves, however, were left to commit suicide.

But now there was euphoria—for a few moments. Then the commanders began to have second thoughts about the document. Was it a trick? Did Varela
plant it to mislead the Loyalists? And if it was genuine, did the general know that

the Loyalists had gotten hold of it? If he did, certainly he would change his plans. Could the Loyalists now base their whole defense strategy on this document without knowing the answers? If they lost the gamble, they would lose Madrid.

Rojo and his staff officers left the table to study the plan in his office and determine its authenticity. They had hardly eight hours to redistribute their troops to counter Varela's moves—if they decided the document was valid. They soon agreed it was. The main rebel force would attack from the west through Casa de Campo, rather than from the south through Carabanchel. The plan rather hurt Rojo's feelings, for it mirrored the contempt Franco felt for Madrid's defenders. Instead of attacking on a broad front, the generalissimo was flinging a mere spearhead into Madrid's heart, apparently convinced the city would then hemorrhage to death. The main assault was to start that day, November 7, the document indicated, but evidently had been postponed for a day.

Now Miaja and Rojo decided to gamble and switch their troops around, massing their strongest forces west of the Casa de Campo so they could strike with maximum effect from Yagüe's rear and left flank. Troops were placed to block every route of attack designated in the enemy plan.

A surprise awaited Franco—if he wasn't playing a dirty trick on them after all.

2

On November 8, Madrid reverberated with the emotional voice of Fernando Valera, undersecretary of communications, as he thundered over the radio: "People of Madrid! . . . Put your eyes, your will, your fists at the service of Madrid. . . . It is here . . . that two incompatible civilizations undertake their great struggle: love against hate; peace against war; the fraternity of Christ against the tyranny of the Church. Citizens of Madrid . . . today we fight . . . tomorrow we conquer. . . . This is Madrid. It is fighting for Spain, for humanity, for justice. . . . Madrid! Madrid!"

These stirring words little impressed the determined Varela—or the international community. That same morning, the American embassy sent a terse message to Washington:

"City is in tense state of quietness awaiting rebel entry."

But the battlefield was far from quiet, and the defenders were not sitting around waiting for the rebels to enter. The two rebel columns in Carabanchel could only inch their way toward the Toledo and Segovia bridges, at nearly prohibitive cost. And the three columns storming eastward through the Casa de Campo found themselves under withering fire from the left flank, far more deadly than the welcome given them the day before. As Colonel Castejon, one of the column chiefs, walked into the park, a grenade exploded near him and he fell, his hip shattered.

As he was being evacuated, he despairingly told an American reporter: "We made this revolt, and now we are beaten."

But to his men, he bravely cried: "Not one step backwards, boys!"

The problem was, they couldn't move one step forward. They were too busy trying to repel the counterattack. Finally, the rebels, despite tremendous casualties, managed to advance slightly, but far short of the Manzanares River, which they should have reached on the previous day.

Varela was enraged. How was it that the enemy was resisting most fiercely at precisely the points where his troops should have broken through? And his mood did not brighten when he learned that more Loyalist forces were heading toward the front.

Early that misty morning, few people were yet on the street, but the cry rang out from balconies all along the Gran Vía: "The *Rusos* have come! The *Rusos* have come!"

For who else would help Madrid in this crucial hour when the whole democratic world was waiting, almost with relief, for the city to collapse? The men marching briskly down the boulevard in corduroy uniforms and steel helmets, followed by two squadrons of prancing cavalry, looked like a real army, even though their trousers were baggy and their rifles of varied caliber.

"*Salud! Salud!*" the *Madrileños* cried.

The troops saluted with the clenched fist and shouted back: "*Salud!*"

An old woman, weeping with joy, held up a child who closed her small fist and returned the salute, while a cleaning woman, standing in the entrance of a hotel, was also in tears.

"Long live the *Rusos!*"

But they were not "*Rusos,*" except by proxy. They were nineteen hundred members of the XI International Brigade who had arrived in Spain only about three weeks earlier, and were ill-trained and poorly armed. Originally, they were not to go into battle before mid-November, presumably to *take back* Madrid after it fell. But now they had come, even in their sorry state, to keep Madrid from falling—thanks to Miaja and the Russians. Most were idealists and political refugees who expected to fight "for Spain, for humanity, for justice," not dreaming they would simply be fighting for Stalin in a wider power struggle in which Spain, humanity, and justice would be ruthlessly sacrificed.

Three battalions marched down the Gran Vía: the German Edgar André, the Franco-Belgian Commune de Paris, and the Polish Dabrowsky, with small British units attached to the first two. And leading the brigade was a powerfully built man of forty-one with a lined face, prematurely gray hair, lively brown eyes, and a whimsical mouth. General Emil Kléber's career was as intriguing as his appearance. Born Emil Stern, a Hungarian Jew, Kléber served in the Austrian army during World War I and was captured by the Russians and whisked off to a Siberian prison. He escaped when the Russian Revolution broke out and fought for the Bolsheviks. After the revolution, the Comintern sent him to lead the Hamburg rising of 1923, then to command Communist Chinese forces in battle against Chiang Kai-shek and the Japanese. Rumor had it that he helped to plot the czar's assassination and advised Emperor Haile Selassie during the Italian invasion of Ethiopia.

Now Stalin had given him his biggest troubleshooting role, though Kléber, like most of the Russians sent to Spain, apparently thought his job was to help win the war. By the afternoon of November 8, he had set up his headquarters in the Philosophy Building in University City and was reading a message from Rojo, sent at 2:20 P.M.:

"Enemy carries out foreseen plan. Vanguards have entered Casa de Campo. Proceed with defense in the manner agreed upon last night."

Kléber obeyed. He kept some troops in University City and transferred others to the Casa de Campo and Carabanchel. They were not to fight until the following morning, November 9, but later that night one company of Polish troops occupying the Casa de Velázquez in University City was heavily shelled. A note arrived from Kléber: "Resist—K."

The company did, for five hours, and when relief arrived, only six men remained. The commander, one of the six, tried to shoot himself, feeling responsible for the massacre, but comrades disarmed him and took him to Kléber. The two men spoke and shook hands, and the Pole returned to his post .

He went on fighting for Madrid, for the great dream that made men willing to die, that made Stalin willing to see them die—after they had selflessly served him.

Meanwhile, General Varela, equally fearful and contemptuous of dreamers, desperately tried to wipe them out with shells and bombs—while he still could.

One of the fleeing Russians who had returned to Madrid on learning of Miaja's stand was Colonel N. Voronov, the artillery expert, who now stood on the top floor of the skyscraping Telefónica gazing through his binoculars at the enemy cannons in the Casa de Campo. He pointed them out to a Loyalist battery chief, who corrected his own fire—and then suddenly radioed his men:

"Cease fire!"

"What's going on?" asked Voronov. "Why has the battery stopped firing?"

"It's lunch time," replied the Spaniard.

Voronov was startled. The artillerymen couldn't just sit down and eat in the middle of an operation! But they did. Don't worry, the chief promised, after lunch they would demolish the battery.

But the enemy would move their cannons away!

No, they wouldn't, was the reply. The rebels were also eating lunch.

Voronov nervously kept his eyes on the half-destroyed enemy battery for two hours and then, promptly at 4:00 P.M., the chief got up and cried:

"Fire!"

And the Loyalist barrage resumed.

Voronov was incredulous, he later reported. The chief had been right. The enemy hadn't moved their guns during lunchtime!

Varela loosed aerial bombs as well as artillery shells to break the city's will. Hitler's Condor Legion had started to arrive, and the general now had new planes, tanks, and other weapons, though the superior Russian fighters had knocked down several rebel aircraft on November 6 and seemed, at least temporarily, to rule the skies.

With Madrid resisting and foreign volunteers pouring in, many people who had fled a few days before returned, while others who had stayed indoors came out into the streets to celebrate the miracle of their "triumph." They were now unruffled by fifth-column rumors that the capital was about to topple, and that Miaja had even sent emissaries to rebel headquarters. In fact, Miaja had announced to his troops that morning:

"I don't expect any of you to retreat a single step, for the only order you'll get from me is to advance."

The Puerta del Sol was thus as crowded as ever. Bootblacks were still doing a brisk business on the corners, with militiamen, in a remarkable burst of self-esteem, lined up for a bootshine between battles at the front. Streethawkers were still trying to unload their stocks of militia dolls, badges, and trinkets neatly laid out on the sidewalk. Book and magazine vendors prospered as people tried to absorb the blast of guns in old comics or film-star scandals.

The zigzag Spanish fever chart had zigged again, this time from panic to pluck, and everything seemed back to normal despite the chronic tension—even when five giant bombers, escorted by seven mosquitolike fighters, sailed out of the low gray clouds. The crowd jamming the Puerta del Sol merely looked up.

"*Nuestras!*" ("Ours!"), a man cried proudly.

Who could challenge "our" new planes?

As if in a trance, the people did not move even when several black specks plummeted earthward from the planes. Only when the square shook under a chain of explosions nearby did they realize that the aircraft were not "*Nuestras.*" They then stampeded into the nearest subway entrance or doorway, while fifth columnists capitalized on the chaos by hurling bombs of their own into the crowds.

Geoffrey Cox, a British correspondent, dived into the doorway of a house and crouched under a stairway with several other people.

"The roars stopped," Cox later wrote, "to be followed by shouting in the street. Past the door went an anarchist in a red-and-black cap, spraying the wall on either side with a submachine gun. A fifth-column sniper, forewarned of the raid, had fired on the crowd from a rooftop, wounding one of the guards.''

Shrieks resounded from behind a screen of dust and smoke, and on the street lay four dead women in print dresses and aprons, one still holding in her hand the cloth she had been washing dishes with. Firemen climbed a ladder to the second floor of a shattered building and brought down a four-year-old girl who had one hand blown away.

Another roar in the sky—but this time from *"Nuestras."* They arrived five minutes too late. But not too late to renew Loyalist confidence that the rebels were beaten despite their murderous tantrum. As General Miaja had ordered, Madrid held alone for forty-eight hours.

3

But on the night of November 8, Miaja still could find little time to sleep, for he knew that Madrid might fall at any moment. And even the XI International Brigade might be of little help for it had, after all, less than two thousand men, and many were as green and poorly armed as his own fighters. Meanwhile, Varela was heavily reinforcing his columns and would now attack with everything he had.

What Miaja needed were massive new reserves of his own, but nobody was listening to him. Didn't the high command realize Madrid was fighting for its life? Only once did General Pozas even send a courier, and then simply to find out whether Madrid was still holding! And there was almost no contact at all with the government in Valencia; Prime Minister Largo Caballero seemed too busy to deal with Madrid's pleas.

Finally, on November 9, a dust-coated car drew up to Miaja's headquarters and a courier from Caballero stepped out. He saluted left and right, and walked up to Miaja's office where staff officers excitedly surrounded him while the general shook his hand. At last there would be action.

The officer sat down, removed a large envelope from his briefcase, and handed it to Miaja. As tension mounted, the general frantically looked for a paper-cutter but could not find one, so, with impatience, tore open the envelope with a paper clip, took out a letter and read it silently. His cheeks flushed. He glanced up at the officer and scanned the letter again, then rose and with heavy steps walked toward the door. But suddenly he turned around, came back, and threw the letter into a wastepaper basket, grunting to the courier: "Tell the minister for me that we who have remained in Madrid are still eating."

Miaja's officers were puzzled and, as soon as he left the room, rushed to the basket to retrieve the letter and hurriedly read it. Caballero was making an urgent request: Miaja should turn over to the courier the table linen, dishes, and napkins that War Ministry officials had left behind in their wild flight to Valencia!

While the supreme command in Valencia fretted about dining without proper tableware many of its soldiers in Madrid had even greater problems. Throughout the day of November 9, Varela, relentlessly prodded by Mola, sent wave upon wave of suicide fighters to storm almost every bridge spanning the Manzanares River. The five main bridges were the San Fernando, French, Segovia, Toledo, and Princesa. If the rebels crossed any one of these they would be in Madrid proper, and they were determined to do this before the day was over.

At San Fernando Bridge, north of University City, a thousand anarchists stood ready to halt them, waiting for Major Miguel Palacios, the medical officer who was now their commander, to give the signal—though they were devoted to Cipriano Mera, his political commissar, and would only obey Palacios if Mera ordered them to. These were the men whom Mera had sent to save Madrid for the anarchists, or at least *from* the Communists.

Mera did not yet trust his own military skills despite his audacious exploits in the field, and so agreed that Palacios, a rugged craggy-faced officer who had learned tactics in Morocco and was sympathetic to the anarchists, should lead the column. Not all his men had as much faith in a professional military man, and one even threw a bomb at Palacios, barely missing him but killing another officer.

Palacios, however, would not give up trying to make soldiers of them—especially Mera himself. And he did indeed make a soldier of Mera, helping him to reconcile his ideological purity with the brutal reality of war. Mera strongly opposed "militarizing" his militia despite Palacios's entreaties but the major kept hammering.

"Discipline might be contrary to anarchist philosophy," he argued, "but if an anarchist loses his ideals when he becomes a soldier then he was never a real anarchist to begin with."

This argument gradually made sense to Mera as he saw hundreds of his comrades lying dead in the fields around Madrid, cut down because they had acted according to personal whim. And one day, he even demanded that his men stop calling him "Cipriano."

"From now on," he said, "I am Colonel Mera!"

Palacios was delighted, though Mera still opposed integrating the column into a new brigade and eventually into a real army.

"You've promoted yourself pretty fast," he told Mera with a smile.

In fact, Mera now "outranked" Palacios, the column commander!

On the morning of November 9, the Palacios Column would face its greatest test. If the anarchists broke and ran at this crucial moment they would not only leave the way open for Franco, but they would be ridiculed around the world and the dream of an anarchist Spain would dissolve in disgrace.

At 8:00 A.M., with the Moors closing in on the bridge, the anarchists crossed to the west bank behind a shield of artillery fire and headed south into the Casa de Campo to meet them. Suddenly, amid the trees, dark goblinlike figures emerged from the mist hardly a hundred yards in front of them. Stricken with fright, the anarchists burst toward the rear, but Palacios calmly aimed his rifle at a "goblin" and fired.

The shot somehow paralyzed his men in flight. They turned around and also started firing, refusing to budge despite a blistering rebel barrage. Finally, it was Yagüe's Moors who broke and ran, with the anarchists on their heels. Palacios's men chased the foe to Garabitas Hill in the northern part of the park—the enemy's most important toehold on the Madrid front—and surged to the peak. But shortly they came running down. Palacios was furious.

"Why did you leave the hill?" he asked the commander who had led the attack.

"Because they're shooting up there," the man replied blandly. "And down here they're not."

Palacios glanced at Mera. Their men had fought with supreme courage that day, suffering one-third casualties. They had blocked the path to San Fernando Bridge. But once that was done, why should they die for a hill?

Palacios didn't have the nerve, nor Mera the heart, to say: Because they were ordered to.

The fighting at French Bridge, south of University City, was just as hard. Every time Yagüe's men moved toward it, the militia and the XI International Brigade blocked the way. Finally, screaming Moors stepped over the torn bodies of their comrades and reached the river, managing to scramble onto the bridge. At last the rebels seemed on the verge of a breakthrough. Then, in the midst of the battle, General Miaja rushed a message to his troops:

"Hold out until help comes!"

Paulino García Puente, who had helped in July to seize the rifles in Artillery Park in order to arm the people, now left his cluttered desk at the Finance Ministry and issued weapons to his fellow bureaucrats. The group marched to the National Palace to gather the presidential guard and then to the Plaza de España to pick up a virtually unarmed militia company of waiters and bartenders who called themselves the Red Lions. This ragtag cluster of men hurried to French Bridge, where the unarmed took the weapons of the fallen, and in a bloody battle helped to push the enemy back into the Casa de Campo.

"I started shooting Moors out of the trees," says Garcia Puente. "It was like hunting birds."

And so French Bridge held.

* * *

Next came Toledo Bridge—the link with Carabanchel. At about noon, it was suddenly left unguarded when armored cars roared off to get supplies while militiamen sat down for lunch. This time the rebels decided to curb their own appetites and, after battling from house to house, smashed toward the bridge en masse. Panic gripped the defenders, reaching even the general staff. The rebels were crossing Toledo Bridge! Officers almost forcibly dragged Miaja and Rojo from their headquarters into cars, which raced toward a safer haven in eastern Madrid.

But the hungry militiamen, their food hardly chewed, withstood the assault, and rebel bodies were soon piled up along the route to the bridge. The Loyalists, still in control of the span, then finished their lunch—and reportedly cursed the enemy for giving them indigestion.

At Princesa Bridge, farther south, the Moors fought all the way to the river, but again were driven back with heavy losses.

So the rebels couldn't cross any of the bridges even *after* they came to them.

Meanwhile, *El Campesino*'s roughhouse battalion arrived in Carabanchel from the Guadarramas and joyfully joined in the slaughter. Rebel officers there even informed Varela that Russian troops were manning the lines. Who else could butcher their men with such ruthless efficiency?

The rebels were frantic. They had lost every battle that day. In retribution, they cut the throats of everyone they captured in Carabanchel. And in a wild two-day battle in the military hospital there, neither side dreamed of wasting bullets. The Loyalists finally withdrew from the building, but they had massacred so many rebels with knives, bayonets, and grenades that few were left to fight again.

Despite the Loyalists' magnificent stand that day, the rebels were in a good position to keep attacking until they finally battered their way across one of the bridges. The new equipment Hitler had promised Franco was now streaming in, as were reinforcements from other fronts, and rebel artillery on strategic Garabitas Heights could shatter Loyalist forces. Clearly, the miracle of resistance couldn't last much longer.

Generals Miaja, Goriev, and Kléber thus agreed that the time had come for a bold action that would crush Varela's men with a sledgehammer blow, especially since rebel morale was never lower. Anyway, why wait for new reserves that might arrive too late?

So that night of November 9, Kléber brought his full brigade, as well as some Fifth Regiment units, to the northeast corner of the Casa de Campo. Wipe out the enemy forces! he ordered his commanders. That very night, before they could attack the bridges again. And shortly his troops, with fixed bayonets, began marching southward through the park under a brilliant starlit sky, ready for a show-down battle.

Meanwhile, Varela learned of the attack and threw together a great force of his own, sending it northward under an umbrella of shells to meet Kléber's troops. The whole ideological struggle convulsing Europe now seemed centered in a patch of woods on the edge of Madrid as men from dozens of nations cautiously weaved their way among the gnarled oak trees toward a great confrontation. Neither side could conceive of defeat. For one was driven by a crusader's fury, a twisted professional pride, or an intoxicating dream of unlimited loot; the other, by a desperate grasping for dignity lost, a fear for the fate of family and home, and an unshakable faith in a utopian ideal or a god who would later betray them.

Like eyes too frightened to watch, the stars suddenly slid behind a veil of clouds, and mists swirled through the forest, blurring every silhouette into a shimmering gray mass. The two armies met in the center of the park, and the night burst with the bloodcurdling war cries of the Moors, answered by the internationals' "For the Revolution and Liberty!"

The two sides charged at each other like blind men in a locked room, and nobody knew what was happening. At one point, the Loyalists seemed doomed when the Belgian artillery commander, a Fascist infiltrator, sabotaged his cannons. (His men took him prisoner and he was later shot.) Then gradually the Moors and legionnaires, ripped to shreds by machine-gun fire, began to move back as Kléber's men inched forward, ridge by ridge. And by morning the Loyalists held the whole park, except for Garabitas Heights. Under almost every shell-torn tree, bodies of both sides were grotesquely heaped. And amid these great mounds of flesh lay almost a third of the XI International Brigade.

At 3:00 A.M., with victory already certain, General Miaja rose from his desk, stretched his arms, and removed his clothes for the first time in three nights.

"This is the first night I'm going to sleep with a calm mind," he told his aides. "Until now, before lying down, I kept thinking: *Well, Miaja, tomorrow the wall.*"

Madrid, he felt sure now, would survive. He even dreamed of returning to his home town, Oviedo, as a conquering hero. Dressed in his general's uniform, he would visit the arms factory where his father had worked and chat with the men about these three days of glory. That would be like talking with his father himself, who would no longer ask: "Son, when will you be promoted?"

If only his father had lived to share the glory, to share the love the people felt for him.

He was the hero of Madrid—and General Kléber had better understand that.

CHAPTER 9

Breakthrough

1

With Madrid saved, for the moment anyway, General Miaja now tackled another painful problem—the nightly killings of real and suspected fifth columnists being "transferred" from Madrid's jails. The government in Valencia was alarmed to hear of these crimes, especially since it needed international support now more than ever.

"I have news that lamentable acts have occurred in the jails these past days," a government official wired Miaja.

Although it seems unlikely that Miaja did not know of the murders, a member of his staff replied: "The general is completely unaware of the events you complain about and he will try to find out about them."

Shortly, another message followed: "There were some shootings, although the number was much smaller than rumored." This was "the least that could be expected to occur given the number of air-raid victims."

At about the same time, on November 10, Miaja angrily told *junta* members: "Nobody will be 'taken for a ride' anymore. . . . I'm not requesting benevolence toward the enemies of the republic, but respect for the laws. I give you twenty-four hours to make sure that this undignified spectacle is ended."

He then consulted with Santiago Carrillo, who had largely ended house raids by unauthorized groups but not the prison massacres. Why were these kilings being permitted? Miaja asked. He had nothing to do with them, Carrillo replied.

And in fact, it was his deputy who had signed the orders for the removal of the prisoners, though Carrillo, as his boss, could not avoid responsibility. Whatever the truth, orders, decrees, and proclamations did not stop the massacres.

Janet Riesenfeld was embittered and disillusioned. Yet, though Jaime Castanys had used her for his own political ends, even placing her life in danger, she could not forget him. Nor could she flee Madrid. She had asked at the American embassy how she could go home, but was told that, for the moment, there was no way. As Franco pounded at Madrid's gates, she found herself almost alone. All her militia friends were at the front, so she was almost constantly obsessed with thoughts of Jaime.

When she stayed home she dared not even look at the telephone, fearing she would dial his number, and when she walked through the city each street brought back a memory. Often, without intending to, she would walk past his office, hoping she would meet him as he came out. One day as she passed by she noted that the office was closed, with iron shutters pulled down over the door and windows. And on the door a sign read: "Requisitioned."

Janet knew what that meant. She dashed to Jaime's *pension* and the owner answered her ring. The two stared at each other.

"They took them all," said the woman, red-eyed from weeping. "My sister, too."

"When? How?"

"At one o'clock last night—they asked especially for him."

Shortly, Janet was at the gate of the police station where the prisoners had apparently been taken.

"Weren't a group of people brought in here about two o'clock last night?" she asked a guard.

"Yes."

Janet then told him the names of Jaime and his friends, and the guard checked them against his list.

"Yes, they're all here," he said. "But there's no Jaime Castanys."

2

"What's the situation?" asked the *Pravda* editor on the line from Moscow.

Mikhail Koltsov thought carefully before answering. Despite the remarkable Loyalist performance so far, he was worried. Almost every available man had been thrown into the battle, so there were no fresh fighters to help stop a new attack. No matter how brave the *Madrileños*, if new troops didn't arrive soon Madrid would surely collapse, yet the pessimistic Caballero wanted to save his forces to win back the city *after* it collapsed! A word from Stalin, Koltsov apparently felt, would be enough to change Caballero's mind, for the prime minister couldn't afford to ignore his advice at this critical point. To prod Stalin, Koltsov painted a glum though not hopeless picture.

"The Fascists have come closer to the river," he replied. "Their artillery fire makes it difficult to defend the bridges. The air raids also make it difficult. They are slaughtering the workers in the quarters they are capturing. But this has only strengthened the fighting spirit. The battle will be fought courageously."

That was what the editor wanted to hear.

"It will be fought with courage?"

"Yes, it will. We're waiting for reinforcements."

"Are large reinforcements being sent to you?"

"I did not say large reinforcements are being sent to us. I only said we're waiting for reinforcements."

But the voice from Moscow persisted: "Are large reinforcements being sent to you?"

Koltsov realized he wasn't being asked a question but being told the answer. He now shouted into the phone, repeating his message twice:

"Yes, large and powerful reinforcements are being sent to us! Large reinforcements of republican troops are coming to help Madrid!"

"So there will be large reinforcements?"

The editor wanted an even stronger statement. After all, the conversation was no doubt being monitored by friend and foe alike. Koltsov shouted with all his strength:

"Yes, the reinforcements will be considerable! They'll be coming soon, at any moment! We can hold out perfectly until their arrival!"

After Madrid's heroic stand in the first three days of battle, the chances for a stalemate were improving—and Hitler could be stuck in the Spanish quagmire indefinitely. So Stalin agreed: More reinforcements must be sent to Madrid immediately.

"Here in the battlefields of Spain there are no *Croix de Guerre* to be won, we have no stocks of Victoria Crosses for the widows of dead heroes. Be brave, my comrades, but no false heroics—we are here to kill Fascists, not to commit suicide in front of them."

Keith Scott Watson and the other members of the XII International Brigade in Albacete wildly applauded André Marty as he harangued them in the square of the training base. Marty was the Comintern commander of the base, and his warm words of farewell belied his merciless nature. He was a suspicious French disciplinarian, a grotesque Kremlin tool, who expected the same absolute obedience from his men that Stalin expected from him.

Frozen-faced, bulbous-eyed, often dramatically garbed in black cape and beret, Marty was, like his master, a cynical pragmatist with less love for Spain than for personal power. He had won Stalin's trust when, in 1919, he led a French naval mutiny in the Black Sea, going over to the Bolsheviks with ships sent to help crush their revolution. In Albacete he spent almost as much time fingering suspected Trotskyites for a bullet in the brain as trying to whip the men of more than a dozen nations into an effective fighting machine. Since he didn't have much time to train them with guns, he hypnotized them with words.

And so, on the evening of November 10, Watson and his comrades began marching to the train station as inspired as any soldiers in history. But Keith was less impressed than most, for he had come to fight more for the excitement than the ideology. So far, it had been fun, and he hoped to revisit Barcelona soon to see his Rosita. But he remembered with some foreboding the strange future she had seen in the cards:

"You will not do that for which you came here—there is a coach with a fair woman and with it is death."

Watson wondered how anybody could do what they came here for—to fight. His brigade was even less prepared than the XIth already in Madrid, resembling more a confused mob than a combat force. Thirty-six hours earlier only one battalion had been formed—the Italian Garibaldi Battalion. The French André Marty and German Thaelmann battalions were just being organized and some of their members had arrived only the day before, green and wearing civvies. The brigade leader, General Lukacz, who was actually the famous Hungarian writer Mata Zalka, was in a frenzy. Though he had served in the Austrian army in World War I and then, after his capture by the Russians, in the Red army, he had never had so impossible a mission: to create a fighting force literally overnight.

Commanders were chosen haphazardly and often had to give orders while flipping through the dictionary, since the volunteers spoke many different tongues. Cartridge pouches were made from sacks, rifle slings from linen; worse, there were few rifles, even without the sling. To writer Louis Fischer, who, as the first American to join the International Brigades, had become quartermaster, "it seemed stupid to let the men proceed unarmed." Only while André Marty was making his farewell speech did trucks draw up with wooden crates filled with thickly greased rifles.

The men, half equipped, largely untrained, except for the few veterans from World War I, clambered into the train. They would play a key role in a new drive planned by Miaja and Rojo to cut the southern roads to Madrid and keep the rebels from cutting the eastern road to Valencia, the capital's lifeline. Their mission was to wipe out a rebel column entrenched in a great stone monastery atop the towering Cerro de los Angeles (Hill of the Angels) south of Madrid, though they lacked big guns, air support, and communications gear, and knew nothing about battle tactics.

Keith Scott Watson, who belonged to an English group attached to the Thaelmann Battalion, was more confident than most. He had at least learned how to fire a rifle.

On the morning of November 13, troops of the Thaelmann Battalion halted just below a ridge and deployed for the assault.

"This is a rear attack on the Fascist forces besieging Madrid," an officer shouted. "If successful it will save the city. You will be supported by tanks and planes. Follow your officers and you'll get through all right."

Watson and other members of the XII International Brigade were not so sure. They had arrived here after two chaotic miserable days. When they had stepped off the train in a village about twenty miles away, they were bewildered. Would they have to march the rest of the way? Would they have to go hungry, too? No trucks. No food. And no commander of the André Marty Battalion. He had mysteriously disappeared, and was replaced by a Parisian delicatessen worker who knew more about bologna than battle.

However, with or without trucks, food, or able commanders, the men of the Thaelmann Battalion would get to the front. On foot if necessary. And Ludwig Renn, the German commander of the battalion, decided it was necessary. Watson plodded along with the rope handle of a machine-gun ammunition case cutting into each burning hand, but his pain vanished in rage when the other battalions caught up, riding in trucks because *their* commanders had been more patient.

Everything was at last set for the attack. The drivers—if they could be found— would take the entire force the rest of the way to the starting point. They had wandered off and gone to sleep in far-flung houses, and it took hours to round them up and get the trucks rolling. Then another hitch: One driver took the wrong road, and there went part of the Garibaldi Battalion.

The remnants of the brigade reached its destination more than twenty-four hours late, and Watson now felt an "indescribable sensation" as he glimpsed Madrid in the dawn haze only a few miles away. He and his comrades of the Thaelmann Battalion descended a stony slope to a small village they found deserted and entered a house that had been ransacked, with clothing strewn on the floor, furniture overturned. When Watson looked into the bedroom, he was horrified. Lying across the bed was a half-nude woman, her throat a great red gash. The Moors!

The battalion then moved across the plowed fields toward a steep hill less than two miles away—Cerro de los Angeles. There on the crest stood the monastery, reaching into the sky with the scorched claws of a beast ready to pounce. A wounded beast. For when the Loyalists had seized the hill earlier in the war they shelled the building and smashed to pieces a huge statue of Christ that stood in the courtyard of the monastery and was visible for miles around. In their rage they dynamited what was left of the statue. To the rebels this was the darkest sacrilege. To the Loyalists this was a symbolic blow against those who would treacherously use an image of Christ to keep the people submissive in their chains.

A storm of fire suddenly broke from the half-wrecked fortress, and confusion spread. But Watson moved ahead, side by side with Giles Romilly, Winston Churchill's wayward grandson, who had disgraced his illustriously conservative family by turning Communist and rushing off to fight in Spain.

Suddenly Watson felt a blow in his thigh and fell to the ground.

"Christ, I'm hit!" he cried as he touched his wet, sticky leg.

Now he would never get back to Barcelona. But then he saw Romilly roaring with laughter. Was he mad? Romilly pointed to Keith's canteen, which had been filled with wine—before a bullet struck it. And so Watson's life "blood" ebbed away.

As did his passion for battle.

Ludwig Renn couldn't believe the attack was going so well. A tall man with an ascetic bespectacled face still gaunt from serving time in a Nazi jail, Renn was a well-known writer and pacifist. After escaping from Germany he decided to use his World War I experience to fight the Fascists in Spain, but he hadn't expected to command a bunch of raw recruits.

As he moved forward with his men, someone lying on the ground called to him.

"What's the matter?" Renn asked.

"I can't put the cartridges into the rifle."

"Well, show me how you do it."

The youth opened the chamber and tried to push a cartridge in.

"But man! You're putting it in backwards. Have you ever loaded a rifle?"

"No."

"Have you ever fired a rifle?"

"Only in a booth at a fair."

Renn could only shake his head. He was leading his men into suicide, not battle. Yet they were forging ahead, alongside tanks that poured missiles into the monastery while machine guns rattled away. All his units were advancing—except his Polish-Balkan company. It was supposed to secure the battalion's right flank but it seemed to have disappeared. And then he realized that nobody had told him how to get into the fortress. Where was the entrance? His men could never climb the wall.

Meanwhile, the brigade was having other troubles. Part of the Franco-Belgian battalion got lost, and the Italians were mowed down when they placed ladders against the wall and tried to climb them as if they were knights of old attacking a medieval castle. Finally the "lost" Franco-Belgians were found and were ordered to move *quietly* to the foot of the fortress. Instead, they advanced while lustily singing the "Internationale"—until enemy gunfire broke into the chorus.

But despite everything, the brigade managed to practically encircle the monastery. Now if only someone could find the entrance. Suddenly at dusk, men from a Spanish company attached to the brigade shouted:

"*Los Moros! Los Moros!*"

Everyone looked around. Who was encircling whom?

At about this time, with Renn's men bogged down by heavy fire, a German officer crawled over to him and asked: "Are we moving back now?"

Renn was astonished.

"Why?" he asked.

"We can't move forward and we have to eat and sleep."

"That's not a reason to go back!"

Renn ran along the skirmish line and found that the Italians and the French had already marched off. He went back to the German officer, who again asked: "Are we moving off?"

"No!"

"But I have already given the order to withdraw."

"In that case, you will immediately bring your men back to their positions."

"But that's impossible. They are already running back and it is too dark to find them."

"That means that you have not only given an order unauthorized by your commander, but you also started a planless withdrawal! Did you name a destination? Answer!"

"Here you cannot name any destination."

"With this remark you are showing only your military ineptness. You will have to account for your action!"

But Renn knew it was too late. He had to retreat with his men—wherever they were going.

Late that night he and several companions exhaustedly reached a village several miles away and entered a dimly lit church where many of his men were sleeping. As he sat down for some soup and reflected with despair on the rout, the commander of the missing Polish-Balkan company entered. His men had attacked the monastery, he explained, though his mission had been only to secure the battalion's right flank.

Why had he disobeyed orders? Renn demanded.

"But," replied the commander, "the gate of the monastery was right in front of us."

Renn was speechless.

"What?" he finally cried. "None of us knew where the gate was and you were lying right in front of it?"

"Yes, we got very close to it."

''Is that so? The objective of the whole attack lay in our sector and you did not report it! We could have captured the monastery! Now the whole attack was in vain!''

Renn was stunned. Nor did he cheer up when he later learned that a Spanish company had picked up the enemy password, called it out at the entrance, marched into the monastery, and actually captured it—before being thrown out because it received no support!

''Wake up, you bloody fool, we're retreating! The Fascists have heavy reinforcements.''

Giles Romilly violently shook Keith Scott Watson awake as he lay on a deep soft bed in a house they had occupied during the night after the flight from the monastery. The two then ran outside and joined a long stream of men trudging toward villages in the rear. Suddenly an enemy plane sputtering bullets swooped down on the procession, and the Britons piled into an armored car just as missiles bounced off its roof. The vehicle blasted off and did not stop until it reached a base by the Manzanares River. There Romilly and Watson got out and found themselves among strangers—men of the Franco-Belgian Commune de Paris Battalion of the XI International Brigade, which had been in Madrid since November 8.

While Romilly went off to find the English group, Watson stayed behind in case it turned up at this base. But a French officer ordered him to join his company. Keith protested. He was, he pointed out, a member of a British contingent of another brigade.

''Ah, *mon brave*,'' replied the Frenchman, ''we are all good international socialists. What is a nation? We are all brothers—fall in here!''

Seeing little choice, Watson dug in with his new comrades near French Bridge on a slope covered with olive trees. Since the great battles of November 9, when the rebels were thrown back from all the bridges and then almost swept from the Casa de Campo, General Varela had relentlessly pushed forward again day after day despite the enormous cost.

Meanwhile, General Miaja's new offensive had been stopped not only at the Cerro de los Angeles but almost all along the line. In fact, on the morning of November 13, while the XII International Brigade was launching its catastrophic attack on the monastery, the rebels had gotten as far as the riverbank near French Bridge.

But, Watson's French officer promised him, they would never cross the river.

3

Janet Riesenfeld despaired over Jaime Castanys's disappearance and, with all her Loyalist friends at the front, didn't know where to turn for help. Finally she managed to contact her friend José María when he returned for a short time. He must find Jaime, she pleaded on the phone.

"It's the last thing I'll ever ask."

A few hours later Janet and José María were at the morgue. While Janet waited at the door, José María walked in, stopped at each cadaver, and glanced under the shroud. Suddenly he beckoned to Janet and she picked her way over the dead, trembling, feeling faint. José María bent down and turned the head of one corpse to the side.

Janet could see only the profile, but she knew the man was Jaime.

Like most Spaniards, General Miaja wanted to relax during lunchtime, but so worried were Generals Mola and Varela that they even began violating the sanctity of those sacred hours of peace. Thus, shortly after noon on November 13, while Miaja was lunching with his staff and Russian advisers, several Junkers escorted by fighters began dropping bombs on Madrid again.

"When do they eat?" the general asked grumpily. "They don't eat, and they don't let others eat. I ask you not to get up from the table."

But when he learned that Russian *Chatos* were peppering the enemy planes right overhead, he disobeyed his own order and, with a napkin still tied round his neck, rushed to the balcony to watch the most spectacular dogfight since the war began. While the bombers fled, fourteen Fiats and Heinkels and thirteen *Chatos* dived and rocketed in and out of the clouds knocking each other out of the sky. The people watching from the street were ecstatic each time they saw a plane burst into flames, convinced it was an enemy aircraft, though few could tell one from the other. One man parachuted out of his burning plane only to be greeted by machine-gun fire from the ground.

When the battle was over, Miaja went back to the table but was interrupted again; the parachutist, an aide told him, had been taken prisoner. He should be brought to him, Miaja ordered. And shortly a great throng could be heard shouting outside as a man was dragged upstairs.

Mikhail Koltsov, who was at the lunch, was startled when he saw the prisoner. He was apparently Sergey Tarkhov, known as "Antonio," a Soviet air commander. As the man, groaning in pain, was placed on a couch, Koltsov asked him: "Antonio, were you the pilot who parachuted?"

Breathing heavily, the man only muttered: "Give me water. My belly is burning."

"Antonio . . ."

"What kind of madhouse is this? Why do they shoot their own people? Give me water. Then I'll explain what happened. I must put out the fire of the bullets."

Antonio was driven swiftly to the Palace Hotel, which had been turned into a hospital and Koltsov, who went with him, was distraught. What tragic irony. To be machine-gunned by the people he had come to save! He waited for Antonio outside the operating room, staring at basins full of severed fingers and feet, at a poster on the wall showing a couple dancing, with the inscription "Spend the summer in Santander."

Two hours later, four bullets had been extracted from Antonio's body while two remained inside. If he moved, the doctor warned, peritonitis would set in and he would die. As Koltsov sat by his bed, Antonio insisted on dictating a report of the battle.

"Please note this date in the diary . . . I remember it very well. At one forty-eight P.M. . . ."

"But at one forty-eight P.M. they were already operating on you . . ."

"I remember it exactly, yesterday, at one forty-eight P.M. . . ."

"Not yesterday, today. The battle took place today. Three hours ago! . . . All this isn't important. The main thing is that you shouldn't move. You'll get well."

"And the boys? They're all well?"

"Even more than that. Your boys have downed five planes and you, one more; altogether six."

"They are eagles! Oh, my good boys! . . . All of a sudden, six Heinkels, coming from all directions, like hunting dogs, all against me! . . . I went into a spin . . . I jumped and told myself: The wind is blowing . . . in the direction of the Fascists. That's why I must fall rapidly . . . I open it [the parachute] at four hundred meters and drift down . . . and they begin to shoot from the ground . . . but don't tell anyone. My boys shouldn't know. It wouldn't help their morale."

"It's you who must be silent, do you understand? Otherwise, I'll leave at once."

Antonio was depressed. He wanted to fight again—for the people who had shot him. They were, after all, on the right side. Was it not better to risk death than to abandon friends? Isn't that what Stalin had taught him?

4

A little later, Koltsov was with another friend. Buenaventura Durruti had finally arrived in Madrid with about three thousand militiamen to save the city from the

Fascists and, if it held, from the Communists as well. But Durruti and Koltsov, though caught in different ideological webs, rather liked each other and found common ground in the intensity of their commitment to the anti-Fascist cause.

The two men embraced, and Durruti said jokingly: "You see? I haven't taken Saragossa. I haven't been killed. And I haven't become a Marxist. All this belongs to the future."

Koltsov was surprised by the great change in Durruti since he had seen him some weeks earlier. The anarchist leader not only looked like a commander but spoke to his aides like one. He no longer suggested; he ordered. He even took Koltsov's advice and added a Communist military adviser to his staff.

And Durruti marched like a soldier as he led his green-uniformed men up the Gran Vía, red flags flying, to the cheers and applause of people crowding the sidewalks. Durruti, the living legend, was here. Now Madrid would never fall.

Durruti himself was sure his men would see to that. But he was nevertheless uneasy, for he had had to persuade them to come to Madrid against their will, and they were unhappy. They didn't understand that their cause might collapse all over Spain if either the Fascists captured Madrid or the Communists controlled it. And though he was not quite sure he understood this himself, he had passionately said to them before he left Catalonia:

"Will you come with me to Madrid, yes or no? It is a question of life or death for all of us. Either we will win or we will die, for defeat would be so terrible that we would not survive. But we will win . . . I only regret that I am speaking to you today in a barracks. One day these barracks will be dismantled and we will live under a regime of liberty."

Tears welled in the eyes of some men when he described with rustic, vivid imagery how exquisite life would be in a society free of injustice or cruelty. Many volunteered to go, but mainly to please their beloved leader. They remained dubious, as did Durruti himself. His destiny, Durruti lamented to friends, apparently more in bitter jest than in genuine expectation, was to die in Madrid.

Durruti went to see Miaja and Rojo and swept them up in his almost mystical intensity. His men had come to save Madrid, he told them, but the minute they shot the last rebel dead they would return to the Saragossa front. And to finish the job as soon as possible he wanted to attack in the toughest sector, and only with anarchists. No others were going to take credit for *his* successes, Durruti made clear, obviously thinking of the Communists, who claimed almost every Loyalist victory as their own.

Miaja and Rojo agreed. Two days later, on November 15, they would launch an all-out offensive, Rojo said, and victory would break the siege of Madrid. Would Durruti want to attack from University City across French Bridge and help clear the enemy from Casa de Campo and the whole area southwest of Madrid?

He certainly would, Durruti replied.

But when Durruti then met with Cipriano Mera and other local anarchists, he found them less pleased with his mission. Mera, especially, was skeptical. Durruti's men, he stressed, were exhausted after their long, sleepless trip from Catalonia and had no rest before being sent to the front. Yet they would be fighting on unfamiliar ground against a far more formidable foe armed with far more formidable weapons than they had encountered in Aragon. And the troops Rojo had chosen to spearhead the attack, members of another anarchist column from Catalonia, the Libertad, had proven panicky and irresponsible. There was also the problem of morale. Durruti's men might be brave, but they had not been touched by the spirit of Madrid born on November 7 when almost every *Madrileño* was transformed into an invincible fighter. They didn't even want to fight in Madrid.

Mera thought the Loyalists should attack the rebels from two directions and encircle them, or at least force them to retreat. And his own anarchist fighters, who knew the terrain and conditions, should lead the way.

"If they suggest to you that you should make a frontal attack," he told Durruti, "it means they want you to fail. Understand, Buenaventura, that we have enemies not only on the other side. General Miaja may want to act correctly toward us, but he is surrounded by Communists, and they do not want Durruti, the most important anarchist fighter, to be the savior of Madrid. With their posters and tin-pan bands, they are trying to make it seem that they are the only defenders."

Durruti shrugged off the warning. The Communists were in for a big shock. And so were the Fascists.

While the Loyalists planned to save Madrid with one daring sweep, the rebels planned to seize Madrid with an equally daring sweep. And starting at the same time and place.

Mola was both furious and embarrassed. Before the direct assault on Madrid began on November 7, Yagüe had warned him that it would be a mistake, and so far he seemed to be right. *El Director* now had to justify his decision. Since his men could not capture French Bridge, they would have to wade across the Manzanares near it, together with tanks, and make a lightning attack on University City. Mola discussed the plan with Varela, who did not object, since he, too, had to recoup his prestige. And there were no protests from Franco and his German advisers, who were willing to try anything at this point.

Franco had already accepted a demand by Hitler that he start bombing Madrid into submission, and the time seemed ripe since the entire Condor Legion was now in Spain and the rebel aircraft far outnumbered the Loyalist planes. The generalissimo had eagerly bombed workers' quarters earlier in the war, but until now had not deliberately hit civilian targets in most other parts of Madrid. Why inherit a heap of ruins unless you had to? Now he had to.

Hitler wanted to test the psychological effect on the city of massive methodical bombing designed mainly to kill people and destroy homes, hospitals, and cultural centers. The information would be valuable when he would later attack Paris, London, Moscow, and other cities. And Franco, desperately needing the Führer's help, did not dare balk. Nor, it seems, did he wish to. With victory in Madrid no longer certain, it was better to inherit ruins than nothing at all. Still, he bargained with Hitler, who wanted him to throw every plane he had into every raid. Franco apparently argued that thirty to forty at a time would be enough, hoping to save at least part of the city from destruction. And the Führer magnanimously agreed.

Thus, the first mass bombing of any city in history would begin.

It would be synchronized with Mola's ground attack plan—a simultaneous assault on Madrid's seemingly unshakable spirit. But once again, Yagüe who would command the troops, was livid. How could his tanks break through the wall lining the river and climb the steep banks? Anyway, he didn't have enough reserves for such an assault. Mola and Varela, however, again ignored his advice. So, reluctantly, Yagüe drew up the attack order and handed it to his column commander, Lieutenant Colonel Asensio.

Asensio's men would forge a path southeastward through University City and West Park to Moncloa Square, and on the way open up the gates of Model Prison and free the prisoners. The rebels would then have a springboard for an assault on central Madrid. The plan was a miniversion of Varela's original blueprint for the capture of Madrid on November 7.

"I wish you lots of luck, my friend," Yagüe said doubtfully.

"Tomorrow I'll cross with or without tanks," Asensio assured him.

That night of November 14, Yagüe sat restlessly at his desk in the house he had turned into his headquarters. He was nervous, bitter, worried that failure could mean the end of the whole Madrid campaign. His best troops had already been devoured and he had few reserves. Nor could he bring in men from the northern fronts, with the enemy stepping up its pressure there. And no matter how extensive the massacres in the conquered areas, thousands of rebels had to be tied down just to keep the lid on, for too many Spaniards were the enemy.

Yagüe began to feel ill, finding it difficult to breathe. Asensio then telephoned with discouraging news: His men were having a hard time blasting holes in the river wall big enough for tanks to crawl through. Feeling even worse now, Yagüe lay down on a cot and tried in vain to sleep. He then got up at about 2:30 A.M. and collapsed on the floor unconscious.

Shortly, the colonel opened his eyes and, seeing a doctor hovering over him, murmured that he was all right. He would lead his troops at dawn. No, he wouldn't, replied the doctor. And Yagüe's adjutant agreed, though he admitted:

"If you don't lead the attack personally the front will not be broken and Madrid will not be liberated."

"That's what hurts me," Yagüe groaned. "I believe that the order to attack is an error. You know that, and everything has been complicated by the arrival of those foreign volunteers. But if I can be with my men in the morning, God willing, defeating on the one hand the reds, and on the other, José Enrique [Varela], I feel in my bones that I will break the defense of Madrid.''

But Yagüe grew weaker and was evacuated from the front still as dubious about rebel chances as Cipriano Mera was about Loyalist prospects.

King Alfonso XIII, before running out the back door of his palace in 1931, had dreamed of restoring Spain's intellectual greatness. And so he began to build a huge University City, patterned after an American campus, with more than a dozen white-stone and red-brick buildings squatting haphazardly on a green hillside along the east bank of the Manzanares River. On the opposite bank sprawled the Casa de Campo, and to the south, West Park, which led to the center of town.

Alfonso's dream had never been realized completely because the succeeding republican government decided to use educational funds to build schools for the masses, not for the elite. And so some of the structures stood half finished, with crumbling building materials and rusty equipment scattered around amid the tanks and machine guns that had replaced intellect as a means of settling disputes.

At sunrise, November 15, under a cold rainy sky, Durruti's men crouched in shallow trenches on the east bank of the river bordering University City, with the Libertad Column ready to lead the surge across French Bridge. Russian tanks stood behind them, Russian planes flew over them, and Russian artillery exploded in front of them. But as Durruti ordered his men forward, deadly machine-gun fire from Garabitas Heights in the Casa de Campo swept their line, and they fell back.

More artillery, more bombing! Durruti cried. And there was more. But the rebels were returning as much as they received, as if it were *they* who were attacking. Then it dawned. They *were*! The Loyalists, in fear, blew up French Bridge, and the timid Libertad Column would now have to wade across the river—if it moved at all.

Again Durruti ordered it to advance, and again a retreat. A third time he urged it on. But by now the panic of the Libertad had infected all his men. Most fled to the rear while the bravest simply remained where they were.

At 2:00 P.M. an officer at French Bridge sent a short message to Rojo capsuling the situation: "The enemy has furiously attacked . . . French Bridge has been blown up by our troops. Enemy air force has bombed University City. . . . No other news worth mentioning.''

While Durruti urged his men ahead, so did Colonel Asensio, whose Moorish column stood just across the river. It almost seemed as if the two armies might meet in the middle of the shallow waterway. But the leading Moorish battalion was having its troubles, too. The commander was Sifre Carbonel, the "bulletproof" captain who couldn't get himself wounded no matter how hard he tried. Now was the time to challenge his luck again, to prove to his men, and himself, that he was really not a slacker. But how could he get his tanks through the wall along the bank? Dynamite didn't work.

Finally, he found the answer. He used the tanks as battering rams. They smashed through to the river and, though greeted by heavy fire from Russian tanks on the other side, plowed into the water. But some were grounded in the sandy riverbed and others couldn't climb the steep enemy side of the bank and were forced to retreat.

Rebel shells, however, also rained on the anarchists, who began to panic and run back; so with Loyalist fire growing weaker, Carbonel, at about 4:00 P.M., cried: "Everybody into the river!"

And man and machine slid into the knee-deep water, ignoring the Loyalist fire. When they were halfway across, a Russian tank began firing missiles point-blank at the rebels and it seemed the attack would end in disaster. But a Moorish lieutenant halted in midstream and fired an antitank missile just as a shell disemboweled him, and the tank suddenly turned around and slithered off, followed by others. Carbonel's men thus were able to wade all the way to the opposite bank, where they clambered up the slope and fought hand to hand with the few infantrymen still left in the trenches. Then they rushed to the nearest building, the School of Architecture.

Captain Carbonel had opened the door to the city, though, to his chagrin, he was still unscratched.

5

The French commander of the international unit dug in near French Bridge was still guaranteeing Keith Scott Watson that the Moors would never cross the river when suddenly he looked around and saw bearded, turbaned soldiers racing toward his men from behind. He was dumbfounded.

"*Zut!* This should not be!" he gasped.

But it was. The Moors were coming! Everyone turned around in the trench and began aiming to his rear. The scene of the half-naked woman with her throat cut flashed through Watson's mind. Was this simply a melodramatic film? Would it all end when he stepped out into brightly lit Leicester Square and dropped into Lyons for a cup of coffee?

"Fire!" cried the officer as the horses seemed to be almost on top of them.

The volley surprised the Moors, who thought they had surprised the Loyalists, and a wild figure on a white horse caught in Watson's sight toppled to earth, together with about half the others. As a Loyalist machine gun opened up, the rest of the horses galloped down the slope and slapped their way back across the river.

But they soon crossed again under a cover of shells. When one missile exploded behind Watson, killing or wounding several men, someone next to him, noting his paleness, dubiously assured him: "Courage, *mon brave*! It takes twenty shells to kill one man."

The Moors, yelling their terrifying warcries, hurled grenades and the Loyalist machine-gunner slumped dead over his gun. Watson ran out of cartridge clips but continued firing with some taken from a dead man.

"Bayonets ready!" the commander shouted.

There would be a last deadly stand. Then, when all seemed hopeless, a small group of reinforcements arrived, and the Moors turned and fled once more, leaving about twenty of the sixty defenders dead or wounded. Unable to hold any longer, Watson and his comrades withdrew as the enemy got ready for a new assault.

Keith was dazed. So this was what he had come to Spain for. His Rosita had predicted that he wouldn't see it through. Perhaps she was right. Only a fanatic would commit suicide, and he was, after all, a rather moderate fellow with a fondness for the lights of Leicester Square—especially after a massacre.

Jack Max, a seventeen-year-old corporal in the Durruti Column, peered through a hole in the shattered wall of a blockhouse near the river as the Moors crossed the Manzanares and trotted up the hill, storming building after building. Bullets ripped past him, bombs exploded everywhere. Max had never been under such heavy fire. Like Watson, he, too, was given advice by a veteran fighter:

"The enemy tanks will pass us and the Moors will follow and then the dance will begin. Don't open fire on the tanks. Let them go to hell. It's the Moors that interest us. You'll see how much fun it is. Aim at their feet and you'll hit their stomachs. Aim at their stomach and you'll hit their head. Elementary, my dear Watson, elementary."

"Have you read Conan Doyle?" Max asked.

"Of course," the man answered. "I have all his books at home."

And they began to discuss Sherlock Holmes as if they were in a library. But their conversation was soon drowned out by eight tanks that began to machine-gun them.

"What animals!" someone exclaimed. "They're going to run over their own dead soldiers!"

And they did.

Then a whole cloud of Moors appeared.

"Fire!" Max shouted.

And his squad mowed down dozens of Moors, but more followed, together with legionnaires. One defender grabbed a Moor, tore a grenade from the man's belt, and struck him on the head with it. The grenade exploded, killing both.

"In spite of everything, they're brave," Max said, and he hurled his own grenades through the hole in the wall.

He yelled to his machine-gunner: "Come on, fire!"

But the man, Andrés, was dead.

The attackers raced past the blockhouse toward the buildings beyond, then, as darkness set in, the storm subsided and an odd silence reigned. A messenger arrived to find out what had happened to Max's group, and he gasped when he saw the dead machine-gunner, Andrés. His brother! The man bent down and kissed the bloody head of the corpse, crying: "Andrés! Andrés!"

It was strange. Max knew all about death but so little about life. A girl had kissed him on the mouth for the first time as he marched down the Gran Vía on his arrival in Madrid, and even in the midst of battle that kiss had given him erotic thoughts. What would it be like to have a girl in his arms? If only he could live long enough to find out.

"Andrés! Andrés!"

The rebels crossed the river? José Manzana, Durruti's aide, refused to believe it. But Cipriano Mera insisted that the Moors had indeed pushed all the way to Clinical Hospital at the top of the hill, and to prove it he took Manzana to a point where they could see the building and some men standing outside.

"Those are *our* forces," said Manzana.

"Does the Durruti column have horses with padded saddles?" asked Mera.

It didn't.

However, the enemy troops Mera says they saw may have been simply a reconnaissance group, for the rebels had not reached the hospital yet.

The two men hurried to tell Durruti, who was so furious on hearing of the disaster that he immediately ordered several "cowards" shot as an example, though he later changed his mind. He then drove to general staff headquarters and tried to explain the rout. Was it his fault if his men had been given ancient rifles and little artillery support? He demanded a chance to hurl back the enemy the next morning.

Miaja and Rojo had tried to plug the gap in the Loyalist line—now about eight hundred yards wide between the French and San Fernando bridges—with Kléber's troops and other forces. And while Colonel Asensio's whole column had already poured through and seized several buildings, its slender vulnerable wedge was finally contained.

Durruti sat before the two Loyalist leaders like a humiliated child who had boasted of being the smartest in the class and then was the only one to flunk the examination. Despite their alarm they felt sorry for him, since he was a brave commander; he simply did not fully understand yet that an army without iron discipline would easily turn into an unruly mob. Yes, together with the other forces he could try again tomorrow—if he could find his men. But they didn't dare tell him that they expected him to flunk again.

That night young Jack Max and a comrade left their blockhouse, which the enemy had bypassed, to collect arms left by the dead nearby. The moon shone grotesquely on more than three hundred corpses from both sides, and Max thought of the irony of Napoleon's statement:

"How beautiful is a battlefield by moonlight!"

They began to pick up rifles, pistols, and automatic weapons when suddenly they saw two shadowy figures also gathering arms. Legionnaires! After a tense moment, Max said:

"We're in a no-man's-land. We can talk calmly, if you don't feel like fighting."

And he offered them tobacco and cigarette paper.

"I'll accept the paper," said one of the legionnaires, a lieutenant. "It's what we're shortest of."

The two men then shook hands.

"Where are you from?" Max asked.

"From Cádiz. And you?"

"I'm from Barcelona."

"I like the Catalans. You all have businesses. Do you have one?"

"I don't, but my father does."

"In the legion, there are two Catalans whose families also have businesses. How is it that you're on this side?"

"I was a volunteer."

"How old are you?"

"Seventeen."

"So young, and you're already killing Spaniards. Do you realize what you're doing?"

"Yes. It seems that it's destiny."

"Do you believe in God?"

"Well . . . I don't know."

"Maybe we'll see each other again and I'll kill you."

"I could do the same to you."

"You are brave."

"You are braver."

"Do you want to come over to my side? I'll protect you."

"It wouldn't be right. My friends would call me a coward."

Without waiting for a response, Max added: "Well, I have to go back. They're waiting for me."

"Can I embrace you?"

They silently hugged.

"Do you know why I've embraced you?" the legionnaire asked. "You remind me of a brother, just your age."

And they parted.

By November 16, one of the strangest battles in history had begun as every building in University City was converted into a fortress by one side or the other. Some structures changed hands several times within hours, or sheltered both sides at once, with each occupying a different floor and sometimes even adjoining rooms. Shortly after Asensio's men captured the Philosophy Building, Franco-Belgian and German troops of the XI International Brigade smashed in and fought the enemy with grenade and bayonet from landing to landing. Blood dripped down the stairs and twisted handrails gave way, while the wounded and the dead lay piled together in almost every room. Moorish, French, and German curses echoed through the chimneys, mingling with the cries of agony, until finally the few surviving Moors fled to a neighboring fortress.

The new occupants then barricaded all the windows and doors with everything they could find—tables, chairs, desks, and thousands of books found in the basement library. Kant, Goethe, Voltaire, Pascal, Cervantes, Dante, Shakespeare, Plato, all the sages and geniuses of the past, helped bar entry to the enemy.

Similar battles took place in other buildings. Durruti regained some of his lost prestige when his men fought their way into the Science Building. The Polish battalion captured Casa de Velázquez but Captain Carbonel's Moors virtually annihilated them in a counterattack. The rebels also kept their grip on several other buildings, slowly working their way up the slope toward the prized Clinical Hospital at the summit.

Jack Max and his men were ordered to withdraw to a trench right in front of that strategic site so they could protect it. They arrived just in time to halt the enemy in a fierce battle. At night, silence at last—except for the moan of one of Max's fighters who lay in a no-man's-land and could not be reached in his exposed position.

"Mother!" he called all through the night, until his voice grew fainter and finally faded away.

A rat leaped at Max and he stamped on it with his boot, killing it, though not before it had bit into his sole. This grisly encounter seemed to symbolize the savagery and tenacity of the struggle, which, on that evening of November 16, was to convulse all Madrid.

6

It looked like the end of the world. Even the sun had fallen, it seemed, as a Ferris wheel left over from the prewar fair burned brightly in the night. The Junkers came at 7:00 P.M., thunderously but unseen. Wave after wave buried in blackness that suddenly burst into a terrifying spectrum of colors. White flares turned night into day, blue tracers streaked into infinity, red pillars of fire ringed the city center, green rivers of flame poured through the streets, which writhed with monstrous shadows cast by crumbling walls. About twenty bombers escorted by some thirty fighters opened a new era in the art of war as Hitler, with Franco's blessing, turned Madrid into a giant laboratory of horrors.

Dozens of 500- and 1000-ton explosive bombs and countless clusters of incendiary missiles rained down on the city, mainly seeking out hospitals, cultural centers, and private homes. It was a raid designed to spread maximum panic, to test the human spirit and break it at any cost. What city could take such punishment for more than two or three days? And if the popular will cracked, so would the dam holding back the rebel flood, which had already leaked into University City. The battle, and perhaps the war, would then be over.

Since most people at that time could not imagine such massive destruction of a city, no one had even thought of building a system of air-raid shelters like those of World War II. Many *Madrileños* rushed to their cellars, often to be buried alive under burning debris. Others ran into the street carrying bundles, bedding, birdcages, dragging along their children to the doorway of some concrete building or to the nearest subway station, where they trampled over those already sprawled on grimy mattresses. On one platform, while trains taking troops to the front sped past, a mother smiled down on the ragged, hungry refugees from a huge wall poster as she fed her chubby child under the caption "Horxo builds beautiful babies."

Meanwhile, ignoring the holocaust, mothers searched for their children, children for their mothers. One little boy, finding his family buried under the ruins of his house, picked up a stone and hurled it into the air as if trying to bring down one of the invisible murder machines. A mother looking for her three-year-old child found another, about the same age and also blond, crying and lost in the rubble of the Puerta del Sol. Half mad, she clasped the child to her and fed him some chocolate, thinking that he was her own son.

But despite the bombing, some *Madrileños* refused to panic, or even to change their daily habits. During a lull, an old bootblack still knelt at a corner on the Gran Vía.

"They [the bombs] will kill us all, señor, if this continues," he prophesied to a reporter as he shined his shoes. "Certainly me, in any case. I don't know where to hide when they fall. And I have a premonition."

"What will you do?" the reporter asked.

The bootblack took out a coin and flipped it in his blackened hand.

"I play heads or tails. . . . If it's tails I go to the right . . . if it's heads, to the left."

The reporter would shortly find the man's body in the street amid his bottles and brushes. The coin had failed him.

Bombs knocked out the top floors of San Carlos Hospital, killing and wounding more than a hundred patients and terrorizing the others, who crawled under their beds.

And some missiles almost set fire to the Prado, which housed one of the world's greatest art collections. After flares outlined the building, fifteen explosive and incendiary bombs either struck it or fell nearby, though guards managed to put out the flames just in time. But many works were ruined in the San Fernando Academy of Fine Arts and the Convent of the Descalzas Reales, while the Anthropological Museum and the National Library, with its invaluable old manuscripts and rare editions, also suffered damage.

Hardly had the bombing ended when the government began evacuating the masterpieces to Valencia. A special unit of Fifth Regiment militiamen led by the Communist poet Rafael Alberti removed paintings from walls, statues from pedestals, books and manuscripts from shelves, carefully packing them in huge crates that they lifted into trucks. When a reporter asked two little boys sitting on a crate in one of these lorries what was inside, they proudly replied: "The first edition of *Don Quixote*."

The caravans carrying Spain's art works, its Goyas, Grecos, Rafaels, among others, moved only at night, and the thought that one bombing raid could wipe out these immortal treasures at a blow gave the mortal drivers and escorts blacker nightmares than the danger of death itself. The trucks reached their destination safely, but many art experts around the world criticized the government for taking the risk, arguing that the treasures could have been stored in the huge vaults of the Bank of Spain where the gold had been. Better to let Franco have them if he entered Madrid than to take so reckless a chance. But the Loyalists' hatred of Franco was apparently even greater than their love of art.

Ironically, Model Prison was also caught in the inferno as bomb fragments sprayed the cells, killing and wounding a number of prisoners who had been cheering the bombers on. Many of Durruti's men, who were using the prison as a headquarters, were also hit, and inmates were asked or compelled to give them first aid. The prisoners would be moved to another jail—if they weren't selected to die in the ditches of Paracuellos to vilely avenge those dying in the gutters of Madrid.

At the corner of Alcalá and Gran Vía, a hand clung to the leg of Louis Delaprée, the French reporter whom Keith Scott Watson's girl friend in Barcelona had warned of possible death in an air crash. A young woman in a blood-soaked nightgown muttered: "See! See what they have done."

And with a trembling hand she pointed to a small child lying on a bed of broken glass. Then the woman fell back and was motionless. Delaprée called to a passing ambulance, and the driver got out and turned a flashlight on the woman.

"Dead," he said. "We'll pick her up tomorrow. The wounded first."

The driver then noticed the child's corpse, which lay in the middle of the street and could be crushed a second time. He picked it up and placed it on the woman's breast, and the two lay together in a strange, moving scene of maternity and death, a portrait of Madrid and its brood in their martyrdom.

"The strongest sentiment that I have felt today," Delaprée would write, "is not fear, nor anger, nor pity. It is shame. I am ashamed to be a man when humanity shows it is capable of such massacres of innocents."

With a prophetic ring, he added: "Oh, old Europe, always occupied with your little games and your great intrigues. May God keep you from choking on all this blood."

Near the Puerta del Sol, a young man threw himself in the gutter as a bomb tore a great crater in the square and people scrambled blindly in all directions. Keith Scott Watson had fled the battlefield, at least temporarily, because the bombs had been more than he had bargained for. And now, hardly an hour after he had reached the "safety" of Madrid, the bombs were still stalking him. The subway entrance in the plaza was a mass of twisted iron, broken balustrades, and jagged pieces of wall plaster, while the inside was an oven of torn flesh. Two shattered streetcars lay on their sides nearby.

Suddenly a comely blonde woman in a raincoat ran past Watson. "*Aquí! Aquí!* Down!" he shouted to her.

The woman fell flat beside him as sheets of green flame ate up the asphalt, missing them by inches, and pieces of glass showered on them from the building above. Watson guiltily pondered his punishment. Somebody up there had courtmartialed him. Oh, to be back in the trenches, where there was at least a hole to crawl into.

When the hum of the last raiders finally faded away, he stood up and helped his companion to her feet. Embers danced in the smoky air and tongues of fire leaped from the scorched ruins around them, yet right in the middle of the wasteland was a little bar, and the tinkle of wine glasses inside indicated it was still open for business. They entered and sat down to calm themselves over a cognac while Madrid burned. When Watson told the woman he had decided to take a day off from battle, she asked him if he planned to stay at a hotel.

"My last two pesetas paid for our cognac," he replied.

"Then let me help you," she said, handing him some money. "Give it to me when we meet again. Here is my telephone number."

As they parted, Watson was no longer thinking of Rosita.

Another newcomer to Madrid that day was Sefton Delmer, star correspondent of the London *Daily Express*, who had bumped in from Valencia in a ramshackle bus. He immediately went to the British embassy and was greeted by a tall ginger-haired man. Where could he find a hotel? Delmer asked.

"You'd better stay right here," the man said. "The other British correspondents are all camping here, too. . . . You never know when the Moors are going to break in and it would not be funny to be caught by them in a hotel. . . . Mind you, there are no beds for you chaps, just a mattress each on the ballroom floor with the refugees."

The man paused. "By the way, my name is Christopher Lance. I'm a kind of honorary acting assistant military attaché unpaid!"

Lance had returned to Madrid after Franco had freed him on condition that he help some of his supporters escape from the Loyalist zone. And he was planning to do so—unless Franco entered Madrid before he could act. He would at least try to get the most important man on the list out: the son of the generalissimo's chief of staff. Lance had already saved scores of people, but none had the prestige of this man, who was now in hiding. This would be Lance's most daring coup.

Now, however, he played nursemaid to refugees and reporters in the British embassy, though not all his wards were obedient, least of all Sefton Delmer. With darkness falling, Lance warned him it was dangerous outside, but Delmer insisted he had to file a story, and left for the Telefónica. He had not gone far before the tornado broke and he was lying flat on his ample belly while rivulets of flame streamed by.

At that moment reporters in the Telefónica were shouting into the telephone as censors sat with earphones and carbon copies ready to pull a switch if a single word of the approved story was changed. Suddenly editors on the other end could hear the war itself. The building rocked like a reed in the rain as one roar followed another just outside on the Gran Vía.

"Put out the lights!" someone cried while planes rumbled overhead.

"The building's been hit!" another shouted. "Out in the corridor!"

"My God, look out the window—the whole Gran Vía's on fire!"

The girls in the switchboard room next door screamed and rushed sobbing into the corridor, earphones still on their heads. One of them was the mother of an infant, Félix, who had been born in a restroom in the building and was the godson of all the operators. Félix was one of the more than one thousand refugees huddled in the basement who were being cared for by the employees of the American-owned Spanish National Telephone Company; among them was a mother with thirteen children and another about to give birth.

More explosions, and the building almost seemed to be uprooted.

"Out on the stairway! The roof's on fire!"

"Turn on the water!"

"There isn't any. It's off at the main!"

A reporter, apparently Sefton Delmer, then staggered off the elevator crying: "What a story! What a story!"

The hiss of water was heard, and then the lights went on.

"It's all right. The building's not hit—just a small incendiary bomb on the roof. They've got the fire practically out already."

The girls marched back to their switchboards and the reporters ran to a table where two censors were sitting. In the dim light of a lamp covered with carbon paper, one censor stared antagonistically at Delmer when he introduced himself.

"The chief," Delmer later wrote, "was a cadaverous Spaniard with deep furrows of bitterness around his mouth, dug deeper by the shadows from his lamp. He looked the very embodiment of Spanishness, tense and suspicious . . . ready to take national umbrage."

The "cadaverous Spaniard," Arturo Barea, was himself to write of that fiery night: 'I stared at the journalists' reports, trying to make out what they wanted to convey, hunting through pedantic dictionaries to find the meaning of their double-edged words, sensing and resenting their impatience or hostility. I never saw them as human beings, but merely as grimacing puppets, pale blobs in the dusk, popping up, vociferating, and disappearing."

Barea's contempt for these "pale blobs" was greatest when they sat in comfortable chairs by a window high up in the Telefónica with a drink in one hand and a cigarette in the other, watching the struggle in the Casa de Campo as they might a spectacular battle scene in a movie. With a critic's cynicism, they commented caustically, sometimes jovially, as puppet soldiers attacked and toppled, toy cannons spurted drops of fire, little cotton balls rose in the sky. They didn't have to go to the front; the front had come to them. A most agreeable war.

At night the armchairs were usually empty, but Barea, "drunk with tiredness, coffee, brandy, and worry," relieved only by the thought that he would not have to bed down with his wife or mistress, stood by the window and peered into the blackness of what seemed like an almost bottomless well, silent, moldy, crawling with slimy insects, when suddenly the shaft would echo with screams. And on this night, as the *Madrileños* braved the greatest terror they had ever known, the well had never seemed deeper or dirtier, the screams never louder.

From the window could be seen a circle of flames converging toward the Gran Vía, slowly, almost majestically. The roofs burned first, with the fire devouring floor by floor until whole buildings finally collapsed in a pile of sparkling splinters. Over there, on ladders precariously resting against the charred walls of the Savoy Hotel, were a dozen firemen—until the blast of a bomb thrust them into a raging red lake.

To most of the reporters, in Barea's view, all this horror meant only sensational copy. And Sefton Delmer was, in fact, seen as hostile to the victims of this mass carnage, since he had interviewed Hitler, covered the Franco side, and was believed to favor a rebel victory.

When Delmer and the others had phoned their stories and left, another newcomer arrived to be greeted by Barea's withering stare—a young Austrian woman who had also endured the rigors on the road from Valencia. . . .

* * *

She was no beauty, with her round face, blunt nose, and plump figure. But even if she had been, Barea would have resented her. The male journalists were bad enough; a woman would drive him mad. As she sat by his desk waiting to talk with him, she watched him grope for words in an English dictionary, checking on a possible *double-entendre* in a story he was censoring.

"Can I help you with anything, comrade?" she asked.

Barea looked up and since she knew English well agreed to consult with her on a few terms. Anything to reduce the stack of "distorted" copy piled on his desk. Then he asked her:

"Why did you call me comrade?"

"Because we are all comrades here."

"I don't think many of the journalists are. Some of them are Fascists."

Although she contributed to some European newspapers, the woman said, she had come here as a socialist to help the government propagandize.

"All right, then, let it pass at comrades."

Barea shortly sent an aide, Luis, with her to the Hotel Gran Vía, where she would be lodged, and on returning the man exclaimed:

"Now there's a woman for you!"

"What, you find her attractive?"

"She's a fine woman, Don Arturo, but perhaps too much of a good thing for a man. And what an idea to come to Madrid just now! . . . She's got plenty of guts, that woman."

Well, he did need someone who knew those tricky English idioms. And the next day, the woman, Ilsa Kulcsar, moved into the Telefónica.

7

Captain Carbonel's Moors, on the morning of November 17, finally broke through the lines manned by Jack Max's troops and other Loyalist forces and crashed into the sprawling, red-brick Clinical Hospital on the upper fringe of University City. The Loyalists inside, caught by surprise, were calmly cooking a meal on the ground floor when the rebels burst in, and amid the sputter of guns and the clatter of pots and pans, they either fell dead or fled into the labyrinth of corridors.

The Moors looked out of the giant paneless windows of the half-finished building and saw all Madrid at their feet, smoldering and almost certainly crushed in spirit from the pounding of the previous night. They were jubilant. An easy march southward to the Plaza de Moncloa and the road to the Plaza de España would be open.

But then they heard strange noises overhead. Were there ghosts in the building? Or other human beings? In fact, the floors above were seething with so many Loyalists that the rebels would have preferred the ghosts. And thus began a bloody, horrifying, endless battle for every corner of the huge edifice. Each side threw prisoners out of windows. Patrols meeting in the corridors were never sure until the last second whose side the other was on, and if it was on the wrong side such chance encounters usually ended in slaughter.

"It was the roughest fighting I ever went through," Legionnaire Captain Iniesta Cano told the author. "We tore holes in the walls and used flamethrowers to sweep the next room clean. We'd fire from behind sandbags on every floor. The enemy would drop dynamite through holes in the ceiling. Every minute was nerve-shattering."

Later, the Loyalists would place explosives in the sewer beneath the building and set off a blast that would kill almost all the men in Iniesta Cano's company.

While the battle for the Clinical Hospital raged on this day, rebel forces stormed other buildings as well, including the Faculty of Medicine, which was to be captured several times by each side. Some days later, Keith Scott Watson visited this building and a Red Cross orderly showed him around. In the basement his flashlight eerily illuminated a chilling scene—about fifty dead Moors, some sitting in chairs, others sprawled on tables or heaped on the floor.

"Those boys won't do no more looting." said the orderly. "They killed the bloody rabbits, hens, and sheep and ate 'em. What they didn't know was that they had been injected full of germs by the professors. They didn't have time to kill the animals before they beat it, the Moors found 'em and ate 'em, germs and all. There's enough bacilli in here to lay out Madrid."

Actually, whether these Moors died as the orderly claimed or were killed in battle is not certain for while Captain Carbonel confirmed to the author that some of his men had indeed eaten the infected animals and contracted diseases, he said they did not die from them.

Anyway, most of the rebels were well enough to fight with fervor for each building—to the dismay of Durruti's men, who were now pleading with him to send them back to Catalonia. They saw little reason why they should die in Madrid, and began to retreat toward Plaza de Moncloa and their headquarters in Model Prison.

The enemy then surged through the gap they left in the lines.

General Miaja was alarmed when word reached him that the rebels were on the verge of breaking through to the center of Madrid. And his mood was all the more sour because of talks he had just had with government leaders in Valencia. Why hadn't he consulted them on his moves? they asked, apparently jealous of his popularity. While Prime Minister Largo Caballero would not even visit Madrid, fearing the people would taunt him for secretly fleeing on November 6,

Miaja was being touted as the city's savior. Was Miaja planning a coup? his superiors wanted to know. He'd better come to Valencia—and fast!

Impossible, Miaja responded. Let them come to him. He couldn't leave Madrid at this critical moment. The *Madrileños* would never forgive him. This subtle reminder of the government's own departure only fueled Caballero's resentment and suspicion. Miaja, however, had no political ambitions, though he clearly enjoyed being the hero and would not let his less heroic masters tell him what to do in Madrid. Now, on the morning of November 17, he clearly saw the new threat to his domain, and to find out how great it was he decided to inspect the front himself.

With Rojo and other aides, Miaja drove to Model Prison, which had become strictly a military post with all prisoners evacuated. The party arrived just as the enemy began bombing the prison to pave the way for a major assault. Miaja and the others climbed to the top floor of the quivering structure and scanned the battlefield to the north. The scene was chilling. Rebel infantry was sweeping toward the Plaza de Moncloa and the Loyalists were falling back in disorder.

"Trapped within those walls that could bury us," Rojo later wrote, "we felt that perhaps the most critical moment of the attack had come."

They ran downstairs into the plaza and Rojo tried to drag Miaja into the car. Rojo considered his superior a mediocre commander but an indispensable symbol of courage and tenacity. His death would be disastrous. But the general would not listen. He rushed through the rubble toward his retreating men, staggering ahead even after he fell into a bomb crater.

"Cowards!" he shouted, as he met the first group. "Cowards! Die in your trenches! Die with your General Miaja!"

The men stared at him in disbelief. Then they turned around and ran back, crying: "General Miaja is here!"

Planes began to bomb but Miaja would not budge. If Madrid was to fall, this was the place to die. Finally the other officers virtually carried him to the car, aghast at his boldness yet persuaded that he had singlehandedly saved Madrid.

A handful of Moors did actually manage to fight their way through the Plaza de Moncloa and race to the Plaza de España. The Promised Land at last! And there they were shot to the last man.

Meanwhile, the Loyalists scolded by Miaja held against the main rebel force that might otherwise have conquered Madrid and punctured the general's ego.

8

For the next three nights Franco vented his terrible rage for this new failure by spreading terror with ever greater fury, even though several governments urged him to limit his air raids to military targets. He declared bomb-free only the zone of Salamanca, where most of the diplomats and his wealthy friends lived. And about twenty thousand people who had been unable to squeeze into the packed cellars and subways swarmed into this quarter.

Fathers led the way, carrying mattresses or tables on their heads, and women, children, and old men followed, sometimes with overburdened donkeys. They searched for an unoccupied space on the street and settled down in a home without walls or ceiling, while latecomers begged for a few feet of asphalt or sat as near as possible to the "protected" area. Rain poured down, but they preferred to be soaked than sunned, for clouds kept the planes away. The sun was an ally of the enemy, to be feared and cursed.

Elsewhere in the city, Franco was destroying quarter by quarter—public buildings, private homes, hotels, hospitals, schools, markets—while carts loaded with bodies rattled to and from the morgue where relatives waited to see if their loved ones were in them. The noises were more deafening than ever before as explosions, screams, the crash of falling debris, the clang of firebells, the blast of whistles, the screech of ambulances, and the drone of bombers blended into a symphony of insanity. And the smells were stifling—the rotting dead, the swirling smoke, the olive oil and burning fish in the fire-swept Carmen Market.

Even the magnificent abandoned palace of the duke of Alba, which housed an art collection second only to the Prado's, was not spared. As it crumbled into ashes on November 17, militiamen worked in the rain, with missiles exploding around them, to save what they could. Since they knew little about art, the first things they dragged out were a large stuffed polar bear and some armored figures, but they also salvaged some of the world's finest paintings, sculptures, and tapestries, though many treasures were lost. The palace had been turned into a museum when the war started, but the most popular exhibits had been the duchess's hand-painted gold bathroom and the duke's Savile Row suits laid out endlessly, each with appropriate shirt, shoes, and hat.

The Palace Hotel, converted into a hospital, had become, like most hospitals, a trembling madhouse. Ambulatory patients were taken to the basement, but Antonio, the Russian pilot who had been mistakenly shot by Loyalists as he parachuted down, could not move, and so Mikhail Koltsov sat by his bed holding his hands, trying not to shudder when the walls shook. In a cold sweat, Antonio mumbled:

"They won't abandon me here?! They won't leave me? It seems everybody's left. Why are we staying?"

"Nobody has gone," said Koltsov. "Stay quietly in bed . . . I'm with you, by your side. That means nothing serious is happening, doesn't it?"

"Don't go away on any account," Antonio pleaded. "Otherwise I'll get up and follow."

Then Antonio dozed off. A few days later, he would die from his wounds.

Before dawn, on November 19, planes dropped leaflets as well as bombs.

"Unless the city surrenders by four o'clock this afternoon the bombardment will begin in earnest," they warned.

Hitler would now subject his guinea pigs to the supreme test of endurance.

As the deadline approached, the *Madrileños* waited expectantly, and those on the Gran Vía stared at the huge clock on the Telefónica as the black hands jerked ahead minute by minute . . . half-past three . . . a quarter to four. A few minutes before four, eleven bombers and an escort of fighters zoomed over and dropped their loads in the most devastating raid yet. Liars! They had come early.

The people, more angry than fearful, had by now become used to the mass bombings. They came out of hiding—sometimes during forays—and dug in the rubble of their home for things perhaps less valuable than a duke's art collection but just as precious to them. They peeked under every stone and piece of masonry, lifting, sifting, scratching. One woman wept when she found a photo of her child. Another shouted with joy when she salvaged a tiepin.

Still another, dressed in black, elderly and dignified, suddenly collapsed as she rummaged in the ruins, a sliver of shrapnel in her neck. A telephone beside her then began ringing mysteriously—as if Franco were calling to ask if she had had enough. A skywriter was less personal; he tried to spell out the word *surrender!* But he was chased off by Loyalist aircraft while the unfinished demand dissolved into shreds of smoke.

Other citizens replied by seeking safer havens. Some burrowed their way from cellar to cellar, usually with their bare hands since every available spade and shovel was needed to build fortifications. These underground tunnels would help to protect them from being asphyxiated in their own cellars or crushed to death by tumbling debris.

Young anarchist Eusebio Muñoz, who had fled Montaña Barracks in disgust during the executions there, responded in his own way to Franco's ultimatum. He was having his first sexual experience when the bombs started falling.

"We'll be killed!" cried his partner. "Let's get out of here!"

"Not until I finish," he said. "This is my first screw!"

The building shook from an explosion nearby.

"Well, it isn't my first," replied the girl, "and I'll be damned if it'll be my last."

And she desperately tried to get up, but Muñoz wouldn't let her go until he finished. He then quickly dressed and ran off to the front. Now he had to win the war—or they'd shoot him before he could try it again without the bombs.

The Loyalists wanted to live, and so they were ready to die—seriously disrupting Hitler's experiment and Franco's schedule.

It was after midnight, and the planes were spiraling around the Telefónica. Almost everything was burning—except this towering symbol of defiance which, though hit by more than a dozen bombs, suffered little more damage than a man bitten by fleas. But Franco would try again. Arturo Barea knew it, but he was too tired to care. There were no reporters around now and all he wanted as he lay on his hard cot was to sleep. He tried to ignore the whir of the propellers, but Ilsa, across the room on another cot, would not let him.

"What are we going to do?" she asked, sitting up.

What a stupid question! And Barea was utterly dismayed when she removed a powder puff from her handbag and began dabbing at her nose. Was she mad?

"Nothing!" Barea replied.

Yet he admired her. A woman who powdered her nose in the middle of an air raid! And she was turning out to be a good censor. The reporters liked her, and a trace of her influence could already be seen in their copy. Even Sefton Delmer— who offered her a job as his assistant—was showing a certain sympathy for the beleaguered *Madrileños*.

Ilsa's aim was to let the reporters write what they wanted about nonmilitary matters. Better the government let the world understand its problems than feed suspicion by trying to hide every fault and division. Barea persuaded his boss in Valencia to try out the new policy, but it was beginning to annoy the more militant groups, especially the Communists, whose influence was growing daily. If truth started to leak out, where would it end? And Ilsa's foreign origin added to their concern.

A great explosion lifted Barea off the mattress, and the building seemed to sway crazily. He heard cries on the street, glass crashing. Suddenly Ilsa was sitting at the foot of his cot.

"The damp fog, carrying a smell of plaster, came in gusts through the windows," he would later recall. "I felt a furious desire to possess that woman then and there. We huddled in our coats. Overhead the drone of aircraft had ceased." . . .

In the morning the streetcars were running, newsboys were shouting headlines, children were spinning tops on the sidewalk, and people were clearing away debris. As Barea looked out of the window, he saw someone sweep a pile of broken glass from his balcony onto the street, forcing pedestrians to take cover as if from an air raid. The scene was so comical that he would have laughed if his own window had not been shattered, leaving the room exposed to the bitter cold.

No, the people were not ready to surrender. They were acting normally, just as they would on any other day—even to the mortal detriment of their comrades.

Yet by November 19, more than a fourth of Madrid lay in ruins, with over a thousand known dead, a countless number wounded, and tens of thousands homeless. There were never more than thirty-two bombers blasting Madrid at a time, and the death and destruction did not compare with figures during World War II when whole cities were wiped out. But the pattern was set for these more massive raids.

9

Buenaventura Durruti was in a sullen mood on the drizzly morning of November 19. When Mikhail Koltsov met him at the War Ministry he found him with "his big fists . . . . clenched, his erect figure . . . somewhat bent. . . . He embodies the vision of an ancient Roman gladiator slave tensely waiting to make a desperate lunge for freedom." Durruti growled that he was going to his sector to prepare his men for an attack and protect them from the rain.

"Are they made of sugar?" Koltsov joked.

"Yes, they are made of sugar. They dissolve in water. . . . They perish in Madrid."

Then he moved on toward his headquarters in the Civil Guard barracks overlooking the battlefield. Today, he knew, would be crucial—for him, for the anarchist movement, for Madrid, for Spain. His men, the few hundred who survived, would launch a full-scale attack on the Clinical Hospital. If they failed him again . . .

Hungry, exhausted, demoralized, most of his troops were still pleading with him to let them go back to Catalonia, a land they loved and now ruled, a land where they knew how to fight and why they did. But Durruti only exclaimed: "We must hold, hold, hold!"

However, fearing another catastrophe, he had gone to see General Miaja the day before and pointed to his terrible losses. Couldn't his men be replaced and return to fight in Aragon? Several Communist commanders who were present chided him. *Their* men had been fighting in Madrid day after day, week after week. Miaja himself was sympathetic but firm. Could not Durruti try at least to recapture the vital Clinical Hospital? The anarchist chief felt humiliated and also frustrated. How could he explain to these "fools" the mentality of his men? The feeling of being trapped into dying for values repellent to them, for capitalism, communism, bureaucracy?

But his men would remain, he agreed. And they would fight and win.

Durruti was nevertheless tormented. He was forcing them to fight against their will. He even vented his wrath on his wife, Émilienne, when she telephoned him from Barcelona to ask how he was. He was well but too busy to talk! And he hung up.

"In a war one becomes a jackal," he muttered to a comrade.

Durruti stalked into his headquarters at about 6:00 A.M. and with Cipriano Mera and other anarchist leaders went up to the roof to watch the attack. But even with binoculars it was hard to tell what was happening. Then at 7:00 A.M. a messenger rushed to Durruti. The anarchists had seized the upper floors of the hospital but the rebels controlled the basement and ground floor and had thus trapped them.

Durruti immediately ordered the commander of a reserve battalion to capture the lower floors with two companies. And shortly word reached him that the commander was choosing the two companies by lot—as the anarchists usually did. Durruti angrily called the officer in and rasped:

"Choosing by lot is ridiculous! You designate the companies and start the attack immediately! If you delay any longer you'll have to deal with me, captain."

Mera was surprised to see Durruti, the greatest anarchist of them all, imposing discipline on his men.

"Like you," Mera said, "I once supported self-discipline. But I have gradually realized . . . that it is of limited value, for the self-preservation instinct often triumphs over the sense of duty."

Durruti ruefully nodded. How far he had come from those bank-robbing days when compromise was unthinkable. But would his men, who had learned from him the principle of unlimited freedom, follow him that far?

Young Jack Max and his squad were still holding out in the trench in front of the Clinical Hospital while their comrades were battling inside. As Moors and legionnaires attacked, the squad caught them in a cross-fire and cut them down, but they kept coming. Finally some leaped into the trench. Max struck the first one over the head with his submachine gun, and was barely saved when a comrade split open the skull of another who was about to shoot him.

Was this a ghastly dream? Max had learned to kill impersonally from a distance, but not face to face, body to body, to smash a man's brain out and feel a blade penetrate flesh and to know that he was just as vulnerable as the enemy. There were shots, blows, curses, cries of pain. As a Moor bayoneted one of his men, Max again smashed his gun on the attacker's head. Another foe then dented his helmet with a bayonet thrust, and as Max wrestled him to the ground he escaped death once more as the blade sank into the earth inches from him. He then managed to break away and pull his trigger, but the gun jammed. At that moment, international volunteers dived into the bloody free-for-all and the enemy fled.

"To the hospital!" a Loyalist cried.

And suddenly there was a stampede. Swept up in it, Max wondered why his comrades were retreating, but gradually he began to realize why. Like himself, they were almost in a state of shock, their senses dulled by the excitement and horror. They had slaughtered men like animals and had seen their friends slaughtered. They had been bombed and shelled and had gone without sleep for nights. The enemy gave them no peace, and now they had almost no hope—even though they had won the battle!

Max and the others stumbled into the hospital, only to find themselves in a new, terrifying, peekaboo struggle that raged from corridor to corridor, floor to floor, as the sounds of war reverberated through the building. While Max blazed away with his submachine gun and hurled grenades wildly, he heard in the midst of the pandemonium an ominous cry: "They've betrayed us!"

"They," their leaders, had sent them to die meaninglessly.

The Loyalists scrambled for the doors and Max, seeing that he was alone, was forced to run again, too.

For now his death *would* be meaningless.

At about 1:00 P.M., Antonio Bonilla, an aide, ran in to see Durruti. The men were fleeing from the Clinical Hospital, he reported. Durruti was crushed. Not again! He immediately ran out with Manzana and jumped into his Packard; he would personally bar the way to his men. His driver raced off, following Bonilla's car, which would trace a safe path toward the hospital.

As the cars sped down a street near the hospital, Durruti suddenly ordered his driver to stop. He leaped out brandishing a pistol, and faced the men galloping toward him like a herd of animals.

Jack Max was among them. He saw Durruti get out of the car and shout: "Cowards! Go back! You are trampling on the name of the FAI. Let's go and reconquer the Clinical Hospital!"

Max and the others came to a startled halt and some cheered at the sight of their leader. They would recapture the building, one man assured Durruti. Then, as the anarchist leader was about to enter his car, there was gunfire and someone shouted: "Treason!"

Durruti slumped to the ground, blood oozing from his chest. Max ran forward to help him, but others were already lifting him into the vehicle, which turned around and rushed off.

The next morning Durruti was dead.

A half-million people stood or knelt along the roads leading to the cemetery in Barcelona, many weeping as if a close relative had died. Amid the mass hysteria, Loyalist leaders delivered eulogies and an honor guard saluted the flower-covered coffin; inside lay a man dressed in an old leather jacket, threadbare trousers, and shoes with holes in them. Seldom in Spanish history had a funeral evoked such popular emotion. Durruti, the beloved bandit, the *macho* idealist who had wanted to free the human spirit beyond all reasonable bounds, was gone.

Who had killed him? A rebel sniper firing from a window of the Clinical Hospital, claimed the anarchist leaders; the Communists, charged many of his own men; his own men, cried many Communists. Even those who were with him on his last drive could not agree. José Manzana, who rode beside him, blamed the killing on an enemy sniper, while Antonio Bonilla, who had been in the escort car, years later accused Manzana himself, though he did not see the shooting.

Jack Max accused nobody, but his eyewitness account appears to indicate that one of the men fleeing with him from the hospital was the killer. Max had heard the cry "Treason!" just after the shot was fired. And clearly some of Durruti's men felt betrayed because he made them fight what they thought was a senseless, suicidal battle. Who was giving him orders? In their view, a Communist-influenced government that would eventually wipe them all out—the 40 percent who had not already fallen. Some even suspected he had made a secret deal with the Communists, possibly because he was seen chatting with Koltsov and Communist officers and had taken on a Communist military adviser.

One of his men blandly told an international volunteer, Pierre Rösli, only minutes after the shooting: "It was our people who killed Durruti."

And Durruti's wife later confided to an anarchist friend: "Until the day I die, I will accept the official explanation that he was shot by a Civil Guard from an upper window . . . but I know he was killed by one of those standing beside him. It was an act of vengeance."

The fact was that many of Durruti's men could not understand the sudden stress on discipline, the sudden need to adhere to a concept that he had once taught them was abhorrent. As he lay dying in the hospital his last words were, according to anarchist commander Ricardo Rionda, who visited him:

"Too many committees . . . too many committees."

His men had to *obey* commands, not discuss them.

Anyway, powder burns on Durruti's shirt, experts confirmed, showed that the fatal bullet had been fired no more than fifty centimeters from him. When anarchist leaders heard this, some suddenly "revealed" that Durruti had accidentally shot himself when he banged the butt of his rifle against the running board as he was climbing into his car—though Durruti was not known to carry a rifle, only a pistol.

Durruti was dead, but the legend had to live. Nobody must think that one of his own pupils had killed him, that he had been a victim of his own permissive philosophy.

Whatever the truth, the anarchists sensed that the only chance they could have had to save society from the corruption, greed, and dictatorship Durruti hated had gone with him. That the future now belonged either to the Fascists or the Communists—if the Loyalists won. For only Durruti's immense prestige might have countered the growing Soviet-backed Communist influence in Loyalist Spain.

And symbolically, most of the survivors of the Durruti Column—though not Jack Max, who chose to stay and fight in Madrid—hurried back to Catalonia after their leader's death despite the pleas of other anarchist chiefs. Some who might have remained changed their minds when two anarchists were mysteriously shot in the streets of Madrid—by Communists, all were sure. Why be killed in somebody else's war, if not by Fascists on the front line, then by Communists in a back alley, far from home and the revolution?

On the day Durruti died, so did another legendary figure—José Antonio Primo de Rivera, who had been imprisoned in Alicante since spring. Prime Minister Largo Caballero and most of his cabinet did not wish to execute him. They felt a strange affinity to him personally, and some even suspected he was a well-meaning man who had been trapped between his social conscience and his obsession with vindicating his dictatorial father.

José Antonio was known to have little love for Franco and the other right-wing generals, though he needed their support as they needed his. And while he desired a corporate state, he did call for drastic social reforms. Certainly he was not the brutal type of Fascist Hitler was. In fact, did he really order, or even condone, the crimes committed by the thugs and killers in his party? Not all the government leaders were sure.

It clearly seemed a better idea to trade him for several important Loyalist prisoners—among them Caballero's own son. Government officials thus secretly tried to make a deal, but Franco, oddly, would not agree on terms, and the talks fell through, as did several Falangist plots to bribe guards into releasing their star prisoner. And so on November 16, José Antonio went on trial.

He was sentenced to death, but felt confident the government would save him. Especially since he had offered to mediate peace with Franco, though the government had so far rejected the idea. He would try to persuade the generalissimo to accept a constitutional regime led by former Prime Minister Martínez Barrio and including the most important Spanish intellectuals and politicians. And he would leave his family behind as hostages until he returned.

As he waited on the night of November 19 for the government to act on his appeal, his sister and aunt were brought to see him.

"Don't cry, Carmen," he urged his sister. "There is still hope."

"No, it's not possible, José . . . it is not possible that they could do this to you."

"It is understandable. So many of the Falange have fallen that it is quite understandable that I, their leader, should also fall. There is still hope."

He then embraced his visitors and returned to his cell, waving good-bye "for a little while."

The next day, at dawn, a firing squad executed José Antonio.

Caballero and his government seemed more upset than Franco. The cabinet was discussing the condemned man's appeal at the very moment word arrived that he was already dead. The militiamen running the prison did not want to wait for the government's decision—which would probably have cheated them of a prize victim. Caballero feared for his son's life, but somehow the youth survived. Perhaps Franco was repaying the prime minister for his thoughtfulness. With José Antonio gone, no one remained—except perhaps Mola—who might seriously challenge the generalissimo when the war was over.

As the Communists mourned for Durruti, so Franco mourned for José Antonio.

CHAPTER 10

Betrayal

1

The rain falling steadily through the night muffled the sound of sporadic sniper fire, but not enough to let the refugees in the American embassy enjoy a good night's sleep. Janet Riesenfeld and most of the other Americans lying on mattresses spread out on the floor were spending their last night in Madrid. The embassy was moving to Valencia in the morning—Thanksgiving Day—and they would go along and board a ship waiting to take them home.

At 4:00 A.M., they awoke, dressed, and had a breakfast of dry corn flakes and creamless coffee, then stepped into buses, each person carrying a bag with a Thanksgiving dinner of sliced ham, tortillas, bread, and oranges.

When the buses started moving, Janet looked out the window and glimpsed Madrid for the last time—the gutted buildings, the overturned streetcars, the long lines of women in black standing before the markets. Less than three months earlier she had arrived in a carefree sunny Madrid reveling in its "victories," a Madrid of galas, noisy cafés, and candlelit restaurants . . . and Jaime had been there to greet her.

Now she was leaving without Jaime on a cold drizzly morning, and there were only ruins. Yet, if battle had scarred Madrid's face, it had strengthened its character. How calm and resolute were those women in black standing amid the debris. Madrid had matured in the last months, as she herself had.

"Perhaps when we begin all over again," José María had said over a farewell drink, "you can come back and help. We'll have dancing in the streets then."

Yes, she would come back—she loved to dance.

Three cars roared out the gates of the German embassy on the morning of November 24, and within seconds, as whistles blew madly, a gray Hispano Suiza loaded with police tore down the street after them. The most important rebel supporters hiding in the embassy were in the three vehicles, making their getaway just before a police-led mob was to raid the building in search of refugees.

Actually the place was no longer used as an embassy since all German diplomats had already evacuated it and gone to the rebel side. For a few days earlier, on November 18, Hitler—and Mussolini—recognized the Franco regime as the only legal government of Spain. They had expected to do this only after Franco captured the capital so they would have a plausible excuse for intervening so openly on his side.

But things hadn't gone as anticipated. Franco was bogged down outside Madrid and it looked as if he might never enter. And his casualties were so great that he was resorting to a desperate trick to get replacements. He had rounded up eleven thousand more Moors by summoning natives from the Moroccan mountains, then giving them the choice of prison, execution, or enrollment in his army. Nobody wanted prison or execution. Meanwhile, Russia seemed to be pouring arms into Madrid. Hitler had to decide: Should he recognize Franco and thus stake German prestige on a rebel victory? The danger was that Russia might react by staking *its* prestige on a Loyalist triumph. And that could spark a larger war. Don't take a chance, some Nazi generals urged; Germany wasn't ready yet for such a war. But the Loyalists then helped to force Hitler's hand.

On November 16, Foreign Minister Del Vayo warned that the government would attack all vessels entering any Spanish port without its permission. Since seventeen German ships loaded with arms were already on the way to rebel-held ports and more were to follow, the threat could mean a disaster for both Hitler and Franco. For any government had the legal right to use force if necessary to prevent foreign ships from entering its territorial waters, while such ships did not have the right to fight back. But if Germany recognized a Franco regime, German ships could *legally* defend themselves against Loyalist attack since they would have landing permission from Franco.

So Hitler would recognize Franco, virtually guaranteeing the *caudillo's* ultimate victory—unless Russia committed itself similarly to a Loyalist victory. And Mussolini was glad to go along.

Now, on November 24, right after the most wanted refugees had escaped, police set up a machine gun outside the gates of the German embassy and, together with an enraged mob, stormed the building while about fifty people under the care of a German citizen cowered inside. The terrified refugees put up no resistance, though the embassy had been converted into a fortress, with windows sandbagged, light machine guns and German stick bombs in place, and small arms ready for use. In the courtyard the raiders found the "phantom cars" that had once spread terror in the night. The embassy, it appeared, had been fifth-column headquarters.

The mob began dragging out the refugees when some diplomats from other embassies drove up. There would be no *paseos,* they said. And a Mexican diplomat, Nibon, representing the one country besides Russia that had sent arms to the Loyalists, stepped forward with a pistol in one hand and a list of names in the other. He was taking several refugees to his embassy, he declared, and he sought out those he wanted and led them toward his car while the Loyalists looked on in disbelief. But when his car had sped off, they followed and forced it to the curb. Nibon got out, waving his pistol, and threatened to shoot anyone who tried to take his passengers.

"If I kill one of you," he said, "nothing will happen to me. If you kill me, Mexico has soldiers, an army, and it won't send you any more guns."

The militiamen pondered this logic, then gradually moved off, and Nibon's car drove away.

Other diplomats also managed to rescue some refugees, but most of the rebels were arrested and some were later shot.

Meanwhile, in the Telefónica, Arturo Barea was pleasantly surprised when he noted that most correspondents wrote of the links between the embassy and the fifth column. But, ironically, he had to suppress their reports since rules wouldn't permit any mention of police measures unless announced in a communiqué from Valencia. While the reporters vigorously protested about deadlines, Barea called up the War Ministry, and Mikhail Koltsov, the only one there, instructed him to wait for an official statement.

Ilsa was as concerned as the reporters. Because of her leniency, news stories going out were far more sympathetic toward the Loyalist cause than they had ever been. Should this goodwill now be dissipated, she asked Barea, with the German version monopolizing the world press? They decided to release the stories on the embassy raid.

When Koltsov heard about this, he fumed. The two of them would be court-martialed, he threatened—and Barea knew the Russians now had the power to make good on their threats. But the next morning Koltsov apologized; his "superiors" were delighted with the results. However, some Communists grumbled about Ilsa. *She* was responsible, they guessed, and even if she was right she had no business disobeying orders. There was nothing more dangerous than an undisciplined "comrade"—and a foreigner and a socialist at that!

And dangerous people, especially in sensitive positions, had to be dealt with if the Communists were gradually to seize power.

2

At a secret meeting in Valencia, a man with a shaven head and slightly almond eyes greeted Education Minister Jesús Hernández coldly and said: "Our foreign service has learned that certain elements of POUM have taken steps to have Trotsky come to Spain. Do you know something about it?"

"It's the first I've heard of it," Hernández replied to A.A. Slutski, chief of the NKVD foreign division, who had just come from Moscow.

"That proves that the counterespionage services of the republic are deficient."

"That proves simply that we give little importance to what POUM says."

"This is serious. If the responsible men of the party do not give importance to this band of counterrevolutionaries and enemy agents, that helps us to understand many things in this war. . . . We want you to understand that it is necessary to act strongly against Trotskyites. As minister, you must facilitate the work."

"My post of minister was given to me by the party. I will act only after receiving its directives."

"We have in our hands some documents that prove POUM has contacts with the Falange. When we start to make some arrests we might run into some difficulties from the authorities. We need your help."

"Come to see me *then*. Bring me all the elements of proof and I promise to submit the matter immediately to the cabinet."

"I knew that you would finally understand."

Slutski left, greatly relieved, and on his way back to Moscow stopped off in Paris to see Colonel Krivitsky, Stalin's agent there.

"We cannot," he told Krivitsky, "allow Spain to become a free camping ground for all the anti-Soviet elements that have been flocking there from all over the world. After all, it is our Spain now, part of the Soviet front. We must make it solid for us. Who knows how many spies there are among those volunteers? And as for the anarchists and Trotskyites, even though they *are* anti-Fascist soldiers, they are our enemies. They are counterrevolutionaries, and we must root them out."

To do this, an NKVD network would be set up in Spain largely with foreign Communists (not Russian), since Spanish Communists could not be entirely trusted. With Madrid holding, the war would go on and on—serving Soviet foreign policy. And Stalin couldn't take a chance on his left-wing enemies sabotaging his plans. If he could kill Trotskyites in Russia, why not in Spain, too?

Some non-Russian Stalinists, including Spanish ones, found that crying "Trotskyite" was an easy way to get rid of a political competitor or settle a personal score. And, ironically, the Russians, who coined the word and applied it to all leftist anti-Stalinists, had to protect victims from the zeal of their attackers.

General Goriev thus took under his wing the chiefs of the foreign press department in Madrid despite growing Stalinist protests about its activities. Ilsa, cried some Communists, was a Trotskyite, for why else was she letting the correspondents report on so many delicate political matters? She even dared to criticize some foreign Communists! A trusted party member should replace her, demanded her enemies.

But Goriev, as a high Russian official, knew a real Trotskyite when he met one and he wasn't interested in pandering to local political intrigues. He was a practical man, and so he appreciated Ilsa's work. Early each morning Barea and Ilsa would go to see him to discuss the censored press dispatches of the previous day. He gave advice but never orders, and though he sometimes disagreed with the censoring, he was delighted to note the increasing sympathy for the Loyalists reflected in the foreign press.

But the pressure from other Communists on Ilsa mounted and began to damage Barea's position as well. Although he was Ilsa's boss, these Communists charged, he was now under her sway. A foreigner and a Trotskyite was the real power in the Madrid foreign press office!

But the attacks on Ilsa only strenghtened Barea's bond with her. After they had sexual relations early one morning in the censorship office, Barea felt, he later wrote, "an airy sensation, as though I were drinking champagne and laughing, with a mouth full of bubbles which burst and tickled and escaped merrily through my lips."

Yet he denied at first, both to Ilsa and himself, that he loved her. Wasn't his life complicated enough with two women? He hardly needed a third. But soon they were living together and struggling together—to hold back the twin tides of fascism and communism that threatened to overwhelm them.

"May I return a little debt of ten pesetas?"

An attractive woman with golden hair looked up from her table in the Miami Bar as Keith Scott Watson greeted her. She seemed puzzled, then she recognized him.

"*Hombre*! Now I remember. You wear a different hat from our first meeting."

He was wearing a civilian hat rather than the military cap he sported when Elvira had thrown herself next to him on the street as incendiary bombs burst around them. Now he was repaying her the money she lent him for a hotel room that night.

"I am no longer in the Column [International Brigade], but working as a journalist," Watson explained.

"Why did you leave . . . were you wounded?"

"No, I was afraid. I just couldn't stand life in the trenches."

"*Bueno*," Elvira replied with a touch of contempt. "You're honest, that is something at least."

Watson had returned to his British company after that bomb-swept night of their meeting and had fought in several hard battles, but he finally had enough. And so he put down his rifle and went once again into town, this time for good. He remembered his friends from Barcelona, Louis Delaprée and James Minifie, and looked for them at the Telefónica. They weren't there, but he soon found another drinking partner—Sefton Delmer.

Delmer was amused by Watson's story and made him an offer: "You'd better have some official status. . . . I need an assistant . . . does fifty pesetas a day seem reasonable?"

It did, and so Watson became a reporter and moved into the British embassy, viewing the battle for Madrid in far greater comfort from the outside. And then one day, in the Miami Bar, he met Elvira again. He learned that she was the War Ministry secretary, but only later did he realize how important her job was. Delmer, who was not aware that his assistant already knew Elvira, spoke almost in awe of her, even though she was a Communist. At work, he said admiringly, she wore a black leather belt with a pistol in it, and a leather wriststrap with .22 cartridges.

"She is Spain's Joan of Arc. She reorganized the War Ministry's connections with Valencia when things were almost lost. . . . She works harder than any two ministers put together, and anonymously, too."

Watson now understood the contempt in Elvira's voice when she learned he had "resigned" from the International Brigade. But this did not stop her from seeing him, nor prevent him from enjoying his new—and safer—job. He even went to interview members of his old British company between battles. He was glad, and grateful, that they welcomed him without resentment. After all, they said, he was not a Communist and could not be expected to make the sacrifices they made.

On one fateful trip to the front, Watson escorted a tall white-bearded Swedish pastor who, with Bible in hand, had come to the Telefónica to find someone who could take him to see a "little of the gallant men." The pastor commented on each scene with pertinent biblical references, showing a marked bias toward the Loyalist side. He was especially excited when he saw two batteries of artillery fire salvos.

"It is the voice of vengeance," he intoned, waving a gnarled forefinger. "On that day the trumpet shall sound louder."

A bit crazy, Watson thought.

When he returned to the Telefónica, he found an urgent message waiting for him. The police wanted to see him. He rushed to police headquarters with foreboding, for though he had foreign press credentials he could still be punished for deserting the front. As he waited in the station, he was surprised to see Elvira enter.

"You are in a very serious position," she said excitedly. "I must warn you to speak the whole truth when you are questioned. You know what happens to a spy in wartime."

Watson was startled.

"I, a spy?"

A chubby little man suddenly appeared and began questioning Watson in a slightly sardonic tone.

"With your comrades in the column you have some good military information for your paper?" he asked.

"My paper does not specialize in military information . . . they want the wider aspect of the struggle."

"Ah, yes! The human interest, that is what your great public wants."

And then his tone grew more hostile.

"Perhaps you will tell me what human interest the position of our new batteries of Russian guns holds for your readers."

"None at all . . . nor for myself either."

"Then why do you take your friend, Pastor Arnefelt, on a tour of our secret fortifications?"

"He wanted to see some of the fighting men. . . . I met him for the first time today."

The interrogator then showed Watson a black leather-bound Bible—the pastor's.

"Let me translate the inscription . . . your German is not very good perhaps. 'To our beloved pastor from his flock—Grunegarten, 1928.' Do you notice anything odd? . . . His loving flock made this presentation a year before their gift was printed!"

The man then drew out a sheet of paper from under the leather cover and pointed to some lines and figures.

"These, my friend," he said, "are our new positions and artillery emplacements."

Watson was too amazed to reply.

He was free, said the man—for a while; and Keith walked out with Elvira.

"I am glad you have not been shot," she said. "It would have been too bad if you had left the front only to be shot behind the lines."

But that, they knew, could still happen. To her, also, if she showed too much interest in what happened to him.

3

All through November it *was* happening to the prisoners in Madrid, until finally, in the first days of December—due to the courage of two anarchists—it no longer did. García Oliver, the minister of justice in the cabinet who had been jailed many times for criminal activities and had approved Durruti's plot to steal the nation's gold supply, turned out to be a highly efficient and fair-minded man.

"I believe," he said in one speech, "that justice is such a subtle thing that in order to interpret it, it is enough only to have a heart."

Oliver was thus appalled by the killing of prisoners in Madrid and elsewhere, and ashamed that some fellow anarchists were among the killers. He chose another anarchist, Melchor Rodríguez, as his director of prisoners and asked him to end the massacres. Rodríguez didn't have to be told. When he learned that a great crowd was threatening to break into the jail in Alcalá de Henares near Madrid, he rushed there and shouted:

"Are you bloodthirsty? Well! It is apparent that you prefer the rear zone to the front, where the real fighters are struggling, but wish to show your courage in some way. Very well! Forward! You can get in and find your victims, but you won't find them, as you believe, totally defenseless and abandoned to your murderous rage. Right now I'm going to give orders to supply them with weapons so they can defend themselves against you. You can get in whenever you like. They'll receive you armed. . . . Forward!"

But the mob withdrew instead.

In Madrid, Rodríguez had a harder time imposing his authority, so one night he waited on the road leading to Paracuellos, where most of the murders took place, and, at gunpoint, stopped several trucks carrying prisoners to their death. He ordered the drivers to return and put the men back in their cells, and the trucks turned around and raced back.

There would be no more mass killing of prisoners in Madrid.

After the war, Rodríguez would go on trial for simply being an anarchist, and dozens of former prisoners testified that he had saved their lives. He was Christ himself, some said. But Rodríguez disagreed: He was driven by anarchist, not Christian, principles. And so he was sentenced to several years in prison for refusing to give up his principles!

While Melchor Rodríguez helped to save rebel lives openly, Christopher Lance was still doing so secretly. Since his return to Madrid he had already whisked to safety scores of people, and now came the turn of Alvaro Martín Moreno, the son of Franco's chief of staff. If Lance could not help all of the twenty people on Franco's rescue list, he would at least try to deliver the man at the top of the list, despite the tremendous risk.

Martín was hiding in Valencia, Lance learned, but the Loyalists had discovered his hideout and were about to capture him. They had been trying to exchange him for an important prisoner held by the rebels, but apparently to no avail.

Lance decided he must urgently put Martín, as well as another fugitive he was hiding, aboard a foreign ship. He had befriended the guards and workers in Valencia's port, and also the British seamen who came and went with cargoes—and some of his rebels. Now, once more, he returned to the dock and embraced old sailor friends who had just anchored.

He took one skipper aside. How about taking a "couple of customers" aboard? The skipper was game, so Lance revealed his plan. First of all, another British skipper should invite him to lunch aboard his ship so he could advertise he was on a round of parties in the port and would be expected to come and go all day.

No sooner said than Lance was having lunch aboard a British vessel with the crew. Afterward he left in a flurry of loud talk and good cheer, conspicuously stopping to chat with acquaintances on the dock and telling them he would be back later for another party. He then drove to the house where Martín was hiding and, after convincing the landlady that he wasn't a police agent, went up to his room.

"May I come in?" Lance asked as he opened the door. "I have some good news for you."

"Who are you?" Martín inquired suspiciously.

Lance told him, then warned: "If we are seen going out of here, or if you are recognized going into the docks, or if anything should go wrong, it will mean certain death for you."

"And yourself, señor?"

"Of course, for me, too."

"Very well, señor, I will place myself in your hands. You are a brave man."

Lance peeked through the window and wondered whether anybody was lurking behind the curtains in the house directly across the street. The police might be watching but could probably see little because of the heavy rain. Lance left, and minutes later Martín, hiding his face behind an umbrella, stepped into his car parked just in front. The car then raced off to another house where Lance was hiding his other fugitive.

Soon the three men were sauntering into a bar near the dock, where they met a group of British seamen, including the captain who first agreed to help Lance. They piled into the car, with some on the running board hiding from view those inside, all singing, shouting, laughing, as sailors are inclined to do before weighing anchor. As they drove into the port, Lance waved to the guards.

"Here we are back again, you see!"

"*Salud*, comrades," they replied. "Good appetite."

Minutes later the "merrymakers" were all aboard the captain's ship. Lance exulted over his greatest success so far. Within an hour, the ship would be sailing.

The departure, however, was postponed until the next morning, and by that time the police had discovered that Martín was missing and were closing in. They came to search the boat but Lance had managed to flee with his two rebels.

He had to get Martín out of Spain quickly, and there was only one way. He brazenly took him to the dock once more, hoping to put him on the first British ship he could find. Again he cheerfully greeted the guards, this time simply slowing up without stopping—and there on the dock was a British vessel just about to sail. Damn it! How could he get his man aboard with officials and guards standing by the quay? The hell with it! He screeched to a halt before the gangplank, which was just being hauled in, jumped out, and waved a sheaf of papers at the captain aboard.

"Ahoy, there, skipper!" he shouted. "Let it down again. . . . Got some important papers for you."

The gangplank was run out again, and Lance, talking nonstop to the captain so that the astonished officials couldn't ask any questions, motioned Martín to walk up the gangplank. The rebel obeyed, carrying a large official envelope under his arm. And Lance walked right behind him.

Shortly, a group of seamen escorted Lance down the gangplank, gathered around the car, and saw him off—while the officials and guards looked on, not realizing that two men had walked up and only one of them returned.

Later that day Lance was back, and this time he managed to smuggle the second rebel aboard a British warship with the connivance of the admiral!

4

"Ilsa tells me that a car will be here by twelve. You will drive all night to be in Valencia tomorrow," said Sefton Delmer in the bar of the Gran Vía Hotel.

He then gave Keith Scott Watson some French francs to tide him over. The police had decided that Watson, as a "deserter" and suspected spy, should leave Spain, and so he would take a train from Valencia to the French border, where he would switch to the Paris Express. Ilsa, at the press department, had made arrangements so swiftly that he would not even have the chance to see Elvira before he left.

At midnight a black Mercedes drew up in front of the hotel and Watson climbed in, finding to his surprise a woman already seated inside. In the dark, he could not see her clearly.

"Are you glad to be leaving Madrid?"

Watson immediately recognized the voice.

"Elvira! What are you doing here?"

"I am leaving for Valencia, so Ilsa asked if I would take you."

Arturo Barea's aide, Luis, got in beside the chauffeur and the car moved off toward Valencia as Watson exulted in this unexpected encounter. The night was cold and soon he and Elvira were in each other's arms.

"It is just part of things," Watson said, "that we should have met so strangely, only to part like this."

"Don't brood, my dear," Elvira replied. "This war will not last forever, and when it is over I shall take a long, long holiday—I may even write to you."

Suddenly, Elvira's eyes reflected the lights of a car behind them. The vehicle started to pass, then forced the Mercedes over to the edge of the road while the sound of skidding tires mingled with the sputter of machine-gun bullets. Watson's vehicle turned over and came to rest within inches of a sharp precipice. After several moments the crew of a passing food lorry was helping the stunned occupants out of the car. Watson and Elvira had only slight injuries and the chauffeur was unhurt, but Luis was dying from a wound in the spine. Watson shivered. A pile of documents on the back seat of the car had absorbed more than ten bullets.

Three days later Watson was standing by the train in Valencia kissing Elvira good-bye.

"Both of us were sad at heart," he would later say. "There was a terrible finality about that parting."

Then Watson jumped on the train as it started to pull out and they waved to each other until the bend of the platform hid Elvira from view.

As he had sensed, he would never see her or hear from her again. She was a militant Communist but, like Ilsa, had acquired too much power in Madrid and therefore too many enemies. And with Stalin ordering his agents not to take any chances, her enemies would know how to exploit the "danger" of her affair with a foreign "spy."

So Elvira vanished and nobody ever learned what happened to her.

And Watson would often think of Rosita's prophecy: "There is a coach with a fair woman and with it is death."

Arturo Barea sat by Luis's hospital bed and tried to comfort his loyal aide, who was dying in agony from the wounds he had suffered in the attack on the car.

"Don Arturo," groaned Luis, "don't let that woman get lost. I was right. She's a great woman. Do you remember that night she came to Madrid? And she loves you. . . . Don't let her go, it would be a crime, for you and for her."

Then he said good-bye very softly and died.

Luis didn't have to tell Barea. He already knew. He would never let Ilsa go, and would marry her as soon as he divorced his wife and she divorced her Austrian husband, though he realized his life, as well as hers, was in peril. When Ilsa was once arrested "for questioning," he was frantic as he imagined her plump form lying in some field. She was shortly freed, but after that he feared even to let her out of his sight. Finally, they lost their jobs.

Constancia de la Mora, leaving her orphans' home in the hands of her friends, had become Rubio Hidalgo's assistant in Valencia and gradually took over the national office of the foreign press department. Though she didn't appear to distrust either Barea or Ilsa, she resented the independence they asserted and thought that such influential posts should go to her fellow Communists. And so she advised them to take a long-overdue holiday. When they returned, they were told the "holiday" had become permanent.

But some Communists still feared Ilsa. She had many connections in international labor circles and if she talked too much she could undercut the Communist strategy for a gradual takeover of Loyalist Spain. And a "Trotskyite spy," said some, could be dangerous even outside the establishment.

Barea and Ilsa felt helpless to escape the spreading campaign against them. Perhaps they should flee the country. But how could they abandon the cause that was their life, even though Barea, horrified by the cruelty of both sides, had begun to see the war as loathsome and useless? They were caught in a "monstrous mechanism, crushed under the wheels."

The couple decided to seek counsel from Father Leocadio Lobo, an old friend of Barea's and one of the few priests who vigorously supported the republic. Long ago Lobo had chosen a parish of poor workers and now they protected him as zealously as they did their own families. The priest knew that Barea no longer considered himself a Catholic, that he was living in sin with Ilsa, and that both were getting divorces, but this had not affected his attitude toward them. And so the couple now confided their innermost feelings to him.

Father Lobo could understand their reluctance to abandon the cause, and even tried to dispel Barea's doubts about the usefulness of the war.

"It is a terrible, barbarous war with countless innocent victims," he agreed. "But this war is a lesson. It has torn Spain out of her paralysis, it has torn the people out of their houses where they were being turned into mummies. . . . Even if we are defeated, we will be stronger at the end of this than we ever were because the will has come alive."

But if the war was useful, said Lobo, the couple, sadly, were no longer so.

"Now listen to the truth, Ilsa. They don't want you here. You know too many people and you put others in the shade. You know too much and you are too intelligent. We aren't used to intelligent women yet. You can't help being what you are, so you must go, you must go away with Arturo because he needs you and you belong together. In Madrid you cannot do any good anymore, except by keeping quiet as you do."

"Yes, I know," Ilsa replied. "The only thing I can do for Spain now is to not let people outside turn my case into a weapon against the Communists—not because I love the Communist party, for I don't, but because it would at the same time be a weapon against our Spain and against Madrid."

Barea and Ilsa realized that, ironically enough, they could only serve Spain now by *not* serving it. So, penniless, leaving everything behind, they would soon exile themselves to Paris.

CHAPTER 11

Salvation

1

On the dismal rainy night that Durruti died, November 20, Loyalist troops stood ready to avenge him and recapture what his men had lost. Led by General Kléber, foreign volunteers and militiamen smashed into the Clinical Hospital the next morning and, with their bayonets bloody, won back a wing while seizing several other buildings in University City as well.

But the rebels struck back and made a valiant attempt to cross the Manzanares into West Park, just south of University City, so they could widen the precarious wedge they had driven into Madrid. A Polish company of the XI International Brigade with many Jewish soldiers exemplified the resistance here, setting a pattern the ghetto fighters of World War II would diligently follow. Three times Moorish cavalry attacked a key house the Poles were defending just across the river from West Park, and three times they were driven back. The fourth time, tanks replaced horses and the Polish commanders fell one by one. There was no officer left to lead the troops and no machine gun that could still fire.

The rebels finally broke through the front gate and into the ground floor, while hand grenades flew back and forth. After a few hours, as the dead and wounded lay heaped on the stairways and in the corridors, the Poles ran out of grenades and almost out of bullets. Every man, they agreed, would fight until the last bullet, which he would fire into his brain. But then, as they prepared for mass suicide, they burst into the "Internationale" and the rebels fled, apparently thinking a whole happy army was waiting to trap them.

The Poles regained hope. Had the rebels given up? The smell of smoke was their answer—they had set the building on fire. The unwounded fighters decided to remain rather than leave their wounded brothers to die alone, but one of the injured, Juzek, pleaded: "Comrades, you can no longer help us and we cannot jump. . . . We'll be burned alive in this house, but you must jump, get through the enemy lines, and fight again. It's the only way."

Thus, after parting kisses, a dozen able fighters jumped to the ground, never imagining that this scene would be reenacted hundreds of times some years later in the ghettos of their homeland. Seven returned to their lines alive, but soon came back to defend the ashes and help stop the rebels from crossing the river again.

With the Loyalist forces holding everywhere, Enrique Castro Delgado felt it was time to strike back. Why not cut the rebel lifeline at Talavera? Such an attack would draw some of Franco's troops away from Madrid and might even isolate his whole army, forcing it to withdraw from the capital completely. And Castro's optimism grew when a patrol reported that Talavera was clogged with supply trucks that were just waiting to be knocked out.

He went to see General Pozas, the central front commander, to get his approval and found him in an irritable mood because he was ill and the doctors thought he might have to have his testicles removed to avoid further complications. Castro explained his plan to him and asked for two thousand men, one battery of artillery, and air support.

"Do what you like, Castro," Pozas replied. "Talavera or Madrid, what do I care at this moment? All I care about are my balls."

Castro now called on Soviet General Gregori Ivan Kulik, who had recently arrived in Spain to advise Pozas, for the Russians controlled the planes Castro would need to protect his troops. Kulik was a huge man with a large bald head and a blistering temper that kept his aides in a state of constant terror. Castro disliked him, sensing that he held the Spanish in contempt, and was ready for a showdown if necessary.

Pozas, he said, laying his map on a table, had already authorized the operation, but Kulik did not seem impressed as he bent over to study the plan of attack.

"*Nyet*, comrade," he replied. "Out of the question for me."

"Why?"

"That's not your problem."

"It's yours and mine, general."

Kulik's face turned red and he angrily threw the map on the floor. Castro calmly picked it up and said:

"In spite of you, it will be done."

"*Nyet!*"

And Castro left amid shouts of "swine!" in Russian. Shortly, he was with another Russian, General Goriev, who was shocked by the story. For though Goriev was technically the head of the Soviet military mission, Kulik was a more powerful figure in the Soviet bureaucracy.

"With Kulik or without Kulik," said Castro, "I'll carry out this operation."

Goriev puffed on a cigar and replied: "You have committed an error. Comrade Kulik was artillery commander at Tsaritsin [during the Russian Revolution] and is one of Comrade Stalin's closest collaborators. He's an old soldier and an old Bolshevik. You shouldn't have done it!"

"But do you agree with me on the operation?"

"You shouldn't have done it. . . . He is the great general sent by Comrade Stalin to help us win the war. And you treated him badly! Comrade Kulik is my superior . . . you are only a comrade."

"And will that prevent you from aiding me with one or two air sorties if the enemy air force moves against us?"

"I don't know."

"Well, I would certainly like to know before leaving this room."

"I'll help you."

And as Castro rose to leave, Goriev exhaled so much smoke that his visitor could not see his eyes.

Why all this trouble with Kulik? Castro wondered. Hadn't the Russian comrades come to Spain to help the Loyalists win the battle of Madrid—and the war—as soon as possible? Castro did not realize, or did not want to realize, that he was caught in a clash between Soviet foreign policy and his party's political ambition; that Stalin, his idol, had no desire to break the brutal stalemate he had helped to produce with his carefully measured aid.

Another clash flared in the Loyalist camp between Spaniards and foreigners when the International Brigades grabbed the headlines in the world press. General Miaja and Major Rojo were proud of their role in defending a city that the government had abandoned and given up for lost. Their militiamen had held *alone* against the enemy in the crucial first two days of the battle, and also did most of the fighting after the international volunteers arrived, outnumbering them by about ten to one.

True, the volunteers helped to give the Loyalists the extra punch they needed to keep from crumbling under Varela's hammer blows but, in the view of the Spanish commanders, they were still a secondary force. Yet, while the incredible feat of the Spaniards was being largely ignored, the foreigners were getting most of the credit and might even dominate the history books.

The brigades had arrived quietly enough and were kept out of press range at first, with Arturo Barea under strict orders to censor all but the vaguest reference to them. But Ilsa thought the story of the brigades "would be a tremendous inspiration to the workers everywhere, if only they knew enough about it." Wouldn't it be useful to let the correspondents interview General Kléber, the commander of the XI International Brigade? Barea agreed, and without authorization permitted them to do so.

The interview was a huge success, as influential reporters like Sefton Delmer and Louis Delaprée sent glowing reports of Kléber and his men around the world. The Communist commander, in fact, impressed the conservative Delmer "as a superb leader . . . a man who had himself under stern control, weighed carefully what he said and did, and was well aware of the importance of handling his political masters with deference and diplomacy."

The Spanish commanders were delighted by all the space suddenly devoted to Loyalist heroics, but then as the publicity continued day after day, their delight turned into alarm. Kléber was getting so much attention that he overshadowed even Miaja. Rojo, as Miaja's loyal keeper, was especially perturbed. No one must challenge Miaja as the savior of Madrid.

Did Kléber try to? Many reporters didn't think so. He did not seek them out; they sought *him* out, for he was good, colorful copy. But Rojo was convinced the general was trying "to put himself on a pedestal." And on November 26, the day Kléber was given the command of the whole northern front in Madrid, Rojo sent a note to Miaja asking for the man's dismissal.

Kléber, Rojo charged, had disobeyed orders, tried to hide his failures, lied about the size of his forces, withheld vital military information from the general staff and, incidentally, basked in undeserved publicity.

"The press is making an effort to extol this general in an exaggerated and false way," Rojo wrote. "It is true that his men are fighting well, but no more than that. . . . And as for the praise of his leadership, it is also false, as reflected in the very fact that he wants the support of an artificial popularity. . . . He is being presented as a *caudillo* . . . [and] he seems to be the military idol of some of our political parties."

In other words, an unglamorous Spaniard should replace him.

After the war, Rojo would even say, inexplicably, that Kléber's troops had not arrived in Madrid until November 10, though military records (as quoted earlier in this book) show that Rojo started sending messages to him in the Casa de Campo two days earlier.

Rojo's note had explosive repercussions. Miaja had apparently approved Kléber's promotion on General Goriev's advice, and he usually listened to his advice. But now it clashed with Rojo's and Miaja would no more be a puppet of the Russians than of the government. Kléber must go! he thus demanded. And the Russians, who needed Miaja as a "bourgeois" cover for Communist activities as much as he needed *them* for military advice, relayed the demand to the Kremlin.

Kléber was dispensable, in Stalin's view, but Miaja, at this point, was not. So Kléber lost his job, and the newsmen, one of their most fascinating subjects. The world must be reminded that mainly Spaniards were fighting and dying in Madrid.

Among the best of these Spanish fighters was Cipriano Mera, political commissar of the Palacios Column, though his anarchist code constantly collided with military demands. He now approved discipline, but still opposed integrating the column into the large mixed brigades that were to be the backbone of the new Loyalist army. And while he had once ordered militiamen to call him "Colonel Mera," though he was never officially given this or any other rank, he soon again became simply "Cipriano."

However, after one fierce battle which his column won, but at tremendous cost, Mera finally overcame his ideological qualms and arrogance. With Durruti dead and the communists armed by Russia, what chance did the anarchists have anyway of realizing their great dream in the foreseeable future?

"There were moments," he would later write, "when tears came to my eyes at the thought that the profound beliefs I had always cherished about a radical social transformation would be largely abandoned if I accepted militarization."

But facing bitter reality, he added: "The sacrifice of those who fell in battle should not have been in vain. Also, one might hope that when we have won the war, there will be a republic different from the republic we've known until now, a republic that will be greatly concerned with the interests of the workers."

And to make sure the Communist party would never control it, the anarchists had to have a real army to crush not only the Fascists but also the Communists, with all their Russian arms—if they tried to steal the people's victory.

Mera thus went to see Miaja and Rojo and, after sitting subdued and silent for several moments, said:

"General, I know perfectly well that I do not have the necessary knowledge and that I am incapable of commanding a large unit. But . . . I am ready to help militarize [the militia]. . . . Give me the rank of sergeant, corporal, or private, it's the same to me. I'm only interested in being more useful than I've been up to now. I'm here to receive your orders."

"Although it's a bit late, Mera," said Miaja, obviously moved, "the important thing is that you have come to understand the need for this. . . . You must place the interest of winning the war above all others. No personal interest, not even party and organizational ones, can take precedence over the supreme interest."

"That's how I understand it now," Mera replied.

And as he left with the rank of major, he was still subdued, even dazed, like a man who had just pawned his soul.

"Could you have taken Talavera?"

"Who knows?" replied Enrique Castro Delgado.

Castro was meeting with the press shortly after his men had attacked the rebel's right flank in a bid to capture Talavera and cut off the enemy supply line.
The improvised force pushed across the hills overlooking Talavera and at dawn,
November 24, opened devastating fire on the town and its airfield. The rebels
panicked and began retreating, but enemy aircraft soon swept over and pinned
down Castro's men, who waited in vain for their own planes to save them. The
remnants of the force then withdrew in disorder, though only after one of Castro's aims had been fulfilled. The attack had frightened Varela into sending eight
battalions from Madrid to Talavera, weakening his siege of the capital.

After being treated for wounds he received in the battle, Castro now faced the
newsmen.

"What limited the scope of your operation, major?"

"The enemy air force."

"And why didn't the republican air force help you?"

"I don't know. But I'm sure the republican air force had much to do . . .
much."

After the press conference, Castro went to see General Goriev, who greeted
him warmly.

"Everything was magnificent," the Russian said.

"Even the republican air force, Comrade Goriev," Castro sourly replied.

"There were clouds."

"Yes, it often happens that there are clouds in the sky."

Thoughts of his meeting with General Kulik flashed through Castro's mind,
but he immediately cut them off. Kulik was still a close friend of Stalin's, and it
was impossible for Castro to think ill of Stalin. Not after obeying him blindly for
so many years, even mastering the formula in his service.

The rebel generals were edgy, for the scare at Talavera nourished their fear that
Madrid could turn out to be the graveyard of their movement. Only a day before,
November 23, Franco, Mola, Varela, and, apparently, their German advisers
had met in Leganés, a few miles south of the capital. Their situation was critical.
After more than two weeks of savage fighting, they had been able to drive only a
narrow wedge into the city, and it might be chopped off at any time. They had to
admit it—the attack had failed.

Their best professional fighters had been ground up in struggles for each house
and building, and there were few to replace them. At the same time, the Loyalists
were getting not only foreign troops but better arms from Russia than the rebels
were from Germany and Italy. What was worse, the *Madrileños* simply wouldn't
give up. They refused to crack even under the heaviest air raids. Most women
and children, in fact, stayed in the city, though their leaders tried to evacuate
them, and many who did leave turned around before they got to their destination
and came back.

With heavy heart, the three generals decided to call off the direct assault on the city, at least until Hitler and Mussolini could furnish them with more arms—as they would certainly do now that they had recognized the Franco government. They might even send men. Meanwhile, rebel forces would keep Madrid under siege, straighten their lines, and try to surround the city completely, perhaps starving it into raising the white flag.

Their sympathizers in Madrid might never forgive them for postponing their liberation, but they would have to understand that military considerations came first. Besides, Madrid wasn't really that important, militarily or politically. One couldn't afford to be sentimental in war. And so Franco, who had postponed his drive toward Madrid in order to rescue rebels holed up in Toledo's Alcázar, suddenly became the practical soldier again. After all, he was already the *caudillo* and his power was now beyond challenge. But before he ended the direct attack, he would make one last desperate lunge.

Even if his troops failed again, they could perhaps widen the wedge and make it more secure. This decision spawned in Franco a strange new confidence.

He even announced on the radio that he would enter Madrid on November 25!

At dawn that day, in the Plaza de la Moncloa, Mika Etchebéhère lay flat in a trench alongside two comrades when mortar shells whistled past. Their POUM company had heard Franco's announcement and expected the rebels to launch a full-scale attack from University City. If they broke through Loyalist lines they would probably smash all the way into town, and Mika's company, reputed as one of the toughest, was manning a key position.

Mika joined the company after she had managed to escape from the besieged Sigüenza Cathedral in mid-October and became its second-in-command. Lying beside her was the commander, Antonio Guerrero, and if it weren't for the shelling, his nearness would have disturbed her. Since the death of her husband, Hippo, she had tried not to think or act like a woman; the men, she felt, thought of her as neither male nor female but as some kind of strange hybrid.

Then one day Guerrero put his hand on her shoulder and looked at her as if suddenly discovering her femininity, and though she abruptly moved away, she sensed he could see the acquiescence in her eyes. Did she have the right to take a lover among the men? No, she decided. The men thought of her as belonging to *them* and excused her for being a woman only because she didn't try to exploit her sex and remained pure and hard. If they viewed her simply as a woman like any other, they would never follow her orders.

The shells dropped closer and then there was a deafening explosion right in the trench. Mika miraculously escaped injury but her two companions groaned in pain from severe wounds. As stretcher-bearers rushed up, Guerrero, half of his foot torn away, took Mika's hand and whispered: "I'm sorry to leave you in this mess. Be careful, it will be very hard. Take the men well in hand. Luckily they have confidence in you. Make them respect you."

Mika wanted to remove the shoe from his mutilated foot, but she lost her nerve and let someone else do it. After all her battle experience, she could not even look at the wound, yet she would now lead the men into battle and perhaps to their death. Incredibly to her, the salvation of the city seemed now to depend in part on the command ability of a young girl who was squeamish about blood!

During a lull in the shelling, Mika crawled through the trench to encourage the men and to warn them not to drink too much since they were already a little drunk on cognac and whiskey. Suddenly figures could be seen moving among the trees in front of them.

'Fire!'' Mika ordered, and every rifle started crackling while sticks of dynamite, their fuses lit by cigars, sailed into trees, which vanished in huge black clouds.

But enemy shells were also finding their mark and about a dozen more of Mika's men fell. She herself was just wondering how she would die that day when there was a great blast and she was suddenly buried alive under a thick mound of earth. . . . What were her men doing? She couldn't hear them firing. . . . If she could only cry out, but her mouth was full of earth . . . her head was turning . . . then voices.

"Never mind the legs. Lift the head . . . perhaps she isn't dead yet.''

Barely conscious, Mika swallowed some cognac and soon recovered. Nothing was broken. No need to go to the rear. Though still shaky, she remained in command.

Shortly, enemy tanks rumbled toward the trench.

"Use the dynamite!'' Mika ordered.

And missiles zipped through the air.

A veil of dust hid from view the tanks as well as the fate of the company—and perhaps of Madrid—but gradually, the outlines of dark hulks emerged. The tanks had been stopped. Then . . .

"Planes!''

Mika ordered the men to lie flat in the trench or outside it, then dashed to a small wood nearby and flung herself to the ground. This seemed like a pleasant place to die. As the planes circled overhead and dropped their loads, she lay under a tree and breathed in the fresh odor of the leaves, and suddenly all the fatigue of endless battle overwhelmed her and she fell asleep.

But a bomb exploding about fifty yards away shook her awake, and then all was quiet. She returned to the trench and with her men held the enemy off all day. And so did other Loyalist units in other trenches.

Franco's final thrust had failed and Madrid was saved.

But Mika did not celebrate. Too many of her comrades had perished, and for a revolution that Stalin was swiftly crushing. Soon POUM's turn would come, but she would go on fighting the Fascists until the end, whichever side killed her. Better to be betrayed than to betray. And she would betray Hippo and all that he stood for if she stopped fighting and became simply another woman.

2

Louis Delaprée decided to return home. His pro-rebel newspaper, *Paris-Soir*, was publishing reams of copy on the love affair of King Edward VIII and Mrs. Wally Simpson, but found space for only about half his articles from Spain. In a blistering message to his editor, Delaprée wrote:

"I thought you were my friend, and would spare me a useless task. For three weeks I have been getting up at 5:00 A.M. in order to get the news into the first editions. You made me work for the wastepaper basket. Thanks. I am taking a plane on Sunday unless I meet the fate of Guy de Traversay [a French reporter who had been killed], which would be a good thing, wouldn't it, for thus you should have your martyr, too. Meanwhile, I shall send you nothing more. It is not worth the trouble. The massacre of a hundred Spanish children is less interesting than a sigh from Mrs. Simpson."

Dressed in a trenchcoat, red scarf, and gray felt hat, Delaprée boarded a special Air France plane used by the French government to transport supplies to its embassy. Hardly was the aircraft in the air when a fighter plane strafed it, forcing the pilot to make an emergency landing. Delaprée who had been hit, died from his wounds.

Who fired at the airliner? A rebel plane, the government claimed. But some Loyalist airmen admitted that one of their own fighters did, mistaking the aircraft for an enemy bomber—though visibility was excellent. And according to Sefton Delmer, Delaprée told him on his death bed that he had seen Loyalist markings on the plane, remarking: "I cannot understand why they did it. It must have been some stupid misunderstanding."

But was it? many people asked. Some, including Delmer, speculated that the NKVD had ordered the attack because one of the passengers, a representative of the International Red Cross, was carrying incriminating documents on the *paseos* in Madrid.

Whatever the facts, Rosita's cards had been right again. "Here is a journey . . . a large city, death is all around it . . . you must not leave it. From the air there is death for your honor!"

But, to the ironic end, Delaprée had faith in destiny. His own—and Madrid's. He had just written of Madrid as it reeled under the bombs:

"Who would not admire a population submitted to such dangers, menaced by such horrors, not knowing whether their reprieve will come or not, and that nevertheless keeps smiling? Madrid has not enough to eat. Madrid burns the beams of her wrecked houses to warm herself . . . but Madrid holds out and ever shall."

Though the *Madrileños* he so lovingly eulogized held out until the war's end, Delaprée, like them, did not count on Stalin's cynical plot to manipulate the human spirit for his own ends.

Epilogue

After Generalissimo Franco failed to capture Madrid by direct assault in November 1936, he made several attempts to surround the city and starve it to death.

First, in December and January, his troops struck west of Madrid toward the Guadarramas hoping to cut off the Loyalists there and then encircle the capital. But the defenders held.

Then, in February, his forces stormed northward through the Jarama valley trying to sever the Madrid–Valencia highway. There was a terrible bloodbath, but the Loyalists, including the newly arrived U.S. Abraham Lincoln Battalion, kept the road open.

Finally, in March, the rebels, reinforced by Mussolini's soldiers, smashed from the North toward Guadalajara and suffered ignominious defeat.

The Loyalists then took the initiative and in July battered their way north toward the village of Brunete intending to cut off all rebel forces west of Madrid. They fought fiercely but failed to achieve their goal. However, the new stalemate further solidified the lines around Madrid, and they would remain virtually unchanged until the end of the war.

And the end would come only after more than three years of bitter fighting throughout Spain. While aid poured into the rebel zones, the flow to the Loyalist areas gradually dried up, amounting to little more than a trickle in 1938, after Munich. For Anglo-French appeasement of Hitler made it clear that the two Western democracies would not help Russia if the Nazis attacked it, and thus prompted Stalin to woo Germany more vigorously. He even agreed that the International Brigades be sent home.

The Spanish Communists were stunned, for they had been using Russian aid as a lever to enhance their power. In May 1937 they demolished their main competitors when they forced the Largo Caballero government to crack down on anarchist and POUM troops that had dominated Barcelona. After savage street fighting, the Communists emerged politically and militarily supreme in Spain.

They then compelled Largo Caballero to resign because he continued to ignore Stalin's advice, and enticed Finance Minister Negrín to take over, believing they could control him. Although Negrín distrusted them, he gave them almost complete freedom because they were "efficient" and able to squeeze at least some aid out of the Russians. The NKVD even set up its own jails and torture chambers, which it packed with anarchists, Trotskyites, and other suspected enemies, who seldom emerged alive.

Stalin, however, was not interested in helping his Spanish puppets to gain either military victory or political power. Spain had been for him a convenient battleground to drain Hitler's energies and a convenient slaughterhouse to wipe out his leftist rivals, but the time had come to let Franco win and so pave the way for a Soviet-Nazi deal.

By late 1937 the rebels seized northern Spain, by spring 1938, Aragon, and by early 1939, Catalonia. Now the Loyalists held only a small rectangle embracing Madrid, Valencia, Cartagena, and Almería. Though Russian aid had dribbled virtually to a halt, the Spanish Communists, backed by Negrín, refused to consider surrender, though Negrín secretly sounded out the rebels on peace terms. In a few months, he hoped, World War II would erupt, and Britain and France would then help the Loyalists to crush Hitler's Spanish allies.

But other Loyalist leaders, led by Colonel Segismundo Casado, a key commander, conspired to oust Negrín and make peace with Franco, feeling that the rebels would never negotiate with a Communist-dominated government. Casado offered to arrange for a surrender if the generalissimo promised not to take vengeance on the vanquished.

The colonel rebelled against Negrín in early March 1939 and called a clandestine meeting of socialists, anarchists, and republicans to seek their support. They formed a National Defense Council to replace the Negrín government, and soon they were joined by leading non-Communist officers, including General Miaja and Cipriano Mera, now a corps commander. Mera cried over the radio:

"As from this moment, fellow citizens, Spain has one government and one mission—peace."

But with the war lost, he had another mission, too—to crush the Communists, who had earlier crushed the anarchists. He would keep them from setting up a dictatorship of the proletariat before the war ended. And he would weaken the party so severely that it would never again have the strength to challenge anarchism, which, he was confident, would some day reemerge as a power in Spain.

Mera got his chance when Communist forces marched into Madrid to wipe out Casado's forces. Anarchist troops were sent to the rescue and after several days of battle they helped to drive the Communists out of the capital. Mera had his revenge. His once undisciplined anarchists had, paradoxically, defeated the superbly disciplined Communists who had been so contemptuous of them. But Mera's troops did not rule Madrid for long. He had to abandon it to rebel forces on March 28, leaving without even the satisfaction of a Franco pledge of clemency.

At about 9:30 A.M. that day, a Loyalist colonel left behind in Madrid hauled down the republican flag over the Treasury Building and raised the rebel banner. Then he drove to the half-destroyed Clinical Hospital in University City where, at 1:00 P.M., he formally surrendered the capital to a rebel commander. Meanwhile, Franco's troops streamed into the city over all the bridges that the defenders had, until this day, kept them from crossing.

Crowds of civilians, many pallid from years of hiding in embassies and shuttered houses, greeted the conquerors with cheers, tears, and Fascist salutes. And now it was the turn of the great mass of *Madrileños*, who had for three years remained invincible in spirit, come bombs, shells, fire or hunger, to seek refuge against a raging storm of retribution. Many thousands in the following years would die before the firing squad and in the concentration camp from beatings, disease, and starvation.

Most top Loyalist political and military leaders, however, managed to leave Spain in time. In February 1939 President Azaña and former Prime Minister Martínez Barrio fled to France by car, suffering final indignity when the vehicle broke down and they had to cross the border on foot. Once in Paris, Azaña resigned and Martínez Barrio replaced him, serving as president in exile until his death in 1962. Azaña died in 1940, broken in heart and spirit.

Former Prime Minister Largo Caballero, who had gone to Paris earlier, spent World War II in a German concentration camp and died in Paris in 1946, also a shattered man. Indalecio Prieto died in Mexico in 1962, Negrín in Paris in 1956. Among the Loyalist generals, Miaja died in Mexico and Rojo (promoted to general during the war) returned to Madrid after more than twenty years of Bolivian exile and died there shortly after Franco tried him and commuted a death sentence. Rojo's son, Angel, had trained in the Bolivian army, hoping to return to Spain with a conquering guerrilla army after World War II. But Franco remained too powerful and the attack was never launched.

The Communists accused General Asensio of "treason" after the rebels defeated his troops in Malaga in early 1937 and, though they could not prove this charge, had him "exiled" to the Spanish embassy in Washington, where he served as military attaché. He died some years ago in the United States.

Captain Orad de la Torre was sentenced to death by a Francoist court after the war but was saved when attorney Juan Manuel Fanjul, the general's younger son who escaped from Montaña Barracks, pleaded for his life—despite Orad de la Torre's decisive role in crushing the Montaña defenders. Orad de la Torre was released after several years imprisonment and today lives, retired, in Madrid, while Fanjul, who long ago abandoned the Falange, has become the chief legal official in the democratic government of Prime Minister Suarez.

André Malraux wrote a masterful novel based on his experience in Spain, called *Man's Hope*, and after serving with the Free French forces of General Charles de Gaulle in World War II, joined De Gaulle's government and became one of his most important advisers. He died in 1977.

The surviving rebel officers fared very well, of course. Generalissimo Franco became dictator of Spain with the official title of "head of state," and such leading generals as Varela and Yagüe were appointed ministers in his cabinet. General Mola, however, was killed in a mysterious air crash in June 1937, and with his death went the last man who might have challenged Franco for postwar supremacy. People close to Mola made clear to the author their belief that the general's death was not an accident, suggesting that the pilot of his plane was poisoned.

José Antonio's cousin, Luis Sáenz de Heredia, after escaping from the Loyalist zone early in the war, made his way to the rebel sector and took part in many battles against the Loyalists. After the war he returned to film directing, hiring back his old left-wing employees, and is still active in this field. Felipe Gómez Acebo, the Falangist who had several close brushes with death, is today one of Spain's leading attorneys. Father Florinda de Miguel survived the war, though he was jailed for a while, and continued his clerical activities when peace came.

Shortly after Christopher Lance whisked the son of Franco's chief of staff out of Spain, he was captured by Loyalist security police. The NKVD brutally interrogated him and sent him from prison to prison. Though he was at first abandoned by his embassy, British officials finally came to his aid and he was released toward the end of the war, emerging from prison starved, barely alive, and convinced he was being taken to be shot. He returned to England, but came back to Spain in 1961, welcomed as a hero by Franco, who had once suspected he was an enemy spy.

Arturo and Ilsa Barea, forced by Communist threats to flee Spain, lived proudly but bitterly in Paris until late in the war, earning what they could with contributions to European publications. They then went to Britain, where Barea earned modest fame writing books on his life, the war, and Spanish culture, which were translated into English by Ilsa. Barea died some years ago. Keith Scott Watson returned from Britain to Spain during the war to resume his work as a journalist, though no longer for the *Daily Express*. He was unable to discover what happened to Elvira.

Cipriano Mera left for France just before Franco marched into Madrid, but during World War II was extradited to Spain by the Vichy authorities. He was tried and sentenced to death, though the sentence was commuted because of his role in ending the civil war. Eventually he once more managed to escape to France, and until his recent death he lived in Paris, working at his old trade—

bricklaying—unspoiled by his rise to one of the top commands in the war and still convinced that his dream of man's complete liberation would one day come true.

The anarchist-leaning Captain Palacios, Mera's onetime commander who taught him that even anarchists had to make concessions to reality, was saved from death after the war by the intercession of his brother, a leading monarchist. Jack Max (the pseudonym of an anarchist fighter) survived the war and returned to his native Barcelona, where he works today in a textile factory. Mika Etchbéhère continued to lead her POUM group until it was virtually wiped out in a suicidal battle she had been reluctant to fight. Though her unit was then under Mera's command, she suspected that the Stalinists in top army posts had deliberately sent her men to their death. Eventually Mika returned to Paris, where she still lives today amid memories of her husband, Hippo, and a revolution lost.

Most Communist leaders left Spain at the last minute, some feeling doubly betrayed—by Stalin and by Casado. Dolores Ibarruri, José Diaz, Enrique Castro Delgado, Jesús Hernández, and El Campesino all went to the Soviet Union. The last three, already shaken by the Soviet freeze on aid to the Loyalists, grew completely disillusioned with Stalin and fled Russia as bitter anti-Communists. Castro eventually returned to Spain and, while remaining aloof from the Franco government, devoted himself to writing angry tirades against his former gods and comrades until his death several years ago. Díaz mysteriously fell from a window while in Russia in 1942. La Pasionaria, who had become president of the Spanish Communist party, was the only top member to remain permanently in Russia, finally leaving in 1977 to return to Spain and win back a seat in the new democratic parliament. During World War II, one of her sons died fighting at Stalingrad.

Santiago Carrillo eventually became secretary-general of the Communist party, with headquarters in Paris, and today he retains that post in Spain. His party, now legal, has officially abandoned the Leninist label and claims to be Eurocommunist and independent of Moscow. Ignacio Hidalgo de Cisneros and his wife, Constancia, apparently also grew disillusioned with the Moscow brand of communism. Cisneros died recently in Rumania, and Constancia, from whom he separated some years after the war, was killed about twenty years ago in a motor accident in South America. She had been living in Mexico. Ramon Sender fled Spain early in the war, with the help of his friend, Enrique Castro Delgado, after being threatened by Communist commanders who claimed, apparently as a result of a misunderstanding, that he had deserted the front. Still one of Spain's most notable writers, he lives today in Los Angeles.

The Russian and foreign Communist advisers met the cruelest fate of those forced to leave Spain. General Kléber was executed when he returned to Moscow during the war after having been demoted to lower commands. General Goriev, Mikhail Koltsov, Arthur Stashevsky, Marcel Rosenberg, and even Stalin's close friend General Kulik were among the advisers also killed on their return home. (Kulik's turn came during World War II.) One who outwitted Stalin was Alexander Orlov of the NKVD, who defected to the United States and worked secretly with American intelligence.

All these men knew too much about Stalin's calculated betrayal of the Loyalists, while some, especially Goriev and Koltsov, had become emotionally involved in the Loyalist cause. Both of these men were posthumously "rehabilitated" as good Communists by Nikita Khrushchev in his famous 1956 speech denouncing Stalin's crimes.

But more than words, the story of Madrid in November 1936 shall, with brutal vividness, forever attest to one of his greatest crimes.

NOTES

The most important publications consulted and persons interviewed for each chapter of this book are listed below, with the sources of all dialogue shown parenthetically. Additional details can be found in the Bibliography or Acknowledgments. Documentary material used also is specified in the Bibliography. Since the most important general histories were consulted constantly, they are indicated as follows and will not be mentioned in the individual chapter notes:

Life and Death of the Spanish Republic by Henry W. Buckley; *La guerra de los mil días* by Guillermo Cabanellas (2 vols.); *Historia de la guerra civil española* by Ricardo de la Cierva; *The Struggle for Madrid* by Robert Colodny; *Historia de la cruzada española* (35 vols.); *Mil días de fuego* by José María Garate; *The Battle for Madrid* by George Hills; *The Spanish Republic and the Civil War, 1931–1939*, by Gabriel Jackson; *La batalla de Madrid* by Gregoria López Muñiz; *Spain, a Modern History* by Salvador de Madariaga; *La lucha en torno a Madrid* and *La marcha sobre Madrid* by José Manuel Martínez Bande; *Así fue la defensa de Madrid* by Vicente Rojo; *Historia del ejercito popular de la república* (4 vols.) by Ramón Salas Larrazábal; *The Spanish Civil War* by Hugh Thomas; *Historia de la guerra en España* by Julian Zugazagoitia.

Part I
Chapter 1
CONSPIRACY

BOOKS: *José Calvo Sotelo* by Felipe Acedo Colunga; *The Forging of a Rebel* by Arturo Barea (dialogue involving Barea); *Preparación y desarrollo del al-*

zamiento nacional by Felipe Bertrán Güell; *Historia de la Falange española de las JONS* by Francisco Bravo; *La Unión Militar Española* by Antonio Cacho Zabalza; *Hombres Made in Moscú* by Enrique Castro Delgado (dialogue involving Castro); *El General Fanjul* and *Madrid, julio 1936,* by Maximiniano García Venero; *They Shall Not Pass* by Dolores Ibarruri; *El General Mola* by José María Iribarren; *Calvo Sotelo, una vida fecunda* by Aurelio Joaniquet; *Memorias de la conspiración* by Antonio Lizarza; *Mola—aquel hombre!* by Félix B. Maíz (dialogue involving Fanjul); *Iberia* by James A. Michener; *El pensamiento político de Calvo Sotelo* by E. Vegas Latapié; *General Mola, el conspirador* by Jorge Vigón; *Zugazagoitia* (dialogue involving Prieto).

PERIODICALS: *Historia 16,* May 1977, "La reforma militar de Azaña" by G. Kemperfeldt; *Historia y Vida,* December 1975, "Del Alzamiento a la guerra civil; Verano de 1936: la correspondencia Franco-Mola" by J.M. Martínez Bande; *Living Age,* October 1936, "A Portrait of *La Pasionaria.*"

INTERVIEWS: José Calvo Sotelo (dialogue involving his father), Paco Castillo, Irene Falcón, Juan Manuel Fanjul, Elena Medina (dialogue involving Medina), Émilio Mola, Consuelo Morales Castillo (dialogue involving Morales Castillo).

Chapter 2
RETRIBUTION

BOOKS: *Yo fui ministro de Negrín* by Mariano Anso (dialogue involving Anso, Azaña); Barea (dialogue involving Barea); *El Cuartel de la Montaña* by José María Caballero Audaz; Castro Delgado (dialogue involving Castro); *Hombres que decidieron* by José Conceiro Tovar; *Franco* by Brian Crozier; *Ma guerre d'Espagne à moi* by Mika Etchebéhère (dialogue involving Etchebéhères); *Madrid* by Cesar Falcón (dialogue involving streetcar operator); *Defensa de Madrid* by Antonio López Fernández (dialogue involving Miaja); *Falange en la guerra de España* by García Venero (dialogue involving Fanjul from *El General Fanjul* and *Madrid, julio 1936); Asalto y defensa heroica del Cuartel de la Montaña* by Manuel Gómez Domingo; *La muerte de la esperanza* by Eduardo de Guzmán; *Memorias* by Ignacio Hidalgo de Cisneros; *Franco* by George Hills; *Vu en Espagne* by Marguerite Jouve; *Cipriano Mera* by Juan Llarch; *Franco, soldat et chef d'état* by Claude Martin; *I Helped to Build an Army* by José Martín Blasquez; *Guerra, exilio y cárcel de un anarcosindicalista* by Cipriano Mera; *In Place of Splendor* by Constancia de la Mora (dialogue involving de la Mora); *The Spanish Pimpernel* by Cecil Phillips (dialogue involving Lance); *Tres días de julio* by Luis Romero (dialogue involving Balboa, Carratelá, Carmona); *The Tragedy of Manuel Azaña and the Fate of the Spanish Republic* by Frank Sedwick; *El general Miaja* by Lázaro Somoza Silva; *La verdada historia del Valle de los Caidos* by Daniel Sueiro.

PERIODICALS: *Christian Century,* December 16, 1936, "Spain's Syndicalists"; *Commonweal,* June 5, 1936, "President Azaña" by O.B. McGuire; *Liter-*

ary Digest, May 30, 1936, "Azaña"; *New Republic*, October 14, 1936, "Compañero Sogasia Burns a Church"; *Newsweek*, May 16, 1936, "Azaña President"; *Time*, September 7, 1936, "Anarchism."

INTERVIEWS: Antonio Beltrán, Fanjul (dialogue involving Fanjuls), Paulino García Puente (dialogue involving García Puente), Felipe Gómez Acebo, Eusebio Muñoz, Urbano Orad de la Torre (dialogue involving Orad De la Torre); Miguel Palacios (dialogue involving Palacios), Luis de Rivera Zapata, Luis José Sáenz Heredia (dialogue involving Sáenz), Alejandro Sánchez Cabesuda (dialogue involving Sánchez).

Chapter 3
STALEMATE

BOOKS: Etchebéhère (dialogue involving Etchebéhères); *La fiel infantería* by R. García Serrano; *El Campesino* by Valentin González; *El Campesino* by Marcelino Heredia; Ibarruri (dialogue involving Ibarruri); *Nuestra guerra* by Enrique Lister; Mera (dialogue involving Mera); *Reporter in Spain* by Frank Pitcairn; *Counter-attack in Spain* by Ramón Sender (dialogue involving Sender).

INTERVIEWS: Juan José Gallego Pérez, Antonio Gómez (dialogue involving Gómez).

Chapter 4
NONINTERVENTION

BOOKS: *The Grand Camouflage* by Burnett Bolloten; *The Triumph of Treason* by Pièrre Cot; *Palmiro Togliatti* by Marcella and Mauricio Ferrara; *Togliatti en España* by Elasco Grandi; *La grande trahison* by Jesús Hernández (dialogue involving Hernández); Iribarren; *I Was Stalin's Agent* by Walter Krivitsky; *Le Stalinisme en Espagne* by Katia Landau; Maíz; *Communist Intervention in the Spanish War* by José Manuel Martínez Bande; *El communismo en España* by Enrique Natorras.

PERIODICALS: *Contemporary*, February 1937, "Comedy of Non-Intervention" by G. Glasgow; *New Republic*, October 14, 1936, "Fascist Aid to Rebels."

Part II
Chapter 5
TERROR

BOOKS: *Fusilado en las tapias del cementerio, Y Madrid, dejó de reir,* and *La quinta columna* by Santos Alcocer Badenas; *Los presos de Madrid* by Guillermo Arsenio de Isaga; *Tribunales rojas* by Gabriel Avilés; *Obras completas*, vol. 4, by Manuel Azaña; *Memoirs of a Spanish Nationalist* by Antonio Bahamonde y Sánchez de Castro; Barea (dialogue involving Barea); *Les grands cimetières sous la lune* by Georges Bernanos; *Checas de Madrid* by Tomás Borrás y Bermejo; *Madrid pendant la guerre civile* by Federico Bravo Morata; *The Martyrdom of Madrid* by Louis Delaprée; *Así empezó* by José Ignacio Escobar; *La agonía de Madrid* and *Madrid bajo "el terror"* by Adelardo Fernández Arias; *Red Terror in Madrid* by Luis de Fonteriz; *Madrid, de corte a cheka* by Agustín de Foxá; *Madrid, corazon que se desangra* by Gregorio Gallego (dialogue involving Gallego, Muñoz); *Estampas trágicas de Madrid* by Juan Gómez Málaga; Ibarruri (dialogue involving Ibarruri); *La iglesia contra la república española* by Josep María Llorens; *Un cura en zona roja* by Florindo de Miguel (dialogue involving Miguel); *Como fui ejecutado en Madrid* by Jacinto Miquelarena; De la Mora (dialogue involving De la Mora); *Drapeau de France* by Miguel Pérez Ferrero; Phillips (dialogue involving Lance); *El Preso 831; De la cheka de Atadell a la prisión de Alacuas* by Rosario Queipo de Llana; *Red Domination in Spain; Dancer in Madrid* by Janet Riesenfeld (dialogue involving Riesenfeld); *Madrid bajo las hordas rojas* by Fernando Sanabria; *Memorias* by Ramón Serrano Suñer; *La quinta columna española* by Manuel Uribarri; *Todos fuimos culpables* by Juan Simeon Vidarte; Zugazagoitia (dialogue involving last two killings in Model Prison).

Periodicals: *Christian Century*, September 2, "Arrogance in the Name of Christ" by R. Niebuhr; *Current History*, December 1936, "How Many Slain? Anti-Clerical Atrocities"; *Foreign Affairs*, October 1942, "Prelude to War" by J.T. Whitaker (dialogue involving Whitaker); *Journal of Contemporary History*, vol. LV, no. 2, 1969, "Bridegrooms of Death"; *The Nation*, January 9, 1937, "Spain's Red Foreign Legion" by L. Fischer.

Interviews: Acebo, Luisa María de Aramburu (dialogue involving her sister Josefina as quoted to her by Josefina's killer before his execution after the war), Gregorio Gallego, Medina, Sáenz, Ramón Serrano Suñer.

Chapter 6
DESPERATION

Books: *Canaris* by Karl Abshagen; *Freedom's Battle* by Julio Alvarez del Vayo; *Por que fui secretario de Durruti* by Mosen Jesús Arnal; Barea (dialogue involving Barea); *The International Brigades* by Vincent Brome; *Las brigades internacionales de la guerra de España* by Andrew Castells; Castro (dialogue involving Castro); Conceiro Tovar; Crozier; Delaprée (dialogue involving Delaprée); *Les Brigades Internationales* by Jacques Delperrie de Bayac; *The Siege of the Alcázar* by Cecil D. Eby; *La nuit tombe* by Ilya Ehrenburg; Etchebéhère (dialogue involving Etchebéhère); *Men and Politics* by Louis Fischer; *Brigadas Internacionales en España* by Adolfo Lizon Gadea; *La Legion Condor* by Ramón Garriga; González (dialogue involving *El Campesino*); *Nothing but Danger* by Frank Hanighen (ed.) (dialogue involving Weaver); Heredia; Hernández (dialogue involving Hernández); Hidalgo de Cisneros; Hills (*Franco*); *Mis cua-*

dernos de guerra by Alfredo Kindelán (dialogue involving Kindelán, Franco); *Diario de la guerra de España* by Mikhail Koltsov; Krivitsky (dialogue involving arms agent); *André Malraux* by Jean Lacouture; Landau; *Mis recuerdos* by Francisco Largo Caballero; *Le brigate internazionale in Spagna* by Luigi Longo; *Brigadas internacionales* by Martínez Bande; *Voluntaires d'Espagne* by André Marty; *The Epic of the Alcázar* by Geoffrey McNeill-Moss; Miguel (dialogue involving Miguel); *Durruti: le peuple in armes* by Abel Paz; Phillips (dialogue involving Lance); Riesenfeld (dialogue involving Riesenfeld); *Buenaventura Durruti* by Ricardo Sanz; Sender (dialogue involving Sender); *Franco: A Biography* by J. W. D. Trythall; *Single to Spain* by Keith Scott Watson (dialogue involving Watson); Vidarte; Zugazagoitia (dialogue involving last two killings in Model Prison).

Periodicals: *American Mercury*, February 1937, "Russia's Private War in Spain" by L. Dennis; *Collier's*, May 29, 1937, "This Is War" by A. Malraux; *Historia 16*, March 1977, "El mito del oro en la guerra civil: El oro de Francia yel oro de Moscú" by A. Viñas; *Historia y Vida*, March 1977, "André Malraux, un hijo del siglo" by R. Abella; *Living Age*, April 1937, "Soviet Agents"; *The Nation*, October 31, 1936, "Will Moscow Save Madrid?" by L. Fischer; *New Republic*, January 13, 1937, "Shipping Arms to Spain"; *Reader's Digest*, November 1966, "How Stalin Relieved Spain of $600,000,000" by Alexander Orlov (dialogue involving Orlov); *Review of Reviews*, February 1937, "Meet General Kléber" by R. Shaw; *The Slavonic and East European Review*, June 1960, "Soviet Aid to the Republic" by D. C. Watt.

Interviews: María Luisa Asensio Torrado, G. Gallego, Enrique Lister, Mola, Sáenz, Regulo Martínez Sánchez, Serrano Suñer, Luis Valero Bermejo.

Chapter 7
PANIC

Books: Barea (dialogue involving Barea); Yagüe, *un carazón al rojó* by Juan José Calleja; Castro (dialogue involving Castro); *Defence of Madrid* by Geoffrey Cox; *Trail Sinister* by Sefton Delmer; Fernández Arias (*La agonía de Madrid*); Fischer (dialogue involving Fischer) Fonteriz; Gallego; *El General Varela* by Ines García de la Escalera; Hidalgo de Cisneros; Hills (*Franco*); *General Varela* by Francisco Javier Marinas; Jouve; *Correspondent in Spain* by Edward H. Knoblaugh; Koltsov; Largo Caballero; López Fernández (dialogue involving Miaja); De la Mora (dialogue involving De la Mora); Paz; *Un soldado en la historia* by José María Pemán; *Red Domination in Spain;* Riesenfeld (dialogue involving Riesenfeld); Somoza Silva; Vidarte.

Interviews: Acebo, Father José Caballero, Sifre Carbonel, Santiago Carrillo, G. Gallego, Eduardo de Guzmán, Carlos Iniesta Cano, Lorenzo Inigo, Mola, Sanuda Palazuelos, Angel Rojo, Fernando Valera.

Part III
Chapter 8
RESISTANCE

BOOKS: *Bajo la bandera de la España republicana;* Brome; Castells; Conceiro Tovar; Castro (dialogue involving Castro); Cox; Delperrie de Bayac; *L'Epopée de l'Espagne;* C. Falcón (dialogue during rebel attack on Carabanchel); Gadea; Galleja; García de la Escalera; García Venero (*Historia de las Internacionales en España*); Ibarruri; *Madrid es neustro* by Jesús Izcaray; Javier Marinas; Koltsov (dialogue involving Koltsov); Longo; López Fernández (dialogue involving Miaja); *Soy del quinto regimiento* by Juan Modesto; Pemán; *Volunteer in Spain* by John Sommerfield; Somoza Silva.

PERIODICALS: *Foreign Affairs,* "Prelude to War" by J.T. Whitaker (dialogue involving Whitaker); *Literary Digest,* December 5, "Hero of Madrid: Kléber"; *Nueva Historia,* June 1977, "Santiago Carrillo y la represion republicana en Madrid, 1936," by R. Salas Larrazábal.

INTERVIEWS: Carrillo, I. Falcón, García Puente, Iniesta Cano, Palacios, A. Rojo.

Chapter 9
BREAKTHROUGH

BOOKS: Barea (dialogue involving Barea); Becarud; Brome; Calleja (dialogue involving Yagüe); Castells; Cox (dialogue in Telefónica during bombing); Delaprée (dialogue involving shoeshine incident); Delmer (dialogue involving Delmer); Delperrie de Bayac; *L'Epopée de l'Espagne;* Gadea; García Venero (*Historia de las Internacionales en España); The International Brigades, Spain, 1936–39;* Izcaray; Koltsov (dialogue involving Koltsov); Longo; López Fernández (dialogue involving Miaja); Martínez Bande (*Brigadas Internacionales*); Marty; *Memorias de un revolucionario* by Jack Max (dialogue involving Max); Mera (dialogue involving Mera); *The Civil War In Spain* by Robert Payne (ed.) (dialogue involving José Antonio); Penchientati; Riesenfeld (dialogue involving Riesenfeld); *Los procesos de José Antonio* by Agustín de Rio Cisneros; *Boadilla* by Esmond Romilly; Somoza Silva; *Die XI Brigade* by Gustav Szinda; *Der Spanische Krieg* by Arnold Vieth von Golssenau (Ludwig Henn) (dialogue involving Henn); Von Stackelberg.

PERIODICALS: *Historia 16,* November 1976, "Objectivo: Museo del Prado" by J. Lino Vaamonde; *Historia y Vida,* 1974 (Extra). "La defensa de Madrid: Durruti y las brigades internacionales" by J. M. Martínez Bande; *Posible,* July 22, 1976, "Como asesinaron a Durruti" by Costa Muste; *Time,* February 1, 1937, "Treasures Protected."

INTERVIEWS: Carbonel (dialogue involving Carbonel), Carrillo, Iniesta Cano, Muñoz (dialogue involving Muñoz), Palacios.

Chapter 10
BETRAYAL

BOOKS: Araquistain; Barea (dialogue involving Barea); Bolloten; Delmer; Hernández (dialogue involving Hernández); Krivitsky (dialogue involving Krivitsky); Pérez Ferrero (dialogue involving Mexican diplomat); Phillips (dialogue involving Lance); Riesenfeld (dialogue involving Riesenfeld); Watson (dialogue involving Watson).

Chapter 11
SALVATION

BOOKS: Barea; Castro (dialogue involving Castro); Delaprée; Delmer (dialogue involving Delaprée), Etchebéhère (dialogue involving Etchebéhère); Izcaray; Koltsov; Mera (dialogue involving Mera).

INTERVIEWS: Palacios, A. Rojo.

BIBLIOGRAPHY

BOOKS:

Abad de Santillán, Diego. *Por qué perdimos la guerra*, Buenos Aires, 1940.
—————. *La revolución y la guerra en España*, Buenos Aires, 1937.
Abshagen, Karl. *Canaris*, London, 1956.
Acedo Colunga, Felipe. *José Calvo Sotelo*, Barcelona, 1959.
Acier, Marcel (ed.). *From Spanish Trenches*, New York, 1937.
Alba, Víctor. *Histoire des républiques espagnoles*, Vincennes, 1948.
Alcázar de Velasco, Angel. *Serrano Suñer en la Falange*, Madrid, 1940.
Alcocer Badenas, Santos. *Fusilado en las tapias del cementerío*, Madrid, 1975.
—————. *Y Madrid, dejó de reir*, Madrid, 1974.
—————. *La quinta columna*, Madrid, 1976.
Alfonso, José Ramón. *El asesio de Madrid*, Barcelona, 1975.
Alvarez Puga, Eduardo. *Historia de la Falange*, Barcelona, 1969.
Alvarez del Vayo, Julio. *Freedom's Battle*, New York, 1940.
—————. *The Last Optimist*, London, 1950.
Ansaldo, Juan Antonio. *Memoires d'un Monarchiste Espagnol*, Monaco, 1953.
Anso, Mariano. *Yo fui ministro de Negrín*, Barcelona, 1976.
Aparicio, Juan. *La conquesta del estada*, Barcelona, 1939.
—————. *JONS*, Barcelona, 1939.
Araquistain, Luis. *El comunismo y la guerra de España*, Carmaux, 1939.
Armero, José María. *España fue noticia*, Madrid, 1976.
Arnal, Mosén Jesús. *Por qué fui secretario de Durruti*, Andorra, 1972.
Artieri, Giovanni. *Quattro Momenti di Storia Fascista*, Naples, 1968.

Asensio Torrado, General. *El General Asensio: su lealtad a la república*, Barcelona, 1938.

Attlee, Clement R. (with Ellen Wilkinson, Philip Noel Baker, John Dugdale). *What We Saw in Spain*, London, 1937.

Avilés, Gabriel. *Tribunales rojos vistos por un abogado defensor*, Barcelona, 1939.

Azaña, Manuel. *Obras completas*, 4 vols., Mexico, 1966–68.

Aznar, Manuel. *Historia militar de la guerra de España* (1936–1939), Madrid, 1940.

Bahamonde y Sánchez de Castro, Antonio. *Memoirs of a Spanish Nationalist*, London, 1939.

Bailey, Geoffrey. *The Conspirators*, London, 1961.

Bajatierra, Mauro. *Cronicas del frente de Madrid*, Barcelona, 1937.

Bajo la bandera de la España republicana, Moscow, 1970?

Barcia Trelles, Augusto. *La politica de no-intervención*, Buenos Aires, 1942.

Barea, Arturo. *The Forging of a Rebel*, New York, 1946.

Baumelberg, Werner. *Kampf um Spanien*, Berlin, 1939.

Bécarud, Jean. *La Deuxième République espagnole (1931–1936)*, Paris, 1962.

Bécarud, Jean (and Lapouge, Gilles), *Anarchistes en Espagne*, Paris, 1969.

Belforte, Francesco. *La guerra civile in Spagna*, Milan, 1938.

Benavides, Manuel. *El crimen de Europa*, Mexico. n.d.

Benson, Frederick R. *Writers in Arms*, New York, 1967.

Bernanos, Georges. *Les Grands Cimetières sous la lune*, Paris, 1938.

Bertrán, Felipe. *Preparación y desarrollo del alzamiento nacional*, Valladolid, 1939.

Beumelburg, Werner. *Kampf um Spanien, die Geschichte der Legion Condor*, Berlin, 1940.

Billoux, Francois. *985 jours de lutte*, Paris, 1962.

Bolloten, Burnett. *The Grand Camouflage; the Communist Conspiracy in the Spanish Civil War*, London, 1961.

Bonomi, Ruggero. *Viva la muerte, diario dell' 'Aviacion de El Tercio,'* Rome, 1941.

Borkenau, Franz, *The Spanish Cockpit*, London, 1937.

Borrás y Bermejo, Tomás. *Checas de Madrid*, Barcelona, 1956.

——————. *Madrid teñido de rojo*, Madrid, 1962.

——————. *Seis mil mujeres*, Madrid, 1965.

Bouthelier, Antonio (with Mora, José López). *Ocho días de la revuelta comunista*, Madrid, 1940.

Bowers, Claude. *My Mission to Spain*, New York, 1954.

Brademas, Stephen John. *Revolution and Social Revolution*, Oxford, 1953.

Bravo, Francisco. *Historia de la Falange Española de las JONS*, Madrid, 1940.

Bravo Morata, Federico. *Historia de Madrid*, vol. III, Madrid, 1968.

——————. *La República*, Madrid, 1973.

—————————. *Madrid pendant la guerre civile*, Paris, 1973.

Brenan, Gerald. *The Spanish Labyrinth*, Cambridge, 1943.

Brereton, Geoffrey. *Inside Spain*, London, 1938.

Brigada Internacional Militarverlag der Deutschen Demokratischen Republik, Berlin, n.d.

Brome, Vincent. *The International Brigades, Spain, 1936–1939*, London, 1965.

Broúe, Pièrre (and Témime, Émile). *La Révolution et la guerre d'Espagne*, Paris, 1961.

Buckley, Henry W. *Life and Death of the Spanish Republic*, London, 1940.

Burgo, Jaime del. *Conspiración y guerra civil*, Madrid, 1970.

Caballero Audaz, José María. *El Cuartel de la Montaña*, Madrid, 1939.

Cabanellas, Guillermo. *La guerra de los mil días*, 2 vols., Barcelona, 1973.

Cacho Zabalza, Antonio. *La Unión Militar Española*, Alicante, 1940.

Calleja, Juan José. *Yagüe, un corazón al rojo*, Barcelona, 1963.

Carr, Raymond (ed.). *The Republic and the Civil War in Spain*, London, 1971.

Carreras, Luis. *The Glory of Martyred Spain*, London, 1939.

Carrillo, Santiago. *Demain Espagne*, Paris, 1974.

Carrión, Pascual. *La reforma agraria de la segunda República*, Barcelona, 1973.

Casado, Segismundo. *The Last Days of Madrid*, London, 1939.

Casas de la Vega, R. *Brunete*, Madrid, 1967.

Castells, Andreu. *Las brigadas internacionales de la guerra de España*, Barcelona, 1974.

Castro Delgado, Enrique. *Hombres made in Moscú*, Barcelona, 1965.

Catholic Church in Spain. Joint letter of the Spanish bishops to the bishops of the whole world concerning the war in Spain, London, 1937.

Centner, Israel. *From Madrid to Berlin*, Tel Aviv, 1956 (Hebrew).

Churchill, Winston. *The Second World War*, vol. I: *The Gathering Storm*, London, 1948.

Cierva, Riccardo de la. *Historia de la guerra civil española*, Madrid, 1969.

—————————. *La historia perdida del socialismo español*, Madrid, 1972.

—————————. *Leyenda y tragedia de las brigadas internacionales*, Madrid, 1969.

Cirre Jiménez, José. *De Espejo a Madrid con las tropas del general Miaja*, Granada, 1937.

Cleugh, James. *Spanish Fury: The Story of a Civil War*, London, 1962.

Cockburn, Claud. *Crossing the Line*, London, 1956.

Colodny, Robert G. *Spain: The Glory and the Tragedy*, New York, 1970.

—————————. *The Struggle for Madrid*, New York, 1958.

Comín Colomer, Eduardo. *El comisariado político en la guerra española 1936–1939*, Madrid, 1973.

—————————. *Historia del partido comunista de España*, 3 vols., Madrid, 1965.

————————. *El Quinto Regimiento de Milicias Populares*, Madrid, 1973.

Conceiro Tovar, José. *Hombres qué decidieron*, Madrid, 1969.

Conquest, Robert. *The Great Terror*, London, 1968.

Córdoba, Juan de (José Losada de la Torre). *Estampas y reportajes de retaguardia*, Seville, 1939.

Cordón, Antonio. *Trayectoría*, Paris, 1971.

Cossio, Francisco de. *Guerra de salvación del frente de Madrid al Vizcaya*, Valladolid, 1937.

Cot, Pièrre. *The Triumph of Treason*, Chicago, 1944.

Cox, Geoffrey. *Defence of Madrid*, London, 1937.

Crozier, Brian. *Franco*, London, 1967.

Cuardernos de Ruedo Ibérico: 'El Movimiento libertario español,' Paris, 1974.

Cuesta, Teodoro. *De la muerte a la vida*, Burgos, 1939.

Davies, John Langdon. *Behind the Spanish Barricades*, London, 1936.

Delaprée, Louis. *The Martyrdom of Madrid*, Madrid, 1937.

Delmer, Sefton, *Trail Sinister*, London, 1961.

Delperrie de Bayac, Jacques. *Les Brigades Internationales*, Paris, 1968.

Deutsche Widerstandskampfer Band I, Berlin, 1970.

Díaz, José. *Por la unidad, hacia la victoria*, Barcelona, 1937.

————————. *Tres años de lucha*, Paris, 1970.

Díaz-Plaja, Fernando. (comp.). *La guerra de España en sus documentos*, 2nd ed., Barcelona, 1966.

Die Deutsche Politikgegenüber dem Spanischen Bürgerkrieg, vol. 18, Bonn, 1961.

Duclos, Jacques. *Mémoires 1935–1939*, Paris, 1969.

Dupré, Henri. *La 'Légion Tricolore' en Espagne*, Paris, 1942.

Duval, General. *Entwicklung und Lehren des Krieges in Spanien*, Berlin, 1938.

Duval, Maurice. *Los Espagnols et la guerre d'Espagne*, Paris, 1939.

————————. *Les Leçons de la guerre d'Espagne*, Paris, 1938.

Eby, Cecil D. *Between the Bullet and the Lie*, New York, 1969.

————————. *The Siege of the Alcázar*, New York, 1966.

Ehrenburg, Ilya. *The Eve of War (Men, Years and Life*, vol. IV), London, 1963.

Eisner, Alexei. *La 12a Brigada Internacional*, Valencia, 1972.

L'Épopée de l'Espagne; Brigades Internationales, 1936–1939, Paris, 1957.

Escobal, Patricio P. *Death Row: Spain 1936*, Indianapolis, 1968.

Escobar, José Ignacio. *Así empezó . . .* , Madrid, 1974.

Etchebéhère, Mika. *Ma guerre d'Espagne à moi*, Paris, 1976.

Falcón, Cesar. *Madrid*, Madrid, 1938.

Fernández Arias, Adelardo. *La agonía de Madrid*, Saragossa, 1938.

————————. *Madrid bajo 'el terror,' 1936–1937*, Saragossa, 1937.

Ferrara, Marcella and Mauricio. *Palmiro Togliatti*, Paris, 1955.

Fischer, Louis. *Men and Politics*, New York, 1941.

——————. *The War in Spain*, New York, 1937.

Fonteriz, Luis de. *Red Terror in Madrid*, London, 1937.

Fox, Ralph. *A Writer in Arms*, London, 1937.

Foxá, Agustín de. *Madrid, de corte a checa*, San Sebastián, 1938.

Galíndez Suárez, Jesús. *Los vascos en el Madrid sitiado*, Buenos Aires, 1945.

Gallego, Gregorio. *Madrid, corazón que se desangra*, Madrid, 1976.

Gannes, Harry, and Repard, Theodore. *Spain in Revolt*, New York, 1937.

Garate, José María. *Mil días de fuego*, Barcelona, 1972.

García Alonso, Francisco. *Así mueren los españoles*, Buenos Aires, 1937.

García de la Escalera, Inés. *El General Varela*, Madrid, 1959.

García Morato, Joaquin. *Guerra en el aire*, Madrid, 1940.

García Serrano, R. *La fiel infantería*, Madrid, 1973.

García Venero, Maximiniano. *Falange en la guerra de España*, Paris, 1967.

——————. *El general Fanjul*, Madrid, 1967.

——————. *Historia de las Internacionales en España*, 3 vols., Madrid, 1956–1957.

——————. *Madrid, julio 1936*, Madrid, 1973.

Garibaldini in Espagna, Madrid, 1937.

Garriga, Ramón. *La Legion Condor*, Madrid, 1975.

——————. *Las relaciones secretas entre Franco y Hitler*, Buenos Aires, 1965.

Gerahty, Cecil. *The Road to Madrid*, London, 1937.

Gil Robles, José María. *No fue posible la paz*, Barcelona, 1968.

Goldston, Robert. *The Civil War in Spain*, London, 1966.

Gómez Casas, Juan. *Historia del anarcho-sindicalismo español*, Madrid, 1968.

Gómez Domingo, Manuel. *Asalto y defensa heroica del Cuartel de la Montaña*, Valladolid, n.d.

Gómez Málaga, Juan. *Estampas trágicas de Madrid*, Avila, 1936.

González, Valentín, and Gorkin, Julián, *El Campesino*, New York, 1952.

Gorkin, Julián. *El proceso de Moscú en Barcelona*, Barcelona, 1974.

Grandi, Blasco. *Togliatti en España*, Madrid, 1954.

Guérin, Daniel. *L'anarchisme*, Paris, 1965.

——————. *Ni Dieu ni maitre*, vol. 4, Paris, 1970.

Guerra y revolución en España 1936–1939, Moscow, 1966.

Gurney, Jason. *Crusade in Spain*, London, 1974.

Guttmann, Allen, *American Neutrality and the Spanish Civil War*, Lexington, Mass., 1963.

——————. *The Wound in the Heart*, New York, 1962.

Guzmán, Eduardo de, *Madrid rojo y negro*, Buenos Aires, 1939.

——————. *La muerte de la esperanza*, Madrid, 1973.

Hanighen, Frank (ed.). *Nothing but Danger*, London, 1940.

Hemingway, Ernest. *The Spanish War*, London, 1938.

Heredia, Marcelino, *El Campesino*, Barcelona, n.d.

Hernández, Jesús. *La Grande Trahison*, Paris, 1953.

Hidalgo de Cisneros, Ignacio. *Memorias*, 2 vols., Paris, 1964.

Hills, George. *The Battle for Madrid*, New York, 1977.

—————. *Franco*, New York, 1967.

Historia de la cruzada Española (35 vols.), Madrid, 1940–1943.

Hughes, John Emmet. *Report From Spain*, New York, 1947.

Huidobro Pardo, Leopoldo. *Memorias de un finlandés*, Madrid, 1939.

Hull, Cordell. *Memoirs*, 2 vols., New York, 1948.

Ibarruri, Dolores. *They Shall Not Pass*, London, 1967.

In Spain with the International Brigade, London, 1938.

The International Brigades, Spain, 1936–1939, London, 1965.

Iribarren, José María. *El general Mola*, Madrid, 1945.

Iturralde, Juan de. *El catolicismo y la cruzada de Franco*, 2 vols., Bayonne, 1955.

Izaga, Guillermo Arsenio de. *Los presos de Madrid*, Madrid, 1940.

Izcaray, Jesús. *Madrid es nuestro*, Madrid-Barcelona, 1938.

Jackson, Gabriel. *A Concise History of the Spanish Civil War*, New York, 1974.

—————. *The Spanish Republic and the Civil War 1931–1939*, Princeton, 1965.

Jato, David. *La rebelión de los estudiantes*, Madrid, 1953.

Javier Marinas, Gen. Francisco. *General Varela*, Barcelona, 1956.

Jellinek, Frank, *The Civil War in Spain*, London, 1938.

Joaniquet, Aurelio. *Calvo Sotelo, una vida fecunda*, Santander, 1939.

Joll, James. *The Anarchists*, London, 1964.

Jouve, Marguerite. *Vu en Espagne*, Paris, 1937.

Kaminski, H. *Ceux de Barcelona*, Paris, 1937.

Kantorowicz, Alfred. *Spanisches Tagebuch*, Berlin, 1948.

—————. *Tschapaiew*, Berlin, 1956.

Kemp, Peter. *Mine Were of Trouble*, London, 1957.

Kindelán, General Alfredo. *Mis cuadernos de guerra*, Madrid, 1945.

Kisch, Richard. *They Shall Not Pass*, London, 1974.

Kleine, Ahlbrandt. *The Policy of Simmering*, The Hague, 1962.

Knoblaugh, H. Edward. *Correspondent in Spain*, New York, 1939.

Koestler, Arthur, *Dialogue with Death*, New York, 1942.

—————. *The Invisible Writing*, London, 1954.

—————. *Spanish Testament*, London, 1937.

Koltsov, Mikhail. *Diario de la guerra de España*, Paris, 1963.

Krivitsky, Walter. *I Was Stalin's Agent*, London, 1963.

Lacouture, Jean. *André Malraux*, Paris, 1973.

Landau, Katia. *Le Stalinisme en Espagne*, Paris, 1938.

Landis, Arthur H. *Spain: The Unfinished Revolution*, New York, 1975.

Langdon-Davies, John. *Behind the Spanish Barricades*, New York, 1936.

Largo Caballero, Francisco. *Mis recuerdos, cartas a un amigo*, Mexico, 1954.

Larios José. *Combat over Spain*, London, 1966.

Last, Jef. *The Spanish Tragedy*, London, 1939.

Lister, Enrique. *Nuestra guerra*, Paris, 1966.

Lizarza, Antonio. *Memorias de la conspiración*, Pamplona, 1954.

Lizón Gadea, Adolfo. *Brigadas internacionales en España*, Madrid, 1940.

Llarch, Juan. *Cipriano Mera*, Barcelona, 1976.

—————. *Morir en Madrid*, Barcelona, 1976.

—————. *La muerte de Durruti*, Barcelona, 1973.

Llorens, Josep María. *La iglesia contra la república española*, Vieux, 1968.

Lojendio, Luis María de.*Operaciones militares de la guerra de España, 1936–1939*, Barcelona, 1940.

Longo, Luigi. *Le brigate internazionale in Spagna*, Rome, 1956.

López de Medrano, Luis. *986 días en el infierno*, Madrid, n.d.

López Fernández, Antonio. *Defensa de Madrid*, Mexico, 1945.

López Muñiz, Gregorio. *La batalla de Madrid*, Madrid, 1943.

Low, Mary, and Bren, Juan. *Red Spanish Notebook*, London, 1937.

Machado, Antonio. *Madrid 1936–1937*, Madrid, 1937.

Madariaga, Salvador de. *Spain, a Modern History*, London, 1946.

—————. *Memorias, 1921–1936*, Madrid, 1974.

Madem, Gina. *The Jews Fighting for Freedom*, New York, 1938.

Maíz, B. Félix. *Alzamiento en España, de un diario de la conspiración*, Pamplona, 1952.

—————. *Mola . . . aquel hombre!* Pamplona, 1977.

Malaparte, Curzio. *¡Viva la muerte!*, Rome, 1939.

Malefakis, Edward E. *Agrarian Reform and Peasant Revolution in Spain*, New Haven, 1970.

Marañón, Gregorio. *Libéralisme et communisme; en marge de la guerre civile espagnole*, Paris, 1938.

Marinello, Juan. *Hombres de la España leal*, Havana, 1938.

Martin Blázquez, José. *I Helped to Build an Army*, London, 1939.

Martin, Claude. *Franco, soldat et chef d'état*, Paris, 1959.

Martínez Amutio, Justo. *Chantaje a un pueblo*, Madrid, 1974.

Martínez Bande, Colonel José Manuel, *Brigades internacionales*, Barcelona, 1972.

—————. *Communist Intervention in the Spanish War*, Madrid, 1966.

—————. *La lucha en torno a Madrid*, Madrid, 1968.

—————. *La marcha sobre Madrid*, Madrid, 1968.

Marty, André. *Volontaires d'Espagne: douze mois sublimes!*, Paris, 1937.

Matorras, Enrique. *El comunismo en España*, Madrid, 1935.

Matthews, Herbert, *Half of Spain Died*, New York, 1973.

—————. *Two Wars and More to Come*, New York, 1938.

—————. *The Yoke and the Arrows*, New York, 1961.

Max, Jack. *Memorias de un revolucionario*, Barcelona, 1975.

McNeill-Moss, Geoffrey. *The Epic of the Alcázar*, London, 1937.

Mera, Cipriano. *Guerra, exilio y cárcel de un anarcosindicalista*, Paris, 1976.

Merkes, Manfred. *Die Deutsche Politik gegenuber dem Spanischen Burgerkrieg, 1936–1939*, Bonn, 1961.

Miguel, Florindo de. *Un cura en zona roja*, Barcelona, 1956.

Miquelarena, Jacinto. *Cómo fui ejecutado en Madrid*, Avila, 1937.

Modesto, Juan. *Soy del Quinto Regimiento*, Paris, 1969.

Mola, Emilio. *Obras completas*, Valladolid, 1940.

Montero, Antonio. *La persecución religiosa en España*, Madrid, 1961.

Montero Díaz, Santiago. *La política social en la zona Marxista*, Bilbao, 1938.

Mora, Constancia de la. *In Place of Splendor*, New York, 1939.

Moreno Davila, Julio. *Frente a Madrid*, Granada, 1937.

The Nazi Conspiracy in Spain, London, 1937.

Nenni, Pietro. *Spagna*, Milan, 1958.

Nevares Marcos, Sisinio, and Yturriaga, Rafael de. *La primera bandera de Castilla*, Madrid, 1968.

Nin, Andrés. *Los problemas de la revolución española*, Paris, 1971.

Nünez Morgado, Aurelio. *Los sucesos de España vistos por un diplomático*, Buenos Aires, 1941.

O'Donnell, Peadar. *Salud! An Irishman in Spain*, London, 1937.

O'Duffy, Erin. *Crusade in Spain*, London, 1938.

Ortiz de Villajos, Cándido. *De Sevilla a Madrid*, Granada, 1937.

Pacciardi, Randolfo. *11 battaglione Garibaldi*, Lugano, 1948.

Palencia, Isobel de. *I Must Have Liberty*, New York, 1940.

Pasaremos. *Deutsche Antifaschisten in National Revolutionaren Krieg Spaniens*, Berlin, 1966.

Payne, Robert (ed.). *The Civil War in Spain, 1936–1939*, New York, 1962.

Payne, Stanley. *Falange*, Stanford, 1961.

Paz, Abel. *Durruti: le peuple en armes*, Paris, 1972.

Peirats, José. *La CNT en la revolución española*, 3 vols., Toulouse, 1951–1953.

——————. *Los anarquistas en la crisis politica española*, Buenos Aires, 1964.

Peiró, Francisco X. *Fernando de Huidobro, Jesuita y Legionario*, Madrid, 1951.

Pemán, José María. *De la entrada en Madrid: Historia de tres días*, Madrid, 1939.

——————. *Un soldado en la historia: Vida del General Varela*, Cadiz, 1954.

Penchienati, Carlos. *Brigate Internazionale in Spagna*, Milan, 1950.

Pérez Ferrero, Miguel. *Drapeau de France; la vie des réfugiés dans les légations á Madrid*, Paris, 1938.

Pérez Salas, Jesús. *Guerra en España*, Mexico, 1947. *La persecución religiosa en España*, Buenos Aires, 1937.

Phillips, Cecil. *The Spanish Pimpernel*, London, 1960.

Pike, D.W. *Conjecture, Propaganda and Deceit and the Spanish Civil War,* Stanford, 1970.

Pitcairn, Frank. *Reporter in Spain,* Moscow, 1937.

Pons Prades, Eduardo. *Un soldado de la república,* Madrid, 1974.

El Preso 831, Del Madrid rojo. Ultimos días de la Carcel Modelo, Cádiz, 1937.

Prieto, Carlos. *Spanish Front,* London, 1936.

Prieto, Indalecio. *Convulsiones de España,* 3 vols., Mexico, 1967–1969.

Primo de Rivera, José Antonio. *Obras completas,* Madrid, 1942.

Puente, José Vicente. *Madrid Recobrado,* Madrid, 1939.

Queipo de Llano, Rosario. *De la cheka de Atadell a la prisión de Alacuás,* Valladolid, 1939.

Red Domination in Spain: The General Cause, Madrid, 1961.

Regler, Gustav. *The Great Crusade,* New York, 1940.

—————. *Owl of Minerva,* London, 1959.

Rello, Salvador. *La aviación en la guerra de España,* 4 vols., Madrid, 1969–1971.

Reparaz, Antonio. *Desde el cuartel general de Miaja al santuario de la Virgen de la Cabeza,* Valladolid, 1937.

Reynaud, Jean. *En Espagna Rouge,* Paris, 1937.

Riesenfeld, Janet. *Dancer in Madrid,* New York, 1938.

Rio Cisneros, Agustín de (with Pavón Pereira, Enrique). *Los procesos de José Antonio,* Madrid, 1969.

Rivas-Cherif, Cipriano de. *Retrato de un desconocido: vida de Manuel Azaña,* Mexico, 1961.

Rogers, F. Theo. *Spain: A Tragic Journey,* New York, 1937.

Rojas, Carlos. *Por qué Perdimos la guerra,* Barcelona, 1970.

Rojo, Vicente. *Alerta los pueblos!,* Buenos Aires, 1939.

—————. *Así fue la defensa de Madrid,* Mexico, 1967.

—————. *España heroica,* Buenos Aires, 1942.

Romero, Luis. *Tres Días de Julio,* Barcelona, 1967.

Romero Marchent, Joaquin. *Soy un fugitivo,* Valladolid, 1937.

Romilly, Esmond. *Boadilla,* London, 1971.

Rossif, F. *Morir en Madrid,* Mexico, 1970.

Rudel, Christian. *La Phalange,* Paris, 1972.

Ruiz Albéniz, Víctor. *¡Casa de Campo! Ciudad Universitaria!,* Madrid, 1941.

—————. *Del Tajo al Manzanares,* Madrid, 1940.

—————. *Estampas de la Legion,* Madrid, 1940.

—————. *La gran tragedia de Madrid,* Madrid, 1939.

—————. *Leones en el Guadarrama,* Madrid, 1940.

—————. *Madrid, en el cepo,* Madrid, 1941.

—————. *Vida, obra, y muerte del General Don Emilio Mola,* Madrid, 1942.

Rust, William. *Britons in Spain,* London, 1939.

Salas Larrazábal, Jesús. *Intervención extranjera en la guerra de España*, Madrid, 1974.

——————. *La guerra de España desde el aire*, Barcelona, 1969.

Salas Larrazábal, Ramón, *Historia del ejército popular de la república*, 4 vols., Madrid, 1974.

Sanabria, Fernando. *Madrid bajo las hordas rojas*, Avila, 1938.

Sánchez del Arco, Manuel. *El sur de España en la reconquista de Madrid*, Seville, 1937.

Sanz, Ricardo. *Figuras de la revolución española: Buenaventura Durruti*, Toulouse, 1944.

——————. *Los que fuimos a Madrid*, Columna Durruti, 26 división, Toulouse, 1969.

Schlayer, Felix. *Diplomat im roten Madrid*, Berlin, 1938.

Sedwick, Frank. *The Tragedy of Manuel Azaña and the Fate of the Spanish Republic*, Ohio, 1963.

Sender, Ramón, J. *Counter-attack in Spain*, Boston, 1937.

Serrano Suñer, Ramón. *Memorias*, Barcelona, 1977.

Sevilla Andrés, Diego. *Historia política de la zona roja*, Madrid, 1954.

Sheean, Vincent. *Not Peace but a Sword*, New York, 1939.

Sloan, Pat (ed.). *John Cornford, a Memoir*, London, 1938.

Snellgrove, Lawrence Ernest. *Franco and the Spanish Civil War*, New York, 1969.

La solidaridad de los pueblos con la república española 1936–1939, Moscow, 1974.

Sommerfield, John. *Volunteer in Spain*, London, 1937.

Somoza Silva, Lázaro. *El general Miaja*, Mexico, 1944.

Soria, Georges. *Trotskyism in the Service of Franco: facts and documents on the POUM*, London, 1938.

Souchy, Augustin. *Anarcho-Syndikalisten und Revolution in Spanien*, Darmstadt, 1969.

Sperber, Murray A. (comp.). *And I Remember Spain*, London, 1974.

Stackelberg, Karl Georg, Freiherr von. *Legion Condor*, Berlin, 1939.

Stein, Sigmund. *Der Birger-Krig in Shpaanye*, Paris, 1961 (Yiddish).

Strong, Anna Louise. *Spain in Arms*, 1937, New York, 1937.

"Suárez, Andrés," *El proceso contra el POUM*, Paris, 1974.

Szinda, Gustav. *Die XI Brigade*, Berlin, 1956.

Tagüeña, Manuel. *Testimonio de dos guerras*, Mexico, 1973.

Taylor, Foster Jay. *The United States and the Spanish Civil War*, New York, 1956.

Thomas, Hugh. *The Spanish Civil War*, New York, 1961.

Torriente Brau, Pablo de la. *Peleando con los milicianos*, Mexico, 1938.

Toryho, Jacinto. *No eramos tan malos*, Madrid, 1975.

Traina, Richard P. *American Diplomacy and the Spanish Civil War*, Blooming-
    ton, 1968.
Trotsky, Leon. *The Spanish Revolution, 1931–1939*, New York, 1973.
Trotsky, Lev. *Lesson of Spain: The Last Warning*, London, 1937.
Trythall, J.W.D. *Franco: A Biography*, London, 1970.
Tuñón de Lara, Manuel. *La España del siglo XX*, Paris, 1966.
——————. *El movimiento obrero en la historia de España*, Madrid, 1972.
Tusell, Javier. *Historia de la democracia cristiana en España*, 2 vols., Madrid,
    1974.
——————. *Las elecciones del Frente Popular*, 2 vols., Madrid, 1971.
United Nations Security Council. *Report on Spain*, New York, 1946.
United States Government, *Foreign Relations of the United States: 1936* (vol.
    II); *1937* (vol. I); *1938* (vol. I); *1939* (vol. II), Washington, 1954–1956.
Uribarri, Manuel. *La quinta columna española*, Havana, 1943.
Urra Lusarreta, Sinen. *En los trincheros del frente de Madrid*, Madrid, 1967.
Vegas Latapié, M. *El pensamiento político de Calvo Sotelo*, Madrid, 1941.
Venegas, José. *Las elecciones del Frente Popular*, Buenos Aires, 1942.
Vidal Sales, J.A. *Santiago Carrillo*, Barcelona, 1977.
Vidarte, Juan Simeon. *Todos fuimos culpables*, Mexico, 1973.
Vieth von Golssenau, Arnold (Ludwig Renn). *Der Spanische Krieg*, Berlin,
    1955.
Vigón, Jorge. *General Mola, el Conspirador*, Barcelona, 1957.
Vila San Juan, José Luis, *¿ Así Fue? Enigmas de la guerra civil española*, Bar-
    celona, 1972.
Vilanova, Antonio. *La defensa del Alcázar de Toledo*, Mexico, 1963.
Vilar, Pierre. *Histoire de l'Espagne*, Paris, 1952.
Viñas, Angel. *La Alemañia nazi y el 18 de julio*, Madrid, 1974.
Watson, Keith Scott. *Single to Spain*, London, 1937.
Weil, Simone. *Ecrits historiques et politiques*, Paris, 1960.
Werstein, Irving. *The Cruel Years*, New York, 1969.
Wintringham, Thomas Henry. *Deadlock War*, London, 1940.
——————. *English Captain*, London, 1939.
Woodcock, George. *Anarchism*, London, 1963.
Yagüe, María Eugenia. *Santiago Carrillo*, Madrid, 1977.
Zaragoza, Cristobal. *Los generales del pueblo*, Barcelona, 1977.
Zugazagoitia, Julián. *Historia de la guerra en España*, Buenos Aires, 1940.

AMERICAN PERIODICALS:
American Mercury—February 1937 ("Russia's Private War in Spain" by L.
    Dennis).
Atlantic Monthly—November 1936 ("Diary of Revolution" by M. Laird).
Christian Century—September 2, 1936 ("Arrogance in the Name of Christ" by

R. Niebuhr); December 16, 1936 ("Spain's Syndicalists" by H.B. Murkland); April 7, 1937 ("Eyewitness in Spain" by S. Jones).

Collier's—May 29, 1937 ("This Is War" by A. Malraux).

Commonweal—June 5, 1936 ("President Azaña" by O.B. McGuire).

Contemporary—February 1937 ("Comedy of Non-Intervention" by G. Glasgow).

Current History—September 1936 ("Progress of the Revolt"); November 1936 ("Intervention in Spain" by L. Lore); December 1936 ("How Many Slain? Anti-Clerical Atrocities, the Score in Spain" by L. Lore); April 1937 ("I Lived in Madrid" by L. Ziffren).

Foreign Affairs—October 1936 ("Back of the Spanish Rebellion" by L.A. Fernsworth); October 1942 ("Prelude to War" by J.T. Whitaker).

Fortune—December 1936 ("Spanish Kaleideoscope"); March 1937 ("Background of War" by W. Starkie).

Harper's—June–July 1937 ("Eyewitness in Madrid" by G. Cox).

Historical Journal, University of Birmingham—vol. X, no. 2, 1966 ("Calvo Sotelo's Bloque Nacional and its Manifesto" by R. Robinson).

International Affairs—April 1962 ("France and Non-Intervention in Spain, July-August 1936" by G. Warner).

Journal of Contemporary History—vol. LV, no. 2, 1969 ("Bridegrooms of Death: A Profile Study of the Spanish Foreign Legion" by J. N. Galey).

Literary Digest—May 30, 1936 ("Azaña"); July 4, 1936 ("Strike, Riot, and Burn"); July 25, 1936 ("Murder in Spain"); September 12, 1936 ("Dying Spaniards"); October 3, 1936 ("Correspondents in Spain"); October 10, 1936 ("Gallant Spaniards Still Die in Vain"); November 14, 1936 ("Madrid: Shambles of Warring Spain"); November 21, 1936 ("War of the Air"); December 5, 1936 ("Hero of Madrid: Kléber"); December 12, 1936 ("Madrid Impasse").

Living Age—October 1936 ("A Portrait of La Pasionaria", "Franco's War"); April 1937 ("Soviet Agents"); June 1937 ("Franco's Nazi Adviser" by R. Fiestmann).

The Nation—August 1, 1936 ("Issues and Men" by O.G. Villard); August 15, 1936 ("Who's Who in Spain" by A. Brenner); October 31, 1936 ("Will Moscow Save Madrid?" by L. Fischer); November 7, 1936 ("Madrid Keeps Its Nerve" by L. Fischer); November 21, 1936 ("Madrid Fights off Franco" by L. Fischer); January 9, 1937 ("Spain's Red Foreign Legion" by L. Fischer); March 13, 1937 ("Is the State Department Favoring Franco?").

New Republic—August 19, 1936 ("Cable from Spain"); October 14, 1936 ("Fascist Aid to Rebels, Compañero Sogasia Burns a Church" by R. Bates); January 13, 1937 ("Shipping Arms to Spain"); May 5, 1937 ("Reports from the Madrid Battlefront" by E. Hemingway).

Newsweek—May 16, 1936 ("Azaña President"); August 1, 1936 ("Leftist Cabinet in Quandary in Spain''); October 3, 1936 (''Drive on Madrid''); October 10, 1936 (''Franco in Striking Distance of Madrid''); October 24, 1936 (''White Noose Tightens'').

19th Century—December 1936 (''Irishman in Spain'' by P. O'Donnell).

Reader's Digest—November 1966 (''How Stalin Relieved Spain of $600,000,000'' by A. Orlov).

Review of Reviews—September 1936 (''Hell over Spain'' by R. Shaw); November 1936 (''Twilight in Spain'' by R. Shaw, ''Incident in Spain'' by J. T. Whitaker); February 1937 (''Meet General Kléber'' by R. Shaw).

The Slavonic and East European Review—June 1960 (''Soviet Aid to the Republic'' by D.C. Watt).

Time—August 17, 1936 (''Moors to Lusitania''); August 24, 1936 (''The Republic vs. the Republic''); August 31, 1936 (''Long Live Dynamite''); September 7, 1936 (''Anarchism''); September 21, 1936 (''Doing Wonders''); September 28, 1936 (''Queen of Sparrows''); October 7, 1936 (''Fakes''); October 12, 1936 (''Bread and Heat''); October 19, 1936 (''Madrid Digs In''); October 26, 1936 (''Nearer and Nearer''); November 2, 1936 (''Sidewalks of Madrid''); November 9, 1936 (''A Matter of Hours''); November 16, 1936 (''Flight from Madrid''); November 23, 1936 (''Red Stand''); November 30, 1936 (''125 Days''); February 1, 1937 (''Treasures Protected'').

Travel—November 1936 (''In the Ranks of Spain's Republican Army''); February 1937 (''On the Firing Line in Defense of Madrid'' by F. Pitcairn).

AMERICAN NEWSPAPERS:

Chicago *Tribune, Christian Science Monitor,* New York *Herald-Tribune, New York Times.*

SPANISH PERIODICALS:

La Historia se Confiesa—July 1, 1976 (''El Frente Popular'' by R. de La Cierva); July 15, 1976 (''La gran conjura contra el Frente Popular'' by R. de la Cierda).

Historia 16—November 1976 (''Objetivo: Museo del Prado'' by J. Lino Vaamonde); March 1977 (''El mito del oro en la guerra civil: El oro de Francia y el oro de Moscú'' by Angel Viñas); May 1977 (''La reforma militar de Azaña'' by G. Kemperfeldt).

Historia y Vida—December 1968 (''La leyenda negra de la republica española'' by R. de la Cierva); 1974 (Extra) (''La batalla de Madrid: Cuando se intento occupar la capital,'' ''La defensa de Madrid: Durruti y las brigadas internacionales'' by J.M. Martínez Bande (both), ''Documentos: Una decisión del Generalisimo,'' ''Testimonios: El gobierno se traslada a Valencia'' by V. Rojo; December 1975 (''Del alzamiento a la guerra civil. Verano de 1936: la correspondencia Franco-Mola'' by J.M. Martínez

Bande); March 1977 ("André Malraux, un hijo del siglo" by R. Abella, "España 1936–1939. Como se pierde una guerra" by L. Romero; "Origen del 'No pasarán' " by N. Luján; "Oro Español en Moscú" by J.M. Gómez Ortiz).

Nueva Historia—June 1977 ("Santiago Carrillo y la represíon republicana en Madrid, 1936" by R. Salas Larázabal).

Posible—June 22, 1976 ("Cómo asesinaron a Durruti" by P. Costa Muste).

OTHER CURRENT SPANISH PUBLICATIONS:

ABC, La Actualidad Española, El Alcázar, Cambio 16, Diario 16, Interviu, El Pais, Ya.

WARTIME SPANISH NEWSPAPERS:

ABC, Al Frente!, La Ametralladore, Blanco y Negro, Campo Libre!, Cisneros, Claridad, Comisario, Cultura Proletaria, Ejercito, Estampa, Fotos, Frente Libertario, Militia Popular, Mundo Grafico, Mundo Obrero, El Socialista.

DOCUMENTS:

Documents diplomatiques français 1932–1939, Paris.

Documents on German Foreign Policy 1918–1945, Bonn.

Documents secret du ministère des affaires estrangères d'Allemagne, Moscow.

Official documents, military operations, Republican and Nationalist forces, Madrid.

LIBRARIES AND ARCHIVES:

France—Bibliotheque du Ministère des Armées, Paris.

Great Britain—Public Records Office, London.

Italy—Archivio Centrale della Stato, Rome.

Spain—Biblioteca del Cabinete de Documentacion y Estudies Contemporanes, Biblioteca Central Militar, Biblioteca del Ministerio de Cultura, Biblioteca Nacional, Hemeroteca Municipal, Servicio Historico Militar, Madrid.

United States—Brandeis University Special Collections Library, Waltham, Mass.; Columbia University Library, New York Public Library, New York; Library of Congress, Washington, D.C.; National Records Center, National Archives, Washington, D.C., and Suitland, Md.

West Germany—Bibliothek für Zeitgeschichte, Stuttgart; Foreign Ministry Archives, Bonn; Institut für Zeitgeschichte, Munich; Militargeschichtliches Forschungsamt, Freiburg.

Index